Dynamics of Teaching Secondary School Mathematics

Dynamics of Teaching Secondary School Mathematics

Thomas J. Cooney
The University of Georgia

Edward J. Davis
The University of Georgia

K. B. Henderson
Professor Emeritus
University of Illinois at Urbana-Champaign

WAVELAND PRESS, INC.
Prospect Heights, Illinois

For information about this book, write or call:

Waveland Press, Inc.
P.O. Box 400
Prospect Heights, Illinois 60070
(312) 634-0081

Copyright © 1975 by Houghton Mifflin Company. Reprinted by arrangement with Houghton Mifflin Company, Boston.
1983 reissued by Waveland Press, Inc.

Library of Congress Catalog Card Number: 74-19659

ISBN 0-88133-061-2

Printed in the United States of America

12   11   10   9   8

Contents

Preface

Teacher training programs strive to provide a variety of activities to facilitate the development of competent mathematics teachers. Programs usually include investigations into mathematics and a study of basic psychological principles, since a sound knowledge of mathematics and an awareness of how children learn are recognized as essential elements in a teacher's professional knowledge. There is, however, another kind of knowledge essential for effective instruction: knowledge related to the development and implementation of strategies for teaching mathematics.

Teachers are not likely to reach their full capabilities solely by observing and imitating master teachers. As we point out in Chapter 1, observing teachers is more instructive when one has a conceptual framework for analyzing the teaching act. Such a framework can help the observer identify and differentiate among various techniques a teacher uses. By recognizing and classifying such techniques, the observer establishes a basis for making instructional decisions beyond mere common sense. One of the basic tenets of this text is that a teacher who has an understanding of teaching strategies functions at a higher level of competence than a teacher who lacks such understanding.

A major portion of this textbook is devoted to explicating types of knowledge and the ways they can be taught. The analysis we provide involves what we have termed *moves* for teaching mathematics. The concept of a move is important because it enables precise description of various teaching strategies. Further, it provides a means for formulating, utilizing, and evaluating teaching strategies. We also illustrate how a knowledge of moves can facilitate the diagnosis and remediation of students' learning difficulties and aid in constructing instructional objectives. We believe that knowledge and use of teaching moves can be a significant factor in teachers' realization of their potential as professionals.

In addition to chapters dealing with moves for teaching mathematical concepts, generalizations (by exposition and guided discovery), skills, and diagnosis and remediation, we present considerations for other aspects of teaching mathematics. We include a chapter dealing with classroom management, a matter of concern to all teachers and especially beginning teachers, that focuses on principles for developing a desirable classroom atmosphere and maxims for dealing with misbehavior. We devote chapters to problem-solving and the teaching of proof, topics recognized as worthy of explicit instruction in the teaching of secondary school mathematics. The problem-solving chapter includes maxims for helping students solve problems and incorporate problem-solving strategies into their behavior. The chapter dealing with the teaching of proof discusses various strategies of proof and offers suggestions for developing the concept of proof. Other chapters consider teaching the slow learner and the student of high ability. A chapter on planning and evaluating instruction includes questions teachers may use in evaluating their own teaching.

To facilitate comprehension, we have made use of a variety of pedagogical techniques throughout the text. In dialogues, we try to capture some of the dynamic qualities of teaching and to illustrate points in realistic settings. Objectives, or competencies, placed near the beginning of each chapter, help the reader focus on major concerns. At the conclusion of each chapter, the competencies are restated and followed by related questions in "self-tests" to provide the reader with a means of determining his mastery of the competencies. The questions posed are exemplary in nature and can serve as prototypes for further questions. Thought questions are interspersed throughout each chapter to accentuate major points and to serve as points of departure for class discussions.

We are indebted to the people who have influenced our thinking in the writing of this text and to those who assisted in the preparation of the manuscript. We particularly appreciate the constructive criticisms offered by reviewers Jeremy Kilpatrick, Teachers College, Columbia University, Richard Crouse, University of Delaware; William Engel, University of South Florida, and Larry Hatfield of the University of Georgia.

Thomas J. Cooney
Edward J. Davis
Kenneth B. Henderson

Dynamics of Teaching Secondary School Mathematics

1

Introduction

E ach chapter in this book opens with a short section that provides a perspective on what will be discussed in the chapter and a list of competencies—what you should know and be able to do as a result of studying the chapter, answering the thought questions at the ends of sections, and taking the self-test. You can think of the competencies as the objectives of your study of each chapter. At the close of each chapter a self-test is provided to help you decide whether you have attained the competencies. The self-tests contain restatements of the competencies along with activities designed to indicate your attainment of them. The extent to which you can do this adequately will demonstrate your attainment of the competencies.

In this chapter, we begin with a discussion of the satisfactions of teaching, particularly of teaching mathematics. To attain these satisfactions, one must develop competence in teaching by acquiring both practical experience and a knowledge of theory of teaching. Each enhances the other. Students are usually more aware of the need for practical experience than they are of the need for theory. Hence we argue the place of theory in the education of mathematics teachers. Following this, we explain the general point of view that is set forth in the remaining chapters of the book.

At the conclusion of this chapter, you should be able to demonstrate the following competencies:

1   Explain why the characteristics of mathematics make teaching satisfying to many mathematics teachers

2   Explain why a knowledge of the theory of teaching is necessary to a competent mathematics teacher

3   Show how the analysis of teaching that forms the basis of the theory presented in this book is helpful

Satisfactions of teaching

It seems unnecessary to argue at length that teachers are important. The service they render enables society to perpetuate and strengthen its culture. Think of how a society would disintegrate if each generation had to rediscover for itself without the guidance of its teachers what the previous generation knew, believed, and was able to do. The production of goods and services would be crippled. Research—the discovery of new knowledge and the development of theory—would change from its present rapid pace to a very slow pace. We would despair over problems whose solution determines whether society as we know it will wind up in the wastebasket of history. The contribution of the teacher toward maintaining and improving the quality of life is indeed significant.

Teachers also contribute to the individual students they teach by helping them make the most of their inherent capabilities. The potentialities of students with various talents—musical, artistic, literary, mathematical, physical, or social—might not be nurtured were it not for teachers who know how to make the most of them. Students with meager potentialities— the mentally or physically handicapped, the emotionally disturbed, and the slow learners—might be doomed to unhappy lives were it not for teachers whose patience and support help them make the most of whatever their potentialities are.

Would that our society were willing to pay teachers (and ministers and social workers) in accordance with the significance of their contributions! Yet the rewards of teaching go beyond material gain. They are manifested by the feelings of satisfaction that always accompany an activity that makes life more enjoyable and worthwhile for other people. Without such emotional and intellectual satisfactions, even large financial returns would lose much of their significance. Most people would rather take less when they realize that their work is important than receive more when they believe in their hearts that their work makes very little difference, and that life would go along well enough without them.

Among various teachers, the work of mathematics teachers is particularly satisfying. They have a very important body of knowledge and skills to convey, part of which is mandatory if people are to participate successfully in the life of our society. Mathematics has been considered a necessary part of general education by every group that has deliberated about what the content of general education should be, and it is a required subject in the curriculum of practically all junior high schools and many senior high schools.

Over and beyond what mathematics teachers offer in the way of general education is what they contribute toward specialized education for members of professions, like scientists, engineers, statisticians, and accountants. In jobs in which work is based heavily on quantification and measurement, a knowledge of mathematics is necessary to an understanding of the theory of the primary subject matter. Hence the work of mathematics teachers is satisfying because of their realization of the social significance of the subject matter they teach.

There is also an intellectual satisfaction in teaching mathematics. It is a distinctive body of knowledge, characterized by some scholars as "hypothetico-deductive." A minimum set of terms is taken as undefined and, in the case of abstract mathematics, uninterpreted. In terms of these, other terms are defined. These two sets of terms, the undefined and the defined, identify the objects of study such as sets, numbers, points, operations, functions, spaces, groups, rings, and fields. A minimum set of propositions concerning these objects and the relations among them is taken as true. From these, other propositions are deduced. Given any proposition, it is possible with few exceptions to decide whether the proposition is a consequence of the other propositions already established.

Certainly only very little mathematical knowledge can be taught students in secondary schools, yet enough can be taught to give them some insight into the distinctive nature of this kind of knowledge and how it differs from knowledge in an empirical science like chemistry, astronomy, or medicine. Moreover, under the guidance of a teacher who has intellectual objectives, students can be shown how to discover knowledge new to them and how to convince themselves and others that what they have discovered is correct. Thus, in the process of learning mathematics, they concomitantly learn how to learn more about mathematics. This may be of value to them long after they have forgotten particular propositions.

There is additional intellectual satisfaction in teaching mathematics. Mathematics is definite and logical. The rules for determining the truth and falsity of its statements are clear and accepted by all who understand the subject. Should a teacher and student disagree on the truth of a statement, it usually can be readily tested. Students respond to the force of the argument rather than to the force of the arguer; they have recourse to something other than authoritative opinion. Contrast these characteristics with the subjective characteristics of other subjects like literature, social studies, and art, where problems of semantics, esthetics, and ethics abound. This is not to disparage such subjects but only to point to the distinctive intellectual satisfaction that derives from the objectivity that mathematics affords.

Most mathematics teachers enjoy solving problems. Until they came to teach mathematics, many of the problems they sought to solve were mathematics problems. In teaching the subject, different sorts of problems become evident. Mathematics is not easy for all, and students who find it hard to understand offer the teacher challenge. To be sure, this is a problem different from mathematics problems, and in many respects it is harder to cope with. Yet the attack is the same: defining the problem as clearly as possible, entertaining hunches as to the solution, testing the hunches, and arriving hopefully at a solution. Teachers cannot solve all the problems of learning, but they solve many and this becomes an immense source of satisfaction. Mathematics teaching becomes dull only if the teacher does not look for problems to solve and ways of improving methods of teaching.

Thought questions

1   It was asserted that teachers contribute to society and to individual students. Are these contributions disjoint? Why?

2   Subjects other than mathematics have their own logic. What is the difference between the logic of mathematics and that of an empirical subject?

3   Why are differences of opinion more prevalent in subjects like literature, art, sociology, and ethics than in mathematics?

4   It is sometimes said that people can teach themselves by observing, reading, and thinking. How probable is it that a young person without the aid of a teacher can learn the mathematics that is currently taught in high school?

5   Suppose a student is highly motivated to learn mathematics and is willing to study the subject independently. What contributions can a teacher make to the education of such a student?

6   Suppose a student has had a record of lack of success in mathematics and cares to study it no longer than required. What help can a teacher give such a student?

7   In light of the nature of the profession, what professional and personal qualities should a mathematics teacher have?

The theoretical aspect of pedagogical education

It is possible to learn a lot about teaching by observing teachers teaching and imitating what they do. Mathematics teachers can be observed to give assignments, ask questions, explain when students do not understand, write on the chalkboard, assign and correct homework, give tests, admonish students to behave properly, talk to parents, attend meetings, stand in halls during the changing of classes, read announcements, pass out and collect report cards, write reports, and do many other things.

It is well known, however, that people do not see all they look at. Observation discriminates and is guided by preconceptions. An observer who has no concept of motivation might not notice that teachers deliberately use some class time to motivate students. Such an observer, unaware of their logical differences, might not distinguish between the stating of facts, the drawing of inferences, and the stating of value judgments. One might be aware that there are times when a teacher seeks to convince students that some proposition is true by giving an argument, but, unacquainted with the nature of inductive and direct and indirect deductive arguments, he probably would not notice that the structure of various arguments differs. Without didactic instruction from the teacher or from some other source, an observer may not recognize certain things the teacher does or makes use of. Uninstructed observation may not be maximally effective.

Guided only by observation, with no explanations as to why teachers do certain things under certain conditions, an observer gains little new understanding. Assume, for example, that an observer can recognize and distinguish between a generalization and instances of the generalization. This person might notice that on some occasions a teacher gives several instances of a generalization and then states the generalization and on other occasions states the generalization first and then gives several instances of it. Both these practices can be imitated. But under what conditions should one order be used rather than the other? This is not readily learned merely by observation.

Consider also a teacher giving individual instruction. The observer sees the teacher give an assignment that consists in part of exercises. The students set to work on the assignment while the teacher walks around the room and guides different students. Two students are unable to do a particular exercise. To one, the teacher says, "Well, you think about it a while." To the other, the teacher suggests the performance of a particular operation. Both actions can be imitated, but why does the teacher behave one way when working with one student and another with the other? Should the teacher have responded in two different ways? The answers to these questions require an understanding not gained easily by mere observation.

It is doubtful, moreover, that values, which along with facts form the basis of decision and choice, can be acquired rationally just by observation. Suppose a teacher in training is advised to observe two mathematics teachers with good reputations. Their students do well on standardized examinations and report that they enjoy their mathematics classes. The observer notices that one teacher goes to great pains to insure that students understand what they are doing. This teacher relates various items of knowledge, explains the rationale of algorithms, and shows how certain mathematical principles follow from others. The other teacher does not do these things very extensively but tells the students what to do and how to do it and then gives them lots of practice exercises that require them to apply the rules they have been taught. Moreover, this teacher assigns many review exercises. Which teacher should the observer imitate? The answer depends on what the observer values.

It is not being argued here that values cannot be learned by imitation. We know they can, especially if the observer identifies with the person being observed. But values acquired by imitation (identification, as the psychologists put it) usually are not rational. They tend to be unexamined and are held nonevidentially—that is, the person who acquires them is not able to state the grounds for their acceptance. Conflicting values cannot be reconciled by mere observation. Deliberation is required too, and if deliberation is to be sound, it should be predicated on knowledge of concepts and principles, consideration of alternatives, and projection of the consequences of various alternatives. All this requires a knowledge of theory.

Finally, good judgment is a necessary attribute of an effective teacher.

Like all professional workers, a mathematics teacher is called on repeatedly to exercise judgment. What should be the objectives of mathematics education? What subject matter should be selected? What are the reasonable expectations of a class of students and particular students within the class? What individualized instruction will most help a student with certain learning disabilities? How should grades be assigned? How can the desire to learn be cultivated in particular students? How can a student who disrupts the learning atmosphere in class be persuaded to change? The answers to these questions and others similar to them require judgment. It is no wonder that superintendents appraising candidates for a teaching position attempt to assess their judgment.

Before arguing that good judgment in teaching cannot be learned just by observation but needs a theoretical base, let us consider what judgment is—and is not. Judgment is sometimes confused with guessing or stating an opinion. This may be because the outcomes of guessing and opining are the same as the outcome of judging; the result is an assertion of a belief, of a value to be assigned, or of something that should be done. A judgment differs from a guess and an opinion because of the grounds from which they are reached. Making a judgment necessarily implies the application of some standards or principles and the ability to give reasons for the judgment. A guess and an opinion, on the other hand, can be groundless. As Green (1971, p. 175) points out, it is quite natural in certain circumstances "for a person to say, 'I cannot really give a judgment; I can only guess.' And this way of speaking suggests that we often contrast judging and guessing in relation to the grounds for judgment at our disposal."

Another cognitive activity with which judgment is sometimes confused is knowing. The two are distinct; we use "judge" and "know" differently. Suppose we are able to show that $ABCD$ is a parallelogram. Because the opposite sides of a parallelogram are congruent, we would say, "I *know* that the opposite sides of $ABCD$ are congruent"; we would not say, "I *judge* that the opposite sides of $ABCD$ are congruent." The latter is not syntactically or semantically incorrect, but we do not ordinarily use "judge" and "judgment" in this way.

The distinction between judging and knowing rests on the grounds on which the cognitive activity is predicated. Judgment is made in the absence of sufficient evidence or grounds; statements of knowledge are made when the evidence or grounds are sufficient. Thus, a teacher says to a student, "I *judge* (or think) that your work in mathematics is worth an A." It would be both misleading and an abuse of language for him to say, "I *know* your work is worth an A." When the grounds are inconclusive, judgment must be exercised.

Judgments are claims made in absence of grounds sufficient to warrant claims to knowledge but on the basis of some grounds so that they are not mere guesses. Judgments take on value in practical situations in which decisions concerning what ought to be done have to be made. They are good when subsequent evidence shows that the judgments attain the end for which they state means and do not attain undesirable ends. Thus, a mathematics teacher's judgment concerning a kind of remedial teaching for a student who is having trouble solving so-called story problems in mathematics would be considered good judgment if the student improved in solving such problems and did not at the same time develop a dislike for mathematics, a tendency to cheat, or any other undesirable trait.

Two kinds of ground for practical judgments—judgments concerning what ought to be done in a particular situation—can be identified. One is the facts in the situation. A mathematics teacher working with a student who has difficulty solving story problems may notice that the student does not always remember what the problem asks, has trouble setting up an equation, and does not know basic relations such as the relation between time and rate and distance, or percentage. These are facts relevant to the teacher's diagnosis or judgment of the causes of the student's trouble and the teacher's subsequent choice or judgment of remedial teaching. But these facts imply little unless they are coupled with principles based on experience in teaching and learning. The relevant principles constitute the second kind of ground on which judgments are made. In the case of diagnosis and re-mediation, certainly one principle is: If it is necessary to know A in order to understand B, then A must be taught before B. Guided by the facts and this principle and other relevant principles of teaching, the mathematics teacher probably would teach the student to read the problem carefully and ask what is to be found. Additionally, the teacher would reteach the time-rate-distance relation and relations involving percentage. The teacher would probably also offer advice on how to go about setting up an equation.

When observing teachers teaching, it is easy to observe facts, assuming the observer has the guiding concepts. Attaining principles by observation is less readily accomplished; many may not be attained, for the observer may not know which principles the teacher is using in making judgments. Concepts and principles are elements of the theory of teaching.

Theory enables us not only to become aware of certain phenomena and relations but also to understand them—to know why they occur and how to control them insofar as this is possible. Thus, a teacher who knows what it means to define and how to judge a student's comprehension of a definition is better able to adapt to the case of a student who has difficulty comprehending a definition. A teacher who understands logical implication and knows about the nature of students who do not sense implications readily is able to use examples, analogies, or drawings to clarify the logical relations between premises and conclusions. There are few things more practical than good theory.

Theory is most efficiently learned didactically rather than by observation This is not to imply that observation has no part in the learning of theory. Observation helps test and give meaning to theory and provides opportunity for applying it. Where direct observation is hard, indirect observation can substitute. In this book you will find the exposition of theory as well as the theory clarified. Opportunities are given you to apply it in the classroom dialogues that represent indirect observation.

Thought questions

1 Give examples of how concepts guide observation.

2 It is sometimes said that values are caught rather than taught. What does this mean? Would values acquired in this way be rational? Why?

3 What are some kinds of judgment a mathematics teacher has to make?

4 Why is it difficult to learn good judgment by observing instances of it?

5 How does judging differ from knowing? How does it differ from guessing?

6 Teachers often offer students advice. To what extent does this advice represent knowledge and to what extent does it represent judgment?

7 Why can judging be considered somewhere between guessing and knowing?

8 Green (1971, p. 177) writes, "To exercise good judgment is to get optimum results under less than optimum conditions or on grounds which are less than decisive." Is this a satisfactory definition of good judgment?

9 What contributions does theory make toward competence in teaching?

10 It is argued that a knowledge of theory is a necessary condition for competence in teaching. Is it a sufficent condition? Why?

An analysis of teaching

A fruitful way of studying teaching is to observe what teachers do, classify the observations in some way that allows insight, and then study the classes and subclasses. Subsequent studies can be made of the relation between classes of activity and student learning.

When one studies what teachers do, one finds that some activities are related closely to teaching; demonstrating, explaining, defining, correcting students' mistakes, providing motivation, and assessing students' progress are some of these. The acts in this category are the most significant and may be thought of as *teaching-centered acts.* Others are less significantly related to teaching and may be thought of as *institution-centered acts:* taking attendance, attending teachers' meetings, supervising the halls during changes of classes, reading announcements, making out institutional reports. Still other activities are scarcely related to teaching: eating lunch, sneezing, combing one's hair, smoking, driving to and from school. There is little use in giving these a designation.

Institution-centered acts are necessary in our complex society in which formal education is accomplished in an institution—the school. Large numbers of students, teachers, secretaries, custodians, and ancillary pro-fessional personnel such as administrators, guidance counselors, and nurses work together in the restricted environment of the school building and grounds. Hence, some things that have to be done are related not to the mission of the school but to keeping the school going. While the institution-centered acts the teacher performs are necessary and should be performed effectively, they are less interesting than teaching-centered acts. They are largely routine, are readily learned, and have no substantial body of theory associated with them. Hence, when there is not enough time to consider everything a teacher does, as is the case in every teacher education program, little instruction in *how* to execute the institution-centered acts is usually given.

When the teaching-centered acts are examined, we find that some can best be studied by logical analysis. Defining, inferring, explaining, giving reasons, generalizing, applying principles, and proving are examples. Whether a teacher has given a definition instead of, say, an example or a description and whether the definition is satisfactory are determined on logical grounds. Whether an argument constitutes a proof is determined by analyzing the argument in terms of established criteria. Let us call such acts *logic-centered acts*. They predominate whenever a teacher appeals to the rational aspect of a student's personality—that is, when the teacher wishes the student to understand what is being learned and done and to be thoughtful about it.

A second kind of teaching-centered act seems studied best in terms of its consequence rather than in terms of logical structure. Teachers teach so that students can learn; this is the justification for teaching. Hence a teacher does many of the things he or she does because they will facilitate learning. By emphasizing the importance of what is to be learned or by introducing the lesson by a thought-provoking problem, the teacher hopes to induce a desire to learn and a disposition to study what is assigned. By pointing out errors a student commonly makes and suggesting ways of avoiding them, the teacher seeks to improve the student's competence. By focusing on the positive attainments of the student and offering encouragement, the teacher expects to sustain the student's interest in mathematics. In all these cases, the judgments of the teacher are appraised by the consequences relative to the learning of the student. Let us call teaching-centered acts appraised by their effects on students' learning *student-centered acts*.

It should not be inferred that a particular teaching-centered act can be analyzed by only one set of criteria, logical or consequential. Suppose a mathematics teacher gives a particular definition. The definition may satisfy logical criteria in every way, but it may be incomprehensible to the students for whom it is intended because it uses terms the students do not understand. Another definition may be readily comprehended by the students and thus satisfy the reason for defining, but it may be faulty on logical grounds; it may not state all the necessary conditions, for example. Similarly, when an algebra teacher plans to give several instances of the cancellation law for multiplication and expects the students subsequently to generalize from the instances, the act can be appraised in terms of what we know about how students learn—that is, about learning theory. It can also be appraised in terms of whether what the teacher chooses are in fact instances of this law, whether the formulated generalization is consistent with the instances—that is, logical theory. Each kind of appraisal has value.

The methods or acts teachers plan and use to attain general objectives like concepts, principles, and skills, to teach students how to solve problems and prove propositions, and to build favorable attitudes toward mathematics are typically both logic-centered and student-centered. In planning a lesson to teach something—some substantive knowledge, a skill, or an attitude—a mathematics teacher calls on a knowledge of logic and also on a knowledge of psychology. The interplay of these helps the teacher decide what sequence of things to do, what kinds of explanation to give, how to forestall errors students commonly make, what kinds of application and practice to provide, how to provide motivation and reinforcement, and how to assess the students' progress. At times, application of principles of logic is more helpful in making judgments; at other times, application of principles of learning furnishes more insight. The competent teacher can use both kinds of analysis and decide which has more value in a particular situation.

In subsequent chapters of this book, you will find an exposition of both logical and psychological theory as these are relevant to the major activities of mathematics teachers—maintaining a classroom atmosphere that is conducive to learning; teaching such substantive knowledge as concepts, facts, and principles; teaching the skills of operating with mathematical objects and the generalized intellectual skills of solving problems and proving propositions; diagnosing students' difficulties and providing effective remediation; evaluating both the progress of the students and of the teacher's own effectiveness in teaching. In the absence of actual classroom observation, classroom dialogues simulating what might be observed develop and clarify the principles. The questions that follow most of the sections in the chapters provide opportunities for making judgments calling for an application of the concepts and principles you will learn.

Thought questions

1   Name some teaching-centered acts that mathematics teachers typically perform other than those mentioned in this section.

2   What is the distinction between teaching-centered acts and institution-centered acts? Which should be used to define, in the sense of identify, teaching?

3   Is it conceivable that an explanation can be regarded as satisfactory even though the students for whom it is intended do not understand it? Explain.

4   Is motivation logic-centered or student-centered? Explain.

5   Consider a teacher trying to convince the students in a class that a certain statement is true. How can this act be appraised by means of logic? How can it be appraised by means of learning theory?

6   We might define an inference as a conclusion a person reaches on the basis of

certain premises. Given a set of premises, some inferences from these are warranted; others are not. How do we tell whether an inference is warranted?

7 Teachers often try to get students interested in mathematics. Which theory is of more value to a teacher in this case, logical theory or psychological theory?

8 Explain how both logic and psychology can be used in helping students understand indirect proof.

9 It might be said that the purpose of the theory of teaching is to make the teacher rational. What does this statement mean? Give examples.

Self-test on the competencies

1 Explain why the characteristics of mathematics make teaching satisfying to many mathematics teachers.
   a What are some of the characteristics of mathematics that many teachers find satisfying?
   b Why do some of the characteristics you stated make the teaching of mathematics satisfying?

2 Explain why a knowledge of the theory of teaching is necessary for a competent mathematics teacher.
   a Why will only the observation of the actions of a mathematics teacher probably not result in the development of much competence in teaching?
   b Point out some of the contributions a knowledge of teaching theory affords a person who is training to become a mathematics teacher. Give examples.

3 Show how the analysis of teaching that forms the basis of the theory presented in this book is helpful.
   a The things a mathematics teacher does are classified as teaching-centered and institution-centered acts. Teaching-centered acts are analyzed as logic-centered and student-centered acts. What are some advantages of this conception?
   b When considering student-centered acts, what theory is particularly relevant? Give a couple of examples of how a knowledge of this theory will be of help to a mathematics teacher who is considering an act in terms of its consequences for enhancing a student's learning.
   c Give some examples of how a knowledge of logic will be helpful to a mathematics teacher who is considering a logic-centered act.

References

Brown, Claude H. *The Teaching of Secondary Mathematics*. New York: Harper & Row, 1953. Chs. 1–3.
Green, Thomas F. *The Activities of Teaching*. New York: McGraw-Hill, 1971. Ch. 1.

2

Developing a success-oriented classroom

In some respects teaching is analogous to the onstage performance of an actor. An actor must project his role so that the audience is transformed from detached onlookers to sensitized participants. Similarly, a teacher must engage students in such a way that they are transformed from spectators to active participants. This is a difficult task, because the teacher must interact with both subject matter and students.

A teacher's interactions with subject matter take place in a social context—the classroom environment. Two basic components of this social context are the students' perceptions of their status as learners and their perceptions of the teacher as a leader. People behave in situations according to how they view themselves in relation to the world in which they live. Perceptions are determined to some extent by self-concepts, by one's view of oneself as an individual. Students who believe they cannot learn mathematics or perceive the teacher as an antagonist are likely to behave in ways that can make teaching ineffectual. In this chapter we are going to describe actions mathematics teachers can take to affect positively students' perceptions of themselves as learners and their perceptions of the teacher as a leader.

At the conclusion of this chapter, you should be able to demonstrate the following competencies:

1 Identify and illustrate defensive strategies students use

2　Explain why students use defensive strategies

3　Explain why defensive behavior can inhibit learning

4　Identify routine matters occurring in a classroom you have observed and judge the effectiveness of the way these matters were handled

5　Identify and illustrate four uses teachers make of questions

6　Identify uses of maxims for classroom management that occur in a classroom you have observed and judge the effectiveness of the teacher's use of the maxims

Defensive behavior in students

To help get a better understanding of why students use defensive behavior, consider some defensive strategies you may have used or observed. Have you ever heard a teacher ask,

What city in the world has the largest population?

and heard a reply such as,

It wouldn't be Los Angeles, would it?

Similarly, in a mathematics classroom a student might answer the question,

What is the product of $2x$ and $3x$?

by responding,

It isn't $6x^2$, is it?

This strategy can be called **hedging.**

Another strategy students often use can be labeled **guess and look.** Have you ever been asked a question that has only two reasonable responses when you were not sure which one was correct? When students are confronted with this situation, they often respond with one alternative and have the other alternative ready for instant use if the teacher's facial reaction is not affirmative. Perhaps you can recall using such a strategy yourself. This strategy helps the learner maximize his chances for receiving credit or approval.

Sometimes when students are called on, they use a strategy called **incomplete answer.** This strategy entails giving an incomplete answer in the hope that the response will be accepted and elaborated on by the teacher:

Teacher　What is the formula for the sum of the angles of a convex polygon?

Student　180 times . . . um . . . (*pause*)

Teacher　Two less than the number of sides?

Student　$(n - 2)$. That's right!

Another common strategy, especially among junior high school students, is to join in with their more capable classmates once they have initiated a response. A student may use the **joining-in** strategy by nodding his head enthusiastically or by giving some affirmative verbalization after classmates have committed themselves with a response.

Why is it that students employ such defensive strategies? To answer this question, consider why people in general use defensive strategies. Individuals use defense mechanisms as a shield to protect their self-concept. The maintenance and enhancement of one's self-concept makes this shield a psychological necessity. The existence of alibis attests to this phenomenon. Students, like everyone else, must maintain and enhance their self-concept. Students use (consciously or unconsciously) each of the four defensive strategies identified previously to maintain and enhance their intellectual status when challenged by a question they view as threatening.

Holt, in *How Children Fail*, identifies the strategies above and others as exemplifications of how students try to avoid fear. He sees students as being afraid of failure in the eyes of their teachers, peers, and parents and particularly in their own eyes. The constant threat of failure, as portrayed by Holt, is a continuing attack on the student's self-image.

Notice the cleverness of each of the strategies we have described in maintaining and enhancing the self. Consider the strategy implied by the answer "It isn't $6x^2$, is it?" If $6x^2$ is the correct answer, then the student receives credit. However, if $6x^2$ is incorrect, the student still receives some credit (at least in his own eyes) for being the first to challenge the response. A student using this strategy when informed that an answer is wrong will typically respond, "I didn't think it was right." Thus, whatever the outcome, the student has shielded himself against complete failure.

One should not take such strategies for abnormal behavior. These and others occur in every classroom. One could even argue that such behavior is preferable to no response at all: a total lack of response may indicate that fear is present in the classroom to such a degree that learning is severely stifled. The point is that a teacher should be able to recognize a strategy as a defensive behavior and be able to cope with it as such. The teacher must take care not to threaten the student's self-image; such action only promotes further defensive behavior until finally the student ceases to have any desire to communicate in class. On the other hand, the teacher must not allow students always to succeed in using these defensive strategies. Success may reduce classroom interactions to guesses of what is in the teacher's mind as opposed to attempts to understand the subject matter. Understanding the subject matter has taken place when students are able to use their knowledge as a foundation for future learning. This kind of learning is not likely to occur when students are continually preoccupied with answer-grabbing strategies. While a teacher may view mathematics as an organized system of knowledge, students who rely on answer-grabbing behavior are unlikely to conceptualize mathematics in this way. Successfully guessing what is in a teacher's mind may alleviate immediate pressures on students, but it does little to promote understanding.

Thought questions

1 Identify some similarities and differences between acting and teaching not cited in this chapter.

2 The strategies of hedging and guess and look were discussed as ways of protecting one's self-concept when it is threatened with a question. Discuss how the strategies of joining-in and incomplete answer can also be used to maintain and enhance the self-concept.

3 Some students employ the strategy of not trying at all. Explain why this strategy is often defensive.

4 Sometimes a teacher will say to a student, "John, you are a bright boy; you would do well if you would only try." Why is this sometimes a poor strategy for a teacher to use? If a student believes that the teacher thinks he is bright, why may it be to his advantage not to try?

5 As further evidence that a student's behavior is predicated on fear, Holt (1964) identifies a strategy he labels as **don't look back**. An example of this strategy occurs when a student turns in a test paper or some other written assignment without checking the work or the reasonableness of the answers. How does this strategy result in a reduction of tension?

6 Identify additional defensive behavior students use to avoid being embarrassed in the eyes of their peers and their teachers.

The defensive behaviors just discussed are not, in isolated cases, a serious threat to learning. However, when answer-grabbing, absence of student interaction, or defensive behaviors occur frequently, it is unlikely that the classroom atmosphere is conducive to learning. A teacher should be able to perceive when defensive strategies are becoming dominant in the classroom and to take action to alleviate the conditions that promote the defensive behavior.

What action can a teacher take to promote a positive atmosphere toward learning mathematics in the classroom? A teacher must realize that reacting to students in negative ways, such as reprimanding individuals or admonishing the class, may only trigger further defensive behavior. This is not to say that there is no place for reprimands. Direct action to control misbehavior is sometimes necessary, and when it is used judiciously it can have a positive effect on students. But to engender a positive atmosphere, a teacher must promote student behavior that maintains and enhances desirable aspects of each student's self-concept.

Basic ingredients in a desirable classroom atmosphere include the teacher's interest in mathematics and a concern for students as persons and their progress. Mathematics students are keenly aware of their teacher's interest and enthusiasm for mathematics and desire and willingness to help them learn. Students must perceive that the teacher is serious about teaching mathematics. A teacher can convey this seriousness by using a tone of voice and projecting an attitude that portrays the confidence of the teacher as teacher and in students' ability to learn. As an actor must use voice and appearance to create a desired impression, so must a teacher utilize voice and be enthusiastic to convey confidence in and concern for students.

A teacher must be firm yet friendly. This is not easy. It necessitates confidence in discussing subject matter and in dealing with students' problems as they arise. Such confidence is predicated upon a thorough understanding of the subject and the establishment of limits in the student-teacher relationship. The exact limits of a student-teacher relationship must evolve from a teacher's experiences and beliefs about teaching and the nature of the students. Many teachers are unable to establish these limits because of their failure to define their role as a teacher. Each teacher must decide the expectations to be held for students. Only when the teacher has done this can effective communication be achieved. If students are in a constant quandary as to what is expected of them, it is difficult for them to maintain and enhance their status as learners. When a teacher's expectations are not clear, then the students will attempt to define the limits under which they may operate. This often results in various forms of misbehavior and, in general, does not promote an atmosphere conducive to learning.

Let us consider the different tasks that confront a teacher in the classroom. A teacher is involved in such routine matters as keeping records and grading and must involve the students in learning mathematics. In addition to these tasks, a teacher is expected to be in control of classes. The remainder of this chapter will present suggestions for you to consider in defining your role as a teacher in working with the class as a group in matters of routine, questioning, and control.

Establishing a viable routine

The following hypothetical sequence of events is one that could occur in a ninth-grade algebra class.

The bell rings, and the majority of students find their seats and converse with one another, some discussing algebra problems, others generally socializing. Three students are waiting around the teacher's desk and two other students are standing in the doorway. One of these two students leaves the room. The teacher arrives about two minutes later and immediately engages in conversation the three students waiting at the desk. They are discussing a matter that concerns a school club sponsored by this teacher. Meanwhile, the class continues to socialize.

After a few minutes, the teacher concludes the conversation with the three students. At this point the teacher is unable to locate the lesson plans and, hence, is forced to ask the students for the day's assignment. After receiving several conflicting reports, the teacher verifies the assignment and asks students to take out their homework. This request requires several repetitions as some students persist in socializing. While the teacher explains a problem, several students are confused as to what problems are being discussed. Two students ask permission to go to their lockers to retrieve their homework papers. The teacher is slightly annoyed but grants this request.

A hall monitor now knocks on the door and asks the teacher for the attendance slip. After a hurried survey the teacher fills out the slip but fails to note the absence of the student who left before the teacher arrived. While answering an additional question, the two students return from their lockers accompanied by the student who had departed earlier. The teacher wants to know why this student is late. The student replies that he had been called to the office and had come to class to obtain permission but upon finding the teacher missing decided to answer the assistant principal's summons. The teacher is again slightly annoyed and tells the student to return to the office and obtain a note verifying his visit. In responding to still another question the teacher needs some colored chalk to clarify a diagram and steps out of the room to borrow it from a neighboring teacher.

After fielding a number of additional questions the teacher begins to introduce some new material. The students appear to be having some difficulty understanding the teacher's points and interrupt frequently with questions. The bell signaling the end of the period rings as the teacher is answering a student's question. As the students are packing up and leaving, the teacher hurriedly turns to the next problem set and makes a verbal assignment of the odd-numbered problems on that page. A few students stop and write the information down, but the majority seems to make a hurried mental note of the assignment. As he is leaving, one student announces, "I'll never be able to do these problems; I don't understand any of this new stuff we had today."

In this episode are a number of situations that could undermine the teaching and learning of mathematics. If they recur over an extended period of time, not only will the learning of mathematics be adversely affected but the atmosphere in this class could become permanently chaotic.

Let us identify and examine some of the incidents that caused disruptions. One of the first occurred when a student left the room before the teacher arrived. There is a danger inherent in students leaving the classroom without proper authorization: they are likely to engage in disruptive activities. Another disruptive incident occurred when the teacher elected to chat with the three students at the desk. Such behavior encourages a variety of further disruptions from the students who remain. In addition, the teacher, unable to locate lesson plans, was handicapped in starting the lesson. This was compounded by the teacher's having to ask the students to identify assigned homework problems.

One factor that contributed to the teacher's difficulties was being late to class. This accounted for the unauthorized departure of one student and also contributed to the uneasiness with which the lesson began. Furthermore, it is likely that the teacher's tardiness led to the omission of taking attendance, which then caused an additional disruption by the hall monitor. The haste necessary in finally taking attendance probably caused the teacher to overlook the student who was missing from class. The teacher's failure to begin class in a forceful way was due in part to tardiness but was compounded by election to converse with students concerning an extracurricular activity during class time and by misplacement of lesson plans and instructional materials.

The exposition of the new material was not clear to the students, perhaps because of the hurried beginning and the subsequent disruption. The student who commented on this as he was exiting from the classroom indicated this. The teacher's loss of plans and inability to bring the lesson to a close before the final bell resulted in a homework assignment that was apparently not well thought out. Making assignments in this way can result in asking students to complete an inordinate number of exercises or problems that they are not prepared to handle. This situation can result in student animosity. Even if the assignment had been previously thought out, it would have appeared to the students that the teacher was making an ill-conceived assignment. In any event, hastily assigned problems can result in student frustration at home and in subsequent class meetings. Furthermore, in giving a hurried verbal assignment a teacher runs the risk of miscommunication. This is especially true when the students are under the duress of packing up and leaving.

This teacher would have been well-advised to have established certain standard routines. Many of the disruptions could have been averted had the teacher established routines with respect to punctuality of both teacher and students, starting class efficiently with carefully formulated plans and necessary notes and equipment, taking attendance and making announcements promptly, and making assignments clear. Punctual teachers have an advantage in being able to handle, in a calm and unhurried way, many peripheral matters such as students asking to be excused for field trips and student council meetings. In addition, teachers have the opportunity to collect their thoughts, quickly review their plans for the coming period, and secure any equipment needed such as chalk, overhead projector, or visual aids. Being punctual also provides a teacher with an opportunity to interact on occasion with students in matters of interest to them such as last week's ball-game or a forthcoming school event. Had the teacher in our example been on time, he probably could have attended before class started to the student who was called to the office, dealt with the concerns of the club members, located his lesson plans, secured the needed chalk, and avoided a number of disruptions. No doubt the quality of the lesson would have been improved if the teacher had had a moment to collect his thoughts and reflect on his goals in the forthcoming lesson. In general, it is a good idea for teachers to dispense with such matters as taking attendance and making announcements before starting the lesson. In the illustration, the teacher would have avoided at least one interruption by taking attendance at the outset of the class. Furthermore, it is highly advisable that a teacher get everyone's attention before beginning to teach.

One of the students' major contacts with mathematics is homework and classroom exercises assigned by the teacher. Hence, it behooves the teacher to assign exercises that reflect objectives for the course. In the illustration, the teacher apparently did not give careful thought to assigning exercises that would reflect course goals. Teachers must also effectively communicate the assignment and its due date to students under conditions that enable them to record and clarify their responsibilities. Obviously this does not occur when a teacher makes an assignment hurriedly.

Grading is another routine matter teachers must consider in establishing a desirable classroom atmosphere. Grades have a pervasive effect on the morale of the class. When a teacher's evaluation scheme or grading system is unknown, students are unsure of what is expected. The resulting tension often forces students to resort to answer-grabbing and other defensive strategies. In general, teachers are wise to make their grading system clear to students and to keep students informed of their progress through a grading period.

Mathematics teachers usually base their grades primarily on test scores. Therefore, it is important that students perceive tests as having face validity—that they feel the tests are fair evaluations of their mathematical competence. It is also important that the teacher grade and return tests to students promptly as an indication that the tests are viewed as important and that the teacher is keenly interested in each student's progress. Learning theory provides us with ample evidence that, if tests are to be used as a learning device, as they should be, they must be graded and returned as soon as possible.

While it is advisable to establish certain routines with respect to non-academic matters, a teacher must guard against monotonous routines in teaching. Many mathematics teachers have a standard operating procedure for the major portion of the class period. A standard routine such as checking and going over an assignment, presenting new material, and beginning work on a new assignment, repeated day after day, can create an unstimulating atmosphere. To guard against this, teachers should discuss homework assignments and present new material in a variety of ways. Homework problems can be discussed in a number of ways: students can put problems on the board, individual students can explain their solutions, or the teacher can work problems with the help of class members. New subject matter can be presented by means of many expository and discovery strategies that are discussed in detail in later chapters.

In the preceding discussion we have tried to illustrate and examine the advantages of the establishment of certain routines for classroom operation. Routines facilitate the teaching of mathematics by helping to create a stable and well-defined context of classroom management and academic expectations. It is rare that students maintain and enhance desirable aspects of their self-concepts in chaotic situations.

Thought questions

1   Give examples of student behavior that would indicate that defensive strategies are dominating the classroom. Can the teacher combat defensive behavior by demanding that it cease? Discuss your answer.

2   What are desirable aspects of a student's self-concept?

3   Besides voice, what can a teacher use to project confidence and enthusiasm for teaching?

4   What difficulties can arise when students are not sure what is expected of them?

5   Discuss the pros and cons of each of the following positions that teachers might take with respect to student tardiness.
    a "As long as the kids arrive within a few minutes of the bell, I don't worry about it."
    b "When the bell rings, I shut the door and expect any latecomers to secure a late pass from the office."
    c "I handle student tardiness on an individual basis."

6   Discuss the pros and cons of permitting students to obtain materials needed for class from their lockers after the period has begun.

7   Offer explanations as to why the presentation of the new subject matter in the hypothetical episode in the ninth-grade algebra class did not go well.

8   What factors in addition to quiz and test scores should mathematics teachers consider when determining grades? Should disruptive behavior influence grades? Discuss your answer.

9   Discuss how a chaotic classroom atmosphere inhibits the development of desirable aspects of a student's self-concept.

Using questions in the classroom

One of the goals of teaching mathematics is to help students learn mathematics in a meaningful way. To learn mathematics in such a way, students must be involved in doing mathematics. One way a teacher can promote involvement is by employing various questioning techniques. A teacher's questions have many purposes, each serving in some way to facilitate learning. Four purposes of questions will be discussed in the remainder of this section. They are to:

Help promote students' feelings of success

Anticipate and overcome learning problems

Review and evaluate progress

Assist in controlling misbehavior

Each of these four purposes can contribute toward establishing a positive classroom atmosphere.

It is essential that every teacher try to establish and maintain a classroom in which the students feel free to discuss mathematics and to challenge ideas presented by their peers and the teacher. Students who are not successful in learning an academic subject cease to be interested in pursuing it. The truth of this can be illustrated by reflection on one's own interests and pursuits. A teacher can provide opportunity for success by asking a question the student can or is likely to answer correctly. For example, in solving a quadratic equation such as

$$3x^2 + 11x - 20 = 0$$

a weak student could be asked to give possible factors of 20 and 3, and questions pertaining to the remaining steps of solving the problem could be asked of more capable students. While it is hoped that all the students will eventually be able to solve the entire problem, simpler questions can provide the less capable student with opportunities to participate in classroom discussions. Students with learning problems are less likely to be mathematical dropouts if teachers can help them feel they are making progress. In the example above, the student who had given factors of 3 and 20 had an investment in the problem and hence was more likely to follow and benefit from the subsequent discussion. Contrast this situation with one in which the less able student is asked to solve an entire problem and the response is, "I don't know," whereupon a more capable student is called on for the solution. The borderline student is more likely to "tune out" after such failure and thus receive no benefit from subsequent class discussions.

A second way that teachers can stimulate thought is to ask questions that encourage high levels of thinking. A steady diet of questions requiring straightforward recall of facts and generalizations can become boring. While asking for factors of 3 and 20 may be an effective way of involving less able students in class discussions, questions should transcend this low level of thinking. A skillful teacher can provide opportunities for all students to have successful experiences in forming and testing conjectures, comparing and contrasting examples, and forming generalizations from specific instances. "Why" and "what happens if" questions promote higher levels of thinking. For example, a teacher of a seventh-grade mathematics section involved in a unit on number theory could ask the class to find sums of two odd numbers. From these specific instances the teacher could then ask slower students to form a conjecture concerning the nature of this sum. The better students might be asked to provide a justification for the given conjecture. Subsequent questions such as "What happens if one of the addends is even?" could then be asked.

Similarly, in a geometry class studying parallel lines and planes, the following questions can provide challenges for students of varying ability:

1   Describe the set of points that is equally distant from two given points. (This request could pertain to either two-space or three-space.)

2   Suppose that the two given points lie on a pair of parallel lines. Will there always be at least one point that is equally distant from the two given points and also on one of the given parallel lines? Why?

3   Now suppose the two given points lie on a pair of parallel planes. Will there always be at least one point that is equally distant from the two given points and also on one of the given parallel planes? Why?

An algebra teacher can stimulate interesting discussions by asking students to examine the relationship between the roots of a quadratic equation, the number of x-intercepts of its graph, and the value of the discriminant. Teachers often fail to seize the opportunity for student discoveries. Instead they merely inform the students of these relationships.

By using questions a teacher can establish a dialogue with students that can do much to promote a positive classroom atmosphere. Questions can draw students into discussions and kindle whatever interest they may have. By maintaining a dialogue with them, a teacher can thwart potential problems and help insure that students will be positively disposed to learn mathematics.

Thought questions

1   List some "easy" questions concerning the factorization of $3x^2 + 11x - 20$ that all algebra students could be expected to answer correctly.

2   "Why" and "What happens if" questions were cited as vehicles for promoting higher levels of thinking. List other types of questions that require more than recall for their solution.

3   Design "Why" and "What happens if" questions that might be appropriate in discussing the following items of knowledge.
a The product of two negative integers is a positive integer.
b The measure of the angle formed by two secants to a circle is one-half the difference of the measures of the intercepted arcs.

4   Answer the three geometry questions on pages 23–24.

5   Outline an approach that will allow students to discover the relationship between the roots of a quadratic equation, the number of x-intercepts of its graph, and the value of the discriminant.

It has been observed that teachers also use questions to anticipate, diagnose, and resolve student difficulties (Lockwood, 1970). From experience and careful reflection, teachers can anticipate errors that are likely to occur. For example, it is probable that some algebra students will make the error

$$\frac{a + b}{a} = 1 + b$$

A teacher can anticipate this error by examining examples such as

$$\frac{4+8}{4} \quad \text{and} \quad \frac{6+10}{10}$$

and then questioning students about the dangers in canceling common terms in numerators and denominators.

Another error some students commonly make is

$$\frac{2}{3} + \frac{3}{4} = \frac{5}{7}$$

Teachers can head off this error by posing questions that illustrate its obviousness. Students can be questioned about the results of this algorithm when applied to the sum $\frac{1}{2} + \frac{1}{2}$. It is to be hoped that they will realize the futility of adding numerators and denominators. Another approach is to have students use the number line in adding fractions. Use of the number line should indicate that the sum of $\frac{2}{3}$ and $\frac{3}{4}$ is greater than one and, hence, any algorithm that produces an answer of less than one cannot be correct.

Anticipating errors does not always prevent mistakes. When a mistake occurs repeatedly, teachers should diagnose the learning deficiencies that underlie the error. Questions can be valuable in this diagnosis. When students are unable to prove statements, the teacher should determine whether they are unable to deduce a conclusion from the given premise or whether their problem is more basic. They may be unable to determine the hypothesis and conclusion from the original statement, for example. Similarly, when students are unable to solve equations such as

$$\frac{2x}{3} - (2 - 3x) = 15$$

the teacher must ascertain where their difficulty lies. It may be that students are unable to work with fractions in equations or that they are unsure of the rules guiding the operations with integers or that they are unable to apply the basic laws of equalities to the writing of equivalent equations.

After probing through questioning to determine the nature of the error, teachers can take action to correct misconceptions. This may take the form of quizzing students about the choice of a particular principle or the use of the principle. In the equation above, the students' difficulty may arise from a misuse of the principle

$$-(m - n) = m + n$$

It may be that the only mistake a student makes is to misuse this principle and that she is successful in the application of the other mathematical principles necessary to solve this equation. If this is the case, the student should be so informed. This information should provide encouragement to the student.

It is an established fact that students forget a substantial amount of material. Forgetting is inevitable and occurs fairly rapidly. To compensate for this natural phenomenon, it is essential that teachers create and use opportunities to review previous knowledge before discussing new material. As a general practice, it is wise to review prerequisite knowledge at the beginning of a lesson. Questioning can be an effective method in conducting reviews. For example, teachers can review the characteristics of a parallelogram by soliciting them from students. In general, a review of the relevant ideas in previous lessons can help set the stage for learning new material.

In developing and using the distance formula to find the length of a segment between any two points in the xy plane, what knowledge is prerequisite? Students need to know how to represent points in terms of ordered pairs in the Cartesian coordinate system, have a working knowledge of the Pythagorean theorem, be able to find the sum and difference of two real numbers, and be able to find the square and square root of a real number. Similarly, in solving an equation of the form

$$x^a = b$$

where a and b are positive real numbers, students should be able to find logs and antilogs and apply the following principles:

if $m = n$, then $\log m = \log n$, and

$\log x^m = m \log x$

Review of prerequisite knowledge requires mathematical competence and forethought in lesson preparation. Review is important and should not be left to chance, for a teacher cannot merely assume that students have the necessary prerequisites.

In addition to being an integral part of reviewing prerequisite knowledge, questions can provide immediate feedback in ascertaining the effectiveness of an ongoing lesson. Rather than finding out that students do not understand a current lesson in subsequent meetings, teachers should use questions to evaluate and adjust the lesson. If feedback indicates a substantial amount of confusion, then the teacher should adjust the current lesson to include more extensive review, a less rigorous approach, or progress at a slower pace.

Suppose you are teaching students to add algebraic fractions. In response to a question, a large number of your students contend that

$$\frac{-2}{x} + \frac{2x}{x - 2} = 1$$

Clearly these students have a misconception. (What are some of its possible sources?) Through questioning, a teacher should determine whether such misconception stems from inability to add arithmetic fractions or to transfer knowledge of adding arithmetic fractions to adding algebraic fractions. Corrective actions should depend on the diagnosis. That is, a teacher should either review or reteach the addition of arithmetic fractions or provide students with guidance and opportunity to transfer such knowledge.

By using questions at the end of a lesson, a teacher can decide whether students have met the objectives established for that lesson. The evidence of the answers should influence the homework assignment, the material to be reviewed for the next lesson, and the feasibility of proceeding with new material. A teacher who fails to obtain this evidence runs the risk of giving frustrating assignments and presenting new material before students have mastered prerequisite knowledge.

Thought questions

1   Are there any integral values for *a* and *b* for which

$$\frac{a + b}{a} = 1 + b$$

would hold true?

2   A student who adds $\frac{2}{3}$ and $\frac{3}{4}$ and obtains $\frac{5}{7}$ is probably employing the incorrect algorithm

$$\frac{a}{b} + \frac{c}{d} = \frac{a + c}{b + d}$$

Are there any values for *a*, *b*, *c*, and *d* for which this algorithm gives a correct result? Answer the question with the assumption that one or both rational numbers are negative.

3   Suppose that two students, in solving the equation,

$$\frac{2x}{3} - (2 - 3x) = 15$$

obtain answers of $\frac{21}{11}$ and $-\frac{51}{7}$. Both students have made a common error. In each case determine the likely source of the error. What advice would you then give the students?

4   What is the knowledge prerequisite to understanding and applying the following principle?

A polynomial equation of odd degree with real coefficients has at least one real root.

Questions can also be used to reduce inattention and, hence, avoid some potential for misbehavior. When students are inattentive and bored, they often resort to disruptive ways to release their energies. They may daydream, carry on side conversations, fidget, prepare for other classes, and sleep. Attention can be recaptured by providing students the opportunity to answer a question: for example, "Jane (*pause*), how can we represent three more than one-half of *x*?" Notice that in such a question the student has the opportunity to refocus attention by virtue of the fact that the teacher has first called her by name, then paused, and only then asked the question. Notice also that

Jane's chances for a correct answer are maximized because the question is simple. In this way, the teacher can prod students into paying attention without using sarcasm or censure. Contrast this approach with the following behavior.

Teacher   If we use $(3 + \frac{1}{2}x)$ to represent Harry's share, then what equation can we set up from this word problem? Jane?

Jane   Huh? Would you repeat the question, please?

Teacher   I didn't think you were paying attention. Mary, what would the equation be? Remember what it was we let x equal and how much money we had altogether.

The teacher's initial question could in many situations be a good question, but in this illustration it is not appropriate for recapturing Jane's attention. Even if the student's attention has been reclaimed, the chances for a correct response are minimized by the nature of the question. The teacher's subsequent behavior may further alienate Jane by providing Mary with hints for answering the question.

Thought questions

1   Assume that you have been daydreaming in class and that the teacher has called on you after raising a question. Your attention has been recaptured but you have not heard the question. Discuss defensive behavior that you might employ. How would you feel if the teacher refused to repeat the question?

2   What would you do if two students continued to engage in a side conversation after you have tried to bring them back into the class discussion with "easy" questions?

3   Can you envision a situation in which you would permit a student to tune out? Discuss advantages and disadvantages of allowing this to happen.

4   What are some possible consequences of allowing students in your class to engage in side conversations or do homework for another class?

5   Initiating a question by calling a student's name may be effective in recapturing that student's attention. What, if any, is the danger in using this technique for every question?

6   Another technique for recapturing attention is to mention a student's name in the middle of a statement or question—for example, "If we use $(3 + \frac{1}{2}x)$, Tom, to represent Harry's share, then what equation can we set up for this word problem?" The teacher can then call on Tom (or someone else) to answer the question. Discuss the advantages and disadvantages of this technique.

Dealing with behavior problems

In the previous sections a number of guidelines are presented and discussed for consideration in establishing an environment conducive to learning. These guidelines deal with such routine matters as punctuality and assigning homework and the roles questions can play in promoting positive student-teacher interactions. Misbehavior can be thwarted by the teacher's establishment of an atmosphere in which success can occur. Such an atmosphere is essential if learning is to take place and behavior problems are to be minimized. A classroom dominated by fear can reduce discipline problems, but meaningful learning is unlikely to occur there. Every teacher, no matter how well prepared or how capable of generating stimulating lessons, will nonetheless encounter some instances of student misbehavior.

Consider the following hypothetical but not atypical classroom episode. The setting is a ninth-grade general mathematics class. During the first twenty minutes of the period there have been only two specific disruptions, by Jack and Bill, who are the class clowns. The class has been rather noisy in general, however, and as a result the teacher has become increasingly annoyed and has compensated for the noise level by talking louder.

1	**Teacher**	Now let's look at the example in the book on page 156.
		$$2\tfrac{1}{10} + 3\tfrac{5}{12}$$
		Mary, put your comb away. (*Pause.*) What is the first step?
2	**Mary**	(*Puts comb away.*) Probably change the fractions.
3	**Teacher**	Why do we need to change the fractions? Sam?
		(*Jack and Bill, who have been fooling around and trying to get each other in trouble, now attempt to knock each other's books off their desks.*)
		Stop it boys! (*Pause.*) Go ahead, Sam.
4	**Sam**	Because the bottom parts aren't . . . (*Jack now breaks Bill's pencil point.*)
5	**Teacher**	I told you boys to stop it. I don't want to see any more messing around.
6	**Sam**	(*Waiting*) Aren't the same; they have to be.
7	**Teacher**	That's right, the denominators are different. But first we have to change the mixed numbers to improper fractions. Johnny, if you can stop talking for a moment we would appreciate it if you would help us here. (*Students chuckle.*) If we change $2\tfrac{1}{10}$ to an improper fraction, what do we have?
		(*At this point the teacher stops additional side conversations and tells one student to stop reading a book*).
8	**Fred**	(*Blurts out.*) Multiply the 10 times the 2 and add 1.
9	**Teacher**	O.K., and you get $\tfrac{21}{10}$. Johnny, I meant what I said about talking. Tom, change $3\tfrac{5}{12}$ to an improper fraction.
10	**Tom**	Well, we have to change everything to twelfths.
11	**Teacher**	Right, and we get 36 plus 5, or $\tfrac{41}{12}$. For the last time, Johnny, keep quiet. Now we have $\tfrac{21}{10} + \tfrac{41}{12}$. Now what do we do?
		(*Noise level in class increases. Teacher reacts by speaking even louder.*)
		We have to find the least common denominator between 10 and 12. What is that?
		(*Students call out a variety of answers. Teacher calls on Susan.*)
12	**Susan**	(*Half laughing*) I don't know. It wouldn't be 120, would it?

| 13 | **Teacher** | No, it would be 60. |

(Susan turns to a nearby friend and mutters, "I knew it wouldn't be right.")

How can we change each of these improper fractions to fractions with a denominator of 60 ?

(Johnny continues to talk.)

John, *please*!

(A paper wad flies through the air. The teacher does not know who threw it but suspects it was Jack or Bill. However, being uncertain, the teacher decides to ignore the incident.)

We would have to multiply the first fraction by 6 and the second fraction by 5. Is that all right with you, Bill ?

| 14 | **Bill** | It's O.K. by me. |

(Some laughter. This further annoys the teacher. At this point some books fall on the floor. It is not clear whether this occurred accidentally or on purpose.)

| 15 | **Teacher** | That's it! I want it absolutely quiet in here. Turn to page 158 and work all seventy-five problems. These are due tomorrow at the beginning of the period. *(Kids gripe and complain in unison, some loudly.)* The next one that talks out loud without raising his hand goes to the office. |

(Warren, the only A student in class, asks the following question without raising his hand.)

| 16 | **Warren** | What page did you say the problems are on ? |
| 17 | **Teacher** | Page 158, Warren. |

(Dick now turns around and asks for a sheet of paper from Willie.)

To the office, Dick.

18	**Dick**	What for ?
19	**Teacher**	Don't argue with me.
20	**Dick**	Tell me what I did.
21	**Teacher**	I told you not to talk without permission. Dick.
22	**Dick**	But I wasn't talking.
23	**Teacher**	You turned around, didn't you ?
24	**Dick**	Only to ask for some paper.
25	**Teacher**	Either leave now or you're out for the year.

(Dick leaves, muttering angrily to himself.)

It is likely that many of the discipline problems illustrated in this episode came about because the students did not perceive the teacher as an effective leader. It cannot be overemphasized that discipline problems such as this are far less likely to occur when the students perceive the teacher as a confident and forceful leader. When students see teachers as wavering and unable to deal effectively with even the simplest of management problems, they quickly lose respect for the teacher and seek ways to badger them.

When problems occur, as they inevitably do, teachers must have ways of dealing with them. In the remainder of this section we discuss maxims that teachers often find effective in dealing with discipline problems.

Use nonverbal techniques to thwart potential problems

A teacher can often prevent small disturbances from developing into major disruptions by acting quickly to inhibit the development of a potential problem. In the illustration in the section above, if the teacher had circulated around the room, disturbances such as Mary combing her hair, Jack and Bill jostling each other's books, and the student reading could probably have been averted. The teacher would probably not even have had to speak, thus avoiding the distractions caused by verbal reprimands. Nonverbal techniques have the added advantage of preventing attention-seeking students from receiving reinforcement. If the antics of a disruptive student are motivated by a desire to receive attention, verbal reprimands serve only to give the attention sought and also to compound the disruption. Many times, through the use of a simple gesture or by moving toward a student or perhaps by tapping on a student's desk, a teacher can stifle misbehavior. But nonverbal action must be taken quickly to be effective. Can you identify other instances in this episode where the teacher could have used nonverbal techniques?

Don't make a big issue of a problem in class

A teacher can only make a situation worse by making a spectacle of a particular incident, as in the case of the argument with Dick. Arguments seldom serve a useful purpose; they promote antagonism between teacher and students, which in turn can foster subsequent discipline problems as well as affect adversely the learning atmosphere.

A beginning teacher often feels the need to provide an immediate justification for disciplinary actions. This justification seldom convinces the student to whom it is directed, for the student is then involved in self-defense and in maintaining status among the other students. Similarly, once an argument has ensued, the teacher must also undertake self-defense. The teacher usually wins the argument (or more exactly, the student usually withdraws from the argument), but in doing so the teacher loses stature. Often in the heat of the argument a teacher makes unreasonable threats that, if challenged, could not be enforced. (What was the unreasonable threat in the example?) A teacher should be able to justify each action, but this need not occur in the presence of students. Discussions of student misbehavior can best occur away from the actual incident, at a time when both the teacher and the student have had a chance to collect their thoughts. The teacher can ask the student to stop after class or after school or at an appropriate time in the principal's office. Could the situation between Dick and the teacher have been improved had the teacher followed the advice of this second maxim?

Take punitive measures appropriate to the misdeed

It is important for teachers to react to misbehavior in a way that neither underemphasizes nor overemphasizes the seriousness of the situation. Underemphasis often encourages additional occurrences of the problem. For example, if a teacher does not stop students from making relatively innocent wisecracks, the frequency of wisecracking is bound to increase until eventually it becomes less innocent than serious. A teacher who repeats admonitions is probably guilty of underreacting. In the dialogue, the teacher tells Johnny no less than four times to stop talking. What is the effect on Johnny and the rest of the class when the teacher repeatedly tells him to stop talking but takes no further action when Johnny continues to talk? A teacher who fails to enforce such requests will be perceived by students as a weak and wavering leader.

On the other hand, overreaction to a disturbance opens the teacher to the risk of alienating or embarrassing students. They lose respect for a teacher who resorts to drastic methods for relatively minor disturbances. A teacher who sends students to the office for such minor disturbances as writing notes or making innocent wisecracks alienates them. Consider the principal's perception of such a teacher. Furthermore, in overreacting the teacher is likely to make threats that create additional problems or could prove embarrassing to the teacher if challenged. In the illustration, the teacher threatened Dick with permanent expulsion from class if he did not leave the room at once. It is unlikely that such a threat, if challenged, could be carried out; it serves only to undermine the teacher's credibility.

It is essential for a teacher (especially a beginning teacher) to ascertain what the options are in dealing with behavior problems. For example, can students be kept after school and, if so, under what conditions? What are the teacher's beliefs and the school's regulations regarding corporal punishment? If the school system permits suspensions and expulsions, how are they administered? What are the regulations regarding smoking? Drugs? Cutting class? The answers to these questions set the limits of a teacher's actions.

Another danger in overreacting is that the disciplinary measures taken may not be commensurate with the offense. In general, a teacher is wise to try to resolve a problem with a student first and, if this fails, then consult with school officials or parents. The most stringent measures may have to be taken as a last resort—expulsion or suspension or whatever the school policy dictates. The point is that while the student may eventually force drastic measures through continual misbehavior these should not be threatened or taken in the heat of an exchange or in initial confrontations, except in the most dangerous of situations (such as malicious display of a weapon).

Don't punish the entire class for the misdeeds of a few

Teachers who punish an entire class for the misdeeds of a few are generally overreacting. Usually a teacher's disciplinary actions involving the entire class derive from frustration and inability to cope. Group punishment is often in the form of excessive homework assignments, spur-of-the-moment quizzes, and other actions involving the subject matter. Such punitive measures generally have negative effects, including loss of respect for the teacher, potential dislike for mathematics, and increased tension in the classroom. Furthermore, if such action has a detrimental effect on the grades of the better (and perhaps well-behaved) students, the teacher invites the wrath of parents.

There may, of course, be occasions when it is necessary for a teacher to terminate instruction and make an assignment to regain control of the class. This can be an effective strategy. It has the effect of quieting the students, giving the teacher a chance for self-composure, and giving the students something specific and constructive to do. It is when the assignment becomes excessive and punitive that this strategy ceases to have positive effect. What is the likely effect in the hypothetical classroom of the punitive assignment of seventy-five problems?

Make your own behavior consistent

It is difficult to give specific guidelines on consistency, but it is important that teachers establish their limits for student-teacher relation and then maintain these limits consistently. It is extremely difficult for a student to maintain and enhance a self-concept when the teacher's expectations continually shift. For example, a teacher who on some occasions rewards students for calling out correct answers but at other times chastises those who do not raise their hands makes it difficult for students to define appropriate behavior. Students seem to value consistency above almost everything else in a teacher's disciplinary procedures. For this reason, a teacher who is consistently strict will fare better than teachers who admonish students for minor disturbances on one day and overlook them on the next.

To illustrate this maxim, let us consider a basketball game in which officials sometimes call a foul when players barely touch each other and at other times overlook a flagrant foul. Such behavior breeds frustration and resentment in the players. Similarly, students become frustrated and resentful when a teacher is inconsistent. Can you identify instances in the dialogue above when the teacher was inconsistent? Did this inconsistency seem to contribute to subsequent misbehavior?

Thought questions

1 In utterance 13, the teacher makes a statement that is mathematically incorrect. Identify this statement. Assuming the teacher knows better, conjecture as to why he made such an error.

2 Conjure a defense that Dick might present to the principal for being removed from class. While this defense will undoubtedly be slanted in Dick's favor, what valid arguments could it contain?

3 There are thirteen utterances by the teacher in the dialogue. How many deal solely with mathematics? How many deal solely with discipline? Contrast the mathematics discussed in utterances 1–14 with the mathematics discussed in utterances 15–25. What conclusion can you draw about the quality of mathematical discussions when a teacher has continual management problems?

4 "Don't smile until Christmas" is a slogan teachers sometimes follow. What does this slogan imply to you? What are the advantages and disadvantages that result from following it?

5 Some disciplinary problems can be averted by having students change seats. This is particularly effective when disturbances are caused by two or three students sitting close together. For example, the problems Jack and Bill caused might have been avoided if they had been separated. This technique can be effective, but can it be overused? Explain.

6 What is the likely opinion that a principal will have of a teacher who continually sends students with discipline problems to the office?

7 Consider the plight of the teacher who had thrown Dick out for the year had the principal reinstated him the following day. Discuss.

8 How could you as a beginning teacher ascertain your school's policies regarding behavior problems?

9 Answer the questions contained in the discussion of each maxim.

Self-test on the competencies

1 Identify and illustrate defensive strategies students use.
   a List at least five defensive strategies that students utilize.
   b Exhibit in either paragraph form or by use of a fancied dialogue each defensive strategy you listed.
   c Observe a mathematics class in session (or a mathematics lesson that has been taped). Identify the defensive strategies. Discuss how the teacher reacted or failed to react to these strategies. In each case judge whether the teacher's actions were effective or ineffective.

2 Explain why students use defensive strategies.
   a For each defensive strategy you identified above enumerate probable reasons why students employ such a strategy.
   b Suppose the following dialogue occurred in a beginning algebra class.

   Teacher   Consider now the inequality $-\frac{1}{3}x > 6$. To solve this inequality what would you recommend, Jake?

   Jake   Well, I would multiply each side by negative 3.

Teacher O.K. What happens then to the sense of the inequality? Does it change or remain the same? Jane?

Jane I think it would change.

Teacher It would change?

Jane Oh—no—it stays the same.

Identify a defensive strategy illustrated in this dialogue. Give several alternatives as to how you might react to this defensive strategy. Justify each of your reactions.

3 Explain why defensive behavior can inhibit learning.
Discuss why defensive behavior can inhibit learning.

4 Identify routine matters occurring in a classroom you have observed and judge the effectiveness of the way these matters were handled.
Observe a mathematics class in session or a mathematics lesson that has been taped. Identify routine matters (taking attendance, collecting homework) and judge whether the teacher dispensed with these matters efficiently. Justify your judgment.

5 Identify and illustrate four uses teachers make of questions.
  a State the four purposes of questions identified in this chapter. Exemplify each of the four by describing a classroom incident (either hypothetical or one you have actually observed). Your description can be in paragraph or dialogue form.
  b In observing a mathematics class (or one on tape) identify questions used by the teacher for each of the four purposes given in this chapter.
  c Suppose a student makes the following error:

$$(a + b)^2 = a^2 + b^2$$

Design questions that could be used to help the student correct the mistake.
  d Suppose you are going to introduce, discuss, and illustrate the fundamental theorem of arithmetic to a junior high school mathematics class. Create a set of questions students could be asked in an attempt to determine their readiness to learn this new material.
  e Suppose you have just completed a lesson designed to reach the following objective: "The student should be able to transform equations of the form $ax + by = c$ to the form $y = mx + b$, give the slope and y-intercept of the graph of this equation, and then draw the graph of the equation." Design a set of questions that a teacher might use to determine whether the students have attained all or part of this objective.

6 Identify uses of maxims for classroom management that occur in a classroom you have observed and judge the effectiveness of the teacher's use of the maxims.
Observe a mathematics class in session (or one on tape). Identify uses of all or any of the five maxims for dealing with discipline problems that the teacher employed. Judge the effectiveness of the teacher's use of the maxims. Justify your judgments.

References

Gnagey, William J. "Controlling Classroom Misbehavior." *What Research Says to the Teacher Series* (Monograph 32). Washington, D.C.: National Eductional Association, 1968.

Highet, Gilbert. *The Art of Teaching*. New York: Vintage, 1950.

Holt, John. *How Children Fail*. New York: Dell, 1964.

Hunkins, Francis P. *Questioning: Strategies and Techniques*. Boston: Allyn & Bacon, 1972.

Kounin, J. S., P. V. Gump, and J. Ryan. "Explorations in Classroom Management." *Journal of Teacher Education*, 12 (1961), 235–246.

Lockwood, James. *An Analysis of Teacher-Questioning in Mathematics Classrooms*. Ph.D. dissertation. Urbana-Champaign: University of Illinois, 1970.

Purkey, William W. *Self-Concept and School Achievement*. Englewood Cliffs, N.J.: Prentice-Hall, 1970.

Sanders, Norris M. *Classroom Questions—What Kinds?* New York: Harper & Row, 1966.

Vredevoe, L. E. "School Discipline." *National Association of Secondary School Principals Bulletin*, 49 (1965), 215–226.

3

General objectives of mathematics in secondary education

It would seem unwise to start on a journey without knowing where you wanted to go. How would you know what kind of transportation to select, what direction to take, how long the journey would take, and how would you know when you were finished traveling? In education, general objectives tell us where we want to go, what we want to accomplish. From these, we can make decisions such as what subjects to include in the curriculum, in what subjects to prepare teachers, what to include in the design of school buildings, and what the cost of schooling will be. We would also insist that the objectives of any subject in the curriculum—for example, mathematics—be consistent with these general objectives. In turn, we would insist that the objectives of any course in mathematics be consistent with the general objectives of mathematics in secondary education.

Rather than begin with a consideration of the general objectives of secondary education in the United States at the present time, let us assume that whatever these objectives are they imply that mathematics is in the curricula of secondary schools. In light of the nature of our technological society and its needs, this assumption seems tenable. Hence it seems logical to begin with a consideration of the general objectives of mathematics in the curriculum of the secondary school. In this chapter, we begin with the rationale of objectives—that is, possible reasons for having objectives. Then we consider criteria for judging objectives. We ask and answer how one can tell whether a set of objectives is sound. Against these criteria, we consider general objectives of teaching mathematics as suggested by various groups and individuals.

At the conclusion of this chapter, you should be able to demonstrate the following competencies:

1 **Explain why a mathematics department should have objectives for the education it provides**

2 **State defensible criteria for appraising objectives and use them to evaluate any set of objectives**

3 **State and defend general objectives for teaching mathematics**

Rationale for objectives

Why does a department establish general objectives? We offer some explanations, developing each to some extent but leaving it to you to decide the relative merit of each explanation. At the present time, there is much talk about accountability in education. It is believed that because schools are established to educate students and teachers are in turn paid to help students learn, the schools and consequently the teachers should be held accountable for their success. How is success to be judged? It is judged in terms of the extent to which the school and the teachers attain the objectives that the people who support the schools accept. If a school or a department has no objectives, they will be imposed on it by outsiders—parents, businessmen, colleges. Hence it behooves a school, and particularly a department within a school, to establish objectives that it can defend and can be explained to the people in control of the school or department. If this is done, then administrators and teachers can be held accountable for attaining at least these objectives.

A department must establish general objectives to effect internal coordination. Unless there is consensus on what the teachers as a group seek to accomplish, some teachers may have objectives that others do not. The former would stress certain things while the latter would not. The students would emerge from the department's curriculum confused, because the absence of general objectives would make coordination of instruction in the various courses difficult.

A department should establish general objectives to help in the choices that the department has to make; what courses to design, what sequences within the set of courses to allow, which textbooks to select, what topics to teach in the various courses, how long to spend on the topics selected, how much review to provide, and what to present in departmental final examinations, if these are used. The general objectives state the ends to be attained, the outcomes expected once teaching has been carried out. There are various means for attaining these ends, and teachers in a department have to choose among them. General objectives facilitate choice for they offer implications that teachers in the department can consider and realize.

A department must establish general objectives because it is partly in terms of these that it justifies what it proposes and what it does. General objectives permit the department to reason after the fact. General objectives tend to be vague and, although their implications suggest choices to the people who establish them, their vagueness allows them to be used to justify many actions a department has not chosen. Let us take a conceivable situation.

Imagine the principal, the curriculum director, or a small group of parents attending a meeting of your department of mathematics. One of these individuals asks you (that is, your department) to describe its instructional program. In the course of the description, the person asks why some aspect of the program is as it is. An alternative question this person might have asked you is whether that aspect should be as it is, whether it is desirable. This person might also have asked how you know that the instructional program is successful. Good answers to these questions will be based explicitly or implicitly on the department's objectives—that is, on what the teachers as a group in the department hope to accomplish. For example, you would probably explain why the department has certain policies or why the teachers in the department are doing certain things by pointing out how these things enable the department to reach its objectives. If the questioner inquires whether the department should have certain policies or certain general procedures, you would have to ascertain the basis of doubt. Is it that the questioner accepts the department's objectives but doubts that a certain policy or procedure will attain them? Or is it the doubt about the worth of the department's objectives in the first place? Once you have decided what the answers to these questions are, you are in a position to try to convince the questioner that the department's policy or procedure is sound.

Thought questions

1 Four explanations were given for general objectives. Which seems best to you? Why?

2 Are the four explanations for establishing objectives mutually independent? Why?

3 Consider students being able to [do] x—for example, being able to compute quickly and correctly, prove theorems, enjoy mathematics, come to class every day, or pay attention. Is having x as an objective a sufficient condition for attaining x as an outcome? Is it a necessary condition? Defend your answers.

4 Give examples of objectives that support the contention that objectives help teachers in the choice of courses or subject matter.

5 Give one or more counterexamples to the contention that objectives help teachers in the choice of courses or subject matter.

6 Under what conditions do objectives function as facilitators of choices of means?

7 One can imagine the fourth explanation of why a department needs to have objectives (to enable the teachers to justify what they are doing) being attacked as cynical. It enables a department to rationalize. Is there any substance to this attack? If so, what is it?

8   Look up in a dictionary the nonmathematical meaning of *rational*. Explain why it is possible to say that the existence of departmental objectives allows the teachers in that department to become rational in their work.

9   A department chairman says, "Don't ask me what our objectives are. Observe what our teachers do in the classrooms and you can infer what we hope to accomplish." To what extent is this position sound?

10 Some people argue that general objectives are like decorations: they provide aesthetic satisfaction but are not functional in any other way. Do you agree? Why?

Criteria for judging objectives

We have selected and stated some objectives that teachers of mathematics have written. How does one judge the worth of objectives such as these and others that might be written? One way is to develop a set of criteria—standards of judgment—and evaluate the objectives against these criteria.

As you read the following objectives, judge whether each objective is good. For each that you consider not good, ask yourself why you so evaluate it. The reason or reasons you identify will lead to criteria for judging. You may enjoy doing this exercise jointly with other students so that each of you may profit from the ideas of the others.

1   To provide an adequate mathematics program

2   The most important objective is to teach students to think logically

3   To teach knowledge and skills of most importance

4   To develop an appreciation for mathematics

5   To enable students to solve equations of the form $ax + b = c$

6   To enable students to pass the college board examinations

7   To provide courses for students who intend to go to college and also courses for those who do not

8   The most important objective is to teach students how to operate with real numbers

9   To develop the mathematical potential of each student to the maximum

10 Our primary objective is to teach students how to apply mathematical principles to solve problems

11 To teach students how to factor the difference of two squares

12 We want students to have an enjoyable experience in learning mathematics

13 Students should be able to prove theorems

14 To teach knowledge and various skills

15 To help students improve their ability to attack a problem and arrive at a satisfactory solution

16 Our first objective is to teach the mathematics that each citizen must know to get along in our society

It has been asserted that one of the reasons for objectives is to facilitate choices. How can we choose among all the things that might be done? Why do we choose one rather than another? After a little thought, it becomes apparent that choices exist at various levels. There is the institutional level of choices such as whether a vocational educational program should be offered, whether a fourth year of mathematics or a third year of foreign language should be offered, whether a gymnasium should be incorporated in design of the new high school, whether the same teaching time should be allocated to all subjects in the curriculum.

There is the departmental level of choices that follow those made at the institutional level. For example, once a board of education has decided that there should be mathematics courses that will meet the needs of various well-defined groups of students, the mathematics department must choose what courses to provide and what their objectives should be. But there also are choices at the departmental level that do not explicitly depend on decisions made at a higher level. For example, the mathematics department may be free to choose whether the geometry course will continue to be Euclidean geometry or to change to an approach utilizing affine transformations.

An analogous situation exists at the level of a particular course. For example, once the mathematics department has made the decision to offer the geometry of affine transformations, the teacher of the geometry course has to choose the methods of teaching each topic in the course. In the absence of departmental policy concerning the frequency of examinations, an individual teacher is also free to choose the frequency of periodic tests and quizzes.

Following this reasoning, it seems appropriate to demand that objectives should facilitate choices. In light of this, we may decide that objectives 1, 3, and 14 are not helpful. They are indefinite and too vague. In contrast, objectives 5, 8, and 11 are definite and specific. They are helpful for deciding what to teach in a particular mathematics course such as algebra, but they are not helpful for another course such as seventh-grade mathematics or geometry. Moreover, because they are specific, they are not as helpful for making choices at the departmental level. Hence it appears that no one set of objectives is equally helpful with any other at all levels of decision. Instead we need objectives appropriate for each particular level of choice or decision. Hence the following criterion seems reasonable:

Given a particular level of decision (institutional, departmental, course, or lesson), the objectives written for this level should be helpful in making the choices that are possible.

Two corollaries follow from this criterion:

1   Objectives should not be so vague or indefinite that they are not helpful in making choices.

2   If objectives are intended for the departmental level, they should not be so specific that a statement of all the objectives would have to include so many that it would be difficult to remember them all.

To arrive at another criterion, think of why people are willing to tax themselves to establish and support schools. The reason is that they believe schools will change the behavior of students in a desirable direction. Taxpayers hold teachers accountable for this. Hence it can be argued that objectives should focus on student behavior. The behavior of teachers and institutions is a means to influencing student behavior. Note that objectives 5, 6, and 8–14 do this. But objectives 1 and 7 focus on institutional behavior. To determine whether these objectives are realized, we would study the school rather than the students in the school; we would study means rather than ends. Hence a defensible criterion is:

Objectives should be stated in terms of the students.

There is a corollary to this criterion. Consider objective 4. How do we tell whether a student appreciates mathematics? We do not observe appreciation as we do smiling, being present in class, raising a hand, asking a question, or other behavior apprehended by the senses. We infer appreciation from certain behavior that students manifest. Hence, to the extent that an objective can be defined in terms of observable student behavior, it can be stated in terms of the student. Moreover, the degree of its attainment can be determined. Hence, the following criterion seems defensible:

Objectives should permit definition in terms of observable student behavior.

When we think of objectives 6, 8, and 13, we realize that these may be valid for senior high school mathematics but not for junior high school mathematics. Objectives 9, 10, 12, and 15, however, are valid for junior high school mathematics.

If we think of objectives for general mathematics and are aware of the kind of student who is in such a course, we judge objectives 6, 8, and 13 to be inappropriate. It is unrealistic to expect the students in the typical general mathematics course or remedial mathematics course to attain these objectives. However, it is realistic to expect them to attain the goals implied by 10, 14, and 15.

In light of the foregoing, it seems reasonable to expect objectives to satisfy the following criterion:

Objectives should be attainable by the students who are in mind when the objectives are written.

One other criterion is sugested by one of the criteria of a good set of axioms: consistency. If objectives 2 and 8 were to appear in the same set, we would consider them inconsistent. But if they were phrased as "An important objective is to teach the students how to operate with real numbers," they would be consistent. For a definition of consistency in this context, let us say that two objectives are inconsistent if the attainment of one precludes the attainment of the other; otherwise they are consistent.

One final criterion is necessary. Although the idea of the criterion is sound, it is hard to express without a value judgment. The idea is:

Each objective should be justifiable as significant.

We would not be disposed to accept an objective that cannot be justified— that is, an objective for which we could not present a convincing argument that it is worthwhile to spend school time trying to attain it. To take a bizarre example, consider the objective of improving students' skills in computing with an abacus. This objective may satisfy the first six criteria, yet it is an indefensible objective. We have better calculating machines than the abacus. If we want to develop skill in using modern calculating machines, we should teach students to use them. The purpose of the seventh criterion is to eliminate trivial objectives that pass through the net of the other criteria.

Thought questions

1   Would you demand that the objectives in a set be independent? Why?

2   Would you demand that an objective be stated in a certain linguistic form such as: To be able to ——? Why?

3   Are there any criteria for judging objectives that should be identified other than those stated above? If so, what are they?

4   What behavior would dispose you to say that a student appreciates mathematics?

5   How would you tell whether your students have an enjoyable experience in learning mathematics?

6   Evaluate the following objective: The purpose of teaching mathematics in secondary schools is to meet the mathematical needs of the students.

7   Which criterion does the objective "to portray the majesty of mathematics" fail to satisfy?

8   Which criterion does the following objective violate? To show by Galois theory why the general fifth-degree polynomial equation cannot be solved algebraically.

9   Present a justification for objective 10 in the list at the beginning of this section.

10   How would you defend the significance of teaching students to understand the nature of proof as an objective?

11   Some theoreticians contend that objectives should be stated in terms of learning rather than in terms of teaching. They argue that teaching does not always imply learning and that objectives stated in terms of learning are stated in terms of the student rather than the teacher. What is your appraisal of this argument?

12   Write a set of objectives for the teaching of mathematics. Assess their worth by applying the criteria suggested in the present section.

Attempts to establish general objectives

Mathematical Association of America

As early as 1916, the Mathematical Association of America was instrumental in getting the National Committee on Mathematical Requirements established. The purpose of the Committee was to direct attention to the movement for reform in the teaching of mathematics that was under way in various parts of the United States. Its membership was composed of outstanding mathematicians in colleges and universities and also of teachers of mathematics in secondary schools. The Committee was directed to make a comprehensive study of the improvement of mathematical education at both the secondary and collegiate levels. The report of this study was published in 1921.

In Chapter 2 of the Committee's report, aims of mathematical instruction are presented and discussed. Three aims, practical, disciplinary, and cultural, are proposed. Because this report was seminal in its importance at the time, and since these aims have continued to be accepted and discussed, it is well to consider at some length what each of these aims implies.

As to the practical aims, the Committee (p. 5) said, "By a practical or utilitarian aim, in the narrower sense, we mean then the immediate or direct usefulness in life of a fact, method or process in mathematics." The meaning of this general aim is established by the citation of less general aims that appear to be implied by it. Five such aims are identified:

1   To continue practice in the fundamental operations of arithmetic. This was to be done not by an explicit topic but as part of the study of more advanced topics

2   To provide an understanding of the language of algebra and the ability to use it in the quantitative relations that occur in everyday life

3   To provide an understanding of the fundamental principles of the algebra of numbers of which the numbers of arithmetic are subsumed, so that students will be able to use elementary algebraic methods, where appropriate, in the solution of problems

4   To enable students correctly to interpret graphical representations

5   To teach the concepts associated with geometric forms commonly used in industry and the study of nature

As to the disciplinary aims, the Committee (p. 6) said, "Such training involves the development of certain more or less general characteristics and the formation of certain mental habits which, besides being directly applicable in the setting in which they are developed or formed, are expected to operate also in more or less closely related fields—that is, to 'transfer' to other situations." One should not infer from this statement that the Committee accepted the doctrines of faculty psychology and its educational counterpart, formal discipline. In fact, it disavowed these doctrines. But rejection of faculty psychology does not imply that generalized intellectual skills cannot be taught and learned.

A disciplined person is one who governs behavior by certain principles that he or she has accepted as proper to live by. A mathematician, in the role of mathematician, has such principles. One attempts to state precise definitions, to test inferences to make sure they are necessary implications of definitions, axioms, or theorems, continually to ask "Why?" and "How do we know?"; one is not dogmatic in asserting that only certain definitions and axioms are correct. If a person who studies mathematics acquires such principles and governs his or her life by them, we say that he or she is disciplined. And since such principles are teachable, it is appropriate to speak of disciplinary aims.

The Committee identified four specific aims that seemed to be implied by the general disciplinary aim:

1 To teach students the concepts basic to quantitative thinking— measurement, ratio and proportion, rational numbers, and function. It was assumed that the disciplined person uses these concepts consistently

2 To develop students' ability to think logically—to analyze a complex situation, recognize the logical relations among interdependent factors, and be able to discover and state a generalization that describes the relation among objects under study

3 To inculcate such mental habits and attitudes as seeking to under- stand relations, intellectual curiosity, persistence, a love for precision, accuracy, thoroughness, clarity, and orderly and logical organization

4 To train students in what the Committee characterized as "functional thinking," meaning thinking in terms of relationships

By cultural aims, the Committee (p. 8) meant "those somewhat less tangible but nonetheless real and important intellectual, ethical, esthetic or spiritual aims that are involved in the development of appreciation and insight and the formation of ideals of perfection." Since this statement sounds vague and idealistic, the Committee cited some specifics:

1 To teach appreciation of beauty in the geometrical forms found in nature, art, and industry

2 To teach appreciation of logical structure, precision of statement and thought, and logical reasoning

3 To teach appreciation of the power of mathematics, the part it has played in the development of civilization and, in particular, that of science

These specific aims may themselves sound abstract and vague. If they cannot be defined in terms of behavior, to that extent they are not useful. But since they are meaningful, such definition should be possible although it might be that not all persons identify the same behavior as indicative of such appreciations. For example, some people might be willing to say that a student appreciates beauty in the geometrical forms found in nature, art, and industry if he says that he does. Others might have less confidence in this behavioral evidence and say that a student who spends some free time studying natural objects, art objects, and the products of industry and identifies geometrical forms that are represented appreciates such beauty. As far as appreciation of the power of mathematics is concerned, some people might say that here *appreciation* really means *understanding*. Hence, if a student can point out uses of mathematics in various civilizations and aspects of science, can cite instances of how mathematical inventions have been used to solve problems previously unsolved, expresses confidence that the continued growth of mathematics will be correlated with continued growth in scientific knowledge, then that student appreciates the power of mathematics. Other people might want to identify different behavior as indicative of appreciation of the power of mathematics in civilization and science.

As a succinct statement of the objectives of teaching mathematics, the Committee (p. 9) stated:

> The primary purposes of the teaching of mathematics should be to develop those powers of understanding and of analyzing relations of quantity and of space which are necessary to an insight into and control over our environment and to an appreciation of the progress of civilization in its various aspects, and to develop those habits of thought and of action which will make these powers effective in the life of the individual.

Joint Commission of the Mathematical Association of America and the National Council of Teachers of Mathematics

In the 1930's the members of the Mathematical Association of America thought that it was time to take another look at mathematics education and appointed a committee to consider the place of mathematics in secondary education. Coincidentally and at about the same time, the members of the National Council of Teachers of Mathematics also thought the subject was worthy of study and also appointed a committee to conduct such a study. When each organization became aware of the interests of the other, the two committees were joined to form the Joint Commission of the Mathematical Association of America and the National Council of Teachers of Mathematics.

The report of the Joint Commission, subsequently published in 1940 as the Fifteenth Yearbook of the National Council of Teachers of Mathematics, *The Place of Mathematics in Secondary Education*, states its philosophy of mathematics education against the backdrop of general education. Although no objectives are stated explicitly, they are implicit in the philosophy. Because of the needs of society and individuals and because of the distinctive nature of mathematics, the Joint Commission pointed out how mathematics could contribute to the attainment of the following objectives of general education:

1   Development of the ability to think clearly, including the ability to gather relevant data, organize them, represent them, draw conclusions, and establish and judge claims of proof

2   Development of the ability to use information, concepts, and general principles

3   Development of the ability to use fundamental skills

4   Inculcation of desirable attitudes such as respect for knowledge, good workmanship, understanding, social-mindedness, open-mindedness

5   Development of interests and appreciations related to mathematics

More specific objectives are implicit in the section of the report entitled "Essentials of a General Program in Secondary Mathematics." Seven broad categories in the mathematical curriculum are identified in this section. The basic concepts and principles, fundamental skills, and applications, in six of these categories are indicated, together with the strong implication that it would be well for secondary school mathematics teachers to teach them. Hence, they may be regarded as specific objectives phrased in terms of the content of the mathematics courses in the curriculum.

The report of the Joint Commission goes beyond philosophy to present two illustrative curricula in mathematics. It is a comprehensive report, treating problems of retardation and acceleration, evaluation of the progress of students, and education of mathematics teachers. Appendices consider such cognate subjects as the mathematical needs of man; transfer of training; terms, symbols, and abbreviations in elementary mathematics; equipment of the mathematics classroom; and possible selection and arrangement of instructional topics for slow pupils. Being as comprehensive and as authoritative as it is, the report greatly influenced pedagogical theory. That it also influenced practice can be inferred from the number of authors who stated in the prefaces to their textbooks that the content of their books had been influenced by the report.

College Entrance Examination Board

The College Entrance Examination Board (CEEB) was formed to prepare examinations that colleges can use to assess the academic background of applicants. Among the examinations the CEEB prepared each year was one in mathematics. These examinations came to determine the content of college preparatory courses in mathematics, and teachers whose students planned on going to colleges that required CEEB examinations in mathematics made sure that their students were able to answer the kinds of questions frequently asked.

By 1955 the CEEB had become concerned that the mathematics examinations might not be reflecting the advances in mathematics and the changing curricula in progressive high schools and colleges. It appointed the Commission on Mathematics to recommend the updating and improvement of college preparatory mathematics. The Commission was composed of representatives from public and private high schools and colleges.

One of the first publications of the Commission on Mathematics was a statement of its objectives. As a background for these objectives, the Commission stated three assumptions (p. 3):

1   It is not known exactly what career any student will follow.

2   It is not known exactly how the mathematical needs of various occupations will develop in the years ahead.

3   Although much mathematical instruction aims at future usefulness, mathematics for its own sake is a valuable part of the general education of any future citizen.

It then stated five general objectives (p. 4):

1   Thorough competence in the processes of arithmetic and the use of formulas in elementary algebra. A basic knowledge of simple statistics and of graphical methods is also considered important.

2   An understanding of the general properties of geometrical figures and the relationships among them.

3   An understanding of the deductive method as a method of thought. This includes the abstraction of mathematical models from the outside world, just as Euclidean geometry is a model of our physical space. It also includes the ideas of axioms, logical reasoning, methods of proof, and the relationship between proved theorems and physical reality.

4   An understanding of the ideas of statistical inference as a method of drawing conclusions based on incomplete information. It is important that the differences between this and the deductive method be made clear.

5   An understanding of mathematics as a continuing creative endeavor with aesthetic values similar to those found in art and music. In particular, it should be made clear that mathematics is not a finished subject embalmed in textbooks.

National Assessment of Educational Progress

A recent attempt to establish mathematics objectives has been initiated as one of the first steps in a project of the Education Commission of the States. This project, known as the National Assessment of Educational Progress, seeks to assess the educational progress of students in the schools in the United States. In developing the objectives, mathematicians, mathematics educators, experts in test construction, and laymen were consulted. The approach was to consider uses of mathematics. Three were selected. One is social mathematics, needed for the solution of personal problems that have a quantitative aspect and for use generally by citizens in our society. The second is technical mathematics, required for various skilled jobs and professions over and beyond social mathematics. The third is academic mathematics, the formally structured mathematics prerequisite to the study of advanced mathematics.

The objectives are stated in terms of successive levels of developed abilities, which are defined in terms of performance of specific tasks appropriate to the four ages of students at which the assessment is to be made—9, 13, 17, and adult. To find the specific tasks, you should consult the work by the National Assessment of Educational Progress entitled *Mathematics Objectives* cited at the end of this chapter. Here we cite only the six categories in which the specific tasks are listed (pp. 16–30):

1   Recall or recognition of definitions, facts, and symbols

2   Perform mathematical manipulations

3   Understand mathematical concepts and processes

4   Solve mathematical problems—social, technical, and academic

5   Use mathematics and mathematical reasoning to analyze problem situations, define problems, formulate hypotheses, make decisions, and verify results

6   Appreciate and use mathematics

It is expected that tests developed to assess educational progress in mathematics will be built by sampling from the specific tasks. These tasks, then, become specific objectives embedded in the more general objectives—that is, in the six categories—which are appropriate at the department level.

National Council of Teachers of Mathematics

Since its formation in 1920, the National Council of Teachers of Mathematics has been interested in providing direction in mathematics education. The Council's cooperation with the Mathematical Association of America to this end has been described above. When the deficiencies in mathematics exhibited by the men who were inducted into military service for World War II became evident, the National Council of Teachers of Mathematics appointed the Commission on Post-War Plans to propose direction in mathematics education following the war. The Commission made three reports in the second of which (1945) it stated what it considered to be the mathematical "needs" for a person to be "functionally competent in mathematics." There are twenty-eight needs, later extended in the final report (1947) to twenty-nine. These were regarded as specific objectives for mathematics in secondary education.

Since the time this report was published, we have seen changes in science and technology reflected in changes in society. Realizing that the set of specific objectives should be brought up to date, the National Council of Teachers of Mathematics in 1970 appointed a committee "to draw up a list of basic mathematical competencies, skills, and attitudes essential for enlightened citizenship in contemporary society." The report of this Committee, presented in 1972, does not state how the Committee proceeded to develop its list. Hence the validity of the recommendations is weakened. But it did present a list, in the first section of which (pp. 673–674) the Committee stated the skills and competencies considered necessary for adults to participate effectively in contemporary society:

1   Numbers and numerals
    a   Express a rational number using decimal notation.
    b   List the first ten multiples of 2 through 12.
    c   Use the whole numbers in problem-solving.
    d   Recognize the digit, its place value, and the number represented through billions.
    e   Describe a given positive rational number using decimal, percent, or fractional notation.
    f   Convert to Roman numerals from decimal numerals and conversely (e.g., date translation).
    g   Represent very large and very small numbers using scientific notation.

2   Operations and properties
    a   Write equivalent fractions for given fractions, such as $\frac{1}{2}$, $\frac{2}{3}$, and $\frac{3}{5}$.
    b   Use the standard algorithms for the operations of arithmetic of positive rational numbers.
    c   Recognize and use properties of operations (grouping, order, etc.) and properties of certain numbers with respect to operations ($a \cdot 1 = a$; $a + 0 = a$; etc.).
    d   Solve addition, subtraction, multiplication, and division problems involving fractions.
    e   Solve problems involving percent.
    f   Perform arithmetic operations with measures.
    g   Estimate results.
    h   Judge the reasonableness of answers to computational problems.

3   Mathematical sentences
    a   Construct a mathematical sentence from a given verbal problem.

   b Solve simple linear equations such as

$$a + 3 = 12; \ 16 - n = 4; \ \frac{n}{3} = 7; \text{ and } 4a - 2 = 18.$$

   c Translate mathematical sentences into verbal problems.

4 Geometry
   a Recognize horizontal lines, vertical lines, parallel lines, perpendicular lines, and intersecting lines.
   b Classify simple plane figures by recognizing their properties.
   c Compute perimeters of polygons.
   d Compute the areas of rectangles, triangles, and circles.
   e Be familiar with the concepts of similarity and congruence of triangles.

5 Measurement
   a Apply measures of length, area, volume (dry or liquid), weight, time, money, and temperature.
   b Use units of length, area, mass, and volume in making measurements.
   c Use standard measuring devices to measure length, area, volume, time, and temperature.
   d Round off measurements to the nearest given unit of the measuring device (ruler, protractor, thermometer, etc.) used.
   e Read maps and estimate distances between locations.

6 Relations and functions
   a Interpret information from a graphical representation of a function.
   b Apply the concepts of ratio and proportion to construct scale drawings and to determine percent and other relations.
   c Write simple sentences showing the relations $=$, $<$, $>$, and $\neq$ for two given numbers.

7 Probability and statistics
   a Determine mean, median, and mode for given numerical data.
   b Analyze and solve simple probability problems such as tossing coins or drawing one red marble from a set containing one red and four white marbles.
   c Estimate answers to computational problems.
   d Recognize the techniques used in making predictions and estimates from samples.

8 Graphing
   a Determine measures of real objects from scale drawings.
   b Construct scale drawings of simple objects.
   c Construct graphs indicating relationships of two variables from given sets of data.
   d Interpret information from graphs and tables.

9   Mathematical reasoning
   a   Produce counterexamples to test the validity of statements.
   b   Detect and describe flaws and fallacies in advertising and propaganda where statistical data and inferences are employed.
   c   Gather and present data to support an inference or argument.

10   Business and consumer mathematics
   a   Maintain personal bank records.
   b   Plan a budget including record keeping of personal expenses.
   c   Apply simple interest formulas to installment buying.
   d   Estimate the real cost of an article.
   e   Compute taxes and investment returns.
   f   Use the necessary mathematical skills to appraise insurance and retirement benefits.

Although these may be regarded as specific objectives for enlightened citizenship in our present society, the Committee disclaimed a belief that each individual should attain each objective. It advised each teacher to consider them in light of particular situations and use them to determine priorities.

In the second section of the list, a concept of the nature of mathematics is presented with implications for objectives. These are considered appropriate for a student whose interest in mathematics is extensive. Paraphrasing the Committee's list, we can say that such a student should

1   Have an understanding of the deductive nature of mathematics

2   Be able to follow and give a consistent argument

3   Be able to distinguish between a valid argument and an invalid one

4   Understand the basic properties of operations on numbers and be able to determine whether a given system possesses any of these operations

5   Recognize the relations among various operations

6   Be able to perceive patterns

7   Be aware of the extent to which mathematical skills are used by individuals in their daily lives

8   Be aware that mathematics is used not only in the natural sciences but also in the behavioral and social sciences and arts

9   Recognize that some professions require knowledge of sophisticated and complex mathematical techniques

10   Recognize that there are some problems that do not lend themselves to solution by mathematical methods

11   Know the ways in which computers are used in science, technology, business, and government

12   Be aware of the evolutionary development of mathematics and have a knowledge of some of the historical milestones in this development

Thought questions

1 To what extent do the objectives stated by the National Committee on Mathematical Requirements satisfy your criteria for good aims?

2 Several of the aims were phrased "appreciation of . . . ." Is understanding a necessary condition for appreciation? Is it a sufficient condition?

3 Choose any two objectives of general education as identified by the Joint Commission. State more specific objectives of mathematics education that seem to be implied by the general objectives.

4 What are some implications of the three assumptions of the Commission on Mathematics of the College Entrance Examination Board?

5 Are the five objectives stated by the Commission on Mathematics of the College Examination Board restricted to college preparatory mathematics or are they sufficiently general to apply to the entire program?

6 Which of the criteria for evaluating objectives do the five objectives of the Commission on Mathematics of the College Entrance Examination Board satisfy?

7 Show that the specific tasks that the National Assessment of Educational Progress cites for one of its general objectives define the general objective in terms of observable student behavior.

8 Some teachers believe that the specificity of the objectives in the list of the National Assessment of Educational Progress coupled with the testing promoted by this agency will standardize the curriculum to such an extent that experimentation and adaptation to local needs will not take place readily. What is your appraisal of this belief?

9 In reporting on the list of competencies and skills developed by the Committee of the National Council of Teachers of Mathematics, it was stated that failure to describe the way the list was developed weakened the validity of the list. State why you agree or disagree with this statement.

10 Which of the criteria for assessing the validity of objectives does the list prepared by the Committee on Basic Mathematical Competencies and Skills of the National Council of Teachers of Mathematics satisfy?

11 It is suggested earlier in this chapter that one reason for objectives is to enable teachers to justify what they are doing. Which of the sets of objectives stated in this section would make this job easiest? Why?

Self-test on the competencies

1 Explain why a mathematics department should have objectives for the education it provides.
   a What are some reasons why a mathematics department should have objectives?
   b Of the reasons you stated above, which are more important? Why?

2 State defensible criteria for appraising objectives and use them to evaluate any set of objectives. Evaluate each of the following sets of objectives:
   a The aims of our department of mathematics were developed by the members of our department. As outcomes of our instruction in the required junior high school courses, grades 7–9, we expect each student should
      (1) Be able to perform the common arithmetical operations on rational numbers with reasonable speed and accuracy

(2)   Be able to analyze a problem having a quantitative aspect and apply appropriate mathematical principles in solving it

(3)   Understand the nature of measurement—that is, that standard units of measure are necessary, that measurement consists in comparing the object measured with a standard unit of measure, that measurements can be expressed in terms of various units of measure in either the English or the metric system, that measurements are approximations, and that measurements can be made in varying degrees of precision and accuracy

(4)   Be able to interpret graphs and tables of related numbers and construct graphs or tables to represent quantitative relations

(5)   Be able to interpret simple formulas and equations and be able to solve them for values of any of the variables

(6)   Know commonly used geometric concepts and the properties of common geometric figures: triangles, quadrilaterals, parallelograms, rectangles, squares, pentagons, hexagons, octagons, and circles

b   We have the following objectives for our geometry course, ordinarily elected by sophomores.

(1)   Teach the knowledge of the properties of geometric figures that would be possessed by any person regarded as liberally educated

(2)   Reinforce the particular knowledge of geometry prerequisite to a successful study of subsequent courses in mathematics in our high school curriculum

(3)   Teach an understanding of the nature of proof so that students will be able to prove theorems

(4)   Compare synthetic and analytic proof so students will be proficient in both methods of proof

(5)   Illustrate how a mathematician develops his subject—that is, his definition of a problem for investigation, his formation of conjectures, and the subsequent proof or disproof of these conjectures

(6)   Portray the structure of geometry so students will obtain an insight into the nature of mathematics as a distinctive kind of knowledge created by man

(7)   Further improve students' ability to solve problems

Read over the evaluations you wrote of the two sets of objectives given above. State the criteria you evidently used to evaluate these objectives.

3   State and defend general objectives for teaching mathematics.

a   Write a set of general objectives for mathematics in secondary schools.

b   Imagine that someone—your principal or superintendent or a parent—expresses lack of confidence in the objectives you just stated. Write a justification of them that will convince your critic that your objectives are sound.

References

Bassler, Otto and John R. Kolb. *Learning to Teach Secondary School Mathematics.* Scranton, Pa.: Intext Educational Publishers, 1971. Chs. 3 and 4.

Bloom, Benjamin S. (ed.) *Taxonomy of Educational Objectives. Handbook I. Cognitive Domain.* New York: David McKay, 1956.

———. *Taxonomy of Educational Objectives. Handbook II. Affective Domain.* New York: David McKay, 1964.

Cambridge Conference on School Mathematics. *Goals for School Mathematics.* Boston: Houghton Mifflin, 1963.

Commission on Mathematics of the College Entrance Examination Board. *Objectives of the Commission on Mathematics of the College Examination Board.* New York: College Entrance Examination Board, 1957.

Commission on Post-War Plans. "The Second Report of the Commission on Post-War Plans." *The Mathematics Teacher*, 36 (1945), 195–221.

——. *Guidance Pamphlet in Mathematics for High School Students.* Final Report of the Commission on Post-War Plans, 1947.

Committee on Basic Mathematical Competencies and Skills. "Mathematical Competencies and Skills Essential for Enlightened Citizens." *The Mathematics Teacher*, 65 (1972), 671–677.

Johnson, Donovan A. and Gerald R. Rising. *Guidelines for Teaching Mathematics.* Belmont, Calif.: Wadsworth, 1967. Ch. 2.

Mager, Robert F. *Preparing Objectives for Programmed Instruction.* San Francisco: Fearon, 1961.

National Assessment of Educational Progress. *Mathematics Objectives.* Denver: National Assessment of Educational Progress, 1970.

National Committee on Mathematical Requirements. *The Reorganization of Mathematics in Secondary Education.* Bulletin 32. Washington, D. C.: Department of the Interior, Bureau of Education, 1921.

National Council of Teachers of Mathematics. *The Place of Mathematics in Secondary Education.* Fifteenth Yearbook of the National Council of Teachers of Mathematics. Washington, D. C.: National Council of Teachers of Mathematics, 1940. Chs. 1–4.

Popham, J. W. "Objectives and Instruction." *American Educational Research Association Monograph Series on Curriculum Evaluation.* No. 3. Chicago: Rand McNally, 1969. Pp. 32–52.

Secondary School Curriculum Committee. "The Secondary Mathematics Curriculum." *The Mathematics Teacher*, 52 (1959), 389–417.

Whitehead, Alfred North. *The Aims of Education.* New York: Mentor, 1960. Essay 1 and 6.

4

Selecting and sequencing subject matter

By *subject matter*, we shall mean knowledge and beliefs about a subject. Thus some of the subject matter of mathematics is knowledge we have about mathematics and some is beliefs about the relative importance and modes of application of the various items of knowledge. We shall discuss some of the ways in which these different aspects of the subject matter of mathematics can be taught. Many beginning teachers think they really have no choice of subject matter. They think that their department chairman or a course of study will determine the subject matter they have to teach and that they will not be able to exert any discrimination relative to its selection. This belief is incorrect. Every teacher, no matter how restricted a teaching situation is, faces the problem of discriminating among items of subject matter.

The teacher has little control over some factors in the decision, however. These include departmental and school regulations and the aptitudes of the students in the class. Other factors are controllable, such as judgments concerning the relative importance of various topics, their interest to the teacher, and whether the teacher thinks they can be made interesting to and understandable by students. We shall discuss some of these factors and how they affect decisions. Once the subject matter has been selected, the decision of how to arrange it in a teachable sequence has to be faced. We shall discuss some of the factors in this decision, too.

At the conclusion of this chapter, you should be able to demonstrate the following competencies:

1 Identify concepts, singular statements, generalizations, prescriptions, and value judgments

2 State some factors relevant to decisions concerning the selection of subject matter for a particular course in mathematics

3 State some factors relevant to decisions concerning the arrangement of subject matter in a sequence for teaching

4 Select and sequence subject matter on a topic in mathematics that might be taught in some course in mathematics and defend this selection and sequence

The ubiquity of selection of subject matter

A subject is sometimes spoken of as a topic and it differs from the subject matter about that subject or topic. A topic is a *name* of a body of subject matter. On the other hand, the *knowledge* or *beliefs* denoted by that name constitute the subject matter. Thus the area of geometric figures or how to find the area of geometric figures is a topic. Items of subject matter about this topic would be, among others, the following:

The area of a geometric figure is the number of units of square measure in the geometric figure.

To measure area, we need a unit of measure.

Units of measure of area in the English system are the square inch, square foot, square yard, and square mile.

Units of measure of area in the metric system are the square millimeter, square centimeter, square meter, and square kilometer.

To find the area of a rectangle, multiply the length and width.

The area of a triangle is one-half the product of a side and the altitude to that side.

The area A of a circle of radius r is given by the formula $A = \pi r^2$.

The area cannot be more accurate than the least accurate measurement used to compute it.

Don't express the area in more significant digits than there are in the least accurate measurement used to compute the area.

Notice that whereas a topic (in this case, geometric figures) is a name, subject matter about that topic is expressed in sentences. This is to be expected, for knowledge or beliefs in daily life are usually expressed in sentences rather than in phrases.

In selecting subject matter, we usually begin by selecting topics. Then we analyze these into subtopics and further subordinate topics. But eventually we must obtain items of knowledge or belief if we are to have something more than names to teach. Thus we might decide to teach students in a general mathematics class about significant digits. We might analyze this into teaching them what a significant digit is and how to identify the relation of digits to the relative error and to the accuracy of a measurement. Each one of these is a topic. We can obtain subject matter about them by asking such questions as "What *is* a significant digit?" "How *does* one identify the significant digits in a measurement?" "What *is* the relation between the relative error of a measurement and the number of significant digits in the measurement?" and "What *is* the relation between the accuracy of a measurement and the number of significant digits in the measurement?" The answers to these questions, when stated in complete sentences, become items of subject matter to be taught about significant digits.

If a teacher is sufficiently self-disciplined to think through—that is, to analyze—a topic and identify explicitly the items of subject matter to teach, then teaching becomes pointed and students probably will know what they are to learn. But to the extent that the teacher does not do this, students may be vague about what they are to remember and be able to do. Many beginning teachers believe that they do not really have a choice of subject matter. They believe that they will be given a course of study or a textbook and told to follow it, that they will have little or no discretion in departing from the course of study or textbook. It is true that in some high schools and in some mathematics departments teachers have little freedom to adapt courses to the needs of the students. But even in these restricted situations, teachers face the problem of selecting subject matter. Let us consider four situations in which a teacher faces this problem.

We begin with a situation that every teacher faces: the determination of what to put in tests. It is highly unlikely that a teacher can test the attainment of all items of subject matter that have been taught in a course; one must sample from this domain. Taking a sample amounts to selecting. The teacher chooses some subject matter and rejects other. This is very much the case for tests that teachers design, and of this each teacher is probably aware.

But suppose a teacher's department has a policy of using periodic, departmental examinations, whether standardized or made by the members of the department. How is selection of subject matter involved? The examinations do not choose themselves; someone chooses the particular standardized examinations or the particular questions in the examinations prepared by the department. Hence, selection is involved. Usually such an operation proceeds first by the selection from the department of a committee responsible for building a test or selecting a standardized published test. If the committee decides on a published test, then it surely will consider what subject matter is tested. It probably will reject a test of subject matter not taught during the period covered by the test. It will assess the relative emphasis given to various items of subject matter and choose the test that provides the emphasis the committee thinks proper. On the other hand, if the committee writes the test, it faces the same problems that an individual teacher faces when writing one.

It is hard to imagine a situation so authoritarian that teachers in a department would not be able to criticize the content of a test or the relative stress of various items of subject matter in a test selected or written by a department committee. If such criticism is accepted, the teachers are implicitly selecting subject matter or determining emphasis. Hence we see that teachers do face the problem of the selection of subject matter.

It is highly probable that no teacher considers all items of subject matter of equal importance; some are more important than others. The important ones are stressed in teaching, and teachers often tell students which items are important. Even if teachers do not do this, students become aware of the relative importance of various items of subject matter. They infer validly that if a teacher reviews certain items and these appear on tests, they are important. In making such value judgments, a teacher implicitly makes choices relevant to objectives and thus solves the problem of selecting subject matter.

The remaining ways in which a teacher selects subject matter are based on the assumption of freedom to adapt courses to the needs and interests of students. A teacher may decide to supplement a course for the students who learn quickly by adding certain topics (bodies of subject matter) to the course. The teacher may decide to reduce the scope of the course by deleting certain topics for students who learn more slowly. Or certain topics or items of subject matter may be replaced by others. In any event, the teacher has to choose either to add or delete from the course.

The development of textbooks is relevant to the selection of subject matter too. Authors and publishers are interested in selling as many copies of a book as possible, and to do this they have to include subject matter that teachers who might buy the book might want. This would be easy if all potential purchasers wanted the same subject matter, but this is not the case. The committee in Texas that adopts textbooks for schools wants certain subject matter, defined to some extent by the state course of study. On the other hand, the analogous committee in Indiana may want certain other subject matter and so on for other states with state adoptions. New York, for example, has its system of Regents' examinations, given at the end of every course and prepared by people designated by the state Regents. The likelihood that a textbook will be adopted that does not cover what is sampled in the Regents' examination is low, and it behooves authors and publishers who wish to sell a textbook in New York to be sure that it covers the domain from which the sampling for the Regents' examinations are made.

There is nonetheless, considerable consensus among textbook adoption committees on what should be in mathematics courses. But authors cannot write only what the majority of textbook purchasers want. Publishers know that they lose fewer sales by including in a textbook subject matter that teachers may not want than by omitting subject matter teachers want. The result is that textbooks become thicker and thicker. If teachers otherwise like a textbook, they can omit the parts of it that they do not want to teach. But if subject matter that teachers want has been omitted from a textbook, they will not buy it. They will not take the time to write copy for the omitted topics. A teacher exercises bad judgment if he tries to cover all the subject matter that is in the textbook. Thus teachers must discriminate. Once a textbook has been adopted, the selection of subject matter is greatly simplified. The authors of a published book have already coped with this problem, and its contents represents their solution. But, like tests, textbooks do not select themselves; this is done by teachers and persons closely associated with teachers. This one decision selects a huge amount of subject matter.

Kinds of subject matter

Probably all teachers realize that the nature of their students can make a difference in how they teach; they adjust their teaching methods according to how students learn. But not all teachers realize that the nature of the subject matter can also make a difference in how they teach. Some items of subject matter are relatively simple and need little clarification. The concept of a quadrilateral is an example. Other items, such as the concept of a vector space, are more complex and require much clarification.

It is worthwhile considering differences in the logic of various kinds of subject matter, too. We both state and prove theorems, but although we state definitions we cannot prove them. When a student disagrees with a theorem, we respond differently than when the disagreement is with a definition. While we are not reluctant to characterize the sentence

   e is a transcendental number.

as true, we are reluctant to characterize the sentence

   e is a beautiful number.

as true. (We would be just as reluctant to characterize it as false.) Such a sentence is used to state a belief, a value judgment, rather than to state what is the case. We feel that we are not indoctrinating students when we teach them that e is a transcendental number but we may feel that we are if we teach them that e is a beautiful number.

Continuing the contrast, we see that there are theorems that enable us to simplify numerical and algebraic expressions; one example is:

$$\text{For all real numbers } x, y, \text{ and } z \neq 0, \frac{xz}{yz} = \frac{x}{y}.$$

But there is a difference in the logic of such statements and one like

   Reduce all fractions to lowest terms.

The former is an assertion, an item of knowledge. It is true and can be proved to be true. The latter is advice, a belief. If it is to be spoken of as "true," its truth must be determined in a way different from that in which the truth of the former was determined. There is no "oughtness" to the former; it simply states what is the case. But there is an implication of "oughtness" to the latter: one *ought* to reduce all fractions to lowest terms. Because differences in the logic of various kinds of subject matter make (or should make) a difference in how the kinds are taught, we shall offer a classification of subject matter in terms of logic.

Concepts

One kind of subject matter is what we shall call conceptual. A concept is knowledge of what something is, as for example the number 10, the number π, a variable, a circle, congruence, or rigor. Such knowledge is quite basic. We have to know what something is, what its identifying properties are, before we can ascertain what its other properties are and how it is related to other objects.

The logic of concepts is similar to the logic of definitions. In fact, as we shall learn in Chapter 5 on the teaching of concepts, one way of teaching them is by means of definitions. Definitions tell what a term means or is to mean, as for example

> For each vector $[x, y]$, x is called the *first* or *x-component* and y is called the *second* or *y-component* of the vector.

or what some object is, as for example

> A quadrilateral that has one pair of sides parallel is a trapezoid.

Knowing the logic of definitions, you know that you cannot prove that a definition is true as you prove that a theorem is true. Definitions resemble axioms and postulates in that we accept them without proof. It is much the same with concepts. If one person thinks that a trapezoid is a quadrilateral that has at least one pair of parallel sides, and another person thinks that a trapezoid is a quadrilateral that has just one pair of parallel sides, there is no way in which either person's concept can be proved correct and the other incorrect. (It is possible, however, to show that one concept is more elegant or more fruitful than another.) Concepts are not invariant among the people who hold them because of the connotations each person associates with them.

Some definitions define just one object, as in the case of the definition of the number e or the number π, the base vectors i and j, and such unique functions as the greatest integer function, the cosine function, and the logarithmic function base e. Other definitions define a nonsingular set of objects, as in the case of rational number, relations, parallelograms, and vertical angles. The latter definitions are generalizations in that they make statements about all the members of a nonsingular set.

Generalizations

Some generalizations are not definitional, as for example

> A square is a convex polygon.

> All points that satisfy $x^2 + y^2 = r^2$, $r > 0$ are on a circle whose center is the origin and whose radius is r.

> The diagonals of a rectangle bisect each other.

> For all real numbers x and y, $xy = yx$.

Either such generalizations are accepted without proof—that is, they are axioms or postulates—or they are capable of proof or disproof. Hence their logic differs from generalizations that are definitions. We shall regard generalizations that are not definitional as a second kind of subject matter.

Generalizations are easy to recognize when the subject and verb are plural:

> The diagonals of a rectangle bisect each other.

> Functions are a subset of relations.

> Micrometers and vernier calipers are used to make precise measurements.

> Trigonometric functions are periodic.

But frequently a statement having a common noun with the indefinite article "a" or "an" is used to make a generalization. For example,

> A square is a convex polygon.

> The slope of a linear function is constant.

Both are generalizations over a single set, the set of squares and the set of linear functions, respectively. In contrast,

> The diagonals of a rectangle bisect each other.

is a generalization over two sets, the set of diagonals and the set of rectangles. As another example,

> A number can be added to or subtracted from both sides of an equation, thereby producing an equation equivalent to the given equation.

is a generalization over two sets, the set of real numbers and the set of equations. The equation

$$x(y + x) = xy + xz$$

functions as a generalization, even though no domains of the variables are stated and no explicit quantification is presented. Yet when this equation is set in a context, we know that it purports to be a generalization over three sets, the sets of real numbers x, y, and z.

In the generalizations immediately above, the variables are quantified implicitly. The common noun and indefinite article function as both a universal quantifier and a designation of the set over which the quantification is made. Thus the generalization

$y = a$ where $a \in R$ determines a constant function.

means the same as

For every $a \in R$, $y = a$ determines a constant function.

Also the generalization

An ellipse is a conic section.

means the same as

All ellipses are conic sections.

or, using the abbreviated quantifier,

$\forall s \in$ ellipses, s is a conic section.

In the last two sentences, the quantification is explicit.

The generalization,

The slope of a linear function is constant.

means the same as

The slope of each linear function is constant.

or

The slope of all linear functions is constant.

Using the abbreviated quantifier,

$\forall f \in$ linear functions, the slope of f is a constant.

Here again, the quantification is explicit in the last three statements.

It is useful to separate generalizations that are not definitions into theorems or axioms (or postulates) because the truth of these two kinds of statement is determined differently. One accepts the truth of an axiom (or postulate) but proves a theorem.

Singular statements

In contrast to generalizations, which are statements about a nonsingular set of objects, there are statements like

2 is the only even prime number.

and

Gauss first proved that a nonconstant polynomial function has a zero in the set of complex numbers.

These are statements about just one object; in the case of the first the number 2 and in the case of the second the man Gauss. We can think of these as statements about a singular set. Let us call these *singular statements.* (Some people call them facts.) We shall consider singular statements as a third kind of subject matter.

Do not jump to the conclusion that if the verb of a statement is singular, the statement is a singular statement. For example, the verb of

A parallelogram is a quadrilateral.

is singular yet the statement is a generalization. To distinguish between a singular statement and a generalization, it is more helpful to consider the use of the statement than its syntactical form. If it is used to assert something about just one object, it is singular. If it is used to assert something about many objects, it is general.

Prescriptions

A fourth kind of subject matter is sentences used to give advice:

Reduce each fraction to lowest terms.

If you cannot prove a theorem directly, try indirect proof.

You should always check your answers.

and

To multiply two common fractions, multiply the numerators for the numerator of the product and multiply the denominators for the denominator of the product.

Such sentences are imperative or hortatory. Rather than stating what is the case, as do singular and general statements, they tell what is to be done or offer advice concerning what to do. Let us call them *prescriptions* and say that a prescription is a sentence imperative or hortatory in form. Thus

To prove a conditional, assume the hypothesis and deduce the conclusion.

is a prescription imperative in form, whereas

The spindle of a micrometer should be tightened snugly against the object being measured but not so tight that either the object or the micrometer is damaged.

is a prescription hortatory in form. The use of *should* or *ought*, and *must* when its meaning is that of *should* or *ought*, results in a hortatory prescription.

You might be disposed to say that prescriptions are generalizations, for they seem to tell what to do in all cases. We propose to draw a distinction between prescriptions and generalizations because of the difference in their logic; they are proven in different ways. We shall say more about these two kinds of subject matter in Chapter 8.

Value judgments

The fifth and last kind of subject matter to be considered is value judgments, as for example

> The best way to find rational approximations of the irrational roots of higher degree polynomial equations is to use the method of Newton.

> Mathematics is an important subject.

> In deciding between two packages of different size when buying a commodity such as soap flakes, breakfast food, or salad dressing, it is a good idea to figure the cost per unit of measure.

> The conceptualization of a group was a significant advance in mathematics.

Value judgments represent someone's belief about whatever is evaluated. They contain rating words such as *good, right, important,* and *significant* and their opposites. Their logic is not to state what is the case but to evaluate. Hence they depend on the evaluator's judgment and are justified differently than any of the other kinds of subject matter we have identified.

It should be noticed that there is a relation between value judgments and prescriptions. A value judgment in a context of choice implies a prescription. Thus, to say

> In solving a worded problem, it is a good idea to let the quantity you are asked to find be represented by a variable.

implies the advice

> In solving a worded problem, let the quantity you are asked to find be represented by a variable.

Conversely, a prescription usually implies a value judgment. Thus it would be logically odd to say

> The spindle of a micrometer should be tightened snugly against the object being measured but not so tight that either the object or the micrometer is damaged, but I don't think this is a good thing to do.

Giving advice contextually implies that the person offering the advice thinks it is good advice. Yet there is a difference between expressing values and telling someone what to do.

Thought questions

1 Give an example of a subject whose subject matter consists more of beliefs than of knowledge and of one whose subject matter consists more of knowledge than of beliefs.

2 Should prescriptions be regarded as beliefs or as knowledge? Why?

3   From some mathematics textbooks you have, find examples of each of the five kinds of subject matter.

4   Classify each of the following as a concept, singular statement, generalization, prescription, or value judgment.

a π is an irrational number.

b   The method of interpolation is a better method than Horner's method.

c   A cube is a parallelepiped.

d $a^2 = b^2 + c^2 - 2bc \cdot \cos A$

e   A proof is a sequence of statements such that the last statement is the statement to be proved and every other statement is an assumption, a theorem, or the conclusion of an inference from statements that have preceded it in the sequence.

f   To prove a conditional, assume the hypothesis and deduce the conclusion.

g   A good way to find a common denominator, though not necessarily the lowest common denominator, is to multiply the denominators.

h   A function $f(x) = a$ where $x \in R$ is a constant function.

i   The diagonals of a rectangle bisect each other.

j   10 is the base of our decimal system.

k   The base of the common logarithmic function is 10.

l   Through a point not on a given line, there is just one line parallel to the given line.

m   A rhombus is an equilateral parallelogram.

n   To simplify a common fraction, divide numerator and denominator by the same non-zero number.

o $x(y + z) = xy + xz$

p   A triangle two of whose sides are congruent is an isosceles triangle.

5   In the list for question 4, which of the statements might be used as a definition?

6   What will be the most useful form in which to state subject matter if the subject matter is to teach the student how to do something?

Factors affecting selection of subject matter

In selecting subject matter teachers are affected by certain constraints such as regulations of the department of mathematics or the board of education and the variety in student ability. The teacher is affected by personal values concerning the relative importance of various items of subject matter and the significance that should be given to factors such as the interest of students and the difficulty of various topics. We shall consider these and some other factors that tend to shape decisions.

Requirements

In the United States voters of a district elect representatives who vote for or against proposals for laws. Theoretically, the representatives are sensitive to the wishes of their constituents, and we can say that laws and regulations concerning the operation of public schools represent the desires of a majority of the voters in a school district. Teachers should therefore abide by these laws or regulations that pertain to what is or is not to be taught.

In some states there are laws that determine subject matter. In some the regulations of a state officer—the state superintendent, for example—serve to interpret the state laws. There may be regulations of administrative organizations between a particular secondary school and the state superintendent that must be followed. Examples of such administrative organizations are county and district boards of education, who act through superintendents, and the board of education of the school district in which the particular school is located which, in turn, acts through executive officers such as superintendents and principals.

Laws and regulations usually neither prescribe nor proscribe particular items of subject matter. They tend to be general. For example, a state may require that physical education be taken by all students but not specify exactly what subject matter in physical education must be taught. Or a state may require that every student pass a course in American history and civics before graduation. It may even specify some topics that must be studied in the course—the federal and state constitutions, for example, and the Australian method of voting and the principles of republican forms of government. But even these topics are general; subject matter within them must be selected.

Most state laws say little or nothing about mathematics. A regulatory body subordinate to the state government may require that all students take one course in mathematics before graduation, but what the content of this course should be is usually not stated. Mathematics departments in large high schools often have courses of study that teachers are expected to follow. These usually give a list of topics to be covered, and each teacher then has to determine the specific items of subject matter for each topic, unless the textbook provides an operational definition of this.

Regulations are established because they are considered the most effective means to desirable ends. This judgment may be wise or unwise at any given time. If it is wise, then meeting regulations is sound. Otherwise it is unsound. The conditions under which a regulation concerning the content of a mathematics course was determined may change. For example, before the introduction of modern mathematics into college mathematics courses, some high school departments prescribed course content in accordance with the mathematics that their students would study when they entered college. But the objectives and content of college mathematics courses changed. When subsequently the curricular regulations of high school mathematics departments did not change accordingly, following what had become antedated regulations was no longer justified. The point is that regulations must be followed, at least in theory, but they should also be continually evaluated to make sure that they continue to be justifiable. If it is found that regulations cannot be justified, then they should be changed.

Objectives

Specific and definite objectives are of more help in selecting subject matter than are general and indefinite ones. As was pointed out in Chapter 3, objectives seem to be used more to justify subject matter that has already been selected than to choose subject matter in the first place. This is not to depreciate objectives but only to indicate how they are actually employed in decisions concerning subject matter.

Utility

Other factors being equal, teachers tend to select subject matter that they consider useful. With all the knowledge and beliefs there are, it seems odd to teach students knowledge or beliefs for which they will find little or no use. Students who assert that school is not relevant to today's world may simply be unaware of the utility of some of the subject matter they are taught. But the concept of utility is not simple, and it bears analysis. Subject matter is not useful in the abstract; it is useful in a particular situation, at a particular time, for a certain purpose. Given knowledge of these conditions, a teacher is able to determine the utility of some given subject. Hence we shall analyze utility by answering the questions: (1) Useful *when?* (2) Useful *where?* (3) Useful *how?* We shall find that these are not mutually independent.

Subject matter may be useful at the very time it is being learned or it may be useful at some future time. A student who is studying general science together with mathematics probably will find it useful to know how to substitute in a formula and compute answers correctly. A student who wants to spend an allowance wisely will find a knowledge of percent, discount, carrying charges, and compound interest useful. Knowledge of measurement is useful at all ages for secondary school students. And students who hold jobs are likely to become involved in some mathematics. If teachers can find out what mathematics is relevant to students, they can teach to classes what particular students need.

Most mathematics taught in high school is useful at some future time rather than at the time the student is learning it. This makes motivation unfortunately difficult, and students are prone to ask, "When would I ever use this?" Yet teachers must select subject matter with one eye toward the future. Some students will go into occupations in which they will find use for the algebra they are being taught. Some will go to college, where they may find variables, relations, functions, and perhaps matrices and vectors of use.

Utility may pertain to academic or nonacademic situations. Some subject matter in mathematics is useful because it enables students to learn other mathematical subject matter. Learning first how to operate with rational numbers, for example, is useful later in solving equations and inequalities. And these in turn are useful when linear programming is studied. When we speak of prerequisite knowledge, academic utility is what we have in mind. If a knowledge of p is necessary for a knowledge of q, then p must be taught before q. Prerequisite knowledge is the chief factor in highly structured courses like algebra, geometry, and others in college preparatory curricula.

Documentary analysis and job analysis can be employed to determine the academic and nonacademic utility of subject matter. Documentary analysis consists in studying books, newspapers, magazines, and printed forms used by institutions and businesses. The objective is to determine what mathematical subject matter is used in such documents and how frequently it is used. To determine the relative academic utility of subject matter for eighth-grade mathematics, for example, a group of teachers might solve a representative sample of problems in the textbook used in a first course in algebra and determine which and with what frequency generalizations, and prescriptions of arithmetic are used. If it is determined that there is not enough time in the eighth grade to teach all these, the ones occurring most frequently can be taught.

To determine the relative utility of subject matter from algebra, geometry, trigonometry, and analytic geometry, Fagerstrom (1933) solved all the exercises in the calculus textbook written by Granville, Smith, and Longley, at the time the most popular textbook for college calculus courses. He analyzed the solution of each exercise and recorded the number of times various items were used. He then recommended what subject matter to emphasize and what to deemphasize. Of course, his recommendations were based on the assumption that at least one objective of high school mathematics is to prepare students to study calculus successfully.

Teachers might make similar analyses of newspapers, magazines, sales slips, invoices, and the like to determine the relative utility of subject matter for a general mathematics course. Such analysis would tell which mathematical terms are frequently used and whose meaning the students should know, which operations are employed, which formulas (generalizations) are used, and what value judgments appear. These, then, become candidates for inclusion in the course. Obviously documentary analysis can be of use in determining academic and nonacademic utility.

When job analysis is used to determine the relative utility of subject matter, a particular job—secretary, teacher, sheetmetal worker, bank teller, day-care operator, lathe operator—is studied carefully to ascertain the frequency of activities within it. Usually, very specific activities are reported. Thus it might be found that a secretary answers the telephone, types letters, determines the amount of postage needed for letters, arranges meetings and makes appointments for the boss, accounts for the petty cash fund, and so on. Each performance of these activities is recorded, and thus a frequency count of them is obtained.

Such analysis is factual, the result of observation and not inference. But it is not productive of subject matter. Identifying the subject matter necessary for a person to be able to perform a particular job requires a second analysis. This is based on inference and proceeds by conditional reasoning: To be able to do p, a person must know $q, r, s, \ldots$. Then $q, r, s, \ldots$ become subject matter that must be taught.

In the decade of the 1920's there was great interest in using job analysis to determine the content of arithmetic courses. The jobs of workers in banks, department stores, drug stores, building trades, brokerages, newspapers, and many industries, especially the chemical, textile, food, and paper industries, were studied to determine what mathematics these workers used. At the present time, however, there is less interest in this technique.

We now turn to a consideration of how subject matter is used. Broudy *et al.* (1964) identify four uses of what is learned in school: (1) replicative, (2) associative, (3) applicative, and (4) interpretive. **Replicative use,** as the term implies, is the repeated use of an item of subject matter without much thought, if any, on the part of the user. By the time students enter high school, most of the uses of arithmetic ought to be replicative. High school students do not deliberate on the sum of 8 and 4 or the product of 7 and 9; a stimulus leads directly to the correct response. And not much more thinking than this is involved in finding a product like 234×567 or a quotient like $12.58 \div 0.96$. Similarly, once students in algebra have studied operations with rational numbers, it is expected that their use of the knowledge they have acquired will be largely replicative.

Replicative use of subject matter is the most reliable because it is frequent and thus continually reinforcing. It is not surprising that subject matter used replicatively is not forgotten. Overlearning assures virtually perfect performance.

Associative use of subject matter occurs when something other than it is called to mind. Thus a student who reads the term *conic section* and consequently visualizes the curves that are the intersection of a plane and one or more of the nappes of two cones is using a knowledge of the term associatively. A student who learns the formula for the law of a convex lens

$$\frac{1}{f} = \frac{1}{d_0} + \frac{1}{d_i},$$

and then thinks, "This equation has the same form as that for computing the total resistance of two resistors connected in parallel" is using knowledge of the lens law associatively.

A very common associative use lies in the attitudes or appreciations dragged into consciousness as subject matter is recalled. Broudy *et al.* (1964) believe that much of what is commonly called *concomitant learning* is associative. Attitudes toward mathematics are learned concomitantly with the subject matter of mathematics. How often have we heard someone who is speaking of mathematics say, "That was my best subject" or "I never did like mathematics!"

The **applicative use** of subject matter is the one most individuals have in mind when they speak of use. A student decides that some knowledge or belief is relevant to the solution of a problem. The student then applies it— that is, makes a deduction and solves the problem. Replicative use is most effective when the situation in which an item is to be used is practically the same as that in which it was learned. But when the new situation departs from the old one, replicative use breaks down. In the new and different situation, the first problem is determining what subject matter is relevant, and this requires judgment and discrimination. The next problem is drawing the correct conclusion. Hence, the applicative use of subject matter requires thinking in a way that the two previous uses we discussed do not.

We can identify two applicative uses by students. One is the application when the teacher or the textbook tells the student what subject matter is relevant. A teacher has taught the concept of percent for example, and how to find what percent one number is of another. As homework the teacher then assigns a set of problems like this one: "The basketball team won sixteen games out of twenty-two. What percent of the games played did it win?" The student knows what knowledge is relevant; the problems appear at the end of the topic "Finding What Percent One Number Is of Another." One would have to be stupid not to realize that what the teacher had just taught had something to do with the solution of the problems. Yet this use is not replicative. The student does not respond automatically; some thinking is required.

The second applicative use occurs when no one informs the student what knowledge is relevant. Suppose the teacher who had taught about percentage waited until some later time and then posed the following problem: "Our principal wants to find out which homeroom has the best attendance record. How would you tell her to do it?" The teacher does not use the term "percent" or any cognate that would create associations. If the students suggest that the principal compute the percent of attendance of the various homerooms, they are proposing the second applicative use. It is more demanding cognitively and is generally regarded as higher in value.

The great value of generalizations is their applicative potential. A generalization is applied whenever one recognizes that a problem or one aspect of it is an instance of the generalization. The conclusion is then immediately drawn. The form of this inference may be represented as

Generalization $\quad \forall x \in A, p(x)$—where $p(x)$ is some statement about x.

Subsumption $\quad a \in A$

Instance $\qquad \therefore p(a)$

Since much of the subject matter of mathematics consists of generalizations, the applicability of mathematics is great. Therefore mathematics teachers are correct to be favorably disposed toward generalizations and are inclined to choose those that have the greatest potential for the second kind of application.

Broudy *et al.* (1964, p. 54) point out that the **interpretive use** of school learning is the most fundamental use of all:

> Whenever we use our school learnings in these areas [everyday experiences] to perceive, understand, or feel life situations, we say that we are using our learnings primarily for interpretation, and not replicatively, associatively, or applicatively, although, strictly speaking, these uses do not necessarily exclude each other.

It may be argued that the reason the interpretive use is the most fundamental is that one first has to interpret a situation before being able to decide what learning is relevant. Once this has been done, if a replicative use is called for, the person can respond automatically. If the situation is different from that in which the learning was acquired, one carries on the reflective thinking that is the essence of application.

To consider some examples of the interpretive use of mathematical subject matter, suppose a student observes the dials on the gasoline pump as the car's gas tank is being filled. The dial indicating the cost of the gasoline and the dial indicating the number of gallons purchased move in coordination, a cost for each gallon or part thereof. If the student thinks, "Here is an example of a function," we would say that the concept of a function is being used interpretively. If in reading a columnist's argument in a newspaper the student understands that the writer is trying to persuade readers that something is the case and realizes that the argument for it can be analyzed as can a proof in mathematics, the student is using knowledge learned in mathematics to gain insight in a different situation. Then if the student proceeds to analysis of the columnist's argument, interpretation moves into application. If a student who is studying abstract algebra comes to realize without being told that the concepts of group, ring, and field help one organize knowledge of the rational, real, and complex numbers, we can say that the student is using knowledge to interpret.

Whenever we use knowledge or beliefs to explain or organize facts, we are using them to interpret. When an explanation is given, we understand things in a way we did not understand before because facts have been related. The cultural aim of mathematics education, as mentioned in the previous chapter, is based largely on the interpretive use of subject matter. Students "see" mathematics in situations that at first thought do not seem mathematical.

It is of some value to point out the reasoning that the principle of utility implies. By means of certain analyses, we find facts, that such and such is the case—as, for example, housekeepers almost never divide by a common fraction, that sales personnel determine sales tax by using a table, or that professors of engineering speak of single-valued and many-valued functions but professors of mathematics do not. It is then argued that because of these facts, we *should teach* so and so. Yet this reasoning is not always sound. It does not follow that simply *because* housekeepers almost never have to divide by a common fraction we should not teach students how to divide this way. Moreover, if it is found that stockbrokers compute percents by paper and pencil, it does not follow that we should not teach them how to do these computations with a slide rule. Perhaps the reason they perform the computations as they do is that they know no other way. If they had been taught how to do computations by slide rule, they might employ the more efficient method.

The basic assumption of utility is: What is ought to be. But there are too many counterexamples to this proposition to permit us to employ it indiscriminately. Thoughtless application of it would do nothing more than perpetuate an existing situation. How would we ever improve? In short, utility requires value judgments, such as consideration of whether a person is using such and such subject matter *should* be using it. Finally, one must not ignore the judgment of whether the subject matter would be used if it were known. The latter judgment enhances utility.

Interest

When students find subject matter interesting, their motives for studying increase and they are more likely to retain it. Moreover, the teacher does not have to spend much energy controlling students. Everyone benefits.

It is more likely that interest in a subject is derived than that it is inherent. A student is interested in mathematics because he or she has had success in it, because its utility has been perceived, or because the teacher is enthusiastic and competent. There is nonetheless some subject matter interesting to most students. In algebra for example, students seem to like graphing, especially graphing equations. This is enhanced when the teacher is able to generate an air of discovery ("Where do you think the graph will be located?"). They also seem to enjoy solving equations and proving identities. Perhaps this is because of their problematic aura. Students in general mathematics appear to like informal geometry, particularly constructions with straight-edge and compass. Perhaps this is because it is not abstract and involves physical activity. "Story problems" tend to be less interesting, perhaps because they are more difficult. Fundamental operations, such as those with rational expressions in algebra, are usually considered to be less interesting. Students are aware of the need for skill in such operations, yet these do not turn them on as other topics do.

If the teacher thinks that some subject matter not interesting at the outset can be made interesting, it is a candidate for selection. The teacher will have to work harder to develop and sustain interest in such subject matter. Its utility may have to be emphasized. The teacher may have to relate it to subject matter that students have studied previously. The teaching method may have to be varied. But so long as there is interest—whether it is inherent or developed by the teacher seems less important—both teaching and learning will be more enjoyable.

We conclude the discussion of interest with a caveat. Were a lot of time to be spent on a particular topic only because the students are interested in it, it might be that not enough time is left for other topics that are equally justified. To select a topic only because the students are interested in it may also be unsound. Students' interests are fleeting and sometimes disappear when a teacher expects the students to exert effort to pursue them. (The latter indicates a way of distinguishing between whims or evanescent interests and more substantial and abiding interests.) Hence teachers must exercise judgment and balance interest against other determining factors.

Difficulty

Subject matter too difficult for students frustrates them; they may not be able to understand what they are expected to learn. Or they may not be able to do what they are expected to do. When one understands what one is learning and is able to do what is expected, inherent satisfaction accompanies the learning and doing. When understanding and the ability to perform are missing, so is satisfaction. Satisfaction supplies the motivation for continued learning. When it is absent, the student wants some extrinsic justification for continuing study. Evidence of this may be exhibited by the student who says, "Why do we have to learn this?" or "When do you ever use this stuff?" Subject matter that is too difficult aggravates the problem of motivation and may cause discipline problems if frustration becomes too great.

The difficulty some students have is lack of academic aptitude to study mathematics successfully. They may not be able to handle abstractions, conceptualize, identify patterns, or read with comprehension. Or they may have a sufficiently high academic aptitude but be weak in mathematical background; they may not know what certain mathematical symbols mean, may not know certain fundamental principles, or be inaccurate in ordinary arithmetic operations. Finally, they may not be interested in mathematics and take it only because it is required in the curriculum or because their parents insist on it. In such cases, mathematics will seem difficult even though it is not difficult for other students.

Another factor in difficulty is that the more abstract a subject is the more difficult it is. Thus $n \times n$ matrices are more difficult to work with than 2×2 matrices. The algebra of rational numbers is more difficult than arithmetic, and modern, abstract algebra is more difficult than algebra of real numbers.

Complexity, too, determines difficulty. The more complex a subject is, the more difficult it is. Complexity, in turn, depends directly on the number of conditions involved. Thus the generalization

> The square of the sum of two numbers is equal to the square of the first plus twice the product of the first and second plus the square of the second.

contains only words that are in Thorndike's list of two thousand common words yet is often not comprehended by algebra students. The definition of a probability function is also complex; it may be defined in such a way that it expresses five necessary conditions. The definition of a linear function, on the other hand, is less complicated and may be defined with only two conditions. Similarly, the definition of a vector space involves several conditions and hence is more complicated than the definition of a group, which involves fewer conditions. One can expect that the definitions of a probability function and a vector space will be difficult, at least initially.

Rigor influences difficulty. It is possible to argue that difficulty varies directly with rigor. Thus if a teacher expects students to distinguish sharply between numbers and numerals, or between rational numbers and fractions, the subject matter employing these concepts will be more difficult.

Methods of teaching also affect difficulty. Students find subject matter difficult when it is taught by a teacher who cannot explain clearly, who cannot make expectations definite, who does not review, or who does not assign enough exercises. Yet methods are not as basic in determining difficulty as are complexity and rigor. The competent teacher can adjust methods in terms of the students and the subject matter.

It should surprise no one that teachers tend not to select subject matter that is too difficult for themselves. It is too threatening to teach subjects one does not understand well. Now and then one will hear teachers say about a textbook, "This is a good book, but it is too hard for my students." If the book has been used successfully by teachers of students like the ones these teachers have, one is tempted to conjecture that they are projecting a feeling of personal difficulty on the students. What they mean is that the textbook is too difficult for them and this is why they reject it.

Authoritative judgment

It is assumed that authorities, better than anyone else, should know what ought to be taught. They have perspective in mathematics and can judge the relative importance of subject matter. The recommendations of the Commission on Mathematics of the College Entrance Examination Board concerning the content of the mathematics curriculum were influential in determining subject matter. Teachers who adopted the textbooks developed by experimental programs such as the Ball State Program, the School Mathematics Study Group (SMSG), the University of Illinois Committee on School Mathematics (UICSM), and the recent Secondary School Mathematics Curriculum Improvement Study (SSMCIS) were swayed by their judgments because the textbooks had been developed by mathematicians and classroom teachers who are authorities.

How do we decide who is an authority? There is no question that a mathematician is an authority about his specialty of mathematics. Is he or she an authority about what can be learned by high school students? There is little question that a child psychologist is an authority about the growth and development of children. Is he or she an authority about what topics of mathematics should be taught in the various grades? The mathematics that the mathematician and the engineer recommend are not always the same. Finally, we may ask what the classroom teacher does when the authorities disagree, which frequently happens.

The best use of authoritative judgment occurs when a group of authorities (mathematicians, applied mathematicians, and classroom teachers) deliberate together and reach whatever consensus they can. The subject matter selected by the teams of mathematicians and high school teachers who wrote the textbooks in the School Mathematics Study Group's project is an example of effective use of authority. Their judgments were not universally sound, but it is hard to argue for a better use. It is highly probable that in the foreseeable future authoritative judgment will continue to be influential in determining the content of secondary school mathematics courses.

It is worthwhile to point out that the kind of decision concerning the selection of subject matter typically faced by the practicing classroom teacher will be based on the relation $x \leq y$, where the domain of x and y is subject matter and $\leq$ is the partial ordering of such properties as utility, interest, difficulty, recommendation by authorities, and so on. Either x or y is presently in the curriculum, and the other competes with it for a place. The burden is on the one that seeks to replace the other, and this decision is made in terms of the order relation. Not just one property is considered; all must be. The advantage of this point of view is that decisions are grounded in reality. Curricular revisions can be continual and need not constitute upheavals.

Thought questions

1   Choose the term that best completes the following analogy: Numeral is to number as topic is to ———. Justify your choice.

2   Criticize the following principle: Select the subject matter that is most important.

3   State the assumptions which are basic to Fagerstrom's study.

4   Wilson (1951) found that in the twenty industries one of his students studied by job analysis, 51,101 workers of 68,043 used no decimals. He therefore recommended (p. 256) "Omission of all drill on manipulation of decimals." Evaluate this reasoning.

5   Choose one issue of a local newspaper. Analyze the issue and make a frequency count of the uses of mathematics in it.

6   Begle (1958) states, "No one can predict exactly which mathematical skills will be important and useful in the future." Discuss the implications of this for the selection of subject matter.

7   Suggest criteria for identifying authorities who might be used in making recommendations concerning subject matter to be taught.

8   Silberman in *Crises in the Classroom* (New York: Random House, 1970) makes some suggestions concerning the subject matter taught in the schools. On page 172 he questions "whether, when fully developed it [the subject matter] is worth adults' knowing, and whether having known it as a child makes a person a better adult. If the answer to both questions is negative or ambiguous, then the material is cluttering the curriculum." Is this a satisfactory principle for selecting subject matter? Why?

9   A principle for selecting subject matter stated in some textbooks on curriculum construction is: Select the subject matter that meets the needs of the students. Evaluate this principle.

10 Which factor affecting the selection of subject matter was used in each of the following decisions?

   a To find out what to teach in general mathematics in Whoopeedo Junior High School, the mathematics department selected the five industrial plants in the city that employ most of the dropouts of the school system. They studied the various jobs in these companies to find out what elements of mathematics the employees were using. Having found these, they selected the ones having the highest frequency of occurrence.

   b The mathematics department of Twomartinis Junior High School were selecting a textbook for the seventh and eighth grades. For each textbook being considered, the teachers took a random sample of thirty-five pages. On each page they identified the items of subject matter presented. Then for each item they made the following analysis:

   (1) They counted the number of words.
   (2) They counted the prefixes and suffixes in the words.
   (3) They counted the number of words not on the Thorndike list of familiar words.
   (4) They computed the averages of all these over the set of items.

   They chose the books that had the lowest averages.

   c The teacher who was teaching the fourth course in mathematics at Community District No. 4 High School decided to devote the course to analysis. She wrote to the head of the department of mathematics in each of the six universities in the state, asking the department head to list the fifteen most important topics in analysis for high school students in such a course. She received answers from all six, complying with her request. She made a frequency count and included in the course topics listed by three or more heads.

11 Find some examples that counter the proposition: What is ought to be.

12 Thomas Briggs, an early writer on curriculum theory, stated that we ought to teach youngsters to do better the desirable things they will do anyway. Evaluate this as a principle for selecting subject matter for schooling.

13 Dean Inge, an Anglican prelate, observed, "There are two kinds of fools—one says, 'This is old, therefore it is good'; the other says, 'This is new, therefore it is better.'" What is the relevance of this observation to the selection of subject matter?

14 Find examples of subject matter that, although not presently being used because they are not known, would be used if known.

Factors influencing sequence of subject matter

Once subject matter has been selected, or as it is being selected, it has to be arranged in some sequence for teaching. By this we mean a temporal ordering of subject matter such that one item of subject matter is taught first, another is taught second, another third, and so on.

Sequence can be vertical or horizontal. By *vertical sequence* we mean the ordering of subject matter with respect to the grade: kindergarten, first grade, and so on. Vertical sequence is often called grade placement. By *horizontal sequence* we mean the ordering either of subject matter with respect to a particular course in a particular grade or of subject matter in a particular topic in a particular course.

When one analyzes the factors to be considered in selecting subject matter, one realizes that an order relation for some of them can be defined. By exercising judgment, one can order the utility of subject matter as having little, some, or great use. The same can be done for difficulty, interest, and so on.

If a property used to select subject matter can be ordered, this ordering can be used to determine a sequence of presentation of the subject matter. Items of subject matter can be arranged in increasing or decreasing utility. When textbook authors place in the last chapters of their book the subject matter that can be most readily omitted without introducing gaps in the student's knowledge, they are using the principle of decreasing utility. And when they put in the first chapter the subject matter that is very easy for the students, they are employing the analogous principle of increasing difficulty. We shall direct our attention to factors used frequently to determine sequence of mathematical subject matter.

Prerequisite knowledge

Prerequisite knowledge is used more frequently than any other factor for determining a sequence for teaching mathematical subject matter. It is derived from the analogous factor discussed above. If a knowledge of p is necessary for the comprehension of q, then p must be taught before q. To take some examples, suppose it has been decided to teach the definition

A prism all of whose bases and lateral faces are squares is called a *cube*.

It is obvious that to comprehend this definition the student must know what a prism is and what the bases and lateral faces of a prism are. Hence definitions of these geometric objects must be taught before the definition of the cube is taught. If a teacher wants to present the theorem

Every real number has an additive inverse.

using abbreviated quantifiers,

$$\forall x \in R, \exists \, y \in R, \, x + y = 0$$

the students will have to be taught the meaning of the symbols $\forall x$, $\exists \, y$, and $\in$ before they can understand the generalization stated in mathematical notation. If the conventional algorithm for adding two common fractions is taught, the teacher ought to teach beforehand the concepts of numerator and denominator of a common fraction, common denominator, lowest common denominator, factoring, and how to factor natural numbers. Otherwise, the students will not know what the teacher is talking about when these terms are used and will not know how to obtain the lowest common denominator.

Familiarity

Some topics selected for a course are more familiar than others to students. Thus in a general mathematics course, it is highly probably that ratio and percent are more familiar than formulas, even though students may not understand either very well. And it may be that simple geometric figures like square, rectangle, triangle, and circle are more familiar than ratio and percent. Many teachers and textbook writers use familiarity to order the presentation of subject matter. They begin with the most and progress to the least familiar.

Using familiarity for determining sequence is justified on psychological and pedagogical grounds. The familiar is less threatening. Hence, students are more motivated to study it, assuming it is not so familiar that they see no challenge and are bored with it. Teaching is easier then, and students learn better.

Abstractness

Abstracting is a cognitive activity that occurs when an individual becomes cognizant of a pattern, of a set of similarities among differences. For example, suppose a student graphs several instances of $y = ax^2 + bx + c$, $a \neq 0$, and inspects the graphs. If the student realizes that even though the graphs are located at different places in the 2-space and some open upward and some open downward and some are "fat" and others are "thin," they all have the same shape, he or she has abstracted the common property of shape from the differences. The word *abstraction* is derived from a Latin word that means *draw from*, which characterizes the cognitive activity to which it refers.

There may be increasing or decreasing abstractness of subject matter, and either of these orders can be used to determine a sequence. Abstractness increases when restricting conditions are removed. Thus the sequence

> rectangles $<$ parallelograms $<$ quadrilaterals $<$ polygons
> where "$<$" means *precedes*

is in the order of increasing abstractness because the right angle condition is removed in passing from rectangles to parallelograms, the condition of parallel opposite sides is removed in passing from parallelograms to quadrilaterals, and the four sides condition is removed in passing from quadrilaterals to polygons. Similarly, the sequence

> 2×2 matrices $< m \times n$ matrices

is increasing abstractness because the restriction on the number of columns and rows is decreasing.

An example of the use of the relation of increasing abstractness in determining vertical sequence is the sequence

> nonnegative integers $<$ nonnegative rationals $<$ integers $<$ rationals $<$ reals $<$ complex numbers

In the primary grades, children work with whole numbers (nonnegative integers). Then, in effect, the condition that the value of q in p/q be 1 is removed and they work with common fractions and decimal fractions (nonnegative rationals). In junior high school, if not before, the conditions $p > 0$ and $q > 0$ are removed and the students work with the rationals. Then in algebra they are introduced to the reals and complex numbers. Similarly, in high school the students first work with ordered fields—rationals and reals. Then in a second course they encounter a field that is not ordered— the complex numbers. Later, in college, they study groups and rings. In this sequence, restricting conditions are removed in passing from one set of numbers to the others. When groups and rings are studied, even the condition that the elements be numbers is removed.

There are many examples of using the relation of increasing abstractness to effect horizontal sequence. Usually, in the geometry course, figures in 2-space are studied before analogous figures in 3-space. Polynomials are studied before rational expressions. The study of systems of equations typically begins with systems of two linear equations and progresses through systems of three linear equations to systems of a linear equation and a quadratic equation to systems of quadratic equations. The study of quadratic functions such that $f(x) = ax^2 + bx + c$, $a \neq 0$, may begin with those for which $b = c = 0$, pass to those for which $b = 0$ but $c \neq 0$, and wind up with those for which the only condition is that in the definition, $a \neq 0$.

Abstractness decreases when conditions are imposed. Thus the sequence

geometric figures < polygons < quadrilaterals < parallelograms < rectangles < squares

is in decreasing abstractness. This is because one progresses through the sequence by imposing additional conditions on each set of figures after the first. As another example, suppose the general quadratic relation

$$Ax^2 + Bxy + Cy^2 + Dx + Ey + F = 0$$

(where A, B, and C are not all 0) is studied first. Then sequentially the relations for which $B = 0$; $B = E = 0$; $B = D = E = 0$; and $B = C = D = E = 0$ are studied. Obviously additional conditions are being imposed and hence the sequence is determined by decreasing abstractness.

Decreasing abstractness is not used as frequently to determine sequence in mathematics as increasing abstractness. Why? We can find examples of its use. Many textbooks in algebra use the sequence

relations < functions < linear functions

Since conditions are being imposed as one moves through the sequence, the sequence is in terms of decreasing abstractness. Similarly, the popular sequence in abstract algebra

groups < rings

is in terms of decreasing abstractness. So is the popular sequence in geometry

geometric figures $<$ polygons $<$ convex polygons $<$ quadrilaterals $<$ trapezoids $<$ parallelograms $<$ rectangles $<$ squares

and the analogous one in solid geometry

solid (geometric) figures $<$ polyhedrons $<$ prisms $<$ parallelepipeds $<$ rectangular parallelepipeds $<$ right rectangular parallelepipeds $<$ cubes

Given a set of items of subject matter that are amenable to sequencing by abstractness, there is very little research evidence that either increasing or decreasing abstractness will be more effective in learning. The choice seems more to depend on factors extrinsic to the nature of the subject matter as, for example, relative familiarity. Thus the sequence

point $<$ line(as a set of points) $<$ ray $<$ line segment (proper subset of a line)

would seem better than the reverse. Point and line are more familiar than line segment. In many cases, one sequence is as good as the other. For example, it seems to make no difference whether textbooks present relations before or after functions. Some textbooks use one sequence and some use the other, and, as far as we can tell, students learn equally from both.

The genetic principle

Morris Kline (1966) pointed out that the conceptual difficulties mathematicians have experienced with ideas are the very ones students experience when they come to learn the ideas. When negative numbers were first conceived, they seemed strange and their acceptance by mathematicians took time. This was even more true of irrational and imaginary numbers. Their designation (*irrational* having the connotation not reasonable and *imaginary*, not real) indicated the suspicion with which many mathematicians have regarded them. Teachers testify that the concepts of negative numbers, irrational numbers, and imaginary numbers are difficult for students. Another example is the elements of non-Euclidean geometry, which did not appear to fit man's conception of space. It was some time before these elements were accepted as subject for research. Non-Euclidean geometry is harder for students to understand than Euclidean geometry.

Because of his belief, Kline proposed a genetic principle for ordering the presentation of subject matter: the order of presentation of mathematical ideas should be the same as the historical order of their invention. We can find examples that fit this genetic principle in curricula. Informal proof precedes formal proof in most courses in geometry. Negative numbers are taught after positive numbers and imaginaries are taught after reals. The calculus follows the algebra of real numbers, as does abstract algebra. Matrix theory follows a study of the solution of systems of linear equations.

But these sequences also are in terms of increasing abstractness, and some of them are in terms of familiarity. Hence the genetic principle, although plausible enough, is not independent of the other factors. Kline advanced it to counter decreasing abstractness, which he felt was being used too frequently as modern mathematics was being introduced in textbooks late in the 1950's and early in the 1960's. For example, some textbooks of that period placed the study of sets before the study of numbers. This accords with the principle of decreasing abstractness. But sets were invented by mathematicians long after the various kinds of numbers. Hence, if one were to follow the genetic principle, a study of sets would follow a study of various kinds of numbers. The fact is that students learn from both sequences, and at the time Kline advanced his proposal it was not possible to prove that learning was more substantial in either sequence.

Immediacy of application

Suppose it has been decided that subject matter about sets will be taught in some textbook, the first course in algebra, for example. There are two ways in which the subject matter could be presented. It could be concentrated in one chapter, perhaps at the beginning of the book, or the various items could be presented just before they are needed to organize or clarify general-izations about the rational numbers. If the second alternative is chosen, the sequence would be determined by what we might call immediacy of application: subject matter should be presented as close to the point of application as possible.

Another instance of immediacy of application occurs in the sequencing of subject matter about logic, assuming this topic is taught in a course in geometry. Instead of presenting all the subject matter about logic in one chapter, it is portioned out at points just before it is to be used. Thus the logic of conditional statements would be taught just before the students' first experience in proving conditional theorems, the topics of equivalent statements and contrapositives just before a theorem whose proof can be given by proving the equivalent contrapositive, and the topics of contradictory statements and the logic of indirect proof just before a theorem whose proof can be made by this kind of proof.

Sequencing by immediacy of application can be justified on psychological and pedagogical grounds. A student who sees the immediate utility of some subject matter is more highly motivated to study it because it has become more significant. Moreover, application reinforces learning. The teacher does not have to work so hard to develop desire to learn. With enhanced learning, teaching becomes more effective.

What can be said of the relative efficacy of the various factors in deter-mining a sequence for presenting subject matter? Some seem not to vary with subject matter, teachers, and students. An example is prerequisite knowledge. It is hard to see how a teacher can ignore it. Others seem to vary.

One of these is interest and another is utility. Given two items of subject of equal difficulty, there is no substantial body of research evidence that indicates a correlation between a particular ordering in terms of either of these two factors and learning. Abstractness varies with subject matter; some topics lend themselves to increasing but others to decreasing abstractness. Perhaps most depends on the cognitive style of the teacher. Some teachers enjoy showing how a mathematical structure is built and are disposed to increasing abstractness. Others enjoy portraying an existing structure and are disposed to decreasing abstractness. Students of both learn mathematics, although concomitant learning may differ. One value of becoming acquainted with the various factors used to determine sequence is that they can be used to experiment with different sequences until teachers find one that seems to fit their cognitive style and from which students learn what each teacher wants them to learn.

Thought questions

1   Is the order relation that can be defined for such properties as utility, interest, and difficulty a strong or a weak order relation? Why?

2   Suppose two items of subject matter are of equal utility. How may they be ordered? Suppose they are of equal difficulty. How may they be ordered?

3   Why is prerequisite knowledge so frequently used to sequence subject matter in mathematics and so infrequently in history?

4   Which of the properties of an order relation (irreflexive, asymmetric, and transitive) does the property of being prerequisite satisfy? Explain why this property can be used to order subject matter.

5   Suppose a teacher teaches about circles determined by $x^2 + y^2 = r^2$ before teaching about circles determined by $(x - h)^2 + (y - k)^2 = r^2$. Is this increasing or decreasing abstractness? Explain.

6   Explain why the sequence

    polynomials $<$ rational expressions

    is in increasing abstractness.

7   Give some original examples of the use of familiarity to sequence subject matter.

8   Choose some subject matter and order it in terms of decreasing abstractness.

9   Choose a textbook in mathematics and find sequences that can be explained by the property of prerequisite knowledge. By the property increasing abstractness. By the property immediacy of application.

10   A teacher decides to teach about all the quadratic relations determined by $Ax^2 + Bxy + Cy^2 + Dx + Ey + F = 0$ when five, four, three, two, one, and none of the parameters have values of 0. Present and defend a sequence for presenting these relations.

11   Suppose the use of two properties produces different sequences. Which sequence will you choose? Why? If you find yourself saying that you will choose "the better one" or "the one that is more important," or using similarly value-laden phrases, how will you judge which is better or more important or whatever?

12   Point out sets of subject matter for which the sequence of teaching the items seems to make no difference.

Self-test on the competencies

1   Identify concepts, singular statements, generalizations, prescriptions, and value judgements.
   a   Give three original examples (examples not used in this chapter) of:
      (1)   concepts
      (2)   singular statements
      (3)   generalizations
      (4)   prescriptions
      (5)   value judgments
   b   Open a mathematics textbook at any page. Begin reading and classify items of subject matter you find in the first ten pages as concepts, singular statements, generalizations, prescriptions, or value judgments.

2   State some factors relevant to decisions concerning the selection of subject matter for a particular course in mathematics.
   a   What are some factors that influence the selection of subject matter for a course in mathematics?
   b   Under what conditions would any of the factors you listed be most influential in determining the choice of subject matter?

3   State some factors relevant to decisions concerning the arrangement of subject matter in a sequence for teaching.
   a   What are some factors that influence the determination of a sequence of the teaching items of subject matter?
   b   Why can some of the factors that are used to select subject matter also be used to determine a sequence for teaching it?

4   Select and sequence subject matter on a topic in mathematics that might be taught in some course in mathematics and defend this selection and sequence.
      Choose some topic that you see yourself teaching in some course in mathematics. Select subject matter for it, remembering that the items of subject matter should be phrased in sentences. Then arrange this body of subject matter in a sequence for teaching. Defend your choice and sequence.

References

Begle, E. G. "The School Mathematics Study Group." *The Mathematics Teacher*, 51 (1958), 616–618.

Broudy, Harry S., B. Othanel Smith, and Joe R. Burnett. *Democracy and Excellence in American Secondary Education.* Chicago: Rand McNally, 1964.

Fagerstrom, William H. *Mathematical Facts and Processes Prerequisite to the Study of the Calculus.* New York: Teachers College, Columbia University, 1933.

Kline, Morris. "A Proposal for the High School Mathematics Curriculum." *The Mathematics Teacher*, 59 (1966), 322–330.

Wilson, Guy M. *Teaching the New Arithmetic.* New York: McGraw-Hill, 1951.

5

Teaching mathematical concepts

In mathematics we study certain objects such as counting numbers, complex numbers, triangles, systems of open sentences, vectors, functions, and proof. One of the first things we have to learn is what each object is: what a line segment is, what a periodic function is, how to tell whether or not something is a parallelogram, what the definition of a one-to-one correspondence is. Once we have learned what some objects are, how to identify them, we can study the relations among them. Then we can study how we can use them.

When we learn what some object is, for example a function, a polygon, or a slide rule, we are learning a concept of that object. Similarly, when we teach students what some object is, how to identify it, we are teaching a concept of that object. We shall begin by refining and making more precise the notion of a concept. We shall develop a concept of a concept. We do this because not all teachers and writers agree on what a concept is; in pedagogy terms are not as well defined as they are in mathematics.

Concepts are a kind of subject matter; from one point of view, they are the most basic learnable object. They are among the first things learned by young children. By means of concepts, other concepts and other kinds of subject matter are learned. We shall see why this is so.

Next, from dialogues of teachers who are teaching concepts, we shall identify moves used in the teaching of concepts. We shall find that some sequences of moves are used frequently. We shall call such sequences *strategies*, and we shall consider the conditions under which various strategies are successful in enabling students to learn concepts.

> **At the conclusion of this chapter, you should be able to demonstrate the following competencies:**
>
> 1   Identify concepts
>
> 2   Illustrate various uses of a concept
>
> 3   Name and give examples of various moves that can be used to teach a given concept
>
> 4   Plan a strategy for teaching a given concept and explain why this strategy should be successful

Nature of concepts

Over twenty years ago, Van Engen (1953), in the Twenty-First Yearbook of the National Council of Teachers of Mathematics, *The Learning of Mathematics: Theory and Practice*, pointed to the confusion in the meaning of the term *concept*. In the interval since Van Engen's observation, the confusion has not been materially reduced. One cannot always tell what a person means by *a concept*, and one should not assume that a person who uses the term means the same as you when you use it. One possible explanation for this confusion is that concepts are complex objects, and attempts to identify all their salient characteristics have so far been unsuccessful. In any event it is worthwhile, in the interest of clarity, to discuss the nature of concepts taught formally, particularly in mathematics.

Nonverbal and verbal concepts

Theorists tend to conceive of concepts according to their interests. Thus psychologists interested in how children learn concepts in the absence of expository teaching, which Ausubel (1968) speaks of as *concept formation*, might regard a concept as an abstraction from experiences involving examples of concepts. A small child has experiences with animals denoted by adults as dogs. (The child may not hear the word "dog" as part of these experiences.) The child probably becomes aware of similarities: this object is like another in that both have hair, run, pant, bark, eat, scratch, and so on. The child probably also becomes aware of differences: not all dogs are the same color; some are large and others small; some bark more than others; some jump and others do not; some have long hair that fingers can be twisted in and others do not. The child who becomes aware of the similarities among the differences has made an abstraction and has a concept of what adults call *dog*. Similarly, a mathematics student who can distinguish protractors from other objects and uses a protractor for the purposes for which it is intended would be said to have a concept of a protractor. Whether or not it is called by its conventional name or by any name is not particularly significant.

Psychologists and educators interested in how individuals acquire concepts by means of other concepts, which Ausubel (1968) calls *concept assimilation* in contrast to concept formation, might agree that a concept is the meaning of a term used to designate the concept. One definition of a concept in this category is that of Hunt, Marin, and Stone (1966, p. 10): "A *concept* is a decision rule which, when applied to the description of an object, specifies whether or not a name can be applied." Thus a student who knows the definition of *a circle* as the locus of points in a plane equidistant from a given point in the plane has a rule that can be used to tell whether any given object is to be called *a circle*. The definition by Geach (1956) may be paraphrased as: "*N* has acquired concept *p*" is to be read as "*N* has learned how to use the term *p*." Thus a student who knows how to use the term *polynomial*—what to denote by this term, what properties objects called *polynomials* have, and how *polynomial* may be defined—has acquired a concept of a polynomial.

As Henderson (1970) pointed out, these two theoretical positions can be made compatible by conceiving of two kinds of concepts, nonverbal and verbal. Nonverbal concepts are learned by concept formation, by abstracting from examples. Verbal concepts are those for which a conventional name or designating expression exists and they are learned by concept assimilation. A nonverbal concept passes into the verbal category if and only if there is a name or designating expression for it that has enough currency to enable persons having the concept to communicate with each other.

Because practically all the concepts taught in formal education are verbal, and because this is the kind of education being considered in this book, we shall simplify our language and hereafter understand *concept* to mean *verbal concept*. Hence, from now on, whenever we speak of concepts, unless otherwise explicitly indicated, it will be verbal concepts to which we are referring.

Some characteristics of concepts

We shall abide by a convention logicians use to indicate when they are talking about a term—a symbol—and when they are talking about the objects denoted by the term. When a term is set in italics or in quotation marks, it is the term that is the object of discussion; when the term is not so set in type, it is the object denoted by the term that is being discussed. Thus we might say that the term *square* is a noun consisting of six letters denoting a square. But in talking about a square we might say that a square is a quadrilateral; all its angles are right angles; its diagonals bisect each other; its opposite sides are parallel; its perimeter is four times the length of one side; and its area is the square of one side.

Consider the following concepts that probably would be taught in some mathematics course.

square   A rectangle having all sides congruent

even number   A number divisible by 2

matrix of order m × n   A matrix having *m* rows and *n* columns

f(x)   The value of a function *f* at *x*

sufficient condition   If $p \Rightarrow q$ is true, then *p* is a sufficient condition for *q*.

necessary condition   If $p \Rightarrow q$ is true, then *q* is a necessary condition for *p*.

necessary condition   If $\sim p \Rightarrow \sim q$ is true, then *p* is a necessary condition for *q*.

degree   A unit of measure of an angle

degree   A unit of measure of temperature

Three observations emanate from these examples. The first is that some of the terms designating concepts are single words while others consist of more than one word. Some of the terms are English words while others contain mathematical notation. But a common property of all is that they are noun-like in their logic and syntax; they designate something. These observations are true of the whole set of terms.

A second observation results from considering the two concepts of a necessary condition. These are different concepts. (Why?) Yet they are equivalent, for either follows from the other. They illustrate that there can be different but equivalent concepts designated by the same term.

The third observation results from considering the two concepts of a degree. These are different concepts. (Why?) Moreover, they are not equivalent, for neither follows from the other. As another example of different and nonequivalent concepts associated with the same term, suppose the definition of a *trapezoid* in one textbook is

A quadrilateral having one pair of sides parallel is called a *trapezoid*.

This definition establishes a concept of a trapezoid. Now suppose in another textbook the definition is

A quadrilateral having just one pair of sides parallel is called a *trapezoid*.

This definition establishes a different concept of a trapezoid; the meanings of the term *trapezoid* are different. The first concept subsumes parallelograms as a kind of trapezoid; the second makes parallelograms and trapezoids disjoint. Hence the concepts are not equivalent. Thus we can designate by the same term concepts that are different but equivalent and concepts that are different but not equivalent.

Thought questions

1   Show that the term *concept* is used ambiguously in pedagogical literature by finding in such literature definitions of the term other than those given in this section.

2   Select a mathematics textbook and find five concepts that are taught in it. Express each as a term and its meaning as proposed in this section.

3   Why is it unreasonable to consider every symbol as designating a concept? Consider prepositions, interjections, adjectives, and adverbs.

4   Show that either of the concepts of a necessary condition given in this section can be deduced from the other.

5   Consider that a concept is a meaning of a term and show that there are several possible concepts of the geometric object called *square*. Why can these concepts be considered equivalent?

6   Consider these two concepts of an angle: (1) An angle is the amount of turning of ray *OA* about point *O* to make it coincide with ray *OB*; (2) an angle is the union of two rays having a common endpoint. Are these different concepts? Why? Are they equivalent? Why?

7   How can you tell whether a student has acquired a concept you have taught? Which kinds of evidence are most valid? Why?

8   We might say that a concept is the set of inferences permitted by a term designating the concept. For each of the following concepts, give some permitted inferences.

a	rational number	*e*	sine function
b	rectangle	*f*	π
c	theorem	*g*	assumption
d	micrometer	*h*	similarity

Uses of concepts

It has been stated that concepts are the most basic kind of subject matter. Let us see why this is so. You have a concept of a circle. One thing you can do with this concept is to recognize examples of circles. Moreover, you can tell why you classify some objects as circles and do not classify certain other objects as circles. That is, you can argue that your classifications are correct. Assuming that the person with whom you are arguing has the same concept of a circle that you have, you can *prove* that your classifications are correct. The following is the form of your proof:

If something has properties, $p_1, p_2, \ldots p_n$, it is a *G*.
This object has properties $p_1, p_2, \ldots p_n$.
Therefore, this object is a *G*.

We can characterize the use of concepts illustrated above as using concepts to draw deductions or conclusions. In other words, we can reason by using concepts. Subsumed in this general use are other particular uses. We have discussed one of these—classification of objects. And since we can classify, we can discriminate. For example, a student who has a concept of a rational number can pick out rational numbers from other numbers.

We who have concepts of the natural (counting) numbers can discriminate in the size of any set of objects. The aborigines without these concepts may be able to discriminate only a few sizes (one, two, three, many). Since concepts enable us to discriminate, we can label things; the student who can discriminate between rational numbers and other numbers can call the rational numbers "rational numbers" instead of "integers" or "irrational numbers." Consequently, this student can communicate with other people who have this same concept and related ones and can discuss some of the properties of rational numbers and check the computations of other people who use them.

Communication breaks down when people do not have certain concepts. Suppose you are teaching students how to add fractions whose denominators are unlike. You point to two fractions to be added and say, "We have to change each of these fractions to an equal fraction so that both have the same denominator. We can do this by finding the least common multiple of the denominators." Suppose also that some of the students do not have one or more of the concepts equal fractions, denominator, and least common denominator. In other words, they do not know what these terms mean. You can see why they will not learn how to add fractions: you are not communicating; you are talking over their heads.

How can you avoid talking over the heads of your students? Knowing the definitions of terms is helpful. A definition of a term tells you both how to use the term and also how to avoid using it. Consider the definition

A rhombus is an equilateral parallelogram.

This definition tells you how to use the term *rhombus*—that it means "equilateral parallelogram"—and how to avoid using it by using its equivalent, *equilateral parallelogram*. And if you think some students do not have the concept of an equilateral parallelogram, you can think of the definition

An equilateral parallelogram is a four-sided figure whose sides are line segments having the same length.

using the longer expression *four-sided figure whose sides are line segments having the same length* to avoid using the term *equilateral parallelogram*. Even though this expression (term) is longer, it may be better understood by some students because it is composed of terms that are meaningful to them; they have the concepts associated with these terms. You and the students then communicate.

Another use of concepts is to enable us to *generalize*. Since we can discriminate between circles and other objects and hence identify circles as a class of objects, we can study circles and find some of the properties other than those that identify or define them. Utilizing the concepts diameter, circumference, area, chord, central angle, and arc, we can make generalizations about circles. You recognize these as the theorems typically studied in informal and demonstrative geometry.

Another use of concepts, related to the two just discussed, is to discover new knowledge. For example, the physicist who has a concept of the sine function is able to define the index of refraction of a translucent substance (roughly the amount of bending of light rays as they pass from air into the substance) as the reciprocal of the sine of the angle of refraction—the angle between the ray passing through the substance and a perpendicular to the point of entrance. The physicist then can study the refractive properties of various translucent substances. An optometrist, using the generalizations the physicist has discovered and others, can prescribe lenses to improve a person's vision. An oculist, using these and other generalizations, can make the lenses. Concepts are the screen through which we observe the world and draw our conclusions about it.

Because concepts enable us to deduce, classify, extend knowledge, and communicate with others, they are indeed important objects of thought. They can be justified as basic subject matter.

Thought questions

1   Choose five concepts that you see yourself teaching sometime. For each, show how students can use the concept to classify, discriminate, generalize, and name things correctly.

2   One way of motivating students to learn some item of subject matter is to show them that it is useful. Tell how you could motivate students to learn the concept of a function and the concept of the metric system.

3   Explain how the concept of eccentricity of an ellipse enables you to discriminate among ellipses.

4   Illustrate how the concept of a triangle enables people to solve problems they could not solve so readily if they did not have this concept.

5   A taxonomy is a classification system that enables one to subdivide a large set (for example, geometric figures) into nonempty, proper subsets. Why are concepts necessary for a taxonomy?

6   You have been using the following terms at various times in your explanations. You find out that some of your students do not know what these terms mean. How can you avoid using these particular terms but still talk about objects denoted by them?
    a   *power set*   f   *converse*
    b   *oblique angle*   g   *contrapositive*
    c   *abscissa*   h   *domain of a function*
    d   *ordinate*   i   *truncated prism*
    e   *hypothesis*   j   *congruent*

7   Why do some students not comprehend what they read in their textbooks? How can you find out whether they are comprehending what they read?

Moves in teaching a concept

Some concepts are taught deliberately and, usually, learned; others are learned but not deliberately taught. That is, the teacher consciously takes time in class to teach some concepts. For others, the teacher simply uses a term that designates the concept; with repeated use the students acquire a concept designated by it. Thus, a teacher who has deliberately taught a concept of a constant function might not take class time to teach a concept of a nonconstant function but would simply use the term and the students would probably make the correct inferences and acquire the concept.

More concepts are learned without being taught than we realize. Typically, a concept formed by restricting another concept is not taught deliberately. Thus, assuming students have concepts of a circle and area, a teacher probably would not take time to teach the concept of the area of a circle but would simply use the term and assume that the students could conjoin the two concepts and thereby attain the concept of the area of a circle. Similarly, if a teacher knows that students know what an exponent, an integer, and what a fraction are, the teacher could feel safe in using the term *integral exponent* and *fractional exponent* without taking time to define them; in other words, he or she would use these concepts without teaching them.

In the analysis that follows, we shall be concerned with the deliberate teaching of concepts—that is, with the teaching of a concept as a conscious objective. We shall base this analysis on classroom dialogues and on the expositions in textbooks from which concepts are being taught.

When we analyze classroom dialogue or exposition, we can identify patterns of language usage—defining, giving examples, asserting, classifying, comparing, or contrasting—that we shall call *moves*. The moves are used by the teacher or author, by the students, or by both. The purpose of the moves is to teach—present or clarify—a concept. Then we can consider under what conditions moves will be effective. Are some more effective for certain kinds of concepts? Are some more effective for certain kinds of students?

In the following (as throughout this book), we shall use the convention of setting in boldface type the term that designates the concept under consideration. This will distinguish this concept from others used to teach it.

Defining

Because most concepts in mathematics are precise, definitional moves can be used. But for concepts that are not precise, definitions alone may not result in useful concepts. For example, one can offer a definition of *integrity* or *good judgment*, but these concepts are so vague and complex that the definitions are academic; they do not help a person do the things with a concept that were recognized in the earlier section on uses of concepts. Other moves have to be used.

Definition is an elegant move since it employs a minimum of language. The more formal the presentation is, the more definitions are used to teach concepts. But the very elegance may be a block to learning. Some students cannot comprehend the conjunction of the necessary conditions and do not understand the logic of a definition. For example, they do not know that from the definition

A **binomial** is a polynomial having just two terms.

four conclusions can be drawn:

1   If something is a binomial, it is a polynomial having just two terms. (This is a paraphrase of the definition.)

2   If something is a polynomial having just two terms, it is a binomial. (This is the converse of the definition.)

3   If something is not a binomial, either it is not a polynomial or, if it is a polynomial, it does not have just two terms.

4   If something is not a polynomial having just two terms, it is not a binomial. (This is the contrapositive of the definition.)

And they may not realize that from the contrapositive it follows that if something is not a polynomial, it is not a binomial; and if it is a polynomial but does not have just two terms it is not a binomial.

Definitions are often written in the form of the definition of a binomial given above. This form is

—— is a —— such that ——

where the lefthand space is filled by the term being defined, the middle space is filled by a term denoting a superset in which the set of objects denoted by the term defined are included, and the righthand space is filled by one or more conditions that differentiate the set of objects denoted by the term defined from all the other subsets of the superset. The logic of such a definition is its assertion that the set determined by the term defined and the set determined by the defining expression are identical.

Definitions in this form are often called *classificatory definitions.* They are characterized by conciseness and the portraying of structure. Yet these very properties make them hard for some students to comprehend. Of necessity, the term denoting the superset in which objects denoted by the term being defined are classified is more abstract than the term being defined. Unless a student has a concept designated by this term, he will not comprehend the definition given in terms of it. The same can be said of other terms in the definition. For such students, the teacher will have to use other moves.

We can identify other moves in teaching a concept by analyzing classroom dialogues. Consider the following, which occurred in an eighth-grade mathematics class. It was recorded on tape and later transcribed. "T" identifies utterances of the teacher and "S_1," "S_2," etc., those of students. The utterances are numbered to facilitate references to the dialogue in future discussions. As you read the dialogue, try to decide what moves the teacher is using to teach a concept of skew lines.

1	T	We have talked about lines that lie in the same plane. Now if two lines don't lie in the same plane, they are skew. Skew. s-k-e-w (*writes the word on the board*). For example, the edge of the ceiling where the ceiling meets the right wall and the edge of the front wall where it meets the left wall are skew lines because there is no plane that contains these lines.
2	S_1	But the front wall contains the vertical line and also hits the horizontal one.
3	T	Does it contain all the horizontal line or just one point of it?
4	S_1	Oh, just one point.
5	T	Yes. It doesn't contain the whole line. No plane that contains the vertical line can contain more than one point of the horizontal line. To think of all planes like this, imagine the front wall rotating around the vertical edge. What about the front edge of the ceiling and the rear edge of the floor, are they skew? S_2?
6	S_2	No, there is an invisible plane that slopes from the front edge of the ceiling to the rear edge of the floor and contains both those lines.
7	T	What kind of lines are they, then?
8	S_2	Parallel lines.
9	T	What do parallel and skew lines have in common? S_3.
10	S_3	They are sets of points.
11	T	True. You're right, but I didn't have that in mind. How else are they alike?
12	S_3	They don't intersect.
13	T	Why, then, can't intersecting lines be skew? S_4?
14	S_4	Because two intersecting lines determine a plane which contains them both.
15	T	Can anyone give me some more examples of skew lines? S_5 then S_6.
16	S_5	The front edge of the desk top and the left edge of the back wall.
17	S_6	(*Holds two pencils to illustrate positions of two skew lines in space.*) How about these two lines?
18	T	They are skew, aren't they? Could you call any two lines drawn on the black-board "skew"? (*Points to a student.*) Yes?
19	S_7	No.
20	T	Why not?
21	S_7	Because they are in the same plane.
22	T	That's right; they are in the same plane and by definition they are not skew.

Stating a sufficient condition

In the first utterance, the teacher states, "if two lines don't lie in the same plane, they are skew." Some teachers might regard this as a definition; evidently the teacher does from utterance 22. However, it is not explicitly a definition and would not be accepted as such by people who consider definition as an operation on symbols. (Why not?) It does state a sufficient condition for lines to be skew; knowing that two lines do not lie in the same plane is enough to warrant saying that they are skew lines. This move is used frequently by teachers to teach a concept. In light of its form, we shall call it **stating a sufficient condition** or, more simply, **a sufficient condition move.**

Notice that it is the form in which a characteristic or property of an object is stated that identifies it as sufficient condition. Hence if a teacher wants students to be aware of a sufficient condition, a linguistic form that signals this must be used. Consider the following characteristics or properties of a rhombus:

A rhombus is an equilateral parallelogram.

A rhombus is a figure used in design.

Being an equilateral parallelogram is sufficient for being a rhombus, but being a figure used in design is not. A teacher would know these facts. But a student who is learning a concept of a rhombus could not tell from this language whether either or both of these characteristics were sufficient for identifying a rhombus. Once the teacher says, "If a quadrilateral is an equilateral parallelogram, it is a rhombus," or "If a parallelogram is a square, it is a rhombus," the teacher has provided more useful information.

We have seen one linguistic signal of a sufficient condition: "if." There are others among which are the following, used frequently in the context of teaching concepts:

provided that	A function is a **linear function** provided that its graph is a straight line.
because	$4x^2 + 9y^2 = 36$ is an **ellipse** because it is of the form $a^2x^2 + b^2y^2 = a^2b^2$.
since	20 is an **even number** since it is divisible by 2.
for the reason that	A circle is a **locus** for the reason that it is a set of points satisfying a condition.

The logic of a move of sufficient condition enables a student to find examples of objects denoted by a concept, assuming such exist. In the dialogue concerning skew lines, the move of sufficient condition the teacher used in the first utterance allowed the choice of an example of skew lines. Provided the students comprehend the statement, this move will also help find examples of skew lines. Hence a move of sufficient condition facilitates application of a concept.

Take some examples. If a student knows that a polygon is a pentagon provided that it has five sides, she knows that the building in Washington, D.C., in which the headquarters of the Defense Department are located is a pentagon. The form of this building satisfies the sufficient condition for being a pentagon; it is a polygon of five sides. Suppose the concept of a polygon is taught by the sufficient condition move: if the sides of a closed, convex geometric figure are line segments, the figure is a *polygon*. Then students should be able to decide whether a square, rectangle, and a triangle are polygons. They are, because they meet the sufficient condition for being a polygon.

Giving one or more examples

Notice that immediately after stating a sufficient condition for being skew, the teacher employs this condition to select examples. Examples are objects denoted by the concept—that is, members of the set determined by the concept. These are exemplification moves—giving one or more examples. Examples clarify concepts. Perhaps this is because they are definite, specific, and, if well chosen, familiar.

Exemplifying is used frequently by teachers. The teacher solicits exemplification moves in utterance 15. Perhaps the teacher asks the question in this utterance to help decide whether the students have acquired the concept. If they can give examples, the teacher might assume they comprehend the concept. If they cannot, the teacher would have to use additional moves to clarify it.

It should not be assumed that an example can be given for every concept. Because there is no even, prime number greater than 2, a teacher could not give an example for this concept as a move in teaching it. A similar statement can be made for such concepts as greatest integer, smallest real number, and rational number equal to $\sqrt{2}$. Of course, no examples can be given for self-contradictory concepts like square circle, six-sided pentagon, negative mantissa, and extraneous root. A teacher does not deliberately teach such concepts, however, but may use them and the students can comprehend them because they have the concepts that are used to form them.

Some theoreticians argue that there are concepts at a high level of abstraction for which examples cannot be given. Consider rigor, an abstraction of the property common to all rigorous arguments. It is argued that one can give an example of a rigorous argument but not of rigor. Similarly, it is argued that one can give examples of elegant proofs, but one cannot give an example of elegance, the property of all elegant things.

Giving an example accompanied by a reason why it is an example

In utterances 16 and 17, two students give examples. These are correct, but the teacher evidently chooses not to ask the students to justify that they are. But in utterance 1, the teacher not only gave an example but supplied a reason that it is an example, "because there is no plane that contains these lines." The reason is the sufficient condition identified in the sufficient condition move.

It seems reasonable to believe that accompanying an example with a reason that it is an example is an effective move; in a way, it couples an exemplification with a move of sufficient condition. Its logic is that of conditional reasoning as, for example,

> If two lines don't lie in the same plane, they are skew. The edge of the ceiling where it meets the right wall and the edge of the front wall where it meets the left wall don't lie in the same plane. Therefore they are skew.

Giving an example along with a reason that it is an example appears to be helpful to students who learn slowly. Why this is so may perhaps be explained by what was pointed out in the previous paragraph, the interaction of the example and the sufficient condition for its being an example. The slow students may not understand this logical connection unless it is made explicit; the students who learn faster are aware of it.

Comparing or contrasting objects denoted by the concept

In utterance 9, the teacher asks, "What do parallel and skew lines have in common?" This language solicits a comparison of parallel lines and skew lines. A student compares these in utterance 10 ("They are sets of points"). But this evidently is not the comparison that the teacher wants and a further comparison is elicited in utterance 11. The teacher then gets the comparison that was wanted.

We find that in teaching concepts, teachers often compare objects denoted by the concept they are teaching with objects with which they think the students are familiar. This establishes a bond or association between the familiar and the less familiar. In teaching a concept of the metric system, for example, the teacher may compare it with the English system.

It is useful to contrast objects denoted by the concept with comparable objects to point out differences. Comparison points out similarities, but since objects compared are not identical there must be differences. A contrast identifies some of these differences, if not all. Suppose a teacher is teaching a concept of the graph of the cosine function after having taught a concept of the graph of the sine function. The teacher would probably not only compare the graphs of the two functions but also contrast the graphs in order that the students not miss the difference between them. Similarly, if a teacher has taught a concept of a half-line and then teaches a concept of a ray, the next step may be to contrast half-lines and rays in order that the students not miss the distinction between them.

Thought questions

1 Give examples of concepts other than the ones presented in this section, that probably would not be deliberately taught.

2 How will you decide whether deliberately to teach concepts like circular protractor, congruent pentagons, equilateral hexagon, nonsquare matrix, root of a quadratic equation, subset of a graph, and polynomial with integral coefficients or to use them without taking time to teach them?

3 Give an example of a definition. Point out the necessary and sufficient conditions in the definition.

4 Explain how you can show a student that he or she has given an incorrect definition.

5 There are concepts for which only one example can be given—10, greatest integer function, Pythagoras. Name some others.

6 In using examples to teach a concept of a rational number, why would it be unwise to use only $+6$, -2, 0, $+1$, -45, and $+324$ as examples? From your answer to this question, offer some advice on the selection of examples when using this move to teach a concept.

7 Explain how you can use the move of giving examples to decide whether a student has acquired a correct concept.

8 How likely is it that a student can acquire a precise concept if the teacher uses only exemplification? Defend your conjecture.

9 Suppose a concept has only a small number of examples, as does a standard unit of measure in the metric system. Why will citing all the examples result in a precise concept? Compare this with determining a set by specification or listing.

10 For each mathematical object below, state a sufficient condition for something to be such an object:

a	circle	f	common denominator
b	odd number	g	square matrix
c	median	h	real number
d	coefficient	i	oblique triangle
e	equation	j	perpendicular lines

To identify additional moves in teaching a concept, read the dialogue below. As you read it, do two things: see if you can recognize moves we have already identified and try to identify additional moves used to teach a concept of a rhombus.

This particular venture was chosen because it illustrates an approach to teaching a concept different from that in the previous dialogue. In the previous dialogue, the teacher used an expository approach, beginning with a move of sufficient condition and then using examples to clarify. In the following dialogue, the teacher begins by reviewing concepts basic to a comprehension of the concept of a rhombus, which the teacher expects to teach later. When the new concept has been introduced in utterance 8, the teacher gives some examples and some nonexamples, hoping that the students will compare and contrast them and abstract the distinctive characteristics of the rhombi. A student does this in utterance 10. The teacher then reinforces the concept by means of a definition in utterance 11. The teacher then obtains examples and accompanies them with a reason and chooses nonexamples and accompanies them with a reason, to make sure that the students are aware of the conditions necessary and sufficient for a quadrilateral to be a rhombus. We shall now identify some moves we did not find in the first dialogue.

1 **T** Yesterday we talked about a special kind of geometric figure. We started with a closed four-sided plane figure. What do we call these? S_1?

2 **S$_1$** Quadrilaterals.

3   T   Good. We talked about some quadrilaterals that we called parallelograms. Can anyone tell me what makes a quadrilateral a parallelogram? S_2 can.

4   S_2 If two sides are parallel, it's a parallelogram.

5   T S_2 said that if we have a quadrilateral with two sides parallel, then it's a parallelogram. Can anyone draw a quadrilateral with two parallel sides that isn't a parallelogram? S_3, you draw the figure.
(*The student draws a trapezoid.*)

6   T   Very good. This isn't a parallelogram, so we must need some other specification to make sure we'll get a parallelogram. What is it?

7   S_3 Both pairs of opposite sides have to be parallel.

8   T   Very good. Now, just as we found some special quadrilaterals that we called parallelograms, we're going to talk about some special parallelograms that we shall call *rhombi*. *Rhombi* is the plural form of *rhombus*.

A set of drawings of parallelograms is shown to the class. Some are rhombi and labeled that way; others are not rhombi and are so labeled. Measurements of adjacent sides are included in all the drawings.

9   T   These labeled with an "R" are rhombi; these others are parallelograms that aren't rhombi. Is there anything the rhombi have in common that doesn't occur in any of the ones that aren't rhombi? Let's look at the measurements. S_1?

10   S_1 The sides next to each other are equal.

11   T   Excellent! The word *rhombus*, which we've been using for this group, means a parallelogram with two equal adjacent sides. S_3 come draw another rhombus on the board. S_5, why is this a rhombus?

12   S_5 It is a parallelogram with two equal adjacent sides.

13   T   Good. (*Draws a quadrilateral with two equal adjacent sides that isn't a parallelogram.*) Why isn't this a rhombus?

14   S_6 It isn't a parallelogram.

15   T   O.K. but wait for me to call on you. There are two necessary conditions for a quadrilateral to be a rhombus. What are they? (*Points to a student.*)

16   S_7 It must be a parallelogram, and it must have two equal adjacent sides.

17   T   Right. If a quadrilateral is not a parallelogram, it isn't a rhombus. And if it doesn't have two equal, adjacent sides, it can't be a rhombus.

Giving a counterexample

In utterance 3, the teacher asks, "Can anyone tell me what makes a quadrilateral a parallelogram?" S_2 responds, "If two sides are parallel, it's a parallelogram." According to the concept of a parallelogram that had probably been taught earlier, this is an incorrect generalization. The teacher, instead of stating that the answer is incorrect, gets a student to give an example of a quadrilateral with two parallel sides that is not a parallelogram—namely, a trapezoid. This example disproves the false generalization that S_2 stated. The teacher then induces (utterances 6 and 7) the correct necessary condition.

The example S_3 gives to disprove the false generalization that S_2 stated is a counterexample. A **counterexample** is an example that disproves a false generalization. The trapezoid the student exhibited was an example of a quadrilateral having two parallel sides and hence satisfied the condition for being a parallelogram that S_2 had stated. But it failed to satisfy the consequent condition (being a parallelogram) and hence showed that it is possible for a hypothesis of the generalization that S_2 stated to be true while the conclusion is false.

When a student gives an incorrect definition, two kinds of counter-examples are possible. Let us see why this is true. As was pointed out earlier, the logic of a definition is that it asserts the identity of two sets, the one determined by the term being defined and the one determined by the defining expression. Hence one kind of counterexample is a member (an example) of the set determined by the term defined that is not a member of the set determined by the defining expression. The other kind of counterexample is a member (an example) of the set determined by the defining expression that is not a member of the set determined by the term defined. Some examples will be helpful. Suppose a student states as a definition that adjacent angles are a pair of angles with a common side. The teacher might give a counterexample such as the one in Figure 5.1 or elicit one from another student. This example satisfies the condition that the student stated, a pair of angles having a common side. The example gets into the set that is determined by the defining expression. But the angles are not adjacent angles and hence it does not get into the set determined by the term defined. Therefore it disproves the definition the student gave.

Figure 5.1

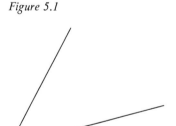

To illustrate the other kind of counterexample possible from a false definition, let us suppose a student states as a definition of an exponent that it is a number written to the right and slightly above another number that tells the number of times the number is taken as a factor. The following dialogue is conceivable:

T In 4^{-2}, is -2 an exponent?

S Yes.

T I agree that the -2 is written to the right and slightly above 4, but what does it mean to say that it tells us how many times 4 is taken as a factor? How can a number be taken as a factor -2 times?

S The exponent has to be positive.

T Ah, yes. Is $1/2$ in $4^{1/2}$ an exponent? It's positive.

S Yes.

T Does $1/2$ tell us how many times 4 is taken as a factor? What does it mean for a factor to be taken $1/2$ times?

S Well, an exponent is a whole number written . . . No, it's any number written to the right and slightly above another number.

T Is there an exponent in 4^4?

S Sure. 4.

T But you said "to the right and slightly above *another* number," which seems to say the numbers are different. In 4^4 the two 4's are the same number.

S O.K. Slightly above and to the right of any number.

T Well, you're getting there. Is 0.5 in $a^{0.5}$ an exponent? And how about b in x^b? Is b an exponent?

S Yeah. They're both exponents. O.K. Slightly above and to the right of any number or any variable.

T Just to be sure we've got it right, state the definition as it ought to be.

S An exponent is a number or a variable that is written to the right and slightly above any number or variable.

T I'll buy that.

At the outset of the dialogue, the teacher gives an example the student is willing to accept as an exponent—that is, it gets into the set determined by the term being defined. But it does not satisfy all the defining conditions and hence does not get into the set determined by these conditions. Hence it is a counterexample that proves that the student's definition is false.

The teacher, not liking the implication of the phrase *another number*, exhibits the same kind of counterexample as before: an object that satisfies the condition of being an exponent but does not satisfy the conditions the student has stated as defining conditions. The student revises the definition to remove the unnecessary restrictions.

The teacher still is not satisfied and poses additional examples 0.5 and b, which the student is willing to accept as exponents. But, again, they do not satisfy the defining conditions. They are not members of both the set determined by an exponent and the set determined by the defining conditions. The student, realizing that these disprove the new definition, revises it so that 0.5 and b become members of both sets.

This dialogue affords examples of the kind of counterexample possible when a person wants to call an object by the term being defined but the object does not satisfy the defining conditions. Although a teacher might proceed as in this dialogue and finally get convergence on the correct concept of an exponent, it might be that students would feel that the teacher was badgering and embarrassing them and would resent this kind of direction. Teachers have to exercise good judgment when deciding how frequently to use counter-example moves, even though this kind of move is effective in sustaining thinking and ultimately facilitates comprehension of the concept desired.

Stating a necessary condition

The counterexample the student exhibits in utterance 5 on page 99 indicates the absence of a necessary condition for a quadrilateral to be a parallelogram. The teacher makes sure in utterance 6 that the students realize this: "This isn't a parallelogram, so we must need some other specification to make sure we'll get a parallelogram. What is it?" S_3 states this necessary condition in utterance 7.

The student's assertion is an instance of a form often used to state a necessary condition. This form uses the locution *has to* or, alternatively, the locution *must* to introduce the necessary condition or conditions. Notice that "must" is used by S_7 in utterance 16.

The student's assertion of the necessary condition in utterance 7 is equivalent to

If both pairs of opposite sides are not parallel, a quadrilateral is not a parallelogram.

This is an instance of another form often used to state a necessary condition. The necessary condition is stated in the hypothesis. The teacher used this form in utterance 17 to identify the two conditions necessary for a quadrilateral to be a rhombus.

A third form in which a necessary condition is stated utilizes *only if*. In this form the statement above is equivalent to

A quadrilateral is a parallelogram only if both pairs of sides are parallel.

The conditions following the *only if* is a necessary condition. Thus a textbook might have, "A parallelogram is a rhombus only if it is equilateral," thereby identifying the condition equilateral as necessary for a parallelogram to be a rhombus.

In light of the form of this kind of move, we shall speak of it as **stating a necessary condition** or, simply, **a necessary condition.** Judging by our analyses so far, the statement of a necessary condition is not as frequent in teaching concepts as is the statement of a sufficient condition. Yet it is useful to prevent misconceptions.

The logic of a move of necessary condition enables a student to identify examples of objects *not* denoted by a concept. Usually, this is not so important as identifying examples but, still, is a kind of discrimination that needs to be made on occasion. A student who misclassifies an object as an example of something it is not could draw some wrong conclusions. As an example, a student who regards arcsin, arccos, and the other analogous relations unrestricted as to domains as functions should logically expect only one value of each "function" at each member of the domain but then probably would miss solutions to equations containing these relations.

As in the case of a sufficient condition, the teacher knows whether a condition is necessary. But if the teacher does not use language that explicitly signals the necessity of a condition, the students will not know for sure. Some will make the correct inference. Others will not, and for these the move will lose its power.

Stating a necessary and sufficient condition

If a condition by which objects can de denoted by a concept is both necessary and sufficient, the teacher can signal this. One form for this is the explicit use of the terms *necessary* and *sufficient*, as

It is both necessary and sufficient that a parallelogram be equilateral for it to be a rhombus.

Another form is the use of *if and only if*. Thus the statement above is equivalent to

A parallelogram is a rhombus if and only if it is equilateral.

Many definitions are given in terms of necessary and sufficient conditions. This is particularly the case if the definition proceeds by subsuming the set of objects to be defined in a superset and then distinguishing the set of objects to be defined from all other subsets of the superset. Thus, a definition of a rhombus might be

A parallelogram that has a pair of adjacent, congruent sides is a rhombus.

This definition proceeds by subsuming rhombi in the set of parallelograms. It then distinguishes rhombi from all other subsets of parallelograms—that is, it states that a rhombus has a pair of adjacent, congruent sides. The definition implies that there are two conditions necessary for an object to be a rhombus: (1) being a parallelogram and (2) having a pair of adjacent, congruent sides. The conjunction of these two necessary conditions is sufficient. If the student knows that this is a definition and knows the logic of a definition (that it is the assertion of the identity of two sets), the implication of the conditions being both necessary and sufficient will be clear. But if the student is unsure that the teacher is using a statement like the one above to make a definition, this implication may be missed. The teacher can make the conditions explicit as necessary and sufficient by using the locution *if and only if*. For example, the teacher who says "A regular polygon is equilateral and equiangular" has not made it as clear that the two conditions are necessary and their conjunction is sufficient for a polygon to be regular as has the teacher who says "A polygon is regular if and only if it is equiangular and equilateral."

Because a sufficient condition enables examples to be identified and a move of necessary condition enables nonexamples to be identified, a necessary and sufficient move enables both these discriminations to be made. Thus logically it is a powerful move. It is appropriate for precise concepts.

Giving one or more nonexamples

Let us say that an object not in the set determined by a concept is a **nonexample** of the concept. In the concept venture we have been analyzing, nonexamples of rhombi are exhibited along with examples so students can induce necessary and sufficient conditions.

Like the move of giving one or more examples, giving nonexamples helps clarify a concept. Giving examples and nonexamples are natural moves with which to follow a definition. Teachers give nonexamples when their past experience has shown that students typically make common confusions out of neglect of one or more necessary conditions. Thus a teacher, after giving a definition of a common factor of two or more numbers, might select the numbers 14 and 24 and give 7 as a nonexample of a common factor. (The teacher might not use the term *nonexample*.) The teacher would point out that while 7 divides 14 it does not divide 24. The teacher might also cite 3 as not a common factor because it does not divide 14 even though it divides 24. Using these nonexamples would be an attempt to impress students with the necessity that a common factor be a factor of every number in the set.

Giving a nonexample accompanied by a reason why it is a nonexample

This move is similar to that of giving an example together with a reason that it is an example. The reason that accompanies the nonexample is the failure to satisfy a necessary condition.

In utterance 13 on page 99, the teacher asked for a reason that the quadrilateral drawn is not a rhombus. The student supplied the reason in utterance 14. Notice that the student implied a necessary condition and also a lack of the quadrilateral in meeting this condition.

As in the move of accompanying an example with a reason that it is an example, accompanying a nonexample with a reason that it is a nonexample is effective. In a way, it couples a nonexample with an implied necessary condition. Its logic is that of conditional reasoning:

If a quadrilateral is not a parallelogram, it is not a rhombus. This quadrilateral (the one the teacher drew) is not a parallelogram. Therefore, it is not a rhombus.

The utility of giving a nonexample together with a reason that it is a nonexample, like the analogous move concerning an example, is evident when teaching students who learn slowly. These students do not always see the connection between a nonexample and the related necessary condition. The teacher helps them by deliberately associating the two.

Giving a characteristic which is neither necessary nor sufficient

When a teacher states characteristics of objects denoted by a concept—for example, having three sides and three angles as characteristics of a triangle, having the same number of rows and columns as a characteristic of a square matrix, having many axes of symmetry as a characteristic of a circle, or utility as a characteristic of periodic functions—the characteristics may be sufficient, necessary, or neither sufficient nor necessary. Thus, utility in design is neither necessary nor sufficient for a triangle; facilitation of computation is a characteristic of the $\log_{10}$ function, but this is neither necessary nor sufficient for a function to be the $\log_{10}$ function; and being the basis of statistics is neither sufficient nor necessary for being a probability function.

Sometimes in teaching a concept a mathematics teacher will state characteristics that are irrelevant for identifying objects either denoted or not denoted by the concept, characteristics neither necessary nor sufficient. Instead, they are, in a way of speaking, accidental, yet they are characteristics and seem to help some students learn the concept.

Mathematics teachers appear not to use this move as frequently as other teachers. Perhaps this is because the concepts in mathematics are, generally speaking, more precise than many of the concepts in some other subjects like social studies, driver training, physical education, art, and literature. A concept is precise just because we know the necessary and sufficient conditions. In teaching such concepts, these moves are easy to use and provide students with more power when they apply these concepts. Mathematics teachers properly employ these moves rather than stating characteristics that are neither necessary nor sufficient.

It may be well to reinforce a statement that was made earlier in this section about the moves of sufficient and necessary condition. If a teacher does not use language that explicitly identifies a characteristic or condition as sufficient or necessary, all a student knows is that it is a characteristic of objects denoted by the concept. How the student can use this information may not be clear.

Thought questions

1   For each of the following false generalizations, give a counterexample:
    a   If a symbol holds a place, it is a variable.
    b   A four-sided geometric figure that has one pair of sides parallel and one pair of sides congruent is a parallelogram.
    c   If the graph of an equation is a straight line, the equation determines a linear function.
    d   A polygon that is equiangular is a regular polygon.

e   If the two congruent sides of a trapezoid are not adjacent, it is not an isosceles trapezoid.

f   A prime number is not divisible by any other number.

g   For every real number x, $|x| > 0$.

h   If $x < y$, then $\log_a x < \log_a y$.

i   An altitude of a triangle is a line inside the triangle from a vertex to the opposite side.

j   Conic sections are closed curves.

2   In planning a lesson for teaching a concept, why is it not possible to include a particular move of counterexample in the plan?

3   When a move of counterexample is appropriate, some teachers give counterexamples; others ask students to give one. Which of these two alternatives would you use most frequently? Why?

4   What is a difference between a nonexample and a counterexample?

5   In stating a condition, the locution *provided that* is frequently used, as in "Two complex numbers are equal provided that their real components are equal and their imaginary components are equal." Does *provided that* signal a sufficient condition or a necessary condition?

6   Translate each of the following sentences into sentences that contain the terms *sufficient condition* or *necessary condition*.

a   If $x^2 - 4 = 0$, then $x = 2$.

b   Each circle has an interior.

c   The lateral faces of a prism are perpendicular to the base if the prism is a right prism.

d   If two lines do not intersect, they are not perpendicular.

e   Only adults will be admitted.

f   Flowers won't grow if they are not watered.

g   If you don't have a ticket, you can't be admitted.

h   A geometric figure is a circle if and only if it is the locus of points in a plane which are equidistant from a given point.

i   If two lines in a plane do not intersect, they are parallel.

j   You buy the coffee if and only if you don't match me.

7   The following expressions contain conditions that are related by being necessary or sufficient. State a correct relationship.

a $3x + 2 = 14$; $x = 4$.

b   Being a geometric sequence; the ratio of each pair of consecutive terms of the sequence being constant.

c   A function P is a probability function; for any event E, $P(E) \geq 0$.

d   A function maps x into $f(g(x))$; the function is the composite of f with g.

e   Equal to $\sqrt{a^2 + b^2}$; being the absolute value of the complex number $a + bi$.

f   The diagonals bisecting each other; being a parallelogram.

g   A function has an inverse; no line parallel to the y-axis intersects the graph of the function in more than one point.

h   Being a real number; being a rational number.

i   Being a linear function; the graph of the function being a straight line.

j n is a median of a triangle; n contains a vertex of the triangle.

8   From a set of examples, can you infer a sufficient condition or a necessary condition? Why? From a set of nonexamples, can you infer a sufficient or a necessary condition? Why?

9 If the move of giving a nonexample and accompanying it with a reason is used, how can the reason be chosen? Explain.

10 In this section, you were taught concepts of various moves. What moves were used to teach the various concepts?

11 Assume that you have taught the concept of a polynomial of degree n over a set S. Design some exercises based on exemplification that you might assign as homework to reinforce this concept.

12 Assume that you have taught a concept of symmetry and you intend to give a test that will contain questions that will help you determine whether your students have attained this concept. Write three questions you think are valid for making this judgment. How would you argue that the questions are valid?

13 In the chapter on the teaching of concepts in the Thirty-Third Yearbook of the National Council of Teachers of Mathematics, *The Teaching of Secondary School Mathematics*, there is a more extensive taxonomy of moves for teaching a concept. Do you prefer it to the one presented in this section? Why?

Summary

We provide two summaries of the moves for teaching a concept. The first is a structure that relates the various moves. The second is a set of questions you can ask yourself as you are making a lesson plan to teach the concept.

The tree diagram in Figure 5.2 shows a relation among the moves. In teaching a concept, you name either objects denoted by the concept or objects not denoted by the concept; these are exemplification moves. Alternatively you may mention characteristics or properties that enable students to find examples or nonexamples; these are characterization moves. Exemplification moves are of three kinds: examples, nonexamples, and counterexamples. Counterexamples are possible only in the context of a false generalization.

Figure 5.2

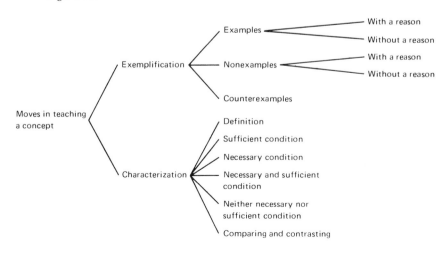

An example can be accompanied by a reason or not; the same can be said for a nonexample.

Of the characterization moves, some are sufficient, some are necessary, some are both necessary and sufficient, and some are neither necessary nor sufficient. Those that are both necessary and sufficient are definitional. Other characterization moves are comparison and contrast. These are appropriately classified as characterization because comparison and contrast are accomplished in terms of the characteristics of examples and nonexamples.

When you plan a lesson in which a concept is to be taught, you will find it helpful to ask the following questions:

1   What is the intellectual ability and conceptual background of your students? If they are intellectually able, characterization moves may suffice; a definition can be readily understood. If they are not intellectually able, you should plan to give examples, probably several with a reason for each. If they are not able to handle abstractions very well, comparison and contrast will be effective, for these begin with particular examples and nonexamples and proceed to distinctive characteristics. If your students have a weak conceptual background, you should review each concept that will be used to teach the new one. The moves used to review a concept can be used to teach the new one.

2   What has been your past experience either in learning this concept yourself or in teaching it to previous classes? If students have not understood sufficient conditions, you may want to stress these. You may want to reinforce them by means of examples with the sufficient conditions as the reason that they are examples. If the students have not understood necessary conditions, you may want to stress these. You may want to give nonexamples to reinforce them, with a necessary condition as the reason that a particular nonexample is a nonexample. If some of your students typically develop a particular, incorrect concept and state it by means of a false generalization, you should have some counterexamples ready to set them straight.

3   How important is this concept? If it is important and will be used to develop several other concepts, you will want to choose moves that make it precise, as a definition would do. You will also want to use moves that clarify the definition—examples, nonexamples if misconceptions must be forestalled, explicit identification of necessary conditions and the sufficient condition. You should ask for examples from students, for the extent of their ability to apply a concept is excellent evidence of the extent of their comprehension of it. If the concept is not particularly important, examples may suffice for providing a practicable comprehension.

Strategies in teaching a concept

It is infrequent that teachers use only one move in teaching a concept; they usually use different kinds of moves and repetitions of a particular move. A **strategy** may be defined as a temporal sequence of moves. Thus giving a definition and following it by two examples is a three-move strategy: definition, giving an example, giving an example. In the dialogue on teaching a concept of skew lines in an earlier section, this strategy was used: sufficient condition, example, nonexample with a reason, nonexample with a reason, example, example, nonexample with a reason; in the dialogue on teaching a concept of a rhombus: examples, nonexamples, comparison, contrast, a characteristic, definition, example with a reason, nonexample with a reason, necessary condition, necessary condition.

A strategy very commonly employed in textbooks is to follow definition by exemplification. In this strategy, authors give the examples or nonexamples or both, either accompanied by reasons or not. This is sound pedagogy. The definition identifies the necessary and sufficient conditions and the exemplification clarifies them. If reasons are supplied for the exemplifications, these reinforce the necessary or sufficient conditions. Judging from the analyses of tapes of classroom dialogues, we may say that teachers also use this strategy and find it successful.

Many textbooks extend this strategy by providing exercises based on exemplification—that is, the exercises present objects and the students are asked to classify, to identify examples and nonexamples. Such exercises require the students to apply the concept in making the discrimination. The feedback the students get as they learn whether their answers are correct helps establish the concept.

A strategy such as the one used in teaching a concept of a rhombus (exemplification followed by the identification of necessary and sufficient conditions) is one by which students are expected to discover distinctive characteristics; the necessary and sufficient conditions of objects denoted by the concept is not frequently employed by teachers. Perhaps this is because this strategy is inefficient; with it usually a large number of moves is required to enable students to attain the concept. Yet many teachers believe that students remember longer concepts learned by this kind of strategy.

Characteristic of an inductive strategy, like that for teaching a concept of a rhombus, is the asking of questions that elicit the defining conditions or characteristics of the objects denoted by the concept. Some teachers state the defining conditions for the students and thus short-circuit the elicitation of them by questioning. Such a strategy might be: one or more examples followed by a sufficient condition. As stated above, exercises based on exemplification (the student is asked to discriminate between examples and nonexamples) are then assigned as homework.

In planning a strategy for teaching a concept, you will find helpful the questions stated in the summary at the end of the previous section; the nature of the students and the relative importance of the concept have been considered in them. If you employ the strategy in the classroom and discover that it is not successful for some students, you can extend or modify it extemporaneously as you become aware of the various moves available in a given situation.

Thought questions

1 Here are concepts you might teach. Design a strategy for each. You will have to determine the characteristics of the students you are teaching (seventh grade, geometry, whatever).

a	compass	f	significant digit in a measurement
b	percent	g	real number
c	hyperbola	h	intersection of two sets
d	inverse of a function	i	limit
e	greatest integer function	j	parameter

2 Show that theoretically there are over ten thousand strategies for teaching a concept.

3 Of the huge number of strategies possible for teaching a concept (question 2), show that some are logically impossible.

4 How will the nature of a concept influence a strategy for teaching it?

5 How will the nature of the students influence strategies for teaching concepts?

6 Assume that you have taught the concept of a polynomial of degree n over a set S. Design some exercises based on exemplification that you might assign as homework to reinforce this concept.

Self-test on the competencies

1 Identify concepts.
   Choose some mathematics textbook and open it to any page. Begin reading and record each use of concepts. Open the same textbook to another page. Begin reading and continue recording concept usage until you have identified five cases of explicit teaching of a concept.

2 Illustrate various uses of concepts.
   State four uses of concepts. For each, give an original illustration, one that was not used in this chapter.

3 Name and give examples of various moves that can be used to teach a given concept. What kind of a move is each of the following? (The term designating the concept being taught is set in boldface type.)
   a A **dihedral angle** is an angle formed by two half-planes having a common edge.
   b *Or* is a signal of **disjunction**.
   c All numbers that satisfy an equation are in the **solution set of the equation**.
   d The figure drawn on the chalkboard is a **parabola**.
   e If a set of numbers $F_0, F_1, F_2, \ldots$ are determined by $F_0 = 1$, $F_1 = 1$, and $F_{n+1} = F_n + F_{n-1}$, then they are **Fibonacci numbers**.
   f π is a **transcendental number**.
   g A set is a **Boolean algebra** only if two closed, binary operations are defined over the set.
   h The number 2 disproves the contention that all **prime numbers** are odd.

4 Plan a strategy for teaching a given concept and explain why this strategy should be successful.
   a Plan a strategy for teaching the concept of **congruent polygons** to seventh graders and present an argument that convinces that this strategy is successful.
   b Plan a strategy for teaching the concept of a **limit** to twelfth-grade students enrolled in the fourth course in mathematics. Why should this particular strategy be successful?

References

Ausubel, David P. *Educational Psychology: A Cognitive View.* New York: Holt, Rinehart and Winston, 1968. Ch. 15.

Geach, P. T. *Mental Acts: Their Content and Their Objects.* London: Routledge and Kegan Paul, 1956.

Henderson, Kenneth B. "Concepts." *The Teaching of Secondary School Mathematics*, Thirty-Third Yearbook of the National Council of Teachers of Mathematics. Washington, D. C.: National Council of Teachers of Mathematics, 1970. Ch. 7.

Hunt, Carl B., Janet Marin, and Philip J. Stone. *Experiments in Induction.* New York: Academic Press, 1966.

Klausmeier, Herbert J. and Chester W. Harris (eds.). *Analyses of Concept Learning.* New York: Academic Press, 1966. See particularly the chapters by Rom Harré, E. James Archer, and David P. Ausubel.

Van Engen, Henry. "The Formation of Concepts." *The Learning of Mathematics: Its Theory and Practice*, Twenty-First Yearbook of the National Council of Teachers of Mathematics, National Council of Teachers of Mathematics, 1953. Ch. 3.

6

Teaching mathematical generalizations by exposition

Once mathematicians have conceived of mathematical objects (numbers, functions, parallelograms, and congruent figures, for example), they can study the properties of these objects and the relations among them. The findings of such study provide generalizations—that is, statements that hold over a set of objects. Generalizations, like concepts, are a kind of subject matter that mathematics teachers teach their students.

Generalizations are usually taught in one of two ways: by exposition or by heuristics (that is, by guided discovery). In this chapter, we shall limit our discussion to the first of these two methods, leaving heuristics to the following chapter. As we did in discussing how concepts are taught, we shall identify moves that teachers use in teaching generalizations.

At the conclusion of this chapter, you should be able to demonstrate the following competencies:

1 State ways of introducing a given generalization

2 Interpret a given generalization by paraphrasing it, analyzing it, reviewing one or more of its constituent concepts, or giving instances of it

3 State a counterexample of a given false generalization

4 Given a generalization to be taught, choose a way of justifying it

5 Design activities that will require students to apply a given generalization

6 Plan an expository strategy for teaching a given generalization

Moves in teaching a generalization

As in the case of teaching concepts, when one analyzes the classroom dialogue that results when a generalization is taught, various moves can be identified. Consider the following transcription of a dialogue. The context is an eighth-grade class studying formulas. The students had learned what a variable is and how to substitute for a variable in formula. The formula under consideration was one for converting Celsius temperatures into Fahrenheit: $F = \frac{9}{5}C + 32$. Some students multiplied the Celsius temperature by $\frac{9}{5}$ and then added 32. Others added 32 to the Celsius temperature and then multiplied the sum by $\frac{9}{5}$. The particular exercise at issue was converting 20° Celsius into Fahrenheit.

1   **T**   Well, who's right? S_1 added first and then multiplied, and S_2 multiplied first and then added. S_2, why did you multiply first—that is. take $\frac{9}{5}$ of 20 and then add 32?

2   **S₂** $\frac{9}{5}$ written next to 20 means multiply.

3   **T**   How did you do—ah—number 12? (*This exercise required the conversion of 48° Celsius into Fahrenheit.*) Did you multiply first?

4   **S₂**   Ah—ah—yes, I guess so.

5   **T**   What did you get as an answer?

6   **S₂**   Ah—118.4°.

7   **T**   118.4°. Let's see (*pausing*). Yes, you multiplied first and then added 32. I just wanted to check to see that you didn't multiply first when changing 20° Celsius just because 5 divided evenly into 20. But you were consistent. S_1, why did you add first and then multiply?

8   **S₁**   The plus sign.

9   **T**   So we see that there is a good reason for doing either operation first. We ought to have a rule to tell which operation to do first. We'll have other problems later where we'll have to know which operation to do first. So let's learn the rule mathematicians use. If there is a combination of multiplication or division combined with addition or subtraction, the multiplication or division is done first, then the addition or subtraction. So for the problem we were doing, who is right, S_1 or S_2? (*Pause.*) Right, S_2. See (*writes on the chalkboard*)

$$F = \frac{9}{\overset{}{\underset{1}{5}}} \times \overset{4}{\cancel{20}} + 32 = 36 + 32 = 68$$

So 20° Celsius equals 68° Fahrenheit. Let's do another—number 12. Who will come to the chalkboard and do that one? All right, S_3.
(*S_3 does the exercise correctly on the chalkboard.*)

10   **T**   One more. No, two more. Numbers 14 and 17. Who'll do 14? All right (*indicating S_4*). Number 17? S_5. While they are putting these on the board, let's talk about the other formula, $C = \frac{5}{9}(F - 32)$. Let's do—mm—number 10. What's given? S_6. (*The teacher writes the formula on the chalkboard.*)

11   **S₆**   212°.

12   **T**   Fahrenheit or Celsius?

13   **S$_6$**   Fahrenheit.

14   **T**   So what do I substitute for what?

15   **S$_6$**   212 for F.

16   **T**   Yeah, 212 for F (*erases "F" and replaces it with "212"*). Now what do we do? We can subtract 32 from 212 and then multiply by $\frac{5}{9}$. Or we can multiply both the 212 and the 32 by $\frac{5}{9}$ and then subtract. Here's a case where it doesn't make any difference which operation we do first; we get the same answer either way. It's usually better to do the operation inside the parentheses first. So we would subtract 32 from 212. (*Does the following on the chalkboard.*)

$$C = \frac{5}{9}(212 - 32)$$

$$C = \frac{5}{\cancel{9}_{1}} \times \cancel{180}^{\,20} = 100$$

Any questions? Let's do one more before we see what S$_4$ and S$_5$ have for us.

Let's analyze this dialogue. The teacher probably knew from experience that there would be differences in the students' answers because of the differing orders of operation employed. In the assignment the previous day, the teacher could have stated the rule mathematicians use and thereby avoided confusion. But the teacher explained to the person who recorded the dialogue that he wanted the students to become aware of two possible orders, and thus demonstrate the need for a convention. In this way he motivated apprehension of the rule (generalization). The teacher ultimately resolved the alternatives by stating, in utterance 9, the rule mathematicians use. He then applied this rule, still in utterance 9, and had two students apply the rule.

The teacher then turned to another formula identified in utterance 10 as $C = \frac{5}{9}(F - 32)$. Why is this a generalization? The teacher applied it in utterances 11–16. Again, he raised the question of the order of operation and proposed a resolution in utterance 16. Finally, he suggested in utterance 16 an application of the generalization $C = \frac{5}{9}(F - 32)$ and the rule he had stated. From this and other dialogues, we are now in a position to identify some moves in teaching a generalization.

Introduction moves

One general kind of move is an **introduction move** in which the teacher sets the stage for the subsequent instruction. Three kinds of introduction moves appear to be used by teachers.

In one, the teacher focuses the students' attention on the topic of instruction. This is often done simply by naming the topic. We shall call this a **focus move**.

The teacher in the dialogue used a focus move in utterance 10 when he said, "Let's talk about the other formula, $C = \frac{5}{9}(F - 32)$." By this language he directed the students' attention to what he wanted to talk about next. Earlier, before the recorded part of the dialogue, the teacher had used another focus move. He had directed the students' attention to the two formulas for converting temperatures in one scale into corresponding temperatures in another scale.

In another introduction move, the teacher states explicitly the goal or outcome of the subsequent study. We shall call this an **objective move.** The teacher in the dialogue had stated an objective at the outset of the day's lesson—that the students needed to learn how to substitute in a formula and solve for the variable that is the subject of the formula. There is no objective move in the dialogue reproduced.

A third introduction move is one in which the teacher tries to convince students that the generalization to be learned is worth learning. We shall call this a **motivation move.**

The teacher of the temperature conversion formulas employed a motivation move when he developed the need for some rule to resolve the dilemma concerning the order of operation. The motivation move became explicit when in utterance 9 he said, "We ought to have a rule to tell which operation to do first. We'll have other problems later where we'll have to know which operation to do first."

Often motivation is attained by pointing out the utility of the generalization. For example, a teacher might point out examples of the use of proportions in daily life in an attempt to persuade students to learn how to set up and solve proportions. Or a teacher who is about to teach the generalizations that are the basis for finding the product of rational numbers might state that these generalizations will be used over and over throughout the rest of the algebra course. The first example makes use of the nonacademic utility of a generalization, the second the academic utility. For most mathematical generalizations in algebra, geometry, and advanced courses in mathematics, the latter appeal is probably more realistic and easier to make than the former.

When one considers the importance of motivation in teaching, it seems that such a move should be used frequently. But if the tapes of classroom teaching on which our analysis is based and the taxonomy of moves developed are representative, teachers do not employ motivation moves at all frequently.

Garth Runion (1972) developed seven ways a mathematics teacher can initiate a lesson and provide motivation. One way is to state the goals of the lesson. This provides the student some direction for study. A second is outlining, in which the teacher states the major points to be covered in the development of the lesson. Like stating goals, this can be regarded as providing the student some direction. Often, motivation increases with the clarity of the objective.

A third way of introducing a lesson is to use an analogue. In this approach the teacher selects, from what the students are familiar with, some object, process, or situation like what the students are to study. This approach relates the unfamiliar to the familiar. Thus, the algebra teacher might remind students of the balance and the operations that can be performed and still maintain a balance. Then the teacher can lead into the solution of equations in which he or she wants to stress performance of the same operation on both sides of the equation.

Using historical material is a fourth way of introducing generalizations. For example, before teaching the Pythagorean theorem, the teacher can tell the students something about Pythagoras, who was a versatile man and did things other than discover this relation. Matrix theory can be introduced by relating the history of the invention of matrices; the same can be done for vectors.

Teachers probably do not use the historical approach frequently because they do not know the history of mathematics as well as they know mathematics. For teachers who would like to use this approach, the Thirty-First Yearbook of the National Council of Teachers of Mathematics, *Historical Topics for the Mathematics Classroom*, contains references to the history of many mathematical ideas, theorems, and processes.

Reviewing subordinate information is a fifth way of introducing a generalization. If motivation is thereby provided, it probably results from relating what will subsequently be studied to what the students presumably already know. The information reviewed is usually prerequisite to understanding the generalization or generalizations to be taught later in the lesson. Should this approach be used, it would be well to ascertain by questioning whether students really do understand the prerequisite information. Thus the review can be diagnostic, with remedial teaching provided if and when it is deemed necessary.

Giving reasons for studying a particular topic is similar to providing the kind of motivation described above. Runion pointed out this approach as particularly effective when combined with another approach—a statement of goals—that makes clear to the students what they are to accomplish.

The last approach Runion identified consists in presenting a problematical situation. This gains the students' attention or arouses their interest in what is to come. Many students are curious, and by posing some sort of problematical situation the teacher can capitalize on their curiosity. Mathematical fallacies represent one kind of problem that can be used. Another concerns how a long and involved process can be shortened by an algorithm. Many teachers use this approach effectively.

Assertion moves

Another kind of move was illustrated in utterance 9, when the teacher stated the rule: "If there is a combination of multiplication or division combined with addition or subtraction, the multiplication or division is done first."

Here a generalization is stated or asserted. We shall call this an **assertion move**.

Sometimes the teacher asserts the generalization, as the teacher in the dialogue did; sometimes the teacher directs the students' attention to its statement in a textbook or helps the students verbalize the generalization, which may have been discovered or identified in a discussion. But however and whenever the assertion is made, the utterance is an assertion move. Often we find the teacher repeating this move, probably for emphasis.

Instantiation moves

Another kind of move is **instantiation**. In this move, the teacher employs one or more instances of the generalization. If the generalization is in mathematical notation with the variables explicitly quantified as, for example,

For each rational number a and for all positive integers m_i,

$i = 1, 2, 3, \ldots, n, a^{m_1} \times a^{m_2} \times \ldots \times a^{m_i} = a^{m_1 + m_2 + \ldots + m_i}$

an instance of the generalization is obtained by dropping the quantifiers and replacing at least one variable by a constant from the domains of the variables. Thus,

$$2^2 \times 2^3 = 2^5 \qquad\qquad 10 \times 10^2 \times 10^3 = 10^6$$

$$a^5 \times a \times a^6 = a^{12} \qquad 5^a \times 5^b = 5^{a+b}$$

are instances of the generalization. If there are no explicit quantifiers, as in

$\mathbf{u} \cdot \mathbf{v} = \mathbf{0} \Rightarrow \mathbf{u}$ and $\mathbf{v}$ are orthogonal

where it is understood that the variables $\mathbf{u}$ and $\mathbf{v}$ range over the domain of vectors, a replacement of either or both variables by a constant yields an instance of the generalization.

If a generalization is not in mathematical notation—that is, if it employs common nouns—an instance is obtained by replacing at least one common noun by a proper noun or constant. Thus, for the generalization

If both sides of an inequality are divided by a negative number, the inequality is reversed,

an instance is

If $-2x < 6$,   then $x > -3$.

Notice that an instance is always a sentence whereas an example is an element of a set. We speak of an example of a concept but of an instance of a generalization. True, some teachers and writers use the two terms synonymously. But since it clarifies pedagogical theory to distinguish between a concept and a generalization, it further clarifies the theory to distinguish between objects denoted by a concept and immediate applications of a generalization. Stipulating a difference between an example and an instance—with an example used to refer to the denotation of concepts and an instance used to refer to immediate implications of generalizations—enables us to preserve this distinction.

In the dialogue, an instantiation move was used each time the rule concerning the order of operations was followed. These instantiations clarified the meaning of the rule and showed how it was applied. In the next chapter, we shall see another use of instantiation moves, to enable students to discover a generalization for themselves.

Application moves

Instantiation moves are closely related to moves in which the generalization is applied. In utterance 9 in the dialogue above, after asserting the generalization, the teacher applied it when he wrote on the chalkboard

$$F = \frac{9}{\overset{}{\underset{1}{\cancel{5}}}} \times \overset{4}{\cancel{20}} + 32 = 36 + 32 = 68$$

The application is an instance of the generalization concerning the order of operations. We shall call moves in which a generalization is applied **application moves.**

An application move always involves deduction. A student analyzes a situation or problem and decides which generalization or generalizations are relevant. The student then uses the data from the given situation or problem along with the generalization and draws a conclusion. For example, the application of the generalization concerning the order of operations asserted in the dialogue may be schematized as follows:

> Where there is a combination of the operations of multiplication or division and addition or subtraction, the multiplications or divisions are done first, then the additions or subtractions. In the formula $F = \frac{9}{5}C + 32$, there is a combination of multiplication and addition. Therefore, the multiplication should be done first and then the addition.

Authors of textbooks often employ application moves either by displaying "examples," which are really instances of the generalization, or by supplying exercises or problems that may be instances of the generalization. In general, an application move is one in which the teacher by means of questions, exercises, or problems seeks to get the students to apply the generalization either by itself or in conjunction with other generalizations.

Thought questions

1   Suggest a different motivation move that the teacher in the dialogue might have used.

2   Suppose you are going to teach the Pythagorean theorem. How might you motivate this generalization?

3   Suppose you plan to teach the distributive principle of multiplication over addition. How might you motivate this principle?

4   You are going to teach the generalization for finding the percent one number is of another. Use a focus move to introduce this generalization.

5   In utterance 9, the teacher demonstrated the application of the rule determining the order of operations. Should he have asked a student to demonstrate the application rather than do it himself? Why?

6   Give at least two instances of each of the following generalizations.
   a $x + z = y \Rightarrow x = y - z$
   b $\sin^2 x + \cos^2 x = 1$
   c   The sum of the measures of the angles of a triangle is $180°$.
   d   If an equation contains fractions, it can be cleared of the fractions by multiplying both sides by a common denominator.
   e   The product of the sum and difference of two numbers is the difference of their squares.
   f   If there are two numbers x and y such that $x < y$, then there is a positive number z such that $x + z = y$.
   g   To divide one rational number by another, the divisor can be inverted and the rational numbers multiplied.
   h   The sum of a number and its additive inverse is 0.
   i $\forall x \in R, \quad \forall y \in R, \quad x + y = y + x$
   j   If the slopes of two lines are negative reciprocals, the lines are perpendicular.
   k   For all real numbers x and y, $x < y$, $x = y$, or $y < x$.
   l   The product of two powers of the same base is that base to the power that is the sum of the exponents of the powers.

7   Offer a conjecture as to why the teacher in the dialogue used so many application moves.

8   Teachers often repeat the answers students give, as in utterances 7 and 16. Why is this a good thing to do on occasion? Why would it be undesirable if it were done continually?

9   Notice what the teacher says in utterance 16 about it making no difference which operation is done first. Does this appear to contradict the generalization asserted in utterance 9? What would be a better way of explaining the difference between computing when using $F = \frac{9}{5}C + 32$ and when using $C = \frac{5}{9}(F - 32)$?

10   Show that if a counterexample of a generalization can be found, an instance using this counterexample will disprove the generalization.

11   The instantiation principle of logic states that every instance of a true, universal generalization is true. Explain how this principle is related to an application move.

12   For each of the following generalizations, design exercises that require application of the generalization.
   a   The volume of a sphere equals $\frac{4}{3}\pi r^3$.
   b   The locus of points equidistant from two parallel planes is a plane parallel to the planes and midway between them.
   c   The number of places in a decimal fraction is the same as the number of zeros in the denominator of its equal common fraction.
   d   By taking time to compare the cost of different kinds of credit, you can often save money.
   e   If a line intersects two sides of a triangle and is parallel to the third side, the measures of the corresponding line segments are proportional.

   f   The converse of "if *p* then *q*" can be formed by interchanging *p* and *q*.

   g   To prove a conditional, assume the hypothesis and show that the conclusion follows from it.

   h $a^2 = b^2 + c^2 - 2bc \cos \angle A$

   i   A geometric sequence whose common ratio is between -1 and 1 has a limit of 0.

13   Study the application exercises in several textbooks. Do there appear to be patterns by which the authors design such exercises? If so, describe them.

Let us now analyze another classroom dialogue. The class has already learned the concepts of an irrational number and a quadratic equation and how to solve (that is, has learned principles for solving) quadratic equations over the integers by factoring. The teacher on this particular day had begun by considering the homework exercises on the solution of quadratic equations by factoring. Whenever some student was unable to solve one of the equations, another student wrote the solution on the chalkboard and explained it.

1 **T**   Let's solve

$$9x^2 - 6x - 1 = 0$$

        Solve it. Each of you solve it. (*The students attempt to solve the equation, presumably by factoring.*) Who has the roots? (*Pause.*) What's the matter? (*Pause.*) What's taking you so long?

2 **S₁** It can't be factored.

3 **T**   Really? Is that what others found? Well, you're right. It can't be factored. Hence we need to learn a way of solving quadratic equations that can't be factored. Our textbook gives us a formula. Look on page 113 just above the middle of the page. (*Reads.*) "The roots of a quadratic equation $ax^2 + bx + c = 0$ are

$$x = \frac{-b + \sqrt{b^2 - 4ac}}{2a} \quad \text{or} \quad x = \frac{-b - \sqrt{b^2 - 4ac}}{2a}."$$

(*Writes on the chalkboard.*)

$$ax^2 + bx + c = 0 \Rightarrow x = \frac{-b + \sqrt{b^2 - 4ac}}{2a} \quad \text{or}$$

$$x = \frac{-b - \sqrt{b^2 - 4ac}}{2a}$$

        Hence to solve a quadratic equation—*any* quadratic equation—it doesn't make any difference whether it can be factored or not. All you have to do is substitute in the quadratic formula. That's what this (*points to the right side of the implication on the chalkboard*) is called, *the quadratic formula:* Now then, what does *b* stand for? S₂?

4 **S₂** The coefficient of the second term.

5 **T**   The coefficient of the *second* term? Suppose the quadratic was

$$bx + ax^2 + c = 0$$

6 **S₂** The coefficient of the *x*-term.

7 **T**   Isn't ax^2 an *x*-term?

8 **S₂** No. That's the *x*-square term.

9 **T** Suppose the equation were $ay^2 + ay + c = 0$. (*S₂ does not answer.*) What's a better way to say what *b* stands for? S₃.

10 **S₃** The coefficient of the first-powered term.

11 **T** Yes. That's it. Do you see, S₂?

12 **S₂** That's what I meant.

13 **T** Maybe so, but that's not what you said. We have to go by what you said. O.K. The coefficient of the first-powered term. And what does *a* stand for? Try that one, S₂.

14 **S₂** The coefficient of the squared term.

15 **T** Now you're cooking; *a* stands for the coefficient of the squared term. And *c* stands for what? Yes? (*Points to a student who has raised her hand.*)

16 **S₄** The constant term.

17 **T** So let's solve

$$9x^2 - 6x - 1 = 0$$

by substituting in the formula.

(*Directs the dialogue to this end and the class obtains*

$$x = \frac{1 + \sqrt{2}}{3} \quad \text{or} \quad x = \frac{1 - \sqrt{2}}{3} .)$$

What kind of roots are these? S₅?

18 **S₅** I don't know what you mean.

19 **T** The roots of quadratic equations you have solved so far, all the roots, have been rational numbers. Are these roots rational numbers?

20 **S₅** No.

21 **T** What kind of numbers are they?

22 **S₅** Irrational.

23 **T** O.K. Now let's see how we get the quadratic formula. I think we have time to develop it. (*Checks his watch.*) Yes, we do.

(*Directs the dialogue toward proving*

$$ax^2 + bx + c = 0 \Rightarrow x = \frac{-b \pm \sqrt{b^2 - 4ac}}{2a}$$

by the conventional method of completing the square. No explicit quantification of the parameters is stated, not even that a ≠ 0. Neither does the teacher prove the converse of the theorem.)

If you didn't understand all the steps, the development is given in your textbook and you can review it. Let's quickly do one more example. Let's do the first exercise in your assignment for tomorrow. Will someone read the equation?

24 **S₆** $6x^2 + x - 12 = 0$

25 **T** (*Directs the dialogue to substituting in the quadratic formula and solving, getting*

$$x = -\tfrac{3}{2} \quad \text{or} \quad x = \tfrac{4}{3} .)$$

> Now these are rational roots, which means that we could have solved the equation by factoring. But using the formula might actually have saved time if we hadn't been lucky in factoring. Remember, the quadratic formula will solve any quadratic equation; it's a general method. (*The bell rings.*) For tomorrow do—ah—let's do the odd-numbered exercises in the set beginning on page 115. Remember, use the formula.

The teacher employed a motivation move in utterance 1 and in the first five sentences of utterance 3. He developed a need for considering the quadratic formula, assuming the students considered it desirable to be able to solve any quadratic equation.

An assertion move was employed in the third utterance. The generalization was stated. It appeared that the author of the textbook believed the students would know the domains of the parameters a, b, and c and the restriction on a (that is, $a \neq 0$), for no mention was made of the extension of the generalization. The teacher then wrote an equivalent generalization on the chalkboard. This may be regarded as an interpretation, by statement of the generalization in different language, of the generalization that appeared in the textbook. Further interpretation occurred in utterances 3 through 16 as the teacher reviewed the meaning of the three parameters a, b, and c, which were constituent terms in the generalization.

Student utterance 4, in response to the teacher's question in the utterance 3, implied a false generalization. The teacher realized this and effectively employed a counterexample to direct attention to this false generalization. He continued the use of this move to correct an additional imprecise generalization that the student evidently had made.

Utterance 17 initiated an instantiation move, probably to clarify the meaning of the generalization. It may also be argued that the instantiation move was used to illustrate the application of the generalization.

The last question in utterance 17 initiated a brief digression as the teacher utilized the concept of an irrational number to imply the existential generalization

Some quadratic equations have irrational roots.

One wonders how many students would be able to express this generalization explicitly.

Evidently the teacher thought the students should see how the quadratic formula is derived. Hence, he proved a theorem. The proof justified the generalization that was the object of the lesson.

At the end of utterance 23, another instantiation move was used. Was this to clarify further the meaning of the generalization? Or was it to illustrate the application of the generalization (in which case it would be an application move)? It is difficult to say.

In the middle of utterance 25, the teacher asserted a generalization: The quadratic formula will solve any quadratic equation. This was an immediate implication of the previous generalization.

Finally, a subsequent application move was used as the teacher made the assignment for the next day.

Interpretation moves

In the first dialogue (on pages 113–114), we identified some moves in teaching a generalization. The second dialogue reveals others. The teacher may decide that not all the students comprehend the generalization. It may involve concepts unclear to them; it may be complex or its implications may be unclear. Should a teacher so decide, he or she may seek to clarify or interpret the generalization. We find that teachers use various moves, called **interpretation moves,** to do this. One of these is **paraphrasing.** The teacher states the meaning of the generalization in different words, presumably easier to comprehend. Teachers often paraphrase in English a generalization asserted initially in mathematical notation.

In a second kind of interpretation move, the teacher **reviews** or leads the students in reviewing the concepts that may be unclear to them. The teacher does this by employing some of the moves in teaching a concept.

A third kind of interpretation move, as we found in the last dialogue, is an **instantiation move.** Like any other, this move is often repeated. One might hypothesize that when the teacher chooses members or examples with which the students are familiar, the instances are more effective in interpreting the generalization.

Analyses of classroom dialogues reveal that when a generalization is complex—as, for example, a conditional whose antecedent is a disjunction or a conjunction, or a biconditional (an if-and-only-if generalization), or a generalization that has exceptions—teachers analyze the generalization by talking explicitly about its components and logic or about its implications. Such moves are called **analysis moves.**

The following dialogue illustrates interpretation by analysis. It had already been established that only square matrices have inverses and that not all these matrices have inverses. The teacher began with a motivation move. But there are other moves in the teacher's complete first utterance. Can you identify them?

1　T　Now it would be nice to know—nice to be able to tell—if a given square matrix has an inverse. You'd like such a—ah, ah—test, wouldn't you? And there is one. A square matrix has an inverse if and only if its determinant is not equal to zero. That's something that's good to know. So far, we have stuck to square matrices of orders 2 and 3. So a square matrix A_2 or A_3 (*writes on the chalkboard*)

A_2 has an inverse A_2^{-1} iff det $A \neq 0$

and similarly for A_3. (*Replaces subscript "2" by subscript "3."*) Now let's see what that proposition tells us. Suppose you have a square matrix and you find that its determinant is not zero. What can you conclude? S_1.

2 **S₁**   That it has an inverse.

3 **T**   Yes. Suppose the determinant of another square matrix is 0. Then what? Let's ask S₂.

4 **S₂**   It doesn't have an inverse.

5 **T**   Good. Suppose a given square matrix doesn't have an inverse. Now what? What do you know? S₃?

6 **S₃**   (*Does not answer.*)

7 **T**   Who knows? What conclusion can you draw? The square matrix doesn't have an inverse. S₄.

8 **S₄**   No use trying to find the inverse.

         (*Some laughter in the class. The teacher ignores both the answer and the laughter.*)

9 **T**   S₁.

10 **S₁**   The determinant is zero.

11 **T**   Of course. If the matrix doesn't have an inverse, it must be that its determinant is 0. Look! (*Points to the generalization on the chalkboard.*) See this "if and only if"? This means that if this (*points to the condition on the left*) is true, then this is true (*points to the condition on the right*). And if this is not true (*points to the condition on the left*)—that is, if the matrix doesn't have an inverse—then this is not true (*points to the condition on the right*). And if this is not true (*points to the condition on the right*), then this is not true (*points to the condition on the left*). See all the information you can get from an if-and-only-if statement?

After the assertion of the generalization, the teacher decided that it should be interpreted. He first employed instantiation moves using A_2 and A_3. In these he also paraphrased the original statement of the generalization by using mathematical notation. He then attempted further interpretation ("Let's see what that proposition tells us") by analysis moves. When a transcript of the dialogue was discussed at a later time with the teacher, he was asked why he had gone into such detail about immediate implications of the generalization. He replied that he had found that many students are unaware of the four immediate implications of an if-and-only-if proposition and therefore he always stresses these. He felt that biconditionals are hard for students to comprehend and that "one has to take them apart and show the individual propositions that you can get."

Thought questions

1   Interpret each of the following generalizations by paraphrasing.

   a   If $a \neq 0$, $ax = b \Rightarrow x = \dfrac{b}{a}$.

   b   The measure of an exterior angle of a triangle is greater than that of either non-adjacent interior angle.

   c   The median helps you compare groups of numbers.

d   The area of a trapezoid equals $\frac{1}{2}(b_1 + b_2)h$.

e   If a triangle is equilateral, it is equiangular, and conversely.

2   Interpret each of the following generalizations by instantiation.

a   You can change a decimal fraction to a common fraction by reading the decimal fraction to yourself and then writing the common fraction you read.

b   The accuracy of a measurement is determined by the number of significant digits.

c   The product of the means is equal to the product of the extremes.

d   The bisector of the vertex angle of an isosceles triangle is the perpendicular bisector of the base.

e   The hyperbola with foci $(c,0)$ and $(-c,0)$ and constant $2a < 0$, $a < c$, is the set of points whose coordinates satisfy

$$\frac{x^2}{a^2} - \frac{y^2}{b^2} = 1 \quad \text{where } b^2 = c^2 - a^2$$

3   Interpret each of the following by analysis.

a   If $a > 1$ and $0 < x < y$, then $\log_a x < \log_a y$.

b   If a statement is true for an integer k, and whenever the statement is true for $n \leq k$ it is also true for $n + 1$, then the statement is true for every integer $n \leq k$.

c   For each complex number z, $|z^n| = |z|^n$ provided $n \in Z^+$.

d z is a zero of a function $f \Leftrightarrow f(z) = 0$.

e   If two lines in space do not intersect, they are parallel or skew.

4   Suppose you can tell from a student's reactions that she does not comprehend the generalization that the smaller a relative error is, the greater will be the number of significant digits in a measurement. Make some conjectures as to why she does not comprehend the generalization.

5   Suppose one of your students does not comprehend this generalization: "The modulus of the product of two complex numbers is the product of the moduli of the numbers, and the amplitude of the product is the sum of the amplitudes of the numbers." For which concepts would you test the student to ascertain the difficulty? How would you do this?

6   From a textbook, find some examples of interpretation of generalizations. How is the interpretation accomplished in each case?

7   A textbook states the identity theorem for polynomials:

If for each $x \in R$,

$a_n x^n + a_{n-1} x^{n-1} + \cdots + a_1 x + a_0 = b_m x^m + b_{m-1} x^{m-1} + \cdots + b_1 x + b_0$
with $a_n \neq 0$ and $b_m \neq 0$,

then $m = n$ and $a_n = b_n, a_{n-1} = b_{n-1}, \ldots, a_0 = b_0$.

The teacher thinks this should be interpreted by paraphrasing it in English. Write a synonymous statement in English that the teacher might use.

8   This and the following questions pertain to the dialogue on the quadratic formula. In utterance 3 the teacher says, "It [the equation] can't be factored." Factoring is performed not on equations but on polynomials. Do you think such imprecise language will confuse students? Can the use of imprecise language be justified? Why?

9   Imprecise language also occurs in utterance 3 when the author of the textbook and the teacher fail to restrict the parameter a to $a \neq 0$. What is your attitude about this? Should the teacher have made an explicit restriction or is this unnecessary since the formula obviously cannot be used when $a = 0$?

10   In utterance 3, the teacher teaches the concept of the quadratic formula. One frequently finds the teaching of a concept hyphenated in the teaching of a generalization. What kind of move was used to teach this concept?

11   In utterance 13, the teacher queries Student$_2$. Why did he do this? Is such practice sound? Why?

12   Notice that in utterance 17 the teacher did not check the answers

$$\frac{1 + \sqrt{2}}{3} \quad \text{and} \quad \frac{1 - \sqrt{2}}{3},$$

that is, he did not prove

$$x = \frac{1 + \sqrt{2}}{3} \quad \text{or} \quad x = \frac{1 - \sqrt{2}}{3} \Rightarrow 9x^2 - 6x - 1 = 0$$

Was this an error? Explain.

13   Again, notice that in utterance 23 the teacher did not prove the biconditional that provided $a \neq 0$;

$$ax^2 + bx + c = 0 \Leftrightarrow x = \frac{-b \pm \sqrt{b^2 - 4ac}}{2a}$$

Is the proof of the biconditional logically necessary? Explain.

14   In utterance 5 (page 120), the word *second* is printed in italics to indicate that the teacher stressed this word, spoke it more loudly than the others. Offer a hypothetical explanation of why he did this. Teachers often deliberately stress certain words when repeating a student's answer. Do you think this is an effective move? Why?

The following dialogue occurred in a general mathematics class. In the days preceding it, the class had been learning how to find the area of various geometric figures—rectangles and squares. The objective of the present day's lesson was to find the area of a parallelogram. The teacher began by teaching a concept of a parallelogram. The class learned that rectangles and squares are parallelograms but that some parallelograms are not rectangles or squares.

1   T   Now let's see if we can find out how to find the area of a parallelogram. Who's got an idea of how to find the area? (*Pause.*) Come on, who's got an idea? Ideas don't cost anything. (*Pause.*) And it doesn't have to be the right idea. Yes (*calling on a student*)?

2   S$_1$ Multiply the length by the width.

3   T   O.K. That sounds like a good idea. I'll draw a parallelogram, and you tell me how to find its area. (*Draws a parallelogram and labels the lengths of two adjacent sides 10 inches and 8 inches.*) O.K. How do you find the area? (*Calls on the same student.*)

4   S$_1$ Multiply 10 by 8. It's 80.

5   T   80 what? 80 what kind of units of area?

6   S$_1$ 80 square inches.

7   T   O.K. How many of you think this is the right answer? (*Some students raise their hands.*) How many don't? (*Some students raise their hands.*) Now imagine me pushing on these two opposite corners and sort of squeezing the parallelogram together (*draws another parallelogram*). Has the area changed? How many think it has? Sure, it has changed. Look at these two parallelograms. There is more area, isn't there, in this (*pointing to the first parallelogram*) than in this (*pointing to the second parallelogram*), isn't there? But have the lengths of the sides changed by my changing the shape of the parallelogram? No. This (*pointing to one side*) is still 10 inches long, and this (*pointing to the other side*) is still 8 inches long. So according to how S_1 figured the area, the area is still 80 square inches. What do you think, S_1?

8   S_1 I don't know. Ah——.

9   T   But you know that the area of both parallelograms is not 80 square inches, don't you? The area is not the same for both, is it?

10   S_1 I guess not.

Figure 6.1

11   T   So your method of finding the area doesn't work, does it? But you had an idea and that's something. Now we need another idea. I'll give you one this time. (*Writes letters at the vertices of the first parallelogram as in Figure* 6.1.) I'm going to draw a perpendicular from vertex *D* to side *AB*. Now imagine cutting along that perpendicular. What is the figure we cut off? It's a (*pause*), it's a triangle. Now I'll move that triangle over here (*points to the right side of parallelogram ABCD*) so that *A* falls on *B* and *AD* falls on *BC* and *D* falls on *C*. Now what kind of a figure do we have? (*Nods to a student.*)

12   S_2 A rectangle.

13   T   Right. A rectangle. How do you know it's a rectangle? You're right; it is a rectangle. But how do you know it is? (*Draws Figure* 6.2 *on the board.*) How do you know it (*pointing to the rectangle*) is a rectangle?

Figure 6.2

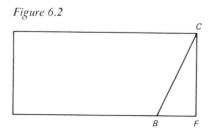

14 S₃ It's got right angles.

15 T How do you know that the angle at *F* is a right angle? S₉, everybody's paying attention, so we can find out how to find the area of a parallelogram. (*Calls on a student other than S₉.*)

16 S₄ It looks like, you know, like a right angle.

17 T That's not good enough. How do we know that it is a right angle?

18 S₅ Measure it.

19 T Well, we could do that and when we did we would find that it measures 90° and hence is a right angle. But don't we know that it is a right angle without having to measure it? Who knows why? How did I draw this line? (*Points to the perpendicular from D in Figure* 6.1.) You remember how I drew this line (*indicates a student*).

20 S₆ Perpendicular.

21 T Perpendicular to what? Let's be precise in our statements.

22 S₆ Perpendicular to side *AB*.

23 T That's better. So if this line is perpendicular to *AB*, what kind of an angle does it make with *AB*? Yes (*calling on a student*)?

24 S₇ A right angle.

25 T A right angle. Right. No pun there. A right angle. So when I move the triangle with the right angle here (*indicates by pointing*) over here (*indicating the right side of the parallelogram*) it's still a right angle, isn't it? So we've got one right angle in this quadrilateral. Is that enough to know that it is a rectangle? Remember what we said a rectangle is? Who remembers? (*Calls on a student who raises her hand.*)

26 S₈ A parallelogram having one right angle.

27 T Yes, having one right angle is enough. Remember? We proved that if a parallelogram has one right angle, all the angles are right angles. O.K. So now we have a rectangle that has the same area as the parallelogram we started with. We know that because all we did was cut off a piece of the parallelogram and move it over to the other side to form the rectangle. Both have the same area. Now we've got it. We know how to find the area of a rectangle. Now we can use your idea, S₁. How do you find the area?

28 S₁ Multiply the length by the width.

The dialogue continued with the teacher leading the students to see that the length of the base of the parallelogram is the same as the length of the rectangle. He showed how to find the height of the parallelogram and stressed that the height is not the same as the length of a side adjacent to the base. The lesson concluded with the assertion of a rule for finding the area of a parallelogram. The teacher assigned as homework some exercises requiring application of the rule.

The teacher introduced the topic by means of an objective move. He was able to solicit a conjecture (assertion in utterance 2) from a student, a conjecture that was a false generalization. From utterance 3 through the first sentence in utterance 11, the teacher employed a counterexample move to disprove the student's conjecture.

Counterexample moves

Just as in teaching a concept, we find teachers using counterexample moves to teach generalizations. These are used for the same reason—namely, to disprove a false generalization. If there exists a counterexample for a generalization (a member of the domain for which the generalization is false), the instance formed by using the counterexample is called a **counterinstance.**

In an exact science, a counterexample proves that a conjecture is not a true generalization. In the less exact sciences (economics, sociology, psychology, for example) it takes more than one counterexample to show that a conjecture is not a true generalization because such sciences admit generalizations that are not universal.

Justification moves

In utterance 13, the teacher asks, "How do you know it's a rectangle?" This may be regarded as a request for a student to justify or prove the contention that the figure is a rectangle. A similar challenge occurs in utterance 15 when the teacher asks, "How do you know that the angle at F is a right angle?" In both cases, the challenge is answered by giving reasons— an informal proof. Notice that the teacher rejects an inappropriate justification (utterances 15–17) when the student seeks to give empirical evidence rather than a deductive argument.

To **justify a generalization** is to give evidence or reasons that the generalization is true. In the dialogue above, the function of utterances 11–28 was to develop and justify a rule for finding the area of a parallelogram. If the students were willing to assume that the parallelogram the teacher chose was typical of all parallelograms (that is, was a paradigm) the rule for finding the area of this parallelogram—actually an instance of the generalization for all parallelograms—was justified for all parallelograms.

Analyses of classroom dialogues that involve justification reveal that four kinds of justification moves are used by teachers. In one, the teacher points out that the generalization is accepted by authorities. Students assume that if a generalization is asserted in a textbook, it must be true. On occasion, teachers make use of this kind of justification with such locutions as

Mathematicians know that . . .

It has been proved that . . .

or the equivalent.

A second kind of justification move is a deductive argument. By starting with premises the student will accept, a deductive argument leads to the generalization. This kind of justification is often used by mathematics teachers to prove theorems once students have acquired the concept of proof. The teacher employed this move in the dialogue on the quadratic formula. (See utterance 23.)

A variation of the move of deductive argument is used in mathematics classes when, instead of giving a proof, the teacher describes how a proof could be given: "by induction" or "We could assume the lines intersect and then show that this leads to a contradiction."

A third kind of justification move employs an instantiation move. One or more instances are given as evidence that a generalization holds. Until students have learned how to prove a theorem other than by citing authoritative opinion, instantiation moves are the only recourse a mathematics teacher has to convince them that a generalization is true. Thus, a teacher may supply several instances to show that the distributive principle of multiplication over addition is true.

The fourth kind of justification move is related to instantiation. Some teachers challenge their students to find a counterexample. Students seem to accept inability to find a counterexample as indication that a generalization is true. (Were a counterexample found, it would imply a counterinstance and disprove the universal generalization.)

In junior and senior high schools, justification moves are infrequently used. This statement is predicated on the assumption that the set of dialogues on which this analysis of teaching a principle is representative. Semilla's findings (1971) also support this conclusion.

Thought questions

1   Find a counterexample for $\dfrac{ax}{ay} = \dfrac{x}{y}$.

2   A student states that if two lines are perpendicular to the same line, they are parallel. Disprove this by a counterexample.

3   Use a counterexample move to disprove the contention that a false generalization yields only false instances.

4   Justify by instantiation that on the left division does not distribute over addition but does on the right.

5   What sample of instances would you use to convince your students that the metric system is easy to use because it is based on a 10's system?

6   By using a model, describe how seventh-grade students might be convinced that the lateral area of a right, circular cylinder is equal to the product of the circumference of a base and the altitude.

7   What is invalid about using only the instances formed from the positive integers to justify that the laws of exponents for multiplication and division hold for all real numbers?

8   What seems unsound about using only integers to show that the remainder theorem—if a polynomial $p(x)$ is divided by $x - a$, then the constant remainder is $p(a)$—holds for all real numbers a?

9   Give an explanation of why mathematics teachers, even in advanced algebra and trigonometry, do not prove all the theorems. Do you approve of such practice? Why?

10 By instantiation, decide which of the following are or are not immediate implications of "*p* if and only if *q*."

    a If *p*, then *q*.   *d* If not *q*, then not *p*.

    b If *q*, then *p*.   *e* If not *p*, then *q*.

    c If not *p*, then not *q*.   *f* If not *q*, then *p*.

11 Read utterance 3 on page 126. In discussing the dialogue with the teacher, the observer asked why the teacher labeled the lengths of the adjacent sides as he did inasmuch as the student had spoken as he did in utterance 2. The teacher replied that he knew that some students in the general mathematics class confused length and width with adjacent sides and wanted to give this confusion a chance to be expressed in order to correct it. Is this sound pedagogy? Why?

12 An alternative to the way the teacher proceeded, by drawing a parallelogram on the chalkboard and talking in terms of it, is to have each student draw a parallelogram on paper, cut off a triangle analogous to the one the teacher figuratively cut off, place it in the position so as to form a rectangle, and then consider the shape of the resultant figure. (The observer asked the teacher why he did not do this, and the teacher replied that he was afraid that he would run out of class time before he had finished the development.) Do you think this would have been better than the approach the teacher used? Why?

13 It was stated at the conclusion of the last dialogue above that the teacher led the students to see that the length of the base of the parallelogram is the same as the length of the rectangle. Write an imaginary dialogue between a teacher and students in which the teacher develops this and justifies it.

14 Describe how you would use instantiation and the absence of a counterexample to show that the height of a parallelogram is not the same as the length of a side adjacent to the base.

We can summarize this section on moves in teaching a generalization by means of questions you will ask yourself as you make a lesson plan to teach the generalization.

1 How can I introduce the generalization, capture the students' attention and induce them into paying attention and trying to learn it? You can choose appropriately among focus, objective, and motivation moves.

2 If it appears that the students do not comprehend the generalization, how can I clarify (interpret or explain) it for them? You can paraphrase it in language more readily understood, review any of the constituent concepts that you conjecture are the source of lack of comprehension, use instances to show what it means, or analyze it into parts and then explain the parts.

3 Should I show the students that the generalization is true—that is, justify it? If so, how should I do it? You can use enough instances to convince them. You can challenge them to find a counterexample, and their inability to find one will satisfy them. If the generalization is provable within their comprehension, you can prove it. Or you can announce that the generalization is true but you are not going to take time to show that it is. Or you can dispense with all justification.

4 Should I select some activities that will require the students to apply the generalization? Or do I expect them only to comprehend and remember the generalization? If you want them to be able to apply the generalization, you will need some exercises. Perhaps you can think of questions that will require the students to use the generalization.

Expository strategies in teaching a generalization

In teaching the generalization about the order of operations in the previous section, the following sequence of moves appeared: objective (used by the teacher before the dialogue opened), motivation, assertion, four interpretation moves by means of instances, focus, assertion, and an interpretation move by use of an instance. In teaching the quadratic formula, the sequence was: motivation, assertion, interpretation by paraphrasing, counterexample, interpretation by instantiation, justification, instantiation, and application. Can you determine the sequence in the other dialogues?

Considering a strategy as a sequence of moves, as we did for teaching a concept, we find that in teaching a generalization mathematics teachers frequently use a strategy in which the assertion move appears early in the sequence. Thus, in teaching the generalization about the order of operations, the assertion move was the third move. In teaching the quadratic formula and in teaching the conditions necessary and sufficient for a matrix to have an inverse, the assertion move was the second move. In teaching the formula for finding the area of a parallelogram, a student asserted a generalization as a conjecture. This was proven false. Then, by what might be regarded as an instance, the teacher developed the generalization that was asserted. The homework required many application moves.

We shall call a strategy in which the assertion move appears early in the sequence an **expository strategy**. The word *expository* is derived from *exposition*, which means an explanation or interpretation in which is given a commentary that seeks to clarify the meaning and implications of the object of exposition. In teaching a generalization, the generalization is the object of exposition.

An expository strategy commonly used by mathematics teachers is composed of an assertion move, one or more interpretation moves, and several application moves, in that order. Other expository strategies, less frequently used, include a motivational move or a justification move. A simple, expository strategy that seems to be based on the old adage "Tell them what you're going to tell them; tell it to them; then tell them what you told them" is employed. It is composed of an introduction move in which the teacher names the subject of the forthcoming generalization to provide focus, asserts the generalization, and then interprets it by paraphrastic language. There is no application move. Teachers who use this strategy seem only to want students to comprehend and remember the generalization.

The textbook is frequently used during an expository strategy. In some cases, the teacher refers to the assertion of the generalization in the textbook. In others, he or she clarifies the meaning of the generalization by various interpretation moves; the teacher may discuss the instances (designated as "examples" in the textbook) used to clarify the generalization. Some justifications of generalizations are given by using proofs in the textbook while the teacher explains the various steps or queries the students as to the reasons for the statements in the proofs. It is almost always the textbook that is the source of application exercises.

Thought questions

1   Assume that you are planning to teach each of the following generalizations by exposition. Form a strategy for teaching the generalization. Defend it.

   a   A number is divisible by 3 if the sum of its digits is divisible by 3. (For an eighth-grade class.)

   b   The smaller the spaces are between the markings on a ruler, the more precise is the measurement that can be derived by using the ruler. (For a general mathematics class.)

   c   The shape of a triangle cannot be changed without changing the length of one or more sides. (For a seventh-grade class.)

   d   If two lines in the same plane are intersected by a transversal forming equal alternate interior angles, the lines are parallel. (For a tenth-grade geometry class.)

   e   The degree measure of a spherical angle is equal to the degree measure of the arc of the great circle whose pole is the vertex of the angle and determined by the sides of the angle. (For a geometry class.)

   f   If $x + w = y + z$ and $w = z$, then $x = y$. (For the first course in algebra.)

   g   For each real number x, $\sin^2 x + \cos^2 x = 1$. (For the second course in algebra.)

   h   Every convergent sequence is bounded. (For a twelfth-grade mathematics class.)

2   Select a mathematics textbook used in high school. From it choose five topics in which a generalization is taught. For each, determine the strategy used to teach the generalization.

3   Considering all the possible moves in teaching a generalization, show that there are over ten thousand expository strategies.

4   Some expository strategies theoretically possible are illogical and hence pedagogically useless. For example, one cannot knowingly apply a generalization of which he is unaware. Hence the strategy, application followed by assertion, for a generalization unknown to a student is illogical. Suggest other illogical strategies.

5   How would you decide whether to use interpretation moves?

6   How would you decide whether to use a justification move?

7   What factors should be considered in determining whether a strategy should be an expository strategy? What difference will each factor make?

8   What are the advantages and disadvantages of an expository strategy?

9   Why can it be argued that the strategy on teaching how to find the area of a parallelogram is not expository?

Self-test on the competencies

1   State ways of introducing a given generalization.
      Assume that you are planning to teach the uniqueness principle for addition: If $x = y$ and $u = v$, then $x + u = y + v$. Describe how you might introduce it.

2 Interpret a given generalization by paraphrasing it, analyzing it, reviewing one or more of its constituent concepts, or by giving instances of it.

   a Interpret the following generalization by paraphrasing: The distance between any pair of points p and q in the plane is

$$\sqrt{(x_P - x_Q)^2 + (y_P - y_Q)^2}.$$

   b Interpret the following generalization by analysis: $\sqrt[n]{x^n} = |x|$.

   c Tell how you would interpret the following generalization by reviewing the constituent concepts that you think may be a source of confusion: If a line segment AB is parallel to the x-axis, then $m(AB) = |x_B - x_A|$.

   d State the instances you would use to interpret this generalization: The process of carrying when adding in base five notation is like the process of carrying when adding in base ten notation except that fives are carried instead of tens.

3 State a counterexample of a given false generalization.

   a State a counterexample for: If $x < y$, then $ax < ay$.

   b Disprove this by exhibiting a counterexample: Matrix multiplication is commutative.

4 Given a generalization to be taught, choose a way of justifying it.

   a Describe a way of justifying this generalization: For all nonnegative real numbers x and y, and for every positive integer n, $\sqrt[n]{xy} = \sqrt[n]{x}\,\sqrt[n]{y}$.

   b Describe a way of justifying the generalization "The empty set is a subset of every set" that is different from the one you used to justify the generalization in 4a.

5 Design activities that will require students to apply a given generalization.

   Write five exercises that require the application of this generalization: All numbers between 1 and 10 have common logarithms between 0 and 1.

6 Plan an expository strategy for teaching a given generalization.

   Write a lesson plan using an expository strategy for teaching the Binomial Theorem.

References

Gagné, Robert M. "The Learning of Principles." *Analyses of Concept Learning*, ed. by Herbert J. Klausmeier and Chester W. Harris. New York: Academic Press, 1966. Ch. 6.

Dodes, Irving Allen. "Planned Instruction." *The Learning of Mathematics: Its Theory and Practice*, National Council of Teachers of Mathematics Twenty-First Yearbook. Washington, D.C.: National Council of Teachers of Mathematics, 1953. Ch. 10.

Hartung, Maurice L. "Motivation for Education in Mathematics." *The Learning of Mathematics: Its Theory and Practice*, National Council of Teachers of Mathematics Twenty-First Yearbook. Washington, D.C.: National Council of Teachers of Mathematics, 1953.

National Council of Teachers of Mathematics. *Historical Topics for the Mathematics Classroom*, Thirty-First Yearbook of the National Council of Teachers of Mathematics. Washington, D.C.: National Council of Teachers of Mathematics, 1968.

Rosenberg, Herman. "The Art of Generating Interest." *The Teaching of Mathematics*. National Council of Teachers of Mathematics Thirty-Third Yearbook. Washington, D.C.: National Council of Teachers of Mathematics, 1970. Ch. 6.

Runion, Garth. "The Development of Selected Activities in the Teaching of Mathematics." Ph.D. dissertation. Urbana-Champaign: The University of Illinois, 1972.

Semilla, Lilia Z. "Moves and Strategies in a Principle Venture in Secondary School Mathematics." Ph.D. dissertation. Urbana-Champaign: University of Illinois, 1971.

7

Teaching mathematical
generalizations by
guided discovery

Teaching by discovery is probably as old as formal education itself. One of the first and most celebrated discovery methods was exemplified for us by Plato in a dialogue between Socrates and a slave boy. This method, called the Socratic method, involves a dialogue between the teacher and a student in which the student reaches the desired conclusion through a carefully arranged sequence of questions. The dialogue below exemplifies this strategy as the teacher tries to guide the student to realize why a^0 is defined as 1.

Teacher What do we know about the quotient of a nonzero number divided by itself?

Student It's 1.

Teacher How about a^m divided by a^m, assuming a is not 0?

Student It is 1 also.

Teacher If our existing laws of exponents were extended to apply to the case a^m/a^m then what would be the result?

Student It would be a^{m-m} or a^0.

Teacher O.K. What then would be a reasonable definition for a^0?

Student a^0 should be 1!

Although teaching by guided discovery has long been advocated, there seems to be no agreement on just what this method is. Hence in the first section of the chapter we try to establish this concept. We do this largely by contrasting guided discovery with exposition. We find that the position of the assertion move in a sequence of moves is the distinguishing characteristic.

Since the moves used in guided discovery are the same as those in expository teaching, we pass immediately to a consideration of strategies in guided discovery. These are organized in two general categories: inductive and deductive. Several examples of lessons taught by these strategies are given.

Finally, we discuss the relative advantages of expository and guided-discovery strategies so you will be better able to decide under what conditions to choose among them. You will find that theoreticians disagree on their desirability. This is the result, in part, of insufficient evidence from experimental research concerning the relative effectiveness of these two modes of teaching.

> At the conclusion of this chapter, you should be able to demonstrate the following competencies:
>
> 1   State what is meant by guided discovery
>
> 2   Distinguish between inductive and deductive discovery strategies
>
> 3   Plan the teaching of a generalization by an inductive discovery strategy
>
> 4   Plan the teaching of a generalization by a deductive discovery strategy
>
> 5   Plan the teaching of a generalization by a combination of an inductive and a deductive discovery strategy
>
> 6   Given that a particular generalization is to be taught to a given group of students, choose wisely among expository and discovery strategies for teaching it

A concept of guided discovery

One of the first books to use discovery techniques was an arithmetic text by Warren Colburn entitled *First Lessons: Intellectual Arithmetic upon the Inductive Method of Instruction.* It was published in 1821. The text emphasized the use of a sequence of questions in developing mathematical concepts and principles. It resembled the Socratic method in which Socrates, by means of the questions he asked, enabled the pupil to answer the question he originally posed.

Various national committee reports—for example, that of the National Committee on Mathematical Requirements, published in 1923, and the Report of the Joint Committee of the National Council of Teachers of Mathematics and the Mathematical Association of America, published in 1940, as the Fifteenth Yearbook of the National Council of Teachers of Mathematics—advocated the use of discovery methods and advised teachers to employ teaching strategies that would increase student participation. In 1963, the Cambridge Conference suggested that students be made actively involved in mathematics and encouraged to hypothesize anticipated results of problems. Such projects as the Madison Project and the University of

Illinois Committee on School Mathematics have developed materials for learning mathematics that rely heavily on discovery.

Although the terms *discovery* or *guided discovery* are used in these and other writings, their meaning is not always the same. To Jerome Bruner, discovery is a process, a way of approaching problems rather than a product or a particular item of knowledge. It is his contention that processes of discovery can become generalized abilities through the exercise of solving problems and the practice of forming and testing hypotheses. In Bruner's view, learning by discovery is learning *to discover* (1960, p. 612). To Bruner, teaching by discovery consists of confronting a student with a problem or seemingly incongruous situation and having the student seek ways of solving or resolving it. An illustration of how Bruner exemplifies a discovery lesson can be found in his book *Toward a Theory of Instruction* (1966, pp. 59–68). In one illustration a student is confronted with a block x by x, strips 1 by x, and small squares 1 by 1. The problem presented to the student is that he must construct larger squares from one square x by x and as many strips and small squares as necessary. Some possible solutions are given in Figure 7.1. It is hoped that from these experiences the student can conjecture a generalization concerning the square of a binomial. (Do you see the relationship?) Bruner believes a student will acquire a generalized way of attacking problems if he is given experiences similar to this one.

Figure 7.1

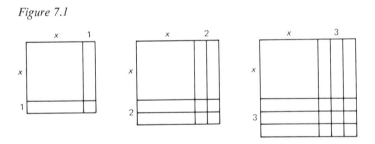

Another advocate of teaching by discovery is Robert Davis, who believes, as Bruner does, that the real essence of discovery is the process of discovering, not the product of the discovery. Like Bruner, Davis would present the student with a problem or, as he might call it, a "crisis dilemma." To illustrate this technique, Davis (1966, p. 119) asks students to find a 2×2 matrix that plays a role analogous to 0 in the rational numbers. Most students suggest the matrix $\begin{bmatrix} 0 & 0 \\ 0 & 0 \end{bmatrix}$. However, when asked to identify a 2×2 matrix analogous to the rational number 1, the students often suggest the matrix $\begin{bmatrix} 1 & 1 \\ 1 & 1 \end{bmatrix}$, in which case a "crisis dilemma" occurs and the students must devise a new plan of attack.

To others, the term *discovery* is used more in the context of discovering something. The attention is on what is to be discovered—a concept, a generalization, or how to do something. Thus Glaser (1966, pp. 14–15) states, "The most prevalent case, learning by discovery is defined usually as teaching an association, a concept, or rule which involves 'discovery' of the association, concept, or rule."

In this chapter, we shall be interested in discovery oriented to a product: the learning of a generalization. The objective of teaching is that students learn some generalization. We can define this kind of teaching by contrasting it with expository teaching. To do this, we start with an example of teaching by discovery. Consider the following transcription of a classroom dialogue. The context is a first-year algebra class in which the students have just learned the concepts of a power, a base, and a positive, integral exponent and how to compute powers. The utterances are numbered for consideration later.

1   **T**   Let's now turn to seeing how powers are multiplied. Let's see if we can discover a rule for multiplying powers of a given base. (*She writes* $2^2 \cdot 2^3$ *on the chalkboard.*) Let's find this product. What does 2^2 mean?

2   **S₁**   Two·square.

3   **T**   Yes, and that means what? How do you find two square?

4   **S₁**   Two times two.

5   **T**   O.K. So for 2^2 I'll write 2×2. And what does 2^3 mean? S₂?

6   **S₂**   Two cube.

7   **T**   And that means . . . ? S₂?

8   **S₂**   Two times two times two.

9   **T**   O.K. So for 2^3 I'll write $2 \times 2 \times 2$. Now we have (*writes on the chalkboard*)

$$2^2 \times 2^3 = (2 \times 2) \times (2 \times 2 \times 2) = 2 \times 2 \times 2 \times 2 \times 2.$$

Now, look at that last product. How many factors of 2 do we have? Count them. Five. And how can we express this product as a power of 2? (*Points to a student.*) All right.

10   **S₃**   Two to the fifth.

11   **T**   Right. (*Writes 2^5 at the end of the chain of equations.*)

$$2^2 \times 2^3 = (2 \times 2) \times (2 \times 2 \times 2) = 2 \times 2 \times 2 \times 2 \times 2 = 2^5$$

Anyone see a relation between this exponent (*points to* 5) and these (*points to the exponents* 2 *and* 3)? S₃?

12   **S₃**   It's the sum.

13   **T**   It's the sum. That is, the exponent of the power that is the product is equal to the sum of the exponents of the two powers being multiplied. Let's do another. Take $3^2 \times 3^5$. What does 3^2 mean?
       (*Dialogue, deleted at this point, is similar to that in utterances* 2 *through* 12.)

14   **T**   It's the sum. So here again we have the exponent of the power that is the product equal to the sum of the exponents of the powers being multiplied. Do you think this would be true for $10^4 \times 10^7$? Try it. Take a piece of paper and work it out. (*Walks up and down the aisles observing the students' work, makes a few comments to individual students.*) Did what we found work here too? (*Some students nod.*) Now take this one. (*She writes $a^5 \times a^4$ on the*

chalkboard and directs a dialogue similar to utterances 2 *through* 12.) So $a^5 \times a^4 = a^9$ and again we see that the exponent of the power equals the sum of the exponents of the powers multiplied. Now let's think. What does a stand for? S_4?

15 S_4 A number.

16 T   A number. A particular number?

17 S_4 No. Any number.

18 T   Right. Any number, that is, every number. So what have we learned? Who can state a rule for finding the product of two powers to the same base? Anyone.

19 S_5 You add the exponents.

20 T   Yeah. That's the general idea. But how about a more precise rule, maybe like: to multiply two powers of the same base? Anyone. S_1?

21 S_1 To multiply two powers of the same base, add their exponents.

22 T   But you haven't told us how to write the product. What's the product?

23 S_1 It's the base whose exponent is the sum of the exponents.

24 T   Well, I suppose you have the general idea, but how about: to multiply two powers of the same base? And remember that you have to have the same base. You can't multiply 2^5 and 3^4 by the rule we discovered. Why not?

25 S_4 Because the bases aren't the same.

26 T   Right. To multiply two powers of the same base, add the exponents and write the product as the base whose exponent is the sum. Like (*writes equation on the chalkboard*) $a^m \times a^n = a^{m+n}$. Do you suppose our rule could be generalized to the product of more than two factors? Three? Five? Any number? S_5.

27 S_5 Yes.

28 T   O.K. Let's try one.
(*The teacher chooses* $2^3 \times 2^4 \times 2^5 \times 2^2$ *and directs a dialogue based on this instance and then the more general instance* $a^4 \times a^2 \times a^4 \times a = a^{11}$, *reminding the students that* $a = a^1$.)

29 T   So we can extend our rule to the product of any number of powers of the same base. Remember, you have to have the same base. Add the exponents and write the product as the power of the base whose exponent is the sum of the exponents of the powers multiplied. Any questions? Now for tomorrow, do exercises 1 through 30 on page 42. You ought to be able to do most of them mentally and write down the answers right away.

In this dialogue, let us see what the teacher was doing with language. In her first utterance, she focused on the topic of discussion: how powers are multiplied. She also stated the objective of the study: to discover a rule or generalization for multiplying powers of a given base. This rule she, of course, knew. She then developed an instance of this rule ($2^2 \times 2^3 = 2^5$), beginning with the third sentence in the first utterance and concluding with the first response in the eleventh utterance. The focusing question in the eleventh utterance served to direct the students' attention to the relevant variables and led to the assertion of what the teacher knew would eventuate as a generalization.

The cycle was repeated twice, using the instances

$$3^2 \times 3^5 = 3^7 \quad \text{and} \quad 10^4 \times 10^7 = 10^{11}$$

obtained by replacing all the variables in

$$a^m \times a^n = a^{m+n}$$

by constants. At the end of the second cycle, the generalization was again stated. It was referred to implicitly at the end of the third cycle.

The teacher in utterance 14 then sought to show the students that the generalization holds for every base. She did this by choosing an instance formed by replacing only the exponents of

$$a^m \times a^n = a^{m+n}$$

by constants and leaving the base a variable. The generalization was formulated again and stated both in English and in mathematical notation in utterance 26. In the formulation, the teacher pointed out a relevant factor: the necessary condition that the bases be the same.

The teacher then stated a subobjective (utterance 26) and chose two instances—a particular instance,

$$2^3 \times 2^4 \times 2^5 \times 2^2 = 2^{14}$$

and the more general instance,

$$a^4 \times a^2 \times a^4 \times a = a^{11}$$

to induce the extension of the generalization previously discovered and asserted. This time (utterance 29) the generalization was stated as a prescription. Finally, homework was assigned that would require the students to apply the generalization, thereby reinforcing their learning.

Notice that in this sequence of moves, the assertion move appeared late, in utterance 13 after a focus, objective, and several instantiation moves. Had the generalization been taught by an expository strategy, the assertion move would have appeared early in the sequence. Hence, let us define a **guided-discovery strategy** as a sequence of moves in which the assertion move, if it appears at all, appears late in the sequence. We say "if it appears at all" because on occasion teachers do not ask students to verbalize (assert) what they have discovered, and the teachers themselves do not assert what should have been discovered. Perhaps they see no reason for having the generalization asserted, for the speed and correctness of the students' responses to the instances is regarded as sufficient evidence that the students have made the discovery. Or perhaps they agree with Gertrude Hendrix (1947) that verbalization interferes with learning and the ability to transfer it to new situations. We shall be saying more about this point of view later in the chapter as we assess the relative advantages and disadvantages of discovery as a general method of teaching.

One or more instantiation moves typically precede the assertion move, if it is used. By adroit questioning the teacher leads the students to abstract the generalization that is the common property of all the instances. Or the teacher starts with knowledge the students have and by skillful questioning leads the students to deduce the generalization. In the next section, we turn to these two general methods of guided discovery. It can be seen that the teacher plays one role when teaching by discovery and another when using an expository strategy. In discovery, the speed at which the class progresses is determined primarily by the learning of the students. The teacher's responsibility is to guide the students as they progress, rather than merely to determine the rate at which material is presented.

Thought questions

1   The strategies considered in this chapter are termed *guided-discovery strategies*. This restriction implies that some strategies are not guided. How would a teacher using a guided-discovery strategy behave differently than a teacher using a discovery strategy?

2   Two of the many characteristics about discovery teaching not included in its definition are having the students actively involved and having a great deal of interaction between the teacher and the student. Why do you think these were not included in the definition? Could these characteristics also be present in expository teaching?

3   Explain why teaching by discovery has long been advocated and yet still not be the dominant strategy of most teachers today.

4   Do the examples of Bruner and Davis satisfy our definition of teaching by discovery? Explain.

5   Does the example of Socratic questioning given earlier satisfy our definition of teaching by guided discovery? Explain.

6   Would you expect a teacher using a guided-discovery strategy to ask more questions than a teacher using an expository strategy? Why?

7   In guided discovery, what moves might logically precede an assertion move?

8   Suppose you intend to teach the rules for testing the divisibility of positive integers by 2, 3, 4, 5, 6, 8, and 9. Propose a sequence for teaching these rules that will make it easy for the students to get hunches as to the rule. Defend this sequence.

9   Notice in utterance 9 of the dialogue that the teacher says, "How many factors of 2 do we have?" Teachers do not always say what they mean. This question is ambiguous. What does she mean? Also, in utterance 29 she says, "You ought to be able to do most of them mentally." What did she mean?

10   Beginning in utterance 20, the teacher seeks to get a precise statement of the rule. Was this wise? Or could she have expected the students to know what was meant by the answer of S_1 in utterance 21?

Inductive discovery strategies

Mathematics teachers use two general discovery strategies. One is inductive in nature and the other is deductive. In this section we shall discuss inductive strategy and present lessons exemplifying induction. An inductive argument comprises two parts. The first consists of evidence that claims to support the conclusion or the second part of the argument. The conclusion of an inductive argument does not necessarily follow from the supporting evidence. The evidence may make the conclusion credible to a greater or lesser extent, depending on the nature of the evidence, but it cannot prove the proposition that it claims to support. For example, the fact that 3, 5, 7, 11, and 13 are all prime numbers makes the generalization that all prime numbers are odd plausible but in no way proves it. One always runs the risk in an inductive argument that the very next instance examined may disprove the concluding generalization. Hence, a conclusion reached by induction must be qualified by words such as "it seems reasonable," "most likely," or "probably."

An argument by induction can be characterized as an inference from the examined to the unexamined. In a mathematics classroom the evidence examined consists of specific examples or instances. Consider the following discovery strategy.

1	T	Today we are going to examine a relation that has challenged mathematicians for a long time. To begin, let us consider the following statements.

$$20 = 17 + 3$$
$$22 = 19 + 3$$
$$24 = 17 + 7$$
$$26 = 13 + 13$$
$$28 = 17 + 11$$

		Does anyone notice a pattern in these statements?
2	S_1	The numbers on the left side are all even numbers in the twenties.
3	T	O.K. How about the addends on the righthand side?
4	S_2	Both of them are odd.
5	T	True. But can you say anything else about them, besides the fact that they are odd?
6	S_2	Well, they are all prime.
7	T	Very good. Can someone summarize the observations of S_1 and S_2?
8	S_3	Any even number in the twenties is equal to two prime numbers added together.
9	T	Do you think this would be true for other even numbers? S_4.
10	S_4	I'm not sure.
11	T	Let's try some other examples, say 30 or 10 or 52.
12	S_5	30 is equal to—27 plus 3.
13	T	Does that follow the same pattern, S_6?
14	S_6	No—27 isn't prime.
15	S_5	That's right. I forgot. O.K. 30 is equal to 17 plus 13.
16	T	How about 10 and 52?

17	S$_7$	10 is equal to 7 plus 3, and 52 is equal to 47 plus 5.
18	T	All right. Everybody pick three even numbers and try it. (*Pause.*) Has anybody found an even number that can't be expressed in this way?
19	S$_8$	4 is equal to 2 plus 2, but 2 is not an odd prime.
20	T	How about 3 plus 1? This equals 4.
21	S$_8$	One isn't prime either.
22	T	O.K. How about 6? Did anybody try that?
23	S$_9$	That's easy. 3 plus 3.
24	T	Will someone venture a final statement concerning even numbers and odd primes?
25	S$_{10}$	Well, any even number greater than 4 is equal to two odd primes added together.
26	T	Very good. This is a famous statement called Goldbach's conjecture. Although mathematicians have been unable to prove it, no one has yet found a counterexample. For this reason we tend to believe that the statement is true.

There are two processes inherent in an inductive discovery lesson: abstracting and generalizing. A student makes an abstraction when he or she realizes properties common to a set of exemplars. In short, the student sees the commonality among the differences. Generalizing occurs when a student predicts that a relationship that holds for a particular sample will also be true for a more inclusive sample.

In the preceding dialogue, the first abstraction is verbalized by S$_1$ in utterance 2. This student abstracted that the commonality of the elements in the set {20, 22, 24, 26, 28} is that they are all even and in the same decade. A second abstraction is verbalized in utterance 4, where the student notices that the pairs of addends consist of odd numbers. Can you identify another situation in the dialogue where abstractions are verbalized?

In the dialogue above, generalizing occurs when S$_{10}$ in utterance 25 extends the original generalization of S$_3$ to the set of all even numbers greater than 4. That is, S$_3$ asserts the following proposition: any even number in the twenties is equal to the sum of two prime numbers. S$_{10}$ then generalizes by making a similar assertion concerning a more inclusive set—the set of all even numbers greater than 4. Is the set {20, 22, 24, 26, 28} a subset of set $\{x | x > 4 \text{ and } x \text{ is even}\}$?

As in the previous lesson, the following discovery lesson also involves abstracting and generalizing. Assuming students have some proficiency in graphing, the teacher begins by asking students to graph the following equation:

$$|x| + |y| = 1$$

Students obtain a graph similar to the one in Figure 7.2 by assigning values to x and calculating the corresponding values for y. Students could then be asked to graph

$$|x| + |y| = 2$$

Figure 7.2

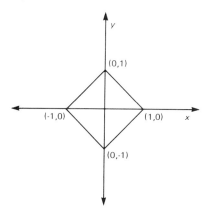

perhaps on the same set of axes. (The reader is expected to draw this graph.) The teacher might then ask students to graph other equations, such as

$$|x| + |y| = 3$$
$$|x| + |y| = 4$$

If and when students have abstracted the pattern, they should be able to describe or construct rapidly the graphs of equations similar to this one:

$$|x| + |y| = 7\tfrac{4}{9}$$

In some cases, the abstraction may be verbalized as a generalization by the student. If the generalization is correct, the teacher knows that the student has made the correct discovery. However, a teacher need not rely on a verbalization to infer that a student has "seen the pattern." Nonverbal evidence, such as a quick and correct response to an instance provides confirmation. Thus, in the case of graphing $|x| + |y| = a$, $a > 0$, rapidly drawing the correct graph of $|x| + |y| = 7\tfrac{4}{9}$ provides evidence that the students have generalized the pattern to all instances of $|x| + |y| = a$, $a > 0$. Notice that the instance used as a test is one whose graph cannot be quickly sketched unless the student has discovered the pattern.

Wills (1970) calls an instance to which a student can apply the generalization to be discovered, only if he has discovered it, a **criterion task**. The criterion task should be difficult enough so that it cannot be done quickly and correctly unless the student has become aware of the pattern. Thus, in graphing instances of $|x| + |y| = a$, $a > 0$, graphing $|x| + |y| = 7\tfrac{4}{9}$ was a criterion task because the student who had not discovered the pattern could not quickly and correctly sketch or describe the graph of this equation. Criterion tasks can be used by teachers to infer whether students have made the discovery. Performance on these tasks is nonverbal evidence of success in discovering a generalization in an inductive strategy.

In having students generalize, teachers should provide ample instances for consideration. Students are prone to generalize from too small a sample. Consider the expression

$$n^2 - n + 11$$

When the replacement set for n is $\{1, 2, 3, 4, 5, 6, 7, 8, 9, 10\}$, the result is a prime number. At this point many students are quick to generalize that all numbers of the form $n^2 - n + 11$ are prime. When n is any multiple of 11, however, the resulting number is not prime. (Try it for $n = 11$, 22, and 33.)

Consider the *maximum* number of regions R formed by drawing all the possible chords between a specified number of points n on the circumference of a circle. For example, if $n = 1$, then no chords can be drawn and there is one region. If $n = 2$, one chord and hence two regions result. If $n = 3$, then three chords are possible and four regions result. If $n = 4$, the number of regions is eight. These relations are illustrated in Figure 7.3. Can you conjecture a relationship between n and R? A reasonable conjecture is

$$R = 2^{n-1} \quad \text{(for } n > 0\text{)}$$

We can test this by constructing a model for $n = 5$ points. (Count the regions in Figure 7.4). It appears, then, that the conjecture $R = 2^{n-1}$ is correct. We leave it to the reader to test the conjecture when $n = 6$.

Even mathematicians may make erroneous conclusions when generalizing from an inadequate sample. A well-known instance of this occurred when the French mathematician Pierre de Fermat (1601–1665) conjected that numbers of the form $n_t = 2^{2^t} + 1$ are prime. His conjecture was based on the cases for $t = 0, 1, 2, 3$, and 4, which results in the prime numbers 3, 5, 17, 257, and 65,537, respectively. As you can see, however, the next value of n when $t = 5$ is very large, and Fermat was unable with the

Figure 7.3

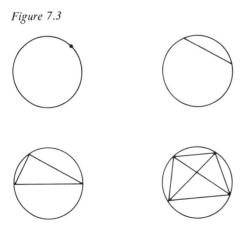

Figure 7.4

techniques he had available to determine whether n_5 is prime. He conjectured on the basis of his sample that all such values of n are prime. The interesting result is that the only values for t for which $2^{2^t} + 1$ are known to be prime are $t = 0, 1, 2, 3$, and 4! It has been determined that for $5 \leq t \leq 16n$ results in a composite number. The case for $t = 17$ has not yet been resolved because the very large number requires a tremendous amount of computer time for analysis.

This is not to say that students should be discouraged to venture hypotheses. Teachers should continually encourage students to examine their guesses critically and to test a large variety of cases before believing their hypotheses are correct. Any conclusion in mathematics based on inductive reasoning is, of course, at best credible only until such time as it has been established deductively. If mathematicians and students were restricted to deductive investigations, however (if guessing were eliminated), then the appeal and the advancement of mathematics would be adversely affected.

Following are examples of discovery lessons using abstracting and generalizing. These are concerned with knowledge that students usually encounter in school mathematics. The first lesson deals with subject matter taken from algebra, the next from geometry, and the next two lessons with knowledge appropriate for junior high school students. The reader is expected to participate in the discussions.

Lesson 1

An algebraic generalization is the focus of this discovery lesson. A teacher might begin the lesson by asking students to find the following products. (The reader is also expected to find these products.)

$$5 \times 5 = ? \qquad 8 \times 8 = ?$$
$$6 \times 4 = ? \qquad 7 \times 9 = ?$$

$$7 \times 7 = ? \qquad 9 \times 9 = ?$$
$$6 \times 8 = ? \qquad 10 \times 8 = ?$$

$$4 \times 4 = ? \qquad 6 \times 6 = ?$$
$$3 \times 5 = ? \qquad 7 \times 5 = ?$$

Have you made an abstraction? If students *have* observed a pattern, then they should be able to do the following criterion tasks very quickly without the aid of paper and pencil.

If $20 \times 20 = 400$, then what is 19×21?

If $25 \times 25 = 625$, then what is 26×24?

If $30 \times 30 = 900$, then what is 29×31?

If students can answer these questions readily (what might a teacher do if students cannot?), then the following problems might be presented:

$6 \times 6 = ?$	$7 \times 7 = ?$
$4 \times 8 = ?$	$9 \times 5 = ?$
$8 \times 8 = ?$	$4 \times 4 = ?$
$6 \times 10 = ?$	$6 \times 2 = ?$

To determine whether students have seen the pattern for these instances, a teacher might ask the following questions:

If $19 \times 19 = 361$, then what is 21×17?

If $30 \times 30 = 900$, then what is 28×32?

If $40 \times 40 = 1,600$, then what is 38×42?

If students can answer these and other criterion questions rapidly, then the teacher can be reasonably assured that the students have made the desired abstraction. If so, the teacher might then turn to the following problems:

If $30 \times 30 = 900$, then $33 \times 27 = ?$

If $40 \times 40 = 1,600$, then $37 \times 43 = ?$

If $25 \times 25 = 625$, then $22 \times 28 = ?$

If students fail to answer these or similar questions without using paper and pencil, the teacher might provide additional instances for their consideration as, for example,

$6 \times 6 = ?$	$5 \times 5 = ?$
$3 \times 9 = ?$	$2 \times 8 = ?$
$7 \times 7 = ?$	$8 \times 8 = ?$
$10 \times 4 = ?$	$5 \times 11 = ?$

Eventually students should be able to answer questions such as:

If $60 \times 60 = 3,600$, then $64 \times 56 = ?$

If $70 \times 70 = 4,900$, then $65 \times 75 = ?$

If $18 \times 18 = 324$, then $14 \times 22 = ?$

If $40 \times 40 = 1,600$, then $33 \times 47 = ?$

If at some point students cannot respond quickly to the questions, the teacher can have the students return to simpler questions involving single-digit numbers.

Eventually, the teacher can lead students to the more general case, which, for students not accustomed to conventional variables, can be stated as follows,

$$\square \times \square = \square^2$$

and hence,

$$(\square - \triangle) \times (\square + \triangle) = \square^2 - \triangle^2$$

For students accustomed to conventional variables, the following equation might evolve:

$$x \cdot x = x^2$$

and hence,

$$(x + y)(x - y) = x^2 - y^2$$

In this lesson, how could a teacher obtain evidence that students had made the discovery without asking them to verbalize the abstraction? Do you think that students who can verbalize the abstraction, either in English or in mathematical notation, have reached a higher level of understanding than students who have seen the pattern and can do criterial tasks?

Lesson 2

The following geometry lesson could take place after students have learned the concepts of parallel lines and parallelogram. This lesson is designed to help students discover some properties of parallelograms. Each student needs a ruler and a protractor.

The teacher could begin with a review of parallel lines and parallelogram. If the students are able to draw or construct parallel lines, then they should be asked to draw or construct four or five parallelograms. If students are not able to draw or construct parallelograms accurately, the teacher can work with the class on this skill or hand out worksheets containing parallelograms already drawn.

The students should then be encouraged to measure the angles and sides of each parallelogram. The students should record their measurements directly on the figures. After making their measurements, they should be encouraged to examine their data for patterns. (What are some abstractions that students could make?) Each student could then make a note of his or her findings on another paper and exchange the sheet containing their parallelograms with another student. Each should then check his or her abstractions against these "new" data.

Figure 7.5

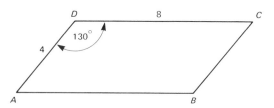

Students should now be ready to form some generalizations. Each student should be able to write a number of statements similar to "If a quadrilateral is a parallelogram then . . . ." If the teacher wishes to delay this verbalization yet provide criterion tasks, the students could be given worksheets containing figures like the one in Figure 7.5 and students could be asked to find the missing data.

A subsequent lesson could use this same approach to investigate the properties of diagonals of parallelograms, including rectangles, rhombi, and squares. Suppose that in drawing parallelograms students draw only rectangles or squares. What words of caution would you have for them concerning their generalizations?

Lesson 3

This lesson could be presented to seventh-grade students at the beginning of a unit on number theory. The teacher could present most of the "drawings" for this lesson on the chalkboard or overhead projector or have each student make an individual set of diagrams.

The teacher could begin by telling the students that they are going to investigate properties of the counting numbers by drawing "dot" pictures of each number. Each number should be represented by a rectangular array of dots equal in number to that counting number.

The teacher could represent the first three counting numbers as follows:

```
     .      . .    . . .
'1       2        3
```

The rectangular arrays are 1 × 1, 1 × 2, and 1 × 3, respectively.

The next counting number can be represented by more than one rectangular array. Both should be drawn

```
    . . . .   or   . .
                   . .
```

The teacher could then have the class proceed (either collectively or individually) to draw all the rectangular arrays for the first twenty-five or thirty counting numbers.

At this point the teacher can encourage students to examine their data and draw conclusions. (What are some probable abstractions that students might make?) If students seem to need direction or encouragement, questions such as the following could be posed:

1 What is the relation between a counting number and the number of rows and columns of its rectangular arrays?

2 Identify some numbers that have more than one rectangular array.

3 What do 11, 13, 17, and 7 have in common? Are there any other numbers that share this characteristic?

4 Are all the numbers you listed in response to question 3 odd?

5 Which numbers can be represented by a rectangular array that is a square?

What is to be learned from each of these five questions? In response to question 3, students may include the number 1. Is this inclusion correct? If 1 is classified the same way as other numbers, such as 11, 13, 17, and 7, what problems arise in discussions of figures? Is 1 a correct response to question 5? Students (and perhaps the reader) have been making abstractions involving the rectangular arrays. At what point in the lesson should a teacher label the various abstractions that students make? That is, when should the teacher introduce the proper terminology?

Lesson 4

The following lesson is also concerned with some ideas from number theory that junior high school students often find interesting. For the lesson to be effective, students must be knowledgeable about prime numbers and divisors.

The lesson could begin by asking students to find the number of divisors for each of the first twenty-five counting numbers. To facilitate our discussion, the number of divisors is given in Table 7.1. Several interesting questions

Table 7.1

Number (n)	Number of divisors of n	Number (n)	Number of divisors of n
1	1	14	4
2	2	15	4
3	2	16	5
4	3	17	2
5	2	18	6
6	4	19	2
7	2	20	6
8	4	21	4
9	3	22	4
10	4	23	2
11	2	24	8
12	6	25	3
13	2		

can arise from this chart. How many numbers have exactly one divisor? Is this number then unique? Suppose someone claimed to have found some number, say 5,627,321, and claimed that it has exactly one divisor. Could you refute the claim?

What kind of numbers have exactly two divisors? Can you characterize the numbers that have exactly three divisors? Exactly four divisors? What conjecture can you form concerning numbers with an odd number of divisors? Notice the following pattern,

$$18 = 9 \times 2$$
number of divisors of 18 = (number of divisors of 9)
$$\times \text{ (number of divisors of 2)}$$

$$20 = 4 \times 5$$
number of divisors of 20 = (number of divisors of 4)
$$\times \text{ (number of divisors of 5)}$$

$$24 = 8 \times 3$$
number of divisors of 24 = (number of divisors of 8)
$$\times \text{ (number of divisors of 3)}$$

Does this pattern hold for other cases? Students can form a variety of conjectures from studying the accompanying table. Can they give at least an intuitive proof of their conjectures? If a proof is too difficult, can the students test their conjectures for numbers not in the original sample? For example, students might observe that numbers with three divisors are of the form p^2 where p is prime. Can this generalization be put in the form of an "if and only if" statement? We suggest the reader test some numbers to explore and analyze this and other conjectures.

Thought questions

1   Discover the maximum number of regions R that result from n lines intersecting a circle. (Hint: create instances and generalize.)

2   Outline a lesson designed to let students discover, through generalizing, that the number of subsets of a set containing n elements is 2^n.

3   Construct an inductive lesson designed to help students discover the relation between the constants m and b in the equation $y = mx + b$ and its graph.

4   Consider the equation that Wills (1970, p. 287) uses:

$$y = \sqrt{x^2 + 10x + 25} - \sqrt{x^2 - 10x + 25}$$

Find the y values when x is replaced by 0, 1, 2, 3, 4, and 5. What conjecture can you form concerning the relation of x and y? Test your conjecture using larger values of x. Do you now wish to revise your original conjecture? Can you prove your result?

5   If students constructed the chart given in Lesson 4, what abstractions would you expect them to make? What generalizations could follow from these abstractions?

6   Select a generalization from high school geometry and one from high school algebra that can be taught by discovery. Construct an inductive discovery lesson for each of these items of knowledge.

Deductive discovery strategies

When a teacher talks about teaching by discovery he is often referring to what we have termed *inductive discovery*. However, discovery teaching does not have to be inductive. Since mathematics consists of a network of interlocking deductive arguments, it would seem reasonable to assume that deduction could play a substantial role in the mathematics classroom. It is, therefore, natural that teachers present premises known to students and ask for implications that follow from them. The essence of deductive discovery is that students be presented with certain mathematical concepts and principles and encouraged to derive additional mathematical knowledge previously unknown to them.

Inductive and deductive discovery require that students be active in acquiring knowledge not previously known to them. In inductive discovery the students do this from examples and instances, by guessing at the properties common among the differences. In deductive discovery they do this by making logical deductions from previously accepted knowledge.

In both kinds of discovery, the teacher necessarily guides them. In an inductive strategy, the teacher presents instances in a carefully chosen sequence to facilitate abstraction of the pattern. He or she may ask questions to direct the students' attention to relevant variables and possible relations. In a deductive strategy, the teacher tends to ask a sequence of questions that guide the students' thinking toward deducing the generalization that is the object of the lesson. At the outset of this chapter, we gave an example of a guided-deductive strategy. Notice the sequence of questions the teacher asked to lead the student to propose that a^0 (where $a \neq 0$) should be defined as 1. The ability to ask a pointed sequence of questions is acquired through practice. We give some examples of deductive discovery lessons below.

Lesson 5

On page 138, we discussed a situation Robert Davis refers to as a "crisis dilemma." That "crisis dilemma" occurs when students are expected to find a 2×2 matrix analogous to the rational number 1. Most students conjecture that the desired matrix is $\begin{bmatrix} 1 & 1 \\ 1 & 1 \end{bmatrix}$. The counterexample here disproves this conjecture:

$$\begin{bmatrix} 4 & 1 \\ 0 & 3 \end{bmatrix} \times \begin{bmatrix} 1 & 1 \\ 1 & 1 \end{bmatrix} = \begin{bmatrix} 5 & 5 \\ 3 & 3 \end{bmatrix}$$

What then is the desired matrix?

Consider the matrix $\begin{bmatrix} a & b \\ c & d \end{bmatrix}$, whose determinant is not 0. If the desired matrix is $\begin{bmatrix} e\,f \\ g\,h \end{bmatrix}$, then

$$\begin{bmatrix} a\,b \\ c\,d \end{bmatrix}\begin{bmatrix} e\,f \\ g\,h \end{bmatrix} = \begin{bmatrix} a\,b \\ c\,d \end{bmatrix}$$

Students can then be led to derive the four equations

1    $ae + bg = a$
2    $af + bh = b$
3    $ce + dg = c$
4    $cf + dh = d$

They can then solve equations 1 and 3 for e and g using Cramer's rule:

$$e = \frac{\begin{vmatrix} a & b \\ c & d \end{vmatrix}}{\begin{vmatrix} a & b \\ c & d \end{vmatrix}} = 1 \quad \text{provided} \quad \begin{vmatrix} a & b \\ c & d \end{vmatrix} \neq 0$$

$$g = \frac{\begin{vmatrix} a & a \\ c & c \end{vmatrix}}{\begin{vmatrix} a & b \\ c & d \end{vmatrix}} = 0 \quad \text{provided} \quad \begin{vmatrix} a & b \\ c & d \end{vmatrix} \neq 0$$

Likewise, when students solve equations 2 and 4 for f and h, they will obtain

$$f = 0 \quad \text{and} \quad h = 1$$

Hence, the desired matrix is $\begin{bmatrix} 1\,0 \\ 0\,1 \end{bmatrix}$. Students can then check their discovery by trying several examples such as these:

$$\begin{bmatrix} -4\,0 \\ 3\,1 \end{bmatrix}\begin{bmatrix} 1\,0 \\ 0\,1 \end{bmatrix} = \begin{bmatrix} -4\,0 \\ 3\,1 \end{bmatrix}$$

$$\begin{bmatrix} 1\,0 \\ 0\,1 \end{bmatrix}\begin{bmatrix} -4\,0 \\ 3\,1 \end{bmatrix} = \begin{bmatrix} -4\,0 \\ 3\,1 \end{bmatrix}$$

Lesson 6

The lesson uses the Socratic method discussed at the beginning of this chapter to instruct students about the determinant formed by the coefficients of the variables of two equations of parallel lines. Socratic questioning is a form of deductive discovery in which the teacher uses leading questions to guide the student toward deducing a particular conclusion. The dialogue below is atypical in that the students have immediate responses to the questions. The sequence can be used in typical classroom settings, however, even though students may need additional guidance. Assume that the dialogue occurs in a second-year algebra class in which the students are solving systems of equations through the use of determinants.

T   In applying Cramer's rule for solving this system of equations:

$$3x - 2y = 6$$
$$-9x + 6y = -3$$

what did you obtain, S_1?

S_1 For $D(x)$ I got 30, for $D(y)$ I got 45, but for the denominator I got 0.

T   Correct. What is your solution, then?

S_1 I don't know.

T   Can anybody tell me what the solution is?

S_2 I don't think we have one.

T   Why not?

S_2 Well 30/0 and 45/0 can't be calculated.

T   That's right. Since we can't divide by 0, we have no solution. Can someone give me a geometric interpretation of this result?

S_3 Well, the graphs of those lines might be parallel.

T   (*Other students agree.*) O.K. If we have a pair of parallel lines, must the determinant formed from the coefficients of the variables always be equal to 0?
(*Students venture different guesses.*)

T   All right. Let's investigate the general case now. Consider $a_1x + b_1y = c$. Give me an equation of a line parallel to this line.

S_4 $ma_1x + mb_1y = d$

T   (*Writes both equations on chalkboard.*) What's m?

S_4 Any real number except 0.

T   O.K. Why did you say d and not mc_1?

S_4 Because then we would have merely represented the same line.

T   Very good! What is the determinant formed from the coefficients of x and y for these two parallel lines?

S_5 $a_1 \cdot mb_1 - ma_1 \cdot b_1$

T   And what does that equal?

S_5 Zero.

T   What does this tell us then? What have we established?

What generalization would you expect the students to assert? What guiding questions did the teacher ask? Was this guidance provided to such an extent that the students were passive?

Lesson 7

This might begin with the teacher drawing the unit circle and central angle θ with its initial side on the positive x-axis. The students could then be asked to express the coordinates of the point formed by the intersection of the unit circle and the terminal side of the central angle in terms of trigonometric

Figure 7.6

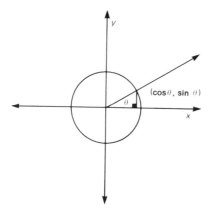

functions of θ. (It is assumed that students are accustomed to doing this.) The teacher could then ask the students to examine a diagram similar to the one in Figure 7.6 and to develop an equation relating $\sin \theta$ and $\cos \theta$.

What relation is the teacher asking the students to discover? If the students could not develop the indicated equations, what hint might the teacher give? Does the equation hold for all values of θ? If so, what is this equation called?

Lesson 8

This lesson is designed for junior high school students. The lesson is intended to help students discover a formula for the area of a circle, given that the students know formulas for the area of a parallelogram and the circumference of a circle.

The lesson can begin by the students or the teacher dividing a circular piece of paper into four congruent parts and then dividing these into two congruent parts each, for a total of eight parts, as illustrated in Figure 7.7.

Figure 7.7

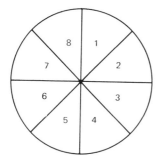

Figure 7.8

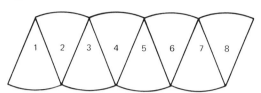

These eight parts can then be rearranged and placed as in Figure 7.8. (To be more effective the odd-numbered and even-numbered parts might be given different colors.) What geometric shape does this figure resemble? In what way does Figure 7.8 differ from the geometric shape? If the circular region were divided into 16, 32, 64, or for that matter any number of congruent parts and placed as shown in the figure, the resulting figure would more closely resemble a parallelogram. (Why can we then use the formula for the area of a parallelogram to find the area of the figure above?)

What is the formula for the area of a parallelogram? In the diagram, how can the base of the "parallelogram" be expressed in terms of the circumference of the original circle? What is the height of the "parallelogram"? What formula can then be given for the area of the "parallelogram" and, hence, the area of the original circle? From this formula, can the more standard formula for the area of a circle ($A = \pi r^2$) be derived?

As we pointed out at the beginning of this section and as we can see from the lessons above, the key to success in a deductive discovery strategy is the teacher's ability to ask a sequence of leading questions that will guide the students to deduce the generalization the teacher wishes to teach. In forming the sequence, the teacher will have to be careful not to use implications the slower students cannot follow. If in doubt as to what question to ask, it is probably better to err on the side of deliberately choosing implications that are readily apparent than those which are less apparent. The brighter students probably will not be offended, and the slower students will profit from being able to follow the development.

Thought questions

1 Assume you wish to teach this generalization: For all rational numbers x, $y \neq 0$, w, and $z \neq 0$, if $x/y = w/z$, then $xz = yw$. You decide to use a deductive discovery strategy.

    a Suggest a motivation move you might use.

    b Suggest a focus move you might use.

    c You write the equation $x/y = w/z$ on the chalkboard. Would it be advisable immediately to ask what restrictions have to be placed on the values of y and z? Why? Suggest another initial question that could be asked.

    d You say, "To get rid of the fractions in this equation, what operation can we use?" None of the students seem to know. What might you do next?

2   In a seventh-grade class you are teaching, you wish to teach the transitivity of set inclusion by a deductive discovery strategy. Should you begin with three particular sets for which the relation holds? Why? Design a deductive discovery strategy you might use.

3   Suppose you decide to use a deductive discovery strategy to teach the generalization that the sum of the roots of the quadratic equation $ax^2 + bx + c = 0$, $a \neq 0$ is $(-b/a)$ to students in a second course in algebra.
   a   State an objective move that you might use that will not give away the generalization to be discovered.
   b   After introducing the topic in some way, what would be a good initial question to ask? Why?
   c   You ask, "What are the two roots of the quadratic equation, $ax^2 + bx + c = 0$?" No student knows the answer. What should you do?
   d   When you ask question c, you infer from the show of raised hands that most of the students know the answer. What should you do?
   e   You suggest to the students that they add the two roots

$$\frac{-b + \sqrt{b^2 - 4ac}}{2a} \quad \text{and} \quad \frac{-b - \sqrt{b^2 - 4ac}}{2a},$$

   but some students do not get the right answer $(-b/a)$. What should you do? Defend your choice.

Strategies involving either induction or deduction or both

Often a generalization can be taught effectively through an inductive or a deductive discovery or a combination of inductive and deductive discovery. If a teacher decides to teach by discovery, then several factors might be considered in selecting and planning the presentation. The mathematical and intellectual competencies of the students together make one such factor. Deductive discovery requires an ability to base logical deductions on content previously studied. Inductive discovery requires an ability to induce a pattern. Both are demanding of students.

Another factor to be considered is the nature of the subject matter. Some generalizations lend themselves to one kind of discovery rather than the other. The teacher should also consider which style of discovery is most commensurate with his or her own individual style of teaching. Some teachers prefer and can use one method more effectively than another. As a teacher you should experiment to determine which method you think is more effective in your teaching of a particular item of knowledge. The following lessons illustrate how inductive or deductive discovery can be used to teach generalizations.

Lesson 9

In lesson 2 an inductive discovery was discussed in which the students were to discover properties of parallelograms. These same properties could also be discovered deductively. The teacher could begin by drawing a diagonal of

Figure 7.9

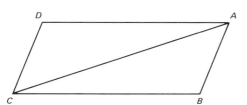

a parallelogram as shown in Figure 7.9. From the definition of a parallel-ogram, it can be deduced that $\triangle ADC \cong \triangle CBA$. (Why?) Once the congruence is established, what properties of parallelograms can then be deduced or discovered? If the other diagonal $\overline{DB}$ is drawn, what triangles would then be congruent? What further properties of parallelograms and their diagonals can then be established?

Lesson 10

In lesson 7 a deductive approach led to the discovery of the generalization

$$\sin^2 \theta + \cos^2 \theta = 1$$

This generalization can also be discovered inductively by having students construct tables similar to Table 7.2. The choice of the angles and the extent to which the tables are completed is a matter for the teacher's judgment.

Table 7.2

θ	$\sin \theta$	$\cos \theta$	$\sin^2 \theta$	$\cos^2 \theta$	$\sin^2 \theta + \cos^2 \theta$
0°					
30°					
120°					
225°					
17°					
155°					
324°					

Lesson 11

This lesson deals with discovering a relation between the sum and product of the roots of a quadratic equation and the coefficients a, b, and c of the equation

$$ax^2 + bx + c = 0, \quad a \neq 0$$

That is, if r_1 and r_2 are the roots of the equation, then what expression, in terms of a, b, and c, can be given for $r_1 \cdot r_2$ and $r_1 + r_2$? First, let us consider how this can be discovered inductively.

In order to discover, inductively, the desired relationship, instances must be generated from which the students can generalize. Equations can be selected by either the teacher or the students for which the roots have been previously determined. Information from these instances can be organized in a table like Table 7.3. On the basis of the instances in this table, what generalizations might you expect from students?

Table 7.3

	r_1	r_2	a	b	c	$r_1 \cdot r_2$	$r_1 + r_2$
$x^2 - x - 12 = 0$	4	−3	1	−1	−12	−12	+1
$x^2 + 3x - 10 = 0$	−5	+2	1	+3	−10	−10	−3
$x^2 + 9x + 20 = 0$	−5	−4	1	+9	+20	+20	−9
$x^2 - 15x + 50 = 0$	10	5	1	−15	+50	+50	+15

Table 7.4

	r_1	r_2	a	b	c	$r_1 \cdot r_2$	$r_1 + r_2$
$2x^2 + 3x - 20 = 0$	$2\frac{1}{2}$	−4	2	+3	−20	−10	$-1\frac{1}{2}$
$6x^2 + 17x + 12 = 0$	$-\frac{4}{3}$	$-\frac{3}{2}$	6	17	12	2	$-\frac{17}{6}$
$2x^2 - 9x + 7 = 0$	$\frac{7}{2}$	1	2	−9	7	$\frac{7}{2}$	$\frac{9}{2}$

Now consider the instances in Table 7.4. In what ways are these equations different from the previous equations? What generalization can now be formed? Is this generalization likely to be a revision of the previous one? Students might now test their revised generalization in the special cases where $b = 0$ or $c = 0$, such as

$$2x^2 - 50 = 0$$

$$x^2 - 3x = 0$$

$$3x^2 = 0$$

If, at some point in the lesson, the students do not abstract the intended relations among the given instances, then additional instances could be generated for their consideration.

To discover this same item of knowledge deductively, the teacher might begin by reminding the students that in general

$$r_1 = \frac{-b + \sqrt{b^2 - 4ac}}{2a} \quad \text{and} \quad r_2 = \frac{-b - \sqrt{b^2 - 4ac}}{2a}$$

The teacher then might ask the students to find an expression for $r_1 + r_2$ and $r_1 \cdot r_2$ in terms of the constants a, b, and c. What are these relations?

Figure 7.10

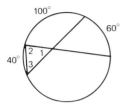

Lesson 12

The following discovery lesson also involves inductive and deductive thinking. It is aimed at helping students discover a particular geometric generalization. It is assumed that the students possess the following prerequisite knowledge:

1   The sum of the measures of the angles of a triangle is 180°.

2   The measure of an angle inscribed in a circle is equal to one-half the measure of its intercepted arc.

The lesson could begin by the teacher asking students to find the measure of $\angle 1$, given the information in Figure 7.10. The students can deduce that $m \angle 2 = 80$ and $m \angle 3 = 50$ and, hence, $m \angle 1 = 180 - 80 - 50 = 50$. They can then find the measure of $\angle 1$ in other such diagrams as illustrated in Figure 7.11.

The teacher can ask leading questions to help students abstract the relation between the measure of the angle formed by two chords intersecting inside a circle and the measures of the arcs intercepted by the indicated angle and its corresponding vertical angle. Do you see the relation?

Figure 7.11

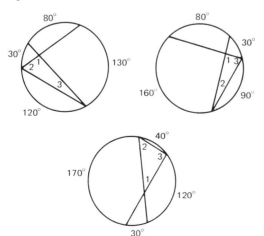

Thought questions

1   Lessons 7 and 10 could be extended to discover additional trigonometric identities. State the identities and discuss what strategies might be used to teach them.

2   Write a hypothetical classroom dialogue in which Socratic questioning is used to guide students to realize that imaginary roots of quadratic equations having real coefficients come in conjugate pairs.

3   State the pro's and con's of each of the inductive and deductive approaches to teaching lessons 9, 10, and 11. In your answer you may wish to define the nature of the students to whom the lessons are directed.

4   Outline a discovery lesson (inductive or deductive) for the following item of knowledge: The area of a rhombus is one-half the product of the measures of the diagonals.

5   Select a generalization and outline inductive and deductive discovery lessons for teaching it.

6   In lesson 12, how does deductive reasoning play a role in the discovery process? What role would inductive reasoning play if the lesson were completed and the students made the desired discovery?

Planning and conducting discovery lessons

In this section we shall present considerations or maxims for planning and teaching discovery lessons and then discuss these maxims with reference to some of the discovery lessons presented earlier in the chapter. While the maxims can serve as guidelines for discovery lessons in general, some maxims will be more applicable than others in specific lessons.

Have the generalization to be discovered clearly in mind

Clearly establishing the generalization to be discovered should assist and guide the teacher in the selection of instances and questions to be presented to students. This is not to say that teachers should be blinded to pursuing interesting avenues of discussion for the sake of making a single discovery. Teachers should always be aware of unexpected conjectures that warrant investigation. However, if the teacher is unclear as to what it is that students are to be discovering, it is likely that they will be engaged in a rather superficial experience. Furthermore, a teacher's assessment of the success of a particular lesson is enhanced if the objective is clearly formulated at the outset.

Consider lesson 1. If the teacher does not establish the generalization below as a goal (at least in his or her own mind), then it is

$$(x + y)(x - y) = x^2 - y^2$$

possible that the lesson may focus on arithmetic manipulations and the students will fail to realize the generalization that is the object of instruction.

Consider the relevant factors before deciding whether to use an
inductive or deductive discovery strategy or a combination

This suggestion assumes that the decision to use a discovery strategy has been made in the first place. Yet this, itself, is a decision that should be made in light of relevant factors. Of particular importance is the nature of the generalization to be taught. Some generalizations are so complex that a discovery strategy would be inefficient and ineffective. De Moivre's theorem could possibly be taught by discovery, but one questions whether the amount of time it would take to teach it in this way is worth the effort. An expository strategy would probably be more efficient.

Assuming that a discovery strategy is viable for teaching a particular generalization, the complexity of the generalization continues to be relevant in choosing between an inductive and a deductive discovery strategy. Generally speaking, the more complex the generalization is the more difficult it is to teach it by induction. The theorem concerning the number of permutations of n objects of which r_1 are alike, r_2 are alike, ... r_k are alike would be difficult to teach by an inductive discovery strategy, but easier to teach by a combination of induction and deduction. A generalization that is a conditional and whose hypothesis is a conjunction will require more instances to indicate the necessity of each of the conditions conjoined. Consider the test for dependence of a system of two linear equations $a_{11}x + a_{12}y = a_{13}$ and $a_{21}x + a_{22}y = a_{23}$. The system is dependent if $a_{11}/a_{21} = a_{12}/a_{22} = a_{13}/a_{23}$ and $a_{21} \neq 0$, $a_{22} \neq 0$, and $a_{23} \neq 0$. It would take many instances to demonstrate the necessity of the conditions in the hypothesis. A deductive discovery strategy would be more efficient.

If students have insufficient aptitude to abstract a pattern from examples or instances, then a great number of inductive strategies may frustrate them; they will be unable to make the discovery and may give up. Until these students improve in their ability to abstract, a deductive discovery strategy determined by a carefully chosen sequence of questions will be more successful. On the other hand, some students have difficulty drawing necessary inferences. For these students, a deductive discovery strategy would likely be ineffective.

If an inductive discovery strategy is to be used, choose instances that
are representative of the domain over which the generalization is to
be made

It is highly desirable for a teacher to encourage students to guess. However, it is well to provide them with a representative sample of instances to consider. For example, if a generalization is to be made over the nonnegative rationals, as is usually the case in the seventh and eighth grades, a teacher presenting instances would be well advised to use nonnegative rationals that are not integers as well as integers. If a generalization is to be made over the rationals, then negative numbers as well as positive numbers should be used to form instances. Consider lesson 11. After examining only instances where $a = 1$, students may conclude that the product of the roots is c and their sum is $-b$. This in itself is not unfortunate, provided the generalization induced is explicitly restricted to $a = 1$. More desirably, other instances in which $a \neq 1$ should be presented for students to consider to enable them to discover the less restricted generalization.

If a sequence in which the instances are presented will facilitate the discovery, plan the sequence

For some generalizations, the sequence in which instances are presented is a determining factor in helping the students make the discovery. Suppose a teacher wishes to teach the relation between the value of m, $m \geq 0$, in $y = mx + b$ and the slope of the graph of the equation. The sequence of instances, reading from left to right,

$$y = 2 \qquad y = x + 2 \qquad y = \tfrac{1}{2}x + 2 \qquad y = \tfrac{1}{3}x + 2$$
$$y = 2x + 2 \qquad y = 5x + 2 \qquad y = 9x + 2 \qquad y = 15x + 2$$

should enable students to see the relation better than if this sequence were permuted in various other ways. Then, if the students are expected to generalize over the values of b, a set of instances in which the value of b is systematically varied can be presented.

When using an inductive discovery strategy, do not force the students to verbalize too soon

Once students have made a few correct responses, there is a temptation to have them verbalize the discovery they seem to have made. This can cause frustration and anxiety among some students, which could result in defensive behavior and thus defeat many of the intended purposes of the lesson. If a teacher insists on early verbalization, the lesson may degenerate into "guess what is on the teacher's mind" rather than remain in the realm of the intellectual processes of abstracting, generalizing, and inferring.

Teachers must judge when the nondiscoverers should be told the desired knowledge. This decision is predicated on time considerations, the nature of the students, and other subjective factors the teacher may wish to consider. Certainly the time to "cue the students in" is not in the initial stages of the lesson, nor should it be prolonged until excessive class time has been devoted to the lesson.

Students who become actively involved in a discovery lesson are going to make responses that are incorrect or divergent from the teacher's expectations. They may offer suggestions that are logically possible but known to the teacher to be unproductive. If such responses or initiatives are given "second class" acceptance by the teacher, students may resort to any one of a number of defensive strategies—guess and look, silence, or qualifying their answers ("It wouldn't be—, would it?"). None of these defensive strategies is likely to have a positive effect on learning.

In lesson 6, S_3 conjectures that the lines represented by the given equations are parallel. Suppose, however, that S_3 had made the following conjecture: "Well, the graphs of those lines might *coincide.*" Is this conjecture reasonable? Is it correct? How would you, as a teacher, react to such a conjecture? Could you react positively to the student and yet question the conjecture? One way to accomplish this is to devise a sequence of questions that will enable the student to critically examine such conjectures.

Have students verify their discovery

Proof of a generalization requires deduction. The degree of rigor in a deductive argument usually varies with the mathematical maturity of the students, however. Deductive discoveries by their very nature require no justification beyond that contained in the lesson, because the discovery is the consequence of a deductive argument. In cases in which strictly deductive verification is judged by the teacher to be beyond the students' existing level of comprehension, the teacher may verify a generalization by having students examine additional instances or challenge the students to produce a counterexample.

Reinforce the discovery by application

Two advantages claimed for teaching by discovery are the potentialities of greater transfer and retention of discovered knowledge. It seems reasonable to assume that both of these goals can be attained better if knowledge discovered by students is used following the initial discovery. In some textbooks this application may be in the form of a variety of exercises. For example, at the completion of lesson 2, a teacher can reinforce discovery by presenting problems necessitating the formula for the area of a circle. Similarly, if students have discovered the generalization

$$\log ab = \log a + \log b, \quad a > 0, \quad b > 0$$

they can apply this knowledge in discovering another generalization,

$$\log a^n = n \log a, \quad a > 0, \quad n \text{ a positive integer.}$$

Thought questions

1   Is the advice given in the first maxim applicable more to inductive or to deductive discovery lessons? Defend your answer.

2   Suppose you wish to use a discovery approach to the following item of knowledge: "The sum of the measures of the interior angles of an n-sided convex polygon is $(n - 2) \times 180$." Sequence two sets of instances you could present to students to

guide their discovery of this generalization. Have one sequence begin with a complex task—for example, finding the sum of the measures of the interior angles of a twelve-sided polygon—and the other begin with the simplest situation (a triangle followed by a quadrilateral, and so on). Which approach would you choose with eighth-grade students of average ability? Would you change to the other approach with tenth-grade geometry students? Give reasons for your choices.

3   What things can a teacher do to prevent more capable students from verbalizing a discovery too soon and thus spoiling the opportunity for other students to make the discovery for themselves? Describe how you would carry out your ideas in teaching lessons 1 and 11.

4   Answer the questions posed in the discussion of the fifth maxim.

5   Devise a sequence of questions that will enable S_3 (lesson 6) to critically examine his own conjecture. In general, do you believe that it is desirable for a student to be given the opportunity to correct his own misconception when he has made a statement or a conjecture that is false? Why?

6   How could the discovery made in lesson 1 be verified?

7   Develop an application item in the form of a story problem that utilizes the generalization discovered in lesson 8.

8   What kind of a strategy would you use to teach each of the following? Defend your choice.
    a   A relation S is symmetric with respect to the y-axis if and only if $(x, y) \; \varepsilon \; S \Rightarrow (-x, y) \; \varepsilon \; S$.
    b $\cos(-x) = \cos x$
    c   If two parallel lines are cut by a transversal, the corresponding angles are congruent.
    d $r_1(\cos \theta_1 + i \sin \theta_1) \times r_2(\cos \theta_2 + i \sin \theta_2)$
        $= r_1 r_2[\cos(\theta_1 + \theta_2) + i \sin(\theta_1 + \theta_2)]$
    e   The rate of interest charged by small loan companies is greater than that charged by banks.
    f   The volume of a rectangular solid is equal to the product of the length, width, and height.

9   Suppose you intend to teach by inductive discovery the generalization that the sum of the measures of the exterior angles of a convex polygon is 360. Determine the sequence of instances you would use.

10 Suppose you have decided to teach each of the following by a deductive discovery strategy. Plan a sequence of questions you would ask.
    a $\cos(x + y) = \cos x \cos y - \sin x \sin y$. (Assume that the students know that $\cos(x - y) = \cos x \cos y + \sin x \sin y$.)
    b   Under an isometry, an angle and its image have the same measure.
    c   If $x + y = z$, then $x = z - y$.
    d   If m and n are nonnegative integers, then $(x^n)^m = x^{nm}$.

    e   If $0° \leq \angle A < 90°$, then $\tan \angle A = \dfrac{\sin \angle A}{\cos \angle A}$

    f $\dfrac{\dfrac{a}{b}}{\dfrac{c}{d}} = \dfrac{ad}{bc}$, assuming the appropriate restrictions as to 0.

11 What applications of the discovered knowledge could be devised for students who had completed lesson 2 ?

12 What applications of the discovered knowledge could be devised for students who had completed lesson 12 ?

A small–group discovery method

In most cases discovery teaching involves a teacher interacting with an entire class. The interactions consist of discussing instances or implications that can be made from established generalizations and other information relevant to the discovery lesson. These interactions often take place between a teacher and twenty or thirty students within the classroom.

An alternative approach has been suggested by Davidson (1971), who has described how students can be organized into small groups of from three to four members with their study so directed that they focus on problems that enable them to discover much of the knowledge they are expected to learn. Such an approach can be used for individual lessons as well as for units of instruction.

The small groups can be formed by students themselves—that is, each student can choose others with whom to work. Students should be encouraged to work cooperatively and achieve a solution satisfactory to all members of the group. New problems should not be attacked until each member of the group has understood the problem just solved. No one student should be allowed to dominate the discussion or do the work of others. Each group could conceivably move at its own pace. While the groups are working, a teacher can visit each group and observe its progress and where necessary make suggestions for improving effectiveness. Also, where necessary, corrections, and clarifications can be made.

In Davidson's experiment, students in the experimental class did slightly better than students in a class taught by a more conventional method. Their attitude was favorable. They reported more interest in this course than in other mathematics courses they had had. Some thought they learned more than if the instruction had been more conventional. Some reported that they no longer feared mathematics.

Like all methods, this small group-discovery method has advantages and disadvantages. As Davidson (p. 789) said, " . . . students learned mathematics by doing mathematics." Rather than reading the finished product of the discoveries in mathematics, the students can produce the product for themselves by their discoveries. The groups can move at their own pace. Social pressure from peers to participate and learn is more effective as motivation than pressure from the teacher. Many students find this method more stimulating, because of the discovery approach and because of the group work. Finally, there is the concomitant learning of how to work cooperatively with others. In our society, this is an important social skill.

Yet there are potential disadvantages. Cognitive styles of students differ. While some students will like this approach, others will not. They have become successful in the usual mode of learning induced by exposition without group work. Forcing them into a mode that is almost entirely discovery and requires them to adjust to the pace of learning of others can be distressing, at least initially.

Learning to work in a group takes time. There are skills which have not been developed in the typical school where instruction is almost exclusively individual. It can be expected that groups will be inefficient initially, and waste time. Some members will be content to allow others to do all the work. For the less mature students, these undesirable conditions are more likely to eventuate. Yet through guidance by the teacher, it can be expected that these conditions can be corrected so that, as time goes by, the groups should be able to work more ideally.

Because of the time required to adapt a textbook or a lesson to the small-group discovery method, it is very demanding on the teacher, at least initially. He will have to write guide sheets containing problems different from the exercises that appear in conventional textbooks. Yet there will have to be exercises to provide for application and develop skills. Also, like the students, the teacher will have to learn how to work with groups. This requires skills somewhat different from those employed in working with individual students. Yet one can argue that learning these skills keeps the teacher alert, makes teaching less routine, and keeps the teacher from getting into a rut. Ideally, each teacher should continue to learn through teaching.

Advantages and disadvantages of teaching by discovery

Those who advocate teaching by discovery make a number of claims for such teaching strategies. Jerome Bruner (1960, p. 612) has suggested numerous benefits that students realize when they experience a discovery lesson:

> Let me propose instead that discovery is better defined not as a product discovered but as a process of working, and that the so-called method of discovery has as its principal virtue the encouragement of such a process of working or if I may use the term, such an attitude.

Bruner believes that students who use their own energy to discover knowledge increase their ability to organize resources in attacking problems, become more adept at problem-solving, and receive intrinsic motivation from being involved in the discovery process.

In summarizing the objectives of the Madison Project, Davis (1966, pp. 167–168) includes the following goals:

> We want the students to have a real feeling for the history of mathematics, derived partly from having been eye-witness observers (or participants) on the occasion of mathematical discoveries.

> We want the student to know that mathematics really and truly is discoverable (something few people believe).

Advantages and disadvantages of teaching by discovery   169

We want each student, as part of the task of knowing himself, to get a realistic assessment of his own personal ability in discovering mathematics.

We want students to come to value "educated intuition" in its proper place.

We want the students to value abstract rational analysis in its proper place.

We want the students—as much as possible—to know when to preserve and when to be flexible.

We want the students to have a feeling that mathematics is fun or exciting, or worthwhile.

Discovery teaching and learning are viewed by the Madison Project staff as basic strategy for realizing the goals listed above.

The majority of the advantages claimed for teaching by discovery attributed to Bruner and Davis are shared by other psychologists and educators. However, almost all the advantages mentioned thus far pertain to educational concerns independent of the particular items of knowledge being discovered. Are there any advantages with respect to the knowledge being discovered? Most proponents claim that students are more likely to retain knowledge learned by discovery. It is felt that when students are involved, they are less likely to tune out and forget the knowledge being discussed. Furthermore, it is hoped that if students do forget the knowledge, there is an increased probability that they can "rediscover." It is also claimed, with some supporting evidence, that students who have acquired knowledge through heuristic strategies are better able to transfer and apply knowledge in a variety of contexts. Also, because the discovery process necessarily involves student interactions and since a student's ability and insights influence the pace and direction of instruction, discovery lessons can prevent the teacher from proceeding with new material when students are confused.

The mathematics educator who turns to research for evidence to support the aforementioned claims can find a number of studies measuring the effectiveness of various discovery and expository approaches in relation to student achievement and the ability to retain and transfer knowledge learned. There are virtually no studies attempting to measure many of the general educational concerns of Bruner and Davis cited above, however. This distressing situation is further confounded by the realization that even in relation to the issues of retention, application, and transfer, the evidence supporting discovery teaching and learning is less than conclusive. Cronbach (1966, p. 76) writes:

In spite of the confident endorsements of teaching through discovery that we read in semipopular discourses on improving education there is precious little substantiated knowledge about what advantages it offers and under what conditions these advantages accrue.

Perhaps Ausubel (1964, p. 291) best expresses the thoughts of those who have reservations about teaching and learning by discovery:

> Actually, a moment's reflection should convince anyone that most of what he really knows and meaningfully understands, consists of insights discovered by others which have been communicated to him in meaningful fashion.

Ausubel points out that if secondary school and university students were taught exclusively by discovery they would fail to progress beyond the basic notions in any discipline. He also maintains that discovery is more appropriate for elementary school students and in general for students of above-average ability. Elementary school students depend on concrete, empirical experience and attain at most a semi-abstract intuitive understanding of abstract propositions. For these pupils a verbal presentation should be accompanied by physical objects; in this context a guided-discovery approach is often successful. However, secondary school students should have the ability, according to Ausubel, to perceive abstract relationships in the absence of physical experience. Hence Ausubel (1964, p. 296) recommends that

> Secondary school and college students, who already possess a sound, meaningful grasp of the rudiments of a discipline like mathematics, can be taught this subject meaningfully and with maximal efficiency, through the method of verbal exposition, supplemented by appropriate problem-solving experience.

Ausubel also cautions that discovery methods can frustrate students of below-average ability in elementary and secondary school. In addition, he challenges discovery teaching and learning as a unique generator and developer of motivation and problem-solving ability. He maintains that a competent, verbal expository presentation of concepts and principles can also produce intellectual stimulation and that schools should focus on the transmission of knowledge.

Ausubel (1964, p. 290) is not totally opposed to teaching and learning by discovery, however:

> Learning by discovery has its proper place among the repertoire of accepted techniques available to teachers. For certain purposes and under certain conditions it has a defensible rationale and undoubted advantages. Hence the issue is not whether it should or should not be used in the classroom, but rather for what purposes and under what conditions.

While research is inconclusive with respect to advantages and disadvantages, it seems reasonable to assume that students are more likely to enjoy mathematics when teachers use a variety of instructional strategies. A continuous sequence of any single approach (expository, laboratory, discovery, tutorial, programmed, or computerized) to the exclusion of others is likely to become routine and unstimulating.

Experienced teachers attest to the fact that a well-planned and well-conducted discovery lesson does stimulate and motivate students. Students do, as teachers have observed, receive a certain amount of gratification in making an intellectual discovery. No doubt this can occur in well-conceived expository lessons as well as discovery lessons. Perhaps retention and transfer are not greater for discovered items of knowledge than knowledge learned by exposition. Nevertheless, one of the most rewarding experiences a human being can have is the realization that he has created, through his own intellectual process, an item of knowledge not previously known to him. To have enabled a student to accomplish this feat through the use of a discovery lesson is a most rewarding experience for a teacher.

Thought questions

1   A number of research studies investigating teaching by discovery have been reported in *The Mathematics Teacher*. Read one of these articles. (See the references at end of chapter.) Summarize and give your reaction to the article.

2   Summarize Ausubel's position on teaching and learning by discovery. Give your reaction to Ausubel's beliefs concerning discovery with respect to:
    a   Inefficiency of discovery as far as instructional time is concerned
    b   Ability of the student
    c   Age of the student
    d   Motivating students
    e   Problem-solving as a primary general educational goal for schools

3   In addition to the claims of Bruner and Davis, enumerate other advantages to using discovery in a mathematics classroom. Discuss and defend your statements.

4   Discuss how each of the following factors can influence a mathematics teacher in deciding whether to present a particular item of knowledge through a discovery or an expository lesson:
    a   Difficulty of the item of knowledge
    b   Student's background and ability
    c   Class time allocated for the lesson
    d   Amount of planning time a teacher has available

5   Would you be more disposed to use discovery or expository strategies with students who learn slowly? Why?

Self-test on the competencies

1   State what is meant by guided discovery.
    a   What are the characteristics of guided discovery?
    b   How do guided-discovery strategies differ from expository strategies?

2   Distinguish between inductive and deductive discovery strategies.
    a   What are the distinguishing characteristics of an inductive discovery strategy in contrast to a deductive discovery strategy?
    b   Which kind of strategy necessitates abstraction from instances?
    c   What would characterize a strategy that is a combination of induction and deduction?

3   Plan the teaching of a generalization by an inductive discovery strategy.
    a Select a generalization amenable to teaching by an inductive strategy and write a lesson plan for teaching it this way.
    b What decisions have to be made when planning the teaching of a generalization by an inductive discovery strategy?

4   Plan the teaching of a generalization by a deductive discovery strategy.
    a Select a generalization amenable to teaching by a deductive strategy and write a lesson plan for teaching it this way.
    b What decisions have to be made when planning the teaching of a generalization by a deductive discovery strategy?

5   Plan the teaching of a generalization by a combination of an inductive and a deductive discovery strategy.
    a Using a strategy that is a combination of induction and deduction, plan a lesson for teaching this generalization: The graph of a quadratic equation with real coefficients will have two, one, or zero *x*-intercepts according to whether the value of the discriminant of the quadratic polynomial is, respectively, positive, zero, or negative.
    b At what point in a combination of an inductive and a deductive discovery strategy does abstraction have to occur?

6   Given that a particular generalization is to be taught to a given group of students, choose wisely among expository and discovery strategies for teaching it.
    a What factors should be considered in choosing between an expository and a guided-discovery strategy?
    b What values of the factors considered in question a will dispose you to choose an expository strategy? Which will dispose you to choose a discovery strategy?
    c Assuming that the decision has been made to use a guided-discovery strategy, what factors should be considered in choosing between an inductive and a deductive discovery strategy?
    d What values of the factors considered in question c will dispose you to choose an inductive discovery strategy? Which will dispose you to choose a deductive discovery strategy?

References

Ausubel, David P. *Educational Psychology: A Cognitive View*. New York: Holt, Rinehart and Winston, 1968. Chs. 2, 3, and 14.
———. "In Defense of Verbal Learning." *Educational Theory*, 11 (1961), 15–25.
———. "Some Psychological and Educational Limitations of Learning by Discovery." *The Arithmetic Teacher*, 11 (1964), 290–302.
Bruner, Jerome S. "On Learning Mathematics." *The Mathematics Teacher*, 53 (1960), 610–619.
———. *Toward a Theory of Instruction*. Cambridge, Mass.: Harvard University Press, Belknap Press, 1966.
———. "Some Elements of Discovery." *Learning by Discovery: A Critical Appraisal*, ed. by Lee S. Shulman and Evan R. Keislar. Chicago: Rand McNally, 1966.
Cronbach, Lee J. "The Logic of Experiments on Discovery." *Learning by Discovery: A Critical Appraisal*, ed. by Lee S. Shulman and Evan R. Keislar. Chicago: Rand McNally, 1966.

Davidson, Neil. "The Small Group-Discovery Method as Applied in Calculus Instruction." *The American Mathematical Monthly*, 78 (1971), 789–791.

Davis, Robert B. "Discovery in the Teaching of Mathematics." *Learning by Discovery: A Critical Appraisal*, ed. by Lee S. Shulman and Evan R. Keislar. Chicago: Rand NcNally, 1966.

Gagné, R. M., and E. C. Smith, Jr. "A Study of the Effects of Verbalization on Problem Solving." *Journal of Experimental Psychology*, 63 (1962), 12–18.

Glaser, Robert. "Variables in Discovery Learning." *Learning by Discovery: A Critical Appraisal*, ed. by Lee S. Shulman and Evan R. Keislar. Chicago: Rand McNally, 1966.

Hendrix, Gertrude. "A New Clue to Transfer of Training." *Elementary School Journal*, 48 (1947), 197–208.

———. "Prerequisite to Meaning." *The Mathematics Teacher*, 43 (1950), 334–339.

———. "Learning by Discovery." *The Mathematics Teacher*, 54 (1961), 290–299.

Polya, George. *How to Solve It*. Garden City, N. Y.: Doubleday, 1957.

———. *Mathematical Discovery: On Understanding, Learning, and Teaching Problem Solving*. New York: Wiley, 1962 (Vol. 1), 1967 (Vol. 2).

Price, Jack. "Discovery: Its Effect on Critical Thinking and Achievement in Mathematics." *The Mathematics Teacher*, 60 (1967), 874–876.

Retzer, Kenneth A., and Kenneth B. Henderson. "The Effect of Teaching Concepts of Logic on Verbalization of Discovered Mathematical Concepts." *The Mathematics Teacher*, 60 (1967), 707–710.

Shulman, Lee S., and Evan R. Keislar (eds.). *Learning by Discovery: A Critical Appraisal*. Chicago: Rand McNally, 1966.

Wills, Herbert. "Generalizations." *The Teaching of Secondary School Mathematics*. National Council of Teachers of Mathematics Thirty-Third Yearbook. Washington, D. C.: National Council of Teachers of Mathematics, 1970. Ch. 10.

Wittrock, M. C. "The Learning by Discovery Hypothesis." *Learning by Discovery: A Critical Appraisal*, ed. by Lee S. Shulman and Evan R. Keislar. Chicago: Rand McNally, 1966.

8

Teaching mathematical skills

In previous chapters we discussed the teaching of cognitive knowledge—that is, knowledge about some topic or knowledge that something is the case. Concepts, singular statements, and generalizations are cognitive knowledge; they are basic to other kinds of knowledge. But another kind of knowledge is also taught in the classroom—knowledge of how to do something. For example, mathematics teachers show students how to square binomials, interpolate, solve equations, and bisect line segments with speed and accuracy. This is commonly referred to as teaching for the acquistion of skills or, more simply, teaching skills.

Teaching skills plays an important role in the teaching of mathematics. If students do not develop skills in performing tasks they will be handicapped in furthering their mathematical learning. It is not enough for students to know how to compute with rational numbers; they must be skilled in doing it if they are to make desirable progress in learning mathematics. Teachers must of course, be wary of developing instructional programs based only on skill acquisition. When this occurs, learning degenerates to continual emphasis on drill. Teachers must provide enough practice for students to let them acquire necessary mathematical skills but strive to strike a balance between teaching concepts and generalizations and teaching skills. It is our purpose in this chapter to discuss how skills are different from concepts and generalizations and to present ways of teaching skills in secondary school mathematics.

At the conclusion of this chapter, you should be able to demonstrate the following competencies:

1 Discuss what implications the difference between skills and cognitive knowledge has for teaching mathematical skills

2 Identify prescriptions useful in teaching a given skill

3 Identify moves used in teaching a skill

4 Discuss, including implications for teaching, the general conditions under which practice can be effective

5 Devise a variety of activities that can promote the learning of a specific skill

6 Using the moves discussed in the chapter, plan a lesson for teaching a skill

The nature of skills

A distinguishing characteristic of learning how to do something is that it can be learned through imitation. Consider the skills of swimming and squaring binomials. Many people learn to swim without formal instruction by observing and imitating others. Similarly, an algebra student may learn how to square binomials by observing and imitating a teacher or another student. Through proper practice he may improve in his ability to square binomials and be able to find products accurately and rapidly, thus acquiring the desired skill.

One should not conclude, however, that the strategy of imitation followed by practice is the best way to acquire a skill. Without some knowledge of theory and principles, imitation and practice tend to be a time-consuming and unreliable approach to learning a skill. A swimmer who understands breathing, kicking, and stroking is likely to improve. Likewise, an algebra student who understands the mathematical generalizations underlying the squaring of a binomial is likely to become proficient in squaring binomials of various complexity. Although students can learn by imitation, providing them with a combination of the cognitive knowledge that pertains to the skill and the right kind of practice enables them to develop skills in a meaningful way. A basic premise of this chapter is that students, in acquiring skills, be provided a basis for understanding what they are doing.

Another characteristic of skills is that speed and accuracy are criteria of their performance. Cronbach (1954) and other educational psychologists use the terms *automatic, rapid, accurate, smooth,* and the like to describe skilled performance. The terms *speed* and *accuracy* apply to someone's ability to square binomials but they do not apply very well to one's knowledge about squaring binomials; it seems odd to say that a student knows the distributive property with great speed and accuracy. It makes sense to say that a student can solve equations quickly and with few errors, but it seems odd to say that he knows such generalizations as the transitive property, the additive property for addition and other basic generalizations which are utilized in solving equations, with speed and accuracy.

To be able to do something very well and quickly requires practice. While students can learn how to use the quadratic formula without practice, they need practice in using the formula in order to solve quadratic equations with speed and accuracy. To teach skills effectively, then, teachers must provide students with opportunity for practice.

Thought questions

1   Identify a nonmathematical skill. Identify the cognitive knowledge that might be useful for a person to learn it. How is the skill different from the cognitive knowledge?

2   What criteria would you use to decide whether a person had acquired the skill in question 1? Justify your choice.

3   Answer questions 1 and 2 for a mathematical skill.

4   State some implications of a teacher's knowing or not knowing whether he or she is teaching a skill. What effect might this have on planning a lesson?

5   Do you think students should be required to factor quadratic expressions quickly?

6   Should speed in solving linear equations be important for ninth-grade algebra students?

The nature and use of prescriptions in teaching skills

Teaching is not limited to nonverbal communication between teachers and students. Teachers communicate directions, called **prescriptions**, to advise, guide, or direct student action. Prescriptions that apply to extensive domains and assist us in guiding our deliberate actions together with true generalizations constitute what we will call **principles.** Principles, then, can be partitioned into generalizations and prescriptions. Concepts and principles constitute some of the cognitive knowledge in mathematics.

We can see the significance of the classification of principles into generalizations and prescriptions when we consider the principles

$$\log x^y = y \log x$$

and

$$\text{antilog} (\log x) = x$$

whose variables are restricted to the proper domains. One might say that anyone who knows these principles can apply them to obtain an approximation of a real number raised to a rational power. But teachers know that many students cannot apply them readily and hence they teach these principles in prescriptive form as, for example,

To form the power of a number, multiply the logarithm of the number by the exponent of the power and find the antilogarithm of the product.

Students can apply this more readily. In general, the implications for action of prescriptions are clearer than for generalizations. A teacher has to judge when to state a principle as a generalization and when to state it as a prescription.

Thought questions

1 Identify the prescriptions you would use to teach the following skills:
   a Factoring trinomial expressions
   b Constructing an angle congruent to a given angle
   c Determining what percent one number is of another number

2 If a teacher is explaining how to do something—for example, finding the centroid of a triangle or using the quadratic formula to solve equations—would generalizations or prescriptions be used? Why?

3 What kind of principles—generalizations or prescriptions—would generally be more effective in teaching slow students to solve problems? Why?

4 Conjecture why the number of principles of mathematics stated as prescriptions decreases from the middle grades to college.

5 Under what conditions would you phrase a principle as a prescription rather than as a generalization?

Moves in teaching skills

Part of a teacher's strategy must be to make sure students know how to complete a task. Usually prescriptive principles accomplish this. They hold over an extensive domain and therefore resemble generalizations. Hence, one might conjecture that moves for teaching generalizations are applicable in teaching students how to do things. Analyzing classroom discourse, Todd (1972) identified moves that mathematics teachers use in teaching skills. Some of these moves are similar to the introduction, interpretation, and justification moves for teaching generalizations. We will discuss these along with practice moves which involve such psychological principles as reinforcement, feedback, and spacing.

Introduction moves

A skill can be introduced in basically the same way as a generalization—through *focus*, *objective*, and *motivation* moves. The teacher may focus students' attention on the skill by describing briefly what it entails. The teacher may state an objective for the skill, such as

> When we finish this material, you should be able to factor quickly and correctly, over a given set, any trinomial I give you or recognize that it is not factorable over that set.

Students are thus made explicitly aware of the teacher's instructional goals.

In Chapter 6 we discussed ways of motivating students by pointing out the utility of the knowledge to be learned. This technique can also be used in teaching skills. Students can be shown that skill in plotting points facilitates the graphing of functions or that skill in interpolating can be of great use in computing trigonometric or logarithmic values. Sometimes the utility of skills can be illustrated by real-life situations: decimals can be used in exercises dealing with making change or determining discount prices. Motivating students to practice is not always easy. Despite its importance, Todd (1972) found only ten occurrences of motivation moves in over fifty hours of classroom discourse.

Sometimes students are motivated to acquire skills and other kinds of knowledge simply because it is fun to learn or they feel a sense of accomplishment in performing a task well. Teachers can capitalize on this by helping students realize when they are successful and by indicating to them their increased proficiency as they perform tasks. Motivation moves can thus be effective at times other than the introductory portions of lessons.

Thought questions

1 Consider the following skills. Identify the level and ability of the students to whom you might be teaching this and briefly outline how you would motivate their learning. State an objective move you might give.
   a Multiplying fractions
   b Converting square feet to square inches
   c Graphing exponential functions
   d Factoring binomials and trinomials
   e Finding the centroid of a triangle
   f Finding the sum of n terms of an arithmetic progression

2 Consider the following three student reactions to learning a particular skill.

   S_1 This is kind of fun, but it seems senseless to me.

   S_2 Why do we have to learn this anyway?

   S_3 I know I'm not going to be able to do this; my father says it's hard.

   As a teacher, how would you react to each of these three students? Why do you think the first thinks it is fun? How could you further motivate this student? Do you think the second student is asking "Why do we have to learn this?" or "Why am I not doing better at learning this?" In either case, how could a teacher motivate this student? How would you motivate the third student?

3 Is the acquisition of algebraic skills likely to be motivated more by illustrating their utility within or without the mathematics classroom?

Assertion moves

We pointed out earlier that prescriptive principles are useful in teaching how to do something because they offer general advice on what to do, how to do it, and perhaps the sequence in which the various steps are to be performed. A teacher teaching students how to bisect a line segment using straightedge and compass might utter this set of prescriptive principles:

1 Open the compass so that it has a radius greater than half the length of the line segment.

2 Place the point of the compass on one of the endpoints of the line segment and draw arcs above and below the line segment.

3 Place the point of the compass on the other endpoint of the line segment and, using the same radius, draw arcs intersecting the arcs drawn in step 2.

4 Using a straightedge, connect the two points of intersection of the arcs. The point at which this line intersects the given line segment is the bisector of the line segment.

It is likely that the teacher would demonstrate the execution of these prescriptions on the chalkboard or with an overhead projector. We shall discuss demonstration moves in a later section.

For more sophisticated students, the teacher might first teach a generalization and then form one or more prescriptive principles from it in order to make explicit what they should do. For example, a teacher of a second course in algebra who wants to teach her students how to find an upper bound of the real zeros of a polynomial function might teach the theorem:

> For each nonconstant polynomial function p and nonnegative real number a, if the coefficients of the terms of $q(x)$, the quotient polynomial, and the coefficient of $r(x)$, the remainder, when $p(x)$ is divided by $x - a$ are all nonnegative or nonpositive, then a is an upper bound of the zeros of p.

She would use whatever strategy she considered most effective. This generalization is the mathematical basis for a set of prescriptive principles such as

> First, make sure that the polynomial $p(x)$ is in standard form. Then choose some nonnegative real number you think might be an upper bound of the real zeros of the polynomial function. By synthetic division, find the quotient polynomial and remainder when the given polynomial is divided by the number you chose. If the signs of the coefficients in the third row in the synthetic division are all nonnegative or nonpositive, the number you chose is an upper bound of the real zeros of the given polynomial function.

The teacher might assert this as advice in applying the theorem.

The theorem—that is, the cognitive knowledge—provides understanding of the process; the prescriptive principles provide knowledge of how to do it. Understanding the process may not be necessary for developing the skill but it is for justifying the prescriptive principles. Whether teachers provide support for the understanding by relating the theorem and the prescriptions depends on how much they value understanding. Some teachers relate the prescriptive principles they assert to substantive theorems; others value the skill above the understanding and spend class time in demonstration and practice.

Thought questions

1 For each of the following skills, state some prescriptive principles you might assert in teaching it:
   a   Bisecting an angle using a protractor
   b   Rounding off numbers to a stipulated unit (10's, 100's)
   c   Checking computations by casting out nines
   d   Finding a lower bound of the real zeros of a polynomial function
   e   Adding two conformable matrices
   f   Proving a conditional theorem
   g   Forming the contrapositive of a conditional
   h   Proving a trigonometric identity
   i   Finding what percent one number is of another
   j   Representing the addition of two vectors in 2-space

2 From each of the following generalizations, deduce prescriptive principles:
   a b is a lower bound of the real roots of a polynomial equation $p(x) = 0$ if and only if $-b$ is an upper bound of the real roots of $p(-x) = 0$.
   b $r_1(\cos \theta_1 + i \sin \theta_1) \times r_2(\cos \theta_2 + i \sin \theta_2) = r_1 r_2[\cos(\theta_1 + \theta_2) + i \sin(\theta_1 + \theta_2)]$
   c   Where $a \neq 0$ and $c \neq 0$, $x/a = b/c \Rightarrow cx = ab \Rightarrow x = ab/c$.
   d   If $\mathbf{v} = a\mathbf{i} + b\mathbf{i} + c\mathbf{k} = [a, b, c]$, then $\|\mathbf{v}\| = \sqrt{a^2 + b^2 + c^2}$.
   e $\begin{vmatrix} a_{11} & a_{12} \\ a_{21} & a_{22} \end{vmatrix} = a_{11}a_{22} - a_{21}a_{12}$
   f   Two lines with directions $[a_1, b_1]$ and $[a_2, b_2]$ are perpendicular $\Leftrightarrow a_1 a_2 + b_1 b_2 = 0$.
   g   A reflection over the y-axis has equation $t(x, y) = (-x, y)$.
   h   If $y \neq 0$ and $z \neq 0$, $xz/yz = x/y$.

Interpretation moves

Many moves used in interpreting generalizations can also be used to help students clarify the meaning of prescriptions. Teachers can review the meaning of terms in prescriptions as well as in generalizations. For example, in teaching this prescription for simplifying complex fractions,

> Multiply each term of a complex fraction by the lowest common denominator of all the fractions within.

a teacher might review the meaning of terms such as *term*, *complex fraction*, and *lowest common denominator*. Students might also be asked to paraphrase the prescription, an interpretation move that applies to generalizations and prescriptions.

Suppose you were teaching students how to find the volume of a cone by using the formula

$$V = \tfrac{1}{3}\pi r^2 h$$

Which symbols would you have the students review? What misconception might the students have concerning the referent of h? In what way could you paraphrase the formula and hence the prescription for finding the volume of a cone?

Sometimes it is necessary not only to review terms but also to review tasks that are prerequisites to acquiring the desired skill. If a teacher is helping students learn how to construct parallel lines by using congruent corresponding angles, it would be wise to remind them how to construct an angle congruent to a given angle. Why? In helping students learn how to square binomials, a teacher should first review how to square monomials. For example, a teacher might see a student make the following error:

$$(x + 3y)^2 = 2x + 6xy + 6y$$

At first glance, the teacher might conclude that the student does not know how to square binomials. This is true in some sense, but the inference does little to diagnose the student's difficulty. A more insightful analysis might indicate that the problem is not in squaring binomials but in squaring monomials, a prerequisite to finding the squares of binomials and other polynomials. The student has forgotten (or never learned) how to square terms such as x and $3y$. The teacher could now devise activities to help the student gain the requisite learning.

In teaching students how to do something, a teacher may select a specific example to elucidate the prescriptive principles being used. For example,

> To find the arithmetic mean of two numbers, find the sum of the two numbers and divide this sum by 2.

is universally quantified over all real numbers. A teacher instructing students how to find the arithmetic mean of two numbers might select a specific pair of numbers, sum them, divide this sum by two, and then inform students that the resulting quotient is the desired mean. Because this move requires the teacher or students to be involved in some overt activity as designated by the prescription, we shall call this a **demonstration move.** By demonstrating a prescription, the teacher clarifies the procedure designated by the prescription by providing students a model of behavior they can then imitate. We mentioned earlier that a unique facet of learning how to do something is that such knowledge can be acquired by imitating the actions of another person, though aping may not be the most effective way of acquiring knowledge. Cognitive knowledge cannot be learned by imitation, however. (Teachers can further elucidate algorithmic procedures by giving advice on how to follow the prescription in concert with demonstration. Such advice might conceivably be given independently as well.)

The importance of interpreting prescriptions by demonstration cannot be overemphasized. Strategies that interpret prescriptions without going through an example are generally less effective than those that model the desired behavior and at the same time give verbal cues as to when to perform a certain task. To perform a task skillfully, procedure must be established to such an extent that actions are, in some sense, automatic. It is unlikely a student who must think through every operation can be skilled in solving equations. The teacher's advice can provide cues for actions to take place.

Let us illustrate these and other points in teaching skills by considering the unlikely prospect that students will be able to compute determinants given only the following definition from Hadley (1964, p. 87):

> The determinant of an nth-order matrix $\mathbf{A} = \|a_{ij}\|$, written $|\mathbf{A}|$, is defined to be the number computed from the following sum involving the n^2 elements in $\mathbf{A}$.
>
> $$|\mathbf{A}| = \sum (\pm)a_{1i}a_{2j} \ldots a_{nr},$$
>
> the sum being taken over all permutations of the second subscripts. A term is assigned a plus sign if $(i, j, \ldots, r)$ is an even permutation of $(1, 2, \ldots, n)$ and a minus sign if it is an odd permutation.

In most cases it would be inappropriate for a teacher to expect students to infer correct operations from this definition. Hence textbooks provide prescriptions for calculation of the determinant of a given matrix. Here is one such set of prescriptions, from Dolciani et al., (1970, p. 569):

1   Multiply each element in the chosen row or column by its minor.

2   Multiply the product obtained by 1 or -1 according as the sum of the row and the number of the column containing the element is an even integer or an odd integer.

3   Add the resulting products.

A teacher using interpretation moves might first review any terms that cause confusion (such as *minor*) and then paraphrase the prescriptions. Finally, the teacher could demonstrate the procedure specified by the prescription. Furthermore, advice such as "Don't forget to multiply the minor by 1 or -1" helps ensure that students will give the proper sequence to their actions in following the prescriptions.

To further illustrate the interplay of demonstration and advice, as well as other interpretation moves, let us consider the dialogue below.

1   T   To simplify a fraction whose denominator contains a complex number, remember to multiply the numerator and denominator by the conjugate of the denominator and then combine like terms wherever possible.

2   S   Huh? What do you mean?

3   T   Well, let me show you. Let's simplify the fraction $(3 + 2i)/(1 - 5i)$. First what do I mean by the conjugate? What would it be for $1 - 5i$?

4   S   Oh, I remember: $1 + 5i$.

5   T   Right. Now what do I multiply the fraction $(3 + 2i)/(1 - 5i)$ by?

6   S $1 + 5i$.

7   **T**   Well, not really.

8   **S**   Oh, let's see. Oh, we multiply by 1.

9   **T**   Yes, but in'what form?

10 **S**   1 + 5*i* over 1 + 5*i*.

11 **T**   O.K. Remember in simplifying a fraction in the form of $(a + bi)/(c + di)$, to multiply numerator and denominator by $c - di$. In our problem, we have $(3 + 2i)(1 + 5i)/(1 - 5i)(1 + 5i)$ (*writes this on board*). What does this fraction simplify to?

12 **S** $$\frac{-7 + 17i}{26}$$

   (*Teacher writes this on board.*)

13 **T**   Fine. Always remember in multiplying two complex numbers that are conjugates that the result is a real number. Also in multiplying $3 + 2i$ times $1 + 5i$, make sure the real number you get in the product is the sum of 3 times 1 *and* 2*i* times 5*i*. I mean, the real part is found by summing the products of the two real components and the two imaginary components.

14 **S**   Isn't this a lot like what we did with a fraction like $(4 - \sqrt{3})/(2 + \sqrt{2})$?

15 **T**   Yes it is. We would multiply $\dfrac{4 - \sqrt{3}}{2 + \sqrt{2}}$ by $\dfrac{2 - \sqrt{2}}{2 - \sqrt{2}}$.

What knowledge is being taught in this dialogue? On what cognitive knowledge is it predicated? Did the teacher review the meaning of any terms? What terms would you have reviewed had you been teaching the lesson? Did the teacher use a paraphrasing move? How many demonstrations did the teacher provide? Do you think this would ordinarily be sufficient for students to acquire the knowledge? In which utterances did the teacher give advice?

Notice a type of move in utterances 14 and 15 that we have not mentioned in interpreting knowledge useful in teaching skills. The student noticed that simplifying fractions of the form $(a + bi)/(c + di)$ is analogous to simplifying fractions whose denominators consist of the sum (or difference) of a rational and an irrational number, such as $5 - 3\sqrt{2}$. If students are proficient in simplifying a fraction such as $(2 + \sqrt{6})/(5 - \sqrt{3})$, the teacher could capitalize on this knowledge to help them acquire the new skill. Reminding students that the procedure for accomplishing a desired task is similar to a previously learned procedure is an **analogy move.** Relating a skill being acquired to previous skills is effective and provides students with continuity in learning. The acquisition of a skill is facilitated when students view what they are learning as connected and not discrete from other acquired knowledge.

Thought questions

1   Consider this prescriptive principle: "When you transform an equation by multiplying by a polynomial, always test each root of the resulting equation in the original equation." In teaching this principle, what terms do you think should be reviewed? How could you paraphrase the principle? What advice would you give students if you were demonstrating it?

2   Compare and contrast a demonstration move with an instantiation move.

3   Suppose a student squared $(x + 3y)$ and obtained $14xy$. What is the apparent mistake? What activities would you devise to help the student overcome misconceptions?

4   Identify at least two tasks prerequisite to skill in
   a   Constructing a tangent to a circle from a point outside the circle
   b   Finding the inverse of a nonsingular 3×3 matrix

5   To clarify a generalization or a prescription, teachers try to select instances that adequately reflect its domain. Give examples you would select to demonstrate the following principles:
   a   To find the geometric mean of two numbers, take the principal square root of their product.
   b   To find the centroid of a triangle, find the point of concurrency of the medians of the triangle.

6   In what way is constructing a perpendicular line to a given line at a given point on the line analogous to bisecting an angle?

7   If you were showing students how to perform the following tasks, state the acquired algorithms you could identify as analogous to the given tasks:
   a   Finding the least common denominator of two fractions
   b   Graphing equations of the form $y = (x - b)^2 + c$.
   c   Solving linear inequalities in one variable.

Justification moves

In Chapter 6, we explicated several moves designed to convince students that a generalization is true. Teachers can also design moves to justify prescriptions. A prescription is assigned a truth value of *true* if following the prescription attains the desired end—that is, in mathematics, a correct result. Hence, one method of justifying prescriptions to students is to enable them to determine whether their answer on following a prescription is correct. A second method of justifying prescriptions is to establish that the prescriptions are predicated on accepted mathematical generalizations. The first of these methods will be termed pragmatic justification; it answers the question "Does it work?" The second will be called deductive justification; it answers the question "Can I prove it?"

   The pragmatic method is not as conclusive as the deductive method but is often more satisfying to the student. Demonstrating that following a prescriptive principle leads to a correct answer requires that the student or the teacher check the work for its accuracy. For example, geometric constructions can often be checked by using a ruler and a protractor—that is, using measurement to justify the constructions.

   Algorithms (sets of prescriptive principles) used to find square roots of numbers are seldom justified deductively. Usually the student is asked to square the answer and show that this result is a reasonable approximation of the original number. Factoring is another task that can be checked pragmatically. We encourage students to check the possible roots of an equation by substituting possible roots into the original equation to see

Figure 8.1

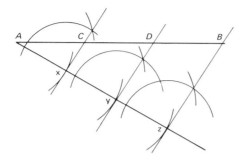

whether, upon simplification, a numerical identity results. In geometry, the procedure for dividing a line segment $\overline{AB}$ into three congruent parts can be justified by measuring $\overline{AC}$, $\overline{CD}$, and $\overline{DB}$ and determining whether they are the same measure. (See Figure 8.1.)

Showing students how to determine whether a number is divisible by 3 or 9 by summing the digits and deciding whether this sum is divisible by 3 or 9 is a procedure seldom justified by a deductive argument. Students accept the teacher's prescriptions because they cannot produce a counter-example. When students generate instances of a prescriptive principle and cannot identify a counterexample, they tend to believe that the principle is true.

Pragmatic justification can be a very effective means of convincing the student that prescriptive principles lead to a correct result. This is especially true with less mathematically mature students who are not interested in whether prescriptions follow from established mathematical generalizations. Their main concern is only if it "works out right."

Deductive justification involves showing that the prescription is pred-icated on previously established generalizations. It is a more powerful strategy than pragmatic justification because once it is seen that a prescription follows from previous knowledge, it can be understood that all applications of the prescription must result in a correct answer. More sophisticated students may not be satisfied unless they can justify prescriptions deductively. For them, the fact that following a prescription leads to a correct result is not sufficient.

Consider the prescription "To divide two fractions invert the divisor and multiply." This can be shown to follow from basic axioms and definitions of arithmetic:

$$\frac{a}{b} \div \frac{d}{c} = \frac{a}{b} \times \frac{1}{d/c}$$

Provided $b \neq 0$, $c \neq 0$, $d \neq 0$. Definition of division.

$$\frac{a/b}{1} \times \frac{1}{d/c} = \frac{a/b}{d/c}$$

Definition of multiplication of rational numbers.

$$\frac{a/b}{d/c} = \frac{(a/b)(c/d)}{(d/c)(c/d)}$$

The value of a fraction remains unchanged when the numerator and denominator are multiplied by the same real number (excluding 0).

$$\frac{(a/b)(c/d)}{(d/c)(c/d)} = \frac{(a/b)(c/d)}{1}$$

The product of a number (excluding 0) and its reciprocal is 1.

$$\frac{(a/b)(c/d)}{1} = \frac{a}{b} \times \frac{d}{c}$$

Division property of one.

$$\therefore \frac{a}{b} \div \frac{d}{c} = \frac{a}{b} \times \frac{c}{d}$$

Transitive property of equality.

The prescription

To multiply two numbers of unlike sign, find the product of their absolute values and assign a negative value to the product.

can be justified deductively by showing that the product of a positive number and a negative number must result in a negative number. Consider the proof below, in which $a > 0$ and $b > 0$ and hence $-b < 0$:

$$0 = b + (-b)$$ Property of additive inverses.

$$a(0) = a[b + (-b)]$$ Multiplicative property of equality.

$$0 = ab + a(-b)$$ Multiplicative property of zero and the distributive property of multiplication over addition.

ab and $a(-b)$ are additive inverses. Why? But ab and $-(ab)$ are also additive inverses. Why?

$ab + a(-b) = ab + -(ab)$ Why?

$a(-b) = -ab$, in other words, the product of a positive and a negative number, results in a negative number. Why?

While some prescriptions are more likely to be justified pragmatically than deductively, some can easily be justified in both ways. For example, the geometric construction of dividing line segment $\overline{AB}$ into three congruent parts (or n congruent parts) can also be justified by using the theorem, "If three or more parallel lines intercept congruent segments on one transversal, they will intercept congruent segments on any transversal intersecting the parallel lines." The principles usually given for solving quadratic equations with the quadratic formula can also be justified by both of these methods. Similarly, prescriptions that assist students in finding perimeters and areas of geometric figures are often justified pragmatically and deductively.

It would seem that acquiring a skill would have more meaning for a student if the prescriptions used in teaching the skills were justified in more than one way. Any algorithm that can be taught by prescriptions can be justified by a deductive argument. That is, the prescription must be predicated on established mathematical definitions, postulates, or theorems. A teacher's decision to justify a prescription deductively is usually based on its difficulty, the maturity and ability of the students, and the value the teacher places on understanding.

Thought questions

1   Suppose you are teaching eighth-grade students and high school geometry students to construct tangents to a given circle from a point outside the circle. What prescriptions would you use? How would your justification of them differ for the two groups of students?

2   If an eighth-grader asked you, "When we find $\frac{1}{2}$ percent of 240, why do we always move the decimal point two places to the left first? Why can't we just multiply by $\frac{1}{2}$?" how would you convince him that the algorithm is correct (assuming it is)? Would such an explanation make the algorithm more meaningful? Suppose an eleventh-grader asked the same question. Would your answer differ, and if so how?

3   Identify a skill and a grade level in which you would justify the prescriptions used to teach the skill primarily through pragmatic means. Outline your strategy of justification.

4   Identify a skill and a grade level in which you would justify the prescriptions used to teach the skill primarily through a deductive argument.

5   Identify a skill and a grade level in which the prescriptive principles you would use to teach it could be justified both pragmatically and deductively. Outline your strategies for both methods.

6   Consider this dialogue:

T_1 When I try to convince my low-ability students that what they are doing is correct, I just show them that it works right.

T_2 With my low-ability students, I first try to show them a logical reason why what they are doing is correct. I try to make the argument simple.

T_1 For me, that doesn't seem to be effective with poorer students.

T_2 Well, I think even slower students should have some experience with proof and logic.

Which teacher do you agree with? To what extent do you think students of low ability should have experience with proof or justifying algorithms deductively? What danger could exist in showing students only pragmatic justification?

Practice moves

The moves we discussed previously deal primarily with the first aspect of learning skills—namely knowing how to do something. The second aspect necessitates practice, for it is only through practice that one develops the ability to complete a task with speed and accuracy. The old adage "Practice makes perfect" still has a ring of truth to it. Swimmers swim, golfers golf, and basketball players practice shooting baskets, all for the purpose of developing their athletic skills. Skills in mathematics also can be acquired only through practice. To speak simply, one must solve equations, graph, and prove theorems to become skilled in these activities.

Practice will not in itself ensure that students will become skilled at the particular task practiced. Practice can be effective, ineffective, or detrimental depending on its context. Effective practice must be related to the achievement of some end that the student is motivated to attain. Students motivated to learn a skill because of its utility, because they enjoy doing it, or because it is a means to attaining some other goal are more likely to be interested and take an active part in the practice sessions rather than viewing them as useless exercises. Doing is not synonymous with learning. Doing can facilitate learning, but for students who are listless, have little interest, or see little relevance to what they are doing, practice is likely to degenerate into a thoughtless activity that may actually develop careless and incorrect responses.

Making practice effective

In this section we will discuss various means of making practice effective. We begin by considering reinforcement and feedback. Later we discuss scheduling and ways to couch practice in a variety of activities.

Reinforcement and feedback

A basic generalization concerning learning asserts that rewarded behavior is more likely to recur. This generalization is sometimes referred to as the law of reinforcement. In reference to this principle, Watson (1961, p. 2) made the following observation:

> This most fundamental law of learning has been demonstrated in literally thousands of experiments. It seems to hold for every sort of animal from earthworms to highly intelligent adults. The behavior most likely to emerge in any situation is that which the subject found successful or satisfying previously in a similar situation. No other variable affects learning so powerfully. The best planned learning provides for a steady, cumulative sequence of successful behaviors.

Practice, then, must occur in a context that ensures success and benefit from effort. Furthermore, correct responses can be promoted by reinforcing, by rewarding, desired responses. In the psychological literature, a reinforcer is defined as any stimulus that increases the probability of a response (Hilgard, 1956, p. 89). Usually positive reinforcers consist of some sort of reward. In teaching mathematics, this may be self-satisfaction from mastering a task, grades, praise from peers, teachers, or parents, recognition from school authorities, or special privileges or prizes. These forms of reinforcement can serve as means of motivating the learning of skills.

Reinforcement must be used judiciously. Bugelski (1964), Watson (1961), Travers (1963), Biehler (1974), and others specify the following constraints that must be adhered to if reinforcement is to be effective:

1   In the initial stages of learning, all desirable outcomes should be reinforced.

2   Reinforcement should follow almost immediately the desired behavior when it occurs.

3   In the mind of the learner, the reinforcement must be clearly associated with the desired behavior.

4   Do not reinforce undesirable behavior.

Another factor to be considered in teaching skills is feedback. DeCecco (1968, p. 290) defines *feedback* as "the information available to the student which makes possible the comparison of his actual performance with some standard performance of a skill." Feedback is sometimes referred to as *knowledge of results*. After reviewing research on the acquisition of skills, Irion (1966) concludes that feedback is the most important variable in determining the learning of a skill. Feedback provides corrective information to the student and thus enables the student to monitor performance. This corrective information can improve a student's performance and hence serve as a reinforcer for the behavior that led to the improvement (Travers, 1963).

DeCecco (1968) stresses the importance of giving feedback immediately after a student's performance. When it is delayed, it is less effective and students tend to be less interested in their tasks. Furthermore, when feedback is immediate it can prompt and motivate subsequent behavior. Let us now consider guidelines for using practice, reinforcement, and feedback in teaching mathematical skills.

1   Strive to provide reinforcement and feedback during practice sessions. It is essential that the teacher supervise the efforts of students in practice sessions started preferably during class time. Immediate feedback is not always possible in the constraints of the typical classroom, but teachers can provide prompt feedback to many students by circulating and checking their progress or by watching their work at the chalkboard. By contacting as many students as possible, teachers have the opportunity to reinforce desirable responses and help students get started on the right track.

2   Make sure reinforcement is associated with desirable behavior. When students are observed doing a task or subtask correctly, they should be reinforced with praise such as "That's right," "That's a good start" or with the directive "O.K. Now don't forget to multiply the other side by 5 also." Be honest. Students are quick to perceive when praise is unwarranted and when it is, its effectiveness is diminished. When students make a mistake they should be informed of their error as soon as possible and provided corrective advice.

3   Do not reinforce inappropriate responses. According to the law of reinforcement, all reinforced behavior is likely to recur. The teacher who reinforces incorrect or substandard responses, then, is in effect increasing the likelihood that undesirable responses will recur. The acquisition of a skill can be hindered if reinforcement accompanies incorrect responses or undue slowness. This is not to say that a student who is making errors should not be encouraged. This encouragement might be couched in language such as, "Now you can get this. Keep trying" or "You haven't quite got it yet. Let's try this one together."

4 *Provide feedback by making answers available to students.* Since it is improbable that a teacher can provide prompt feedback to every student in a given class period, it is often effective to give students answers to selected problems. Students are thus provided feedback that can serve to reinforce correct answers. If their answers are incorrect, they should be advised to solicit help.

5 *Return assignments and test papers as quickly as possible.* Delay in returning papers reduces motivation and can be a factor in development of incorrect algorithms. It is especially important when students are first acquiring skills that teachers return papers or quizzes promptly so that students are aware of their errors and can either correct them or seek advice.

6 *Remind students of their objective.* Teachers should use *objective moves* to introduce a skill and inform students what is expected of them. One form of reinforcement for students is awareness of progress toward objectives. Sometimes students are performing a task correctly but not with the speed that the teacher desires or at a pace to enable them to use the procedure efficiently. For example, a student may be able to compute with percents but be so slow as to become discouraged and perhaps disorganized. The teacher can reinforce such students for accuracy and at the same time encourage them to keep practicing to increase speed.

7 *Try to get students to take pride in their work.* One of the strongest sources of reinforcement is provided by the student himself. Students receive self-satisfaction from mastering a task, especially when they have achieved a high level of proficiency. Teachers can accentuate this reinforcement by complimenting students on their achievement. Unfortunately, teachers only infrequently make deserving comments such as "Excellent John, you are getting very fast at that" or "I'm impressed, Holly. You keep that up and you might just be the world's fastest multiplier" or "You people as a class have done very well."

Thought questions

1   Is it possible for practice without feedback to be detrimental to acquisition of skills? Explain.

2   In discussing the guideline "Do not reinforce inappropriate responses," we suggested that teachers could give encouragement in language such as, "Now you can get this. Keep trying." Is this encouragement a form of reinforcement? If so, does it violate the guideline?

3   Making answers available to students is one means of providing feedback. There are occasions when teachers are reluctant to provide answers to exercises, however. One way to provide answers without "giving everything away" is to give answers in rearranged form so that the order of the answers differs from the order of the exercises. Discuss the advantages and disadvantages of this procedure.

4   Compare and contrast the contexts in which reinforcement would occur in following guidelines 3, 6, and 7.

5   In some general mathematics classes, calculators are provided to assist students who are slow in performing computation. What are some advantages and disadvantages of having calculators available for such students?

6   Programmed instructional materials are often used in teaching mathematical skills. How do these use the principles of reinforcement, feedback, and the spacing and varying of practice?

Scheduling practice

Two additional factors to be considered in providing practice are its distribution and its quantity. *Massed practice* is the distribution of practice over long sessions with little or no interruption. *Distributed practice* denotes shorter practice sessions with allowance for rest periods. Although most of the research on the relative merits of these types of practice has centered on the acquisition of motor skills, some of it offers implications for the teaching of mathematical skills. In general, the research indicates that distributed practice is superior to massed practice (DeCecco, 1968). Cronbach (1954) suggests several reasons for this. First, fatigue and boredom are more likely to accompany massed practice and these, in turn, encourage listless responses counterproductive to skill acquisition. Second, mistakes that occur during massed practice are likely to become fixed and the student may actually retain the wrong pattern of response. Another disadvantage of massed practice identified by Cronbach is that continuous practice makes it more difficult to identify weaknesses. The spacing of practice allows weaknesses to appear and can afford students opportunities to practice the subtasks causing their difficulty. Sometimes the acquisition of a skill is facilitated in the practice of subtasks that have been forgotten. For example, students computing with logarithms may be handicapped by an inability to interpolate. It behooves a teacher, then, to provide practice in interpolating. Of course, distributed practice is not without limitation. Cronbach points out the necessity of having practice sessions close enough together that forgetting is not dominant between the sessions.

Massed practice is cited by Ausubel (1968) as having the advantage of being more effective for the immediate retention of meaningfully learned materials. As Ausubel points out, massed practice in the form of cramming is an effective way of increasing performance for situations such as examinations requiring immediate recall. While such practice is effective in the short-term basis, however, long-term retention is better facilitated by distributed practice. This phenomenon associated with massed practice partially explains why students can perform adequately on a given test (generally after extensive practice or cramming) and yet frustrate the teacher by being unable to perform the same task a week or two later. Such frustration may manifest itself in statements such as, "Ed, don't you remember how to do that? We had the test on that just last week" or "How can you people forget this? We spent four weeks reviewing fractions and decimals at the beginning of the year!" It is difficult for teachers not to get angry in such situations. Anger is usually detrimental to the morale of both students and teachers. Teachers should realize that massed practice contributes to initially correct responses but lack of retention.

When the findings of research on massed versus distributed practice are applied to the teaching of mathematical skills, it is found that students acquire and retain skills more readily when short and frequent practice sessions are devoted to learning a particular skill. Beginning algebra students often have difficulty acquiring proficiency in computing with rational expressions, particularly with subtraction of rational expressions. It is more effective to allocate a certain portion of each day to these operations rather than a larger block of consecutive practice time. Of course, the practice session must be long enough to allow students to reach greater proficiency than they previously had.

Sometimes practice is made effective by increasing the time intervals between sessions. For example, a teacher may have students practice every day for a week, after which the time between practice sessions may be extended to two and then four days or whatever the teacher thinks necessary to help students retain their proficiency.

The amount of practice desirable depends on the complexity of the task, the age and ability of the students, and the importance of acquiring the skill. For example, solving linear equations and dividing polynomials by binomials are both complex tasks, but teachers and textbooks provide more practice for the first because being skilled in solving equations has greater utility in and out of the mathematics classroom. Textbooks generally provide an adequate number of exercises to develop and maintain a skilled performance. When they do not, the teacher is obliged to identify other sources of exercises (such as additional textbooks) and to schedule the spacing of the exercises.

Providing variety

Care must also be taken that practice does not become dull, monotonous, and purely mechanical. Continually practicing the same response in the same context has the effect of producing boredom and apathy. While the initial practice sessions for a particular task can be homogenous, teachers should strive to include variations in subsequent practice sessions. In addition to reminding students of the necessity and purpose for a particular drill exercise, teachers should attempt to provide questions that promote thought in the performance of desired tasks. Teachers can vary the intellectual context of practice in solving algebraic equations by asking students to locate errors in previously worked out solutions or to fill in missing steps. Students can also be required to estimate an answer before actually computing the result. In multiplying 2.3 by 4.7, students sometimes get 1,081, forgetting to place the decimal point and failing to realize that the answer must be approximately 10. Such errors can be averted if students are required to see whether their answers appear reasonable. Helping students to remain intellectually active during practice promotes accuracy.

Game-like situations help prevent practice from becoming monotonous. Various quiz games can be conducted to emphasize computational aspects of algebra and arithmetic. For example, a teacher can divide the class into teams and award points for correct answers, calibrated to the difficulty of the questions. Such games can be modeled after football, basketball, or baseball games or based on some popular TV quiz show. The competition involves students easily and stimulates them more than an ordinary drill. The disadvantage of games is the difficulty of clarifying mistakes when they occur, for the teacher cannot generally afford to let the game drag while explaining a misconception to one or two students. The teacher must also take care that every student participates.

Cross number puzzles and statistical work based on scores from athletic contests not only give students opportunity to learn basic statistics but also require them to practice computing. Codes can also be used in a rather sophisticated way to teach matrices to high school students or rational numbers through linear transformations. In selecting games or activities to promote the learning of skills, teachers must be sure that the activity that they have selected will emphasize the skill that needs to be learned. The role of the teacher is first to decide what skill needs to be learned and then select the learning activity that best enhances it. The teacher should not feel compelled to provide a different activity for each practice. But variance of routine tasks maintains student interest. When that interest is lost, no learning is likely to take place.

When students have acquired some proficiency in following an algorithm, it is appropriate for them to use their skill in solving word problems or other nonroutine exercises. In discussing the effect of practice in such a context, Cronbach (1954) points out that using a response in solving a problem is a superior form of practice. He also states that in such contexts students are motivated to perform responses correctly and will be alert to identifying and correcting errors and when successful be reinforced in their performance. In addition, such practice requires that skills be employed in varied contexts; this improves ability to transfer knowledge. Practicing in problem contexts is also viewed as a way of distributing practice and thus helps maintain proficiency level. For example, trigonometry problems involving angles of depression or elevation provide a context for practicing skills associated with trigonometric functions. Practice in solving equations is embedded in many algebraic word problems such as in money, age, and mixture problems.

Thought questions

1   Identify and explain a situation in your own learning of mathematics in which you knew how to do something but were not skilled in doing it.

2   The slogan "practice makes perfect," like most slogans, has the advantage of being easy to remember and the disadvantage of oversimplifying. Why does practicing golf not make everyone a great golfer? Why do students who try to solve many equations not always become skilled in solving equations?

3   Are the guidelines discussed in this chapter generalizations or prescriptions? Justify your answer.

4   Two teachers discuss the teaching of skills. One says:

T_1 I always make sure students understand the mathematical basis of the prescriptive principles I give. When practice is not guided by understanding, it is unlikely to be effective, for these students will make conceptual errors and will seldom retain the skill I want them to acquire.

The other says:

T_2 You are mouthing the myth of the intellectuals. The proper objective is the skill. As long as students can follow the prescriptive principles and get the right answer, why should they necessarily have to understand the process?

With which teacher do you agree? Defend your position.

5   Identify six mathematical tasks that because of their complexity would require considerable practice for students to become skilled in doing them. Are all these skills of sufficent importance to warrant the time needed for extensive practice?

6   Outline several activities that you could use with a class to practice the skills of multiplying rational numbers, finding the missing dimensions of triangles, and graphing linear equations.

7   What skills are involved by having students
    a   Calculate the distances between cities in a map?
    b   Find the approximate number of square miles in a given state or country?
    c   Construct various geometric patterns?
    d   Figure the cost of buying and maintaining an automobile?
    e   Write a computer program for finding the product of 2 × 2 matrices?

8   Consider the skills of interpolation and solving problems involving proportions. Discuss how you would indicate to students when these skills could be used. Your discussion might include situations inside and outside the mathematics classroom.

9   Identify some algebraic skill and describe a game you might use to provide practice for its acquisition.

10   In some mathematics textbook find five different kinds of word problems. What skills could be promoted in solving these problems? Do some of the problems emphasize the same skills?

Strategies in teaching skills

At this point in the chapter, you should be able to satisfy the first five competencies stated at the beginning. To provide further experience in considering ways of teaching skills, examine this dialogue between a teacher and a ninth-grade algebra class studying the division of algebraic fractions. The questions at the end of the dialogue concern the various teaching moves in it:

1   **T**   Today we are going to learn how to divide algebraic fractions. All of you will be expected to divide such fractions on the test next Friday. Dividing algebraic fractions is essentially the same as dividing ordinary fractions. If we had the problem $\frac{2}{3} \div \frac{4}{9}$ what would we do first? S_1?

2   S_1 Change it to a multiplication problem.

3   **T**   And how could we do that?

4   S_1 Invert the second number and multiply, like $\frac{2}{3} \times \frac{9}{4}$.

5   **T**   Invert the divisor. O.K., we remember that from arithmetic, don't we? All right, what do we do next? S_2?

6   S_2 Divide out like factors.

7   **T**   And what would you get?

8   S_2 (*Computing.*) You get $\frac{3}{2}$.

9   **T**   Fine. Now we are going to study the same sort of problem, only this time it involves algebraic fractions. First, could someone give me some examples of algebraic fractions?

10   S_3 $\dfrac{2}{x}, \dfrac{x+2}{x-4}, \dfrac{x}{z}$ or any fractions like these.

11   **T**   Good. Now if we have the problem $\dfrac{x^2y}{x^2-y^2} \div \dfrac{xy^2}{x+y}$ (*writes this on the board*) how could we change it to a multiplication problem?

12   S_4 Multiply by the reciprocal of the second number and get $\dfrac{x^2y}{x^2-y^2}$ times $\dfrac{x+y}{xy^2}$.

13   **T**   (*Writes this on the board also.*) O.K. Now if we divide out common factors what do we get? (*Students work at seats; finally S_5 gets an answer.*) S_5?

14   S_5 $\dfrac{x}{y(x-y)}$.

15   **T**   Very good. Come on now, S_6, take your eyes off Judy. Go to the board and try one for us. (*Reluctantly goes to the board.*)

16   S_6 What do you want?

17   **T**   Divide out this problem. (*Writes the following exercise on the board:* $\dfrac{x^2y}{x^2-xy} \div \dfrac{xy+y^2}{x^3}$. S_6 *begins by dividing out x^2 from a numerator and a denominator.*) Oh, wait a minute, S_6, I think you forgot something. S_7, what must we do first?

18   S_7 He forgot to turn the second fraction around.

19   **T**   You mean invert it. O.K. What would that give us, S_6?

     (*S_6 erases mistake and writes $\dfrac{x^2y}{x^2-xy} \times \dfrac{x^3}{xy+y^2}$ on board.*)

     Right. Now what, S_6?

20   S_6 I forgot.

21   T   Well, next see if you can divide out any common factors, like you started to do before.

22   S_6 Oh, yeah. O.K. $\left(\textit{Works at the board and with some additional prompting gets}\right.$

$\left.\dfrac{x^4}{x^2 - y^2}\cdot\right)$

23   T   O.K. Good. Suppose we want to check the answer to our first problem. How can we do that? (*No response.*) How could we check our answer of $\frac{3}{2}$ from the other problem? How can we check any division problem?

24   S_7 Oh, by multiplying. Like $\frac{6}{2} = 3$ because $6 = 3 \times 2$.

25   T   Fine, how about the one with $\frac{2}{3} \div \frac{4}{9}$?

26   S_7 Well, $\frac{2}{3} \div \frac{4}{9}$ equals $\frac{3}{2}$ should mean that $\frac{3}{2}$ times $\frac{4}{9}$ equals $\frac{2}{3}$.

27   T   Does it?

28   S_7 Yes.

29   T   How could we check our answer to the first one on the board there? (*Refers to utterance 11.*)

30   S_8 If our answer is correct, then $\dfrac{x}{y(x - y)}$ times $\dfrac{xy^2}{x + y}$ should give us the first

fraction, $\dfrac{x^2 y}{x^2 - y^2}$.

31   T   Everybody check that. (*Class confirms the answer is correct.*)
Are there any other ways we could check our answer to this problem?

32   S_9 We could substitute numbers and see if it works out the same.

33   T   (*Assigns values $x = 2$ and $y = 3$ and the class confirms that a numerical identify results on substitution of the assigned values.*) So we have two ways of checking our answers. Either way will help us determine whether our answer is correct. Could someone tell us, again, what steps we have to follow to divide algebraic fractions?

34   S_{10} Well, first you change it to a multiplication problem by multiplying by the second fraction inverted, the reciprocal I think you call it. Then you divide or cancel out like factors and then multiply.

35   T   Very good. Here are my answers to the first ten exercises on page 162. Work these now and see if you get the same results.

What knowledge was being taught in this dialogue? On what prescriptions was the teacher basing the lesson? Did the teacher use any motivation moves? Objective moves? How did the teacher justify the prescriptions? In what way did the teacher interpret or clarify them? What analogy move did the teacher use? At what point in the lesson did this move occur? Do you think this was effective? Notice that in the problem in utterance 11, the teacher did not specify the domain of the variables. What restrictions should have been placed on the values of x and y? Would stating the restrictions constitute an interpretation move? What demonstration moves did the teacher use? What advice did the teacher give? In what way did the teacher provide practice and feedback? Did reinforcement accompany the feedback? How might the teacher distribute practice to help these students become skillful in dividing algebraic fractions?

The preceding dialogue and following questions illustrate how various moves can be used to construct a strategy for teaching a skill. In developing a strategy you might use, ask yourself the following questions in planning a lesson. First, before actually designing a sequence of moves, ask:

1   What is the skill I am going to teach? As in any lesson, the teacher should be explicitly aware of the mathematics—that is, the object of instruction.

2   What are the prescriptive principles that will be the basis of teaching the students how to perform the desired task?

With this information in mind, ask the following questions.

3   When I introduce and focus the students' attention on acquiring the skill, what objective move should I give? Recall that achievement generally increases when students know what is expected of them. What reasons or other motivation moves can I provide for acquiring this skill?

4   If I explicitly state the prescriptive principles, will there be terms that will be confusing to students or that they may have forgotten? Should I or the students paraphrase the principles? Are there prerequisite tasks that need reviewing? What examples should I select to demonstrate the principles? What advice will be most helpful? Is there an analogous skill students have already acquired that will facilitate the learning of this new skill?

5   How can I best convince students that the procedure they are following is correct? Should I just show them that it always produces the correct result or should I also provide a deductive argument? The answers to these questions depend on the age and ability of the student and how much you value understanding.

The next series of questions deals with the second aspect of acquiring a skill—how to become fast and accurate in doing a task.

6   Before I provide practice, am I convinced the students comprehend and know how to follow the desired procedure? If not, I will need to use additional moves. At this point it might be a good idea to remind students why it is important for them to be skilled in this activity.

7   In designing practice sessions, how much practice should I provide? Certainly the students will need enough practice to enable them to perform the task efficiently. The actual amount of practice will be determined largely by your judgment of the importance of the skill and the nature of the students. How can I best provide feedback and reinforcement for the students? How should I distribute the practice—that is, how much time should I allot each day for practice? How can I vary the contexts of the practice sessions and thus avoid monotonous drill?

Faced with the reality of preparing a variety of lessons for a given day, a teacher may not always have the luxury of completing as detailed an analysis as the one outlined above. The extent to which a teacher identifies the knowledge to be taught and explicitly considers ways of introducing the lesson, of interpreting and justifying required knowledge and carefully designing practice sessions, is the extent to which the presentation will be clear, organized, and hence likely to increase student achievement.

Thought questions

1   Using an imaginary dialogue, illustrate a second strategy for teaching the division of algebraic fractions.

2   Identify a skill and outline a strategy by which you might teach a seventh-grader.

3   Identify a skill and outline a strategy for teaching a geometry student.

4   Return to the first set of thought questions in this chapter and answer question 4. Does your answer now differ in any way from your original answer?

Self-test on the competencies

1   Discuss what implications the difference between skills and cognitive knowledge has for teaching mathematical skills.
   a   How is the skill of finding the least common multiple of two given natural numbers different from knowing how to find the least common multiple of these same numbers? How are each of these different from the concept of least common multiple?
   b   How does this difference affect the planning of a lesson?

2   Identify prescriptions useful in teaching a given skill.
   a   What prescriptions would you use in instructing students how to solve linear equations in one variable?
   b   What prescriptions would you use in showing students how to construct the mean proportional to two given line segments?

3   Identify moves used in teaching a skill.
   a   State a focus and an objective move you might use to teach the skill of factoring trinomials.
   b   Outline how you would motivate students to become skilled in finding the percent of increase or decrease of two given numbers.
   c   Suppose you were using the following prescription for showing students how to find the inverse of a 3×3 nonsingular matrix: "To find the inverse multiply the adjoint of the given matrix by the reciprocal of the determinant of the given matrix." Using this prescription, illustrate the following moves: review terms (and prerequisite skills), paraphrase, and demonstration (including advice you might give).
   d   Suppose you were instructing students on adding algebraic fractions such as $-y/(x^2 - y^2) + y/(x^2 + xy)$. Identify prerequisite skills you should review. What demonstrations and advice would you provide? Identify an analogy move you might use.
   e   Suppose you have directed seventh-graders to find the area of parallelograms by following this prescription: "To find the area of a parallelogram, multiply the length of the base by the length of the height." Indicate two ways you could justify this prescription.

f Suppose you have directed twelfth-graders to find the sum of an arithmetic sequence by following this prescription: "To find the sum of an arithmetic sequence, multiply the sum of the first and last terms by one-half the number of terms in the sequence." Indicate two ways you could justify this prescription.

4 Discuss, including implications for teaching, the general conditions under which practice can be effective.

   a Why is practice necessary for the acquisition of a skill?

   b Suppose you were providing practice in converting decimals to scientific notation. You observe that many students are making errors such as $.0256 = 2.56 \times 10^2$. In all likelihood, what general condition for practice has been violated and what implications does this have for your subsequent teaching?

   c We stated in this chapter that feedback can be a form of reinforcement. Describe a context in which feedback would not be reinforcing and could be counter-productive.

   d In the situation described below, a teacher is violating a guideline for using reinforcement and feedback. What guideline is violated, and how would you have reacted?

     (1) The teacher observes a student solving a quadratic inequality in the following way:

$$(x - 2)(x - 5) > 0$$
$$x - 2 > 0, \text{ or } x > 2$$
$$x - 5 > 0, \text{ or } x > 5$$
$$\text{hence } x > 5$$

     (2) The teacher then makes the following comment to the student: "That's right, Donna, anytime x is greater than 5, you have a correct answer. Keep up the good work."

   e What guideline is being violated in this teacher's statement: "Now here is a worksheet on graphing inequalities. If you get stuck or have questions, come up to my desk for help."

   f Suppose you have just distributed a worksheet on adding and subtracting rational numbers. Discuss a variety of ways that you could maximize reinforcement and feedback for students.

   g A teacher begins the year with an extensive review and practice in computing with fractions. After several long practice sessions, the teacher tests the students. The results range from 80 percent to 100 percent correct, with the median being 92 percent. The teacher is pleased with these results. What conclusions can the teacher justifiably make with respect to acquisition and maintenance of the students' skills?

5 Devise a variety of activities that can promote the learning of a specific skill.

   a Outline activities that a teacher might use to provide practice in bisecting line segments and bisecting angles.

   b Outline activities that a teacher might use to provide practice in graphing points on a coordinate axis system.

6 Using the moves discussed in the chapter, plan a lesson for teaching a skill.

   a Plan a lesson for which the objective is to teach the skill of subtracting rational numbers.

   b Write a lesson plan for teaching students how to construct an indirect proof.

References

Ausubel, David P. *Educational Psychology: A Cognitive View.* New York: Holt, Rinehart and Winston, 1968.

Biehler, Robert F. *Psychology Applied to Teaching,* 2nd ed. Boston: Houghton Mifflin, 1974.

Bugelski, B. R. *The Psychology of Learning Applied to Teaching.* New York: Bobbs-Merrill, 1964.

Cronbach, Lee J. *Educational Psychology.* New York: Harcourt Brace Jovanovich, 1954.

DeCecco, John P. *The Psychology of Learning and Instruction: Educational Psychology.* Englewood Cliffs, N. J.: Prentice-Hall, 1968.

Dolciani, Mary P., Simon L. Berman, and William Wooton. *Modern Algebra and Trigonometry.* Boston: Houghton Mifflin, 1970.

Garrett, Henry. *The Art of Good Teaching.* New York: McKay, 1964.

Glennon, Vincent J., and Leroy Callahan. "What Is the Place of Practice (Drill) in the Contemporary Program?" *Elementary School Mathematics.* Washington D. C.: National Education Association, 1968. Pp. 79–81.

Hadley, G. *Linear Algebra.* Reading, Mass.: Addison-Wesley, 1961.

Henderson, Kenneth B. "Uses of 'Subject Matter.'" *Language and Concepts in Education,* ed. by B. Othanel Smith and Robert H. Ennis. Chicago: Rand McNally, 1961. Pp. 43–58.

————. *Teaching Secondary School Mathematics.* Washington D. C.: National Education Association, 1969.

Hilgard, Ernest. *Theories of Learning.* New York: Appleton-Century-Crofts, 1956.

Irion, Arthur L. "A Brief History of Research on the Acquisition of Skill."*Acquisition of Skill,* ed. by E. H. Bilodeau. New York: Academic Press, 1966. Pp. 1–46.

Quast, N. G., "On Computation and Drill." *The Arithmetic Teacher,* 16 (1969), 627–630.

Ryle, Gilbert, *The Concept of Mind.* New York: Barnes and Noble, 1949.

Sobel, Max. "Skills." *The Teaching of Secondary School Mathematics,* Thirty-Third Yearbook of the National Council of Teachers of Mathematics. Washington, D. C.: The Council, 1970. Pp. 291–308.

Sueltz, Ben. "Drill-Practice-Recurring Experiences." *The Learning of Mathematics: Its Theory and Practice,* Twenty-First Yearbook of the National Council of Teachers of Mathematics. Washington, D. C.: The Council, 1953.

Symonds, Percival. *What Education Has to Learn from Psychology.* New York: Teachers College Press, 1968.

Todd, Howell Wayne. "Moves and Strategies in a Skill Venture in Secondary School Mathematics." Ph.D. dissertation. Urbana: University of Illinois, 1972.

Travers, Robert M. W. *Essential of Learning.* New York: Macmillan, 1963.

Watson, Goodwin, *What Education Has to Learn from Psychology.* New York: Teachers College Press, 1961.

References for instructional material

Brandes, Louis Grant. *Geometry Can Be Fun.* Portland, Me.: J. Weston Walsh, 1958.

Brandes, Louis Grant. *Yes, Math Can Be Fun.* Portland, Me.: J. Weston Walsh, 1960.

Creative Publications Catalogue of Instructional Aids in Mathematics. P.O. Box 328, Palo Alto, California 94302.

Johnson, Donovan. *Games for Learning Mathematics.* Portland, Me.: J. Weston Walsh, 1962.

Midwest Publications Catalogue of Instructional Materials for Mathematics. P.O. Box 307, Birmingham, Mich. 48012.

Peck, Lyman C. *Secret Codes, Remainder Arithmetic, and Matrices.* Washington, D. C.: National Council of Teachers of Mathematics, 1961.

9

Diagnosis and remediation of student difficulties

Students differ in intellectual ability to abstract, generalize, reason, and remember; disposition to try to understand, persist in the face of frustration, seek help, and try to improve; and interest in mathematics and other academic subjects, sports, members of the opposite sex, and vocations. Because of these varying abilities, dispositions, and interests, some students learn readily and usually understand what they are taught the first time it is taught while others are not quick to catch on and need review and reteaching.

A successful teacher can assess the abilities, values, and interest of students and adjust so that most, if not all, students understand what they are learning and are able to apply it in solving problems and making decisions. If some students have trouble understanding, the teacher can diagnose the trouble and provide appropriate remedial instruction. These activities are a normal part of teaching. A teacher should not feel ineffective if some students fail to understand what he or she is teaching the first time a topic is presented. Such students should be regarded as challenges and their temporary lack of understanding as a problem to be solved.

In this chapter we shall present an analysis of the task of coping with the difficulties students typically manifest in learning, making some suggestions about how a teacher can improve diagnosis of these difficulties, and how remedial teaching can remove the difficulties. We begin by setting diagnosis in the context of problem-solving. Each student having difficulty in learning poses a problem to be defined, attacked, and, it is hoped, solved. The teacher proceeds much as a doctor does in conducting diagnosis and pre-scribing treatment.

It is helpful to know some of the basic causes of the difficulties students have in learning mathematics. These become conjectures to test in particular cases and hence we discuss how teachers can secure data to test assumptions of a particular cause.

We then turn discussion to the difficulties students have in learning two of the important kinds of mathematical knowledge: concepts and principles. This is extended to the difficulties they may have when they are expected to solve verbal problems. Finally, we state some principles that can be used to guide remedial instruction designed to remove the difficulties, whatever they may be.

> At the conclusion of this chapter you should be able to demonstrate the following competencies:
>
> 1 State possible causes of a student's difficulties in learning
>
> 2 Identify the kind of difficulty a student has in using concepts, using principles, and solving verbal problems
>
> 3 Form and test conjectures as to the cause of the difficulties stated in competency 2
>
> 4 Having accepted a conjecture concerning the cause of a difficulty provide remedial teaching

Diagnosis as problem–solving

We may approach the consideration of diagnosis by drawing an analogy between what a doctor does and what a teacher does. If you are ill and seek the services of a doctor, she probably asks you what the trouble is. You tell her how you feel and perhaps what you think. Depending on what your discomfort is, the doctor asks you some questions. She may take your temperature and pulse or palpate some region of your body. She may ask you to have an x-ray, one or more blood tests, a urinalysis, or other tests. The doctor does all this to collect data that form the basis of subsequent diagnosis—what the cause of discomfort is. Having made the diagnosis, she then prescribes remediation—medicine, therapy, change of diet, rest, or what not. If the remediation is effective, the problem has been solved. If not, the doctor may reexamine the data and perhaps collect some more. She then makes another prescription. If this, too, is not effective, the cycle is covered again. The end result is, hopefully, removal of the difficulty.

The analogy of the work of a teacher to that of a doctor is not perfect. A doctor is expected to treat only persons who consult her, who want to be helped; a teacher is expected to treat both those who want help and those who do not. Then, too, the teacher has to live with lack of success, in a way a doctor does not. Yet there are great similarities, for basically what is involved is problem-solving. Let us consider this.

As the basis of our analysis, we shall use a model John Dewey proposed in his celebrated book *How We Think*. Dewey pointed out that the first step in solving a problem is becoming aware of it. In the case of the teacher, this occurs when students cannot answer certain questions, cannot apply concepts and principles they have been taught, or make the same mistake repeatedly.

The second step is definition of the problem. Just what kinds of error is a student or a group of students making? What misunderstandings do they manifest? What can they not do? The more analytical and restricted are the generalizations the teacher makes, the clearer is the definition of the problem. A teacher who says that some students do not understand what they have learned is not able to follow through in diagnosis as one who says, for example, that the students do not understand the relation between the definition of a root of an equation and solving an equation or do not see that the conventional algorithm for multiplying two binomials is derived from the distributive principle of multiplication over addition or do not realize that from a definition like

A polyhedron is a closed geometric figure composed of four or more polygonal surfaces, no two of which are in the same plane.

one can draw such inferences as a closed geometric figure composed of four or more polygonal surfaces, no two of which are in the same plane, is a polyhedron, and for a geometric figure to be a polyhedron it is necessary, among other conditions, that it be composed of four or more polygonal surfaces. A teacher who says that students cannot apply what they have learned will find more difficulty in diagnosing the causes of these inadequacies than one who is more analytical and says, for example, that the students cannot recognize a trapezoid, cannot form the contrapositive of a conditional proposition, or cannot solve story problems.

Once the problem has been defined, the next step is to collect data that will enable the person to solve the problem. But not all data are relevant. How is relevancy determined? It is determined in terms of hunches or conjectures as to how the problem may be solved. Hunches indicate the data that are necessary for testing them—in other words, data that are relevant.

Let us now relate this to the process of diagnosis in which a teacher engages. Once the teacher has defined the problem—for example, that the student makes mistakes in subtracting rational (signed) numbers—the teacher has to decide what the cause or causes of the errors are. The teacher recalls how he or she taught this skill. The principle taught was: to subtract b from a, add the additive inverse of b to a. There was plenty of practice with a variety of exercises. The particular student appeared attentive while the operation was explained and did the homework. The teacher gets a hunch as to a possible cause of the student's errors: the student does not know what an additive inverse is, does not have a concept of the additive inverse of a rational number. The teacher tests this hunch perhaps by asking the student to state the additive inverse of several rational numbers. The student's answers are data that enable the teacher to test the hunch. Suppose the student is able to state the additive inverses correctly. It is probable that the teacher's conjecture as to the cause of the student's errors is therefore false, and a new conjecture has to be formed, as for example, that the student does not know how to add rational numbers. The teacher tests this hunch by giving the student several addition exercises and finds the student undependable in addition; the student gets the right answer for a few exercises and the wrong answer for the others. These data test the teacher's conjecture and indicate that it is probably true.

The final step in solving a problem is to act in terms of the hunch that has been found to be true. The teacher we have been considering would probably reteach the student how to add rational numbers. If thereafter the student made no or fewer errors in subtraction, the teacher would be warranted in deciding that diagnosis and remediation had been correct. If the student continued to make errors, however, evidently only one cause of the errors had been identified. The teacher has to go through the cycle again until diagnosis and remediation eliminate the errors.

Let us particularize this model of problem-solving by relating it to the diagnosis that a teacher has to make when students are not learning or have not attained the objectives set for them. We may say that there are four steps in diagnosis. The first is to discover which students are having difficulties. It is these to whom the teacher gives attention. It is of little value teaching cognitive knowledge or skills to students who have already learned it.

The second step is to find out what kind of errors a student or a group of students are making. They may be able to state part of a definition but not the complete definition. They may be able to repeat the statement of a principle given in the textbook but not be able to state it in their own words or give instances of it. They may not be able to abstract a pattern from a set of instances and hence not able to discover a generalization the teacher is trying to teach them. Or they may be able to apply a principle when the teacher or textbook tells them that it is relevant but not be able to decide which principles are relevant when faced with a problem to solve.

The kind of error a student makes leads to the third step in diagnosis— conjecturing the cause of the error. Errors are observable but why an error is made—that is, its cause—is not observed and can only be inferred. Inferred causes explain the errors. For example, if a student is asked to divide 4 by $\frac{1}{2}$ and gives $\frac{1}{8}$ as an answer, the teacher might guess that the student does not know which number is the divisor or knows how to divide by a whole number but not by a fraction. So, given a division by a fraction and expected to come up with an answer, the student divides in the only way he or she knows. Either of these conjectures explains the student's error and implies a cause of error.

Conjectures as to the cause of errors, misunderstanding, or lack of comprehension may be correct or incorrect and hence have to be tested.

Testing is the fourth step in diagnosis and is done in either of two ways. The extent to which a conjecture explains the difficulties a student is having is one test. The better the conjecture explains the difficulties, the more confidence the teacher can have that it is true. A second way of testing is to use the conjecture as a hypothesis and make some predictions by means of it. If the predictions are confirmed by subsequent data, confidence in the hypothesis is enhanced. This second test is more conclusive than the other.

A student teacher who had had some training in diagnosis and was teaching the solution of quadratic equations by factoring gave an example of testing conjectures about the cause of one student's difficulty. As extra-credit problems, she had assigned three quartic equations that were quadratic in form. During a discussion of the homework, she asked how many had not been able to solve the extra-credit problems and several students raised their hands. She asked why they had had trouble. One boy responded that they had not previously had any equations like these.

In the discussion with the student teacher after the teaching had been completed, the supervisor asked whether the student teacher had anticipated that some students would have trouble with these equations. She replied that she had. On being queried as to what she had thought the cause of the trouble would be, she replied that she had anticipated that some students would not recognize that the equations were quadratic in form even though they were fourth-degree equations. She felt that the one student's response that they had not had equations like these verified her conjecture; the conjecture explained the student's response.

After the student had replied that the class had not had equations like these, the student teacher selected the equation $6x^4 - 17x^2 + 12 = 0$ and asked the student whether he could solve a similar equation, like $6a^2 - 17a + 12 = 0$. The student said that he thought he could. The student teacher then suggested that he take a as equal to x^2, solve this equation for a, and then let $a = x^2$ and solve for x. She took his "Oh, I see" as indication that he comprehended. She then asked the boy how he would solve another of the equations she had given for extra credit: $4n^4 - 20n^2 - 25 = 0$. After a minor hesitation, he said he would replace n^4 by a^2 and n^2 by a and solve the resulting equation for a. Then he would set $a = n^2$ and solve for n. The teacher asked him how many roots he would expect for the given equation, and he said four.

In the subsequent discussion, the student teacher was asked by the supervisor how she interpreted the boy's responses relative to her conjecture about the cause of his trouble. She thought that they further confirmed her conjecture, for they were about what she predicted. Since the boy was able to solve the second quartic when she presented it in the manner she had, she believed that he had sensed the pattern.

In general, testing conjectures as to the cause of student difficulties consists in securing additional data, often by questioning, that confirm or disconfirm the conjecture. Once the correct conjecture has been determined, the teacher can decide what kind of remedial teaching to employ. It should be noticed that remedial teaching in itself supplies further data for testing conjectures. If the remedial teaching corrects the difficulty, the conjecture on which it was predicated is probably true; if it does not correct the difficulty, the conjecture is probably false. In this event, the conjecture should be reconsidered and perhaps a new one formed. This then becomes subject to testing in the ways we discussed above.

Notice in the following dialogue how the teacher may be considered to have followed the four steps in making a diagnosis. The teacher had just assigned as homework some equations to be solved. The sentences enclosed in square brackets express what the teacher may have thought; there is no way of knowing whether these thoughts were actual, for the teacher was not interviewed afterward.

1 **T** Look at equations 12, 13, and 14. You haven't solved any like these before. [*The equations contain rational expressions.*] Let's do one like these together. Let's take (*writing on the chalkboard*)

$$\frac{2}{x+2} + 5 = \frac{4x}{x-2}$$

This would be easy to solve if there were no fractions in it. So let's clear the equation of fractions as the first step. We can do this by multiplying both sides by the lowest common denominator. [*I'd better check to see whether the students have the concept of the lowest common denominator. If some of them don't, they won't understand the procedure.*] What's this (*pointing to "x + 2"*) ? S_1.

2 **S_1** A—ah—a binomial?

3 **T** Well, yes. You're right; it is a binomial. But relative to this fraction (*pointing to the fraction in the left member of the equation*), what is it called ? (*Indicates S_1 is to answer, but S_1 does not answer. Calls on S_2, who also does not answer.*) [*Knowing S_2 as I do, she may know the answer but, being as insecure as she is, she may be unwilling to take a chance in being wrong and revealing this to me and the other students. That's why she's decided not to answer. But, then, it is possible she doesn't have the concept of a denominator. Or maybe she knows what a denominator is—can say what a denominator is—but for some reason doesn't see x + 2 as an example of a denominator. I'd better check these possible explanations.*] Who knows what $x + 2$ is called? S_3.

4 **S_3** Denominator.

5 **T** Right, denominator. [*Now to get some more information from S_2.*] Is there another denominator in the equation, S_2?

6 **S_2** $x - 2$.

7 **T** Right. [*Did she make a lucky guess? Improbable. Maybe she reasoned by analogy. If not, she ought to be able to tell how a denominator is identified.*] How do you know?

8 **S_2** It's the expression in the fraction under the line.

9 **T** [*Well, she probably knows what a denominator is. So why couldn't she classify x + 2 as a denominator? I don't know.*] What's the denominator of 5 ? S_4.

10   S_4 There isn't any.

11   S_5 (*To S_4.*) Sure there is. When a denominator isn't written, it is understood to be 1.

12   S_4 (*To S_5.*) You just *said* there isn't any. I know when there isn't one written, it's understood to be 1. But the teacher asked what the denominator of 5 is, and there isn't any.

13   T   O.K., O.K. I think we understand each other. Now what's the lowest common denominator of the two denominators $x + 2$ and $x - 2$? S_6 knows.

14   S_6 (*Pause.*) I guess I don't.

15   T   [*Here we go again! Does S_6 not know because he doesn't know what a lowest common denominator is? Or is it because, while knowing what a lowest common denominator is, he can't apply the concept in this case? If he knows what a lowest common denominator is, he ought to be able to define it.*] Well, let's begin by finding out what a lowest common denominator is. You learned this in grade school. What's the lowest common denominator of two or more denominators, S_6? (*S_6 does not answer.*) [*Well, it looks as though he doesn't have the concept. Knowing him, he'd surely answer if he knew.*]

16   T   Who will tell S_6 what the lowest common denominator is? S_7.

17   S_7 The lowest common multiple of the denominators.

18   T   [*This may not be helpful; it has some of the same words, "lowest" and "common," that the term being defined has. Also they have to have the concept of a multiple. Too risky to use this definition.*] True. But then we have to know what the lowest common multiple is. Let's stick with lowest common denominator. Who doesn't know what a lowest common denominator is or how to find one? (*Three students raise their hands.*) O.K. Let's get the four of us, and anyone else who wants to come, over in this corner, and we'll review l.c.d.'s—lowest common denominators. The rest of you multiply both sides of this equation (*pointing to the chalkboard*) by the l.c.d. This will clear it of fractions, and then you can solve the resulting equation. Be sure you can prove to me that the numbers you find are roots.

In analyzing this dialogue, we see that in utterance 1 the teacher asked for a classification: "What's this (*pointing to* "$x + 2$")?" We cannot be sure why he did this, but perhaps it was an initial move employed to ascertain whether the students had the concept of the lowest common denominator. This is a conjunctive concept, and hence a necessary condition for having this concept is that they have the concept of a denominator. The teacher appeared to be trying to find out first whether the students had this basic concept. Perhaps he reasoned that if they could recognize examples of denominators, they probably had the concept.

Two students could not answer. It may be that these were the only students who could not pick out examples of denominators. But it is probable, and pedagogically a sound hypothesis, that other students were equally unclear even though one student—S_3 in utterance 4—could do this.

The teacher may be regarded as having completed the first two steps in diagnosis; he identified some students who were having difficulties, and he identified what the difficulties were. He may then, in the third step, have conjectured that S_2 did not know what a denominator is even though she picked out an example. Hence he asked, in utterance 7, "How do you know?" The answer S_2 gave disconfirmed his conjecture. He had then completed the fourth step. Notice that although the teacher had tested his conjecture, he had not determined why S_2 was not able to identify $x + 2$ as a denominator. Other conjectures are possible, each of which can be tested.

From utterance 14, the teacher identified a student who could not apply the concept of the lowest common denominator; he could not give the lowest common denominator of $x + 2$ and $x - 2$, an easy application of the concept. Why could the student not do this? Some possible explanations are enclosed in the square brackets in utterance 15. The teacher's question in utterance 15 sought data for testing one of these conjectures—namely, the student who did not have the concept. His conjecture appeared confirmed by the silence of S_6.

The teacher then initiated a definitional move in utterance 16. The response he got was not what he wanted, but he accepted it.

The diagnosis began again; the teacher identified at least three students and their difficulty: they did not know what the lowest common denominator was. In other words, they did not have the concept of the lowest common denominator. He then separated them from the entire class to give them remedial instruction.

Thought questions

1 What kind of move is initiated by the teacher's question in utterance 1?

2 The teacher in utterance 1 could have initiated a definitional move by asking, "What is a denominator?" or "Who will define a denominator for us?" Instead he initiated an example move. Under what conditions would you use the one or the other? Why?

3 As an answer to his question in utterance 3, the teacher evidently wanted the technical name *denominator*. Suppose the student had said, "the expression under the line of a fraction." Would he have had the concept? Why? Should the teacher accept this answer? Why?

4 Are there conjectures, other than those given within the square brackets, as to why S_2 did not answer? If so, state them.

5 If you stated conjectures for question 4, how could they be tested?

6 In utterance 5, the teacher initiated an example move. What other kind of move could he have initiated? Phrase a question to do this. Which move do you think is more effective? Why?

7 Do you agree with the teacher's possible conjecture as stated within the square brackets in utterance 9? Defend your answer.

8 Offer a conjecture other than the ones stated in the square brackets in utterance 15. How would you test this conjecture?

9 In utterance 15, the teacher used a question to solicit a definitional move. He could have given the definition himself. As it turned out, doing this would have avoided the response he did not want. Which alternative is better? Why?

10   Should the teacher have accepted the definition of S_7 in utterance 17? Why?

11   Suppose the teacher had accepted the definition of S_7 in utterance 17 while conjecturing that some students might not have the concept of the lowest common multiple? Tell how you would, if you were the teacher, carry out the four steps in diagnosis.

12   Imagine you were the teacher giving the remedial instruction to the three students. Determine and defend a strategy for reteaching the concept of the lowest common denominator.

13   Did the teacher provide motivation?

14   The teacher chose an equation like but not identical to the ones the students were to solve as homework. How much alike should the equation selected and those assigned for homework have been? Defend your answer.

Basic causes of student difficulties

It is helpful to know and keep in mind basic causes of student difficulties. These become sources of conjecture for inferences concerning causes in particular cases.

Physiological factors

Brueckner and Bond in their useful book *The Diagnosis and Treatment of Learning Difficulties* report on the relation between physiological factors and learning difficulties. In a population of children with visual defects, there is a larger percentage of children with educational disabilities than in a normal population. Conversely, among children having difficulties in learning, there is a slightly greater percentage of children with visual defects. Similarly, there is a positive, though low, correlation between auditory acuity and educational success. Both of these may account for the disability some students have in reading as well as in following a teacher's exposition in class.

Betts (1946) has given a list of symptoms of visual and auditory problems. As symptoms of visual discomfort, he gives (p. 182) reddening and thickening of the margins of the eyelids; scales and crusts on the eyelids; loss of eyelashes; watering of or discharge around the eyes; inflammation or reddening of the eyes; cloudiness of the pupils; drooping of an upper eyelid; widely dilated pupils; difference in the size of the pupils; deviation of one eye; forward thrust or tilting of the head; facial contortions, such as puckering, frowning, or scowling; continual rubbing of the eyes; excessive blinking; excessive head movement while reading. Betts' list of symptoms of auditory problems is (p. 208) monotonous or unnatural pitch of the voice; faulty pronunciation and lack of clear or distinct speech; turning one ear toward the speaker; poor spelling; inattention; frequent requests for repeating questions or statements; difficult breathing, including mouth breathing; earache; discharge from the ears; catarrhal conditions; sinus infection; frequent colds; excessive accumulation of earwax. Some of these symptoms can be observed readily by the classroom teacher; others are not as evident. Should the teacher believe that a student has a visual or auditory problem, the assistance of a specialist such as a doctor or a teacher of the physically handicapped should be consulted.

It is to be expected that students who have defects in vision or hearing will experience difficulties in learning. Typical classroom learning requires extensive use of these senses. For example, any student who cannot see very well will be handicapped by not being able to see clearly what the teacher is writing on the chalkboard. Moreover, the student will find it hard to read textbooks, exercises, and tests. Similarly, a student who cannot hear well will be handicapped by not being able to hear the teacher's explanations and directions and other students' remarks.

Some students do not get enough to eat. If they are hungry, it is hard for them to pay attention to explanations and assignments and hence they miss important parts of the instruction. If they are severely malnourished, their mental activity may be impaired. The teacher may think that their difficulties are caused by mental deficiencies when the cause is actually physiological.

It is possible that students who are inattentive or cannot concentrate may be taking drugs. Such a hypothesis is tenable if their behavior suddenly deviates from their normal behavior and there is no other explanation for this. Symptoms of the influence of drugs, as stated in *Teaching About Drug Abuse* (1972, pp. 22–26), are marked changes in the legibility and neatness of handwriting; unusual degrees of activity or inactivity; sudden and irrational displays of temper, depression, anxiety, tears, or laughter; significant changes in personal appearance such as indifference to appearance and health habits; furtive behavior regarding possessions and actions stemming from fear of discovery; wearing sunglasses at inappropriate or unusual times or places to hide dilated or constricted pupils of the eyes; wearing long-sleeved garments or gloves continually, even on hot days, to hide needlemarks; stealing or frequently trying to borrow money to pay for drugs; being found at odd times in odd places such as closets, storage rooms, or parked cars; having visual or auditory hallucinations; licking chapped and red lips constantly (amphetamines have a drying effect on the mucous membranes of the mouth and nose); drowsiness or excessive yawning; lack of coordination expressed as slurred speech, staggering, stumbling, dropping objects, or cigarette burns on the skin. A teacher who suspects that the use of drugs may be a cause of a student's trouble should seek the advice of a specialist, unless he or she has had specialized education about drugs.

Physiological causes of student difficulties are usually beyond remedy by the classroom teacher. The teacher might be able to identify them and compensate for visual or auditory defects. But more specialized help may have to come from other personnel in the school system such as school psychologists, doctors, and dentists or teachers of the physically or emotionally handicapped.

Social factors

Teachers often do not realize how many social factors influence a student's learning. Consider two students, one whose parents express their value of education and their hope that he or she will do well in school and the other whose parents denigrate education and tell him or her that he or she would be better off not in school. It is easy to see that a student like the second who accepts parental values will not do well in school because there is no motivation or reinforcement at home.

Sometimes parents provide a rationalization for their child to excuse poor performance in mathematics. The mother or father may say, "I never was good in mathematics" or "Mathematics always was hard for me." A parent may even commiserate with the child for poor performance on the basis of the parent's similar poor performance. The child may then cease to work on the assumption of a hereditary shortcoming in this subject.

Lack of cultural advantages in the home may handicap students. A home that has a television set, reference books, magazines, and parents who take their children on trips to museums, exhibits, and libraries provides great advantages for informal learning. Students who do not come from such homes are at a disadvantage, even though they may be intellectually able. It takes them longer to acquire certain concepts and principles because they have had fewer opportunities to manipulate them in nonacademic situations.

Social factors within the classroom may also work against some students. Students who have no friends in the class may feel isolated or suffer ridicule. The atmosphere of the class may militate against doing well; one gets recognition and approval from peers by not doing well. Such unwholesome atmosphere is not common, but it can and does occur in neighborhoods in which social deprivation and disintegration exist.

Emotional factors

The student who has had repeated lack of success in mathematics in elementary school may develop an irrational but deep-seated anxiety and fear or hatred of this subject. Irrespective of how able he or she may be intellectually the student may do poorly in mathematics by making no effort to do assignments, solve problems, or take tests. The student's feeling is that, were one to do these things, he or she would probably only fail as in the past. To preserve self-esteem, such students do not try, then they cannot possibly fail.

There may also be temporary but intense periods of emotional stress. A close relative or friend may be sick or have died. There may have been severe discord between a student's parents just before school. A student may have broken up with a close friend. A pet may have been hurt or died. In such cases, the student may find it impossible to pay attention, be unable to read the textbook, incapable of attending to important explanations in class, and forgetful of assignments. The teacher who is not aware of such factors may entertain as conjectures causes that are not the real ones and remedial treatment probably will not be effective.

Intellectual factors

Intellectual and motivational factors are the ones a teacher usually pays attention to when a student is having difficulty. It is easy, too easy, to explain a student's difficulty in terms of unwillingness to try or lack of intellectual aptitude. Yet this may be a cause. A student who finds it difficult to abstract, generalize, deduce and recall concepts and principles will usually find mathematics difficult even though it is taught by a teacher who attempts to compensate for such lack. The very nature and structure of the subject makes such abilities paramount. Students are expected to be able to solve problems. This kind of intellectual activity requires higher intellectual aptitude than merely comprehension and retention of knowledge.

Lack of intellectual aptitude looms larger as a causative factor when there is group instruction with the progress of the average student determining the pace. Students with intellectual disabilities cannot keep up. They do not comprehend what is being taught and do not readily retain it and cannot apply it in the solution of problems. After a while, they despair and give up.

Pedagogical factors

Obviously, pedagogical factors have a lot to do with how readily students learn. The students of a teacher who is inept in applying the principles set forth in the textbook will experience difficulty; the cause in such cases rests with the teacher. For example, a teacher who selects subject matter too difficult for the students in their existing state of mathematical maturity can cause much of their trouble. A teacher who gives little or no attention to motivation may expect apathetic students. A teacher who attempts to motivate students by punitive actions, intense competition, or invidious comparisons may expect to see them become fearful, refuse to ask questions about points they do not understand, and even express their resentment by overt hostility. A teacher who does not secure enough feedback from students to facilitate decisions as to whether they comprehend what is being taught or who does not provide the right kind of practice—varied, well-spaced, and sufficient— is as much a cause of student difficulties in learning as their shortcomings in academic aptitude, social factors in the home or neighborhood, or any other basic cause may be. It is well that a teacher make self-examination during diagnosis in order not to miss possible causes that may be easier to treat than other causes over which the teacher has little or no control.

A teacher who is inept in giving assignments may cause difficulty. When lessons are unplanned except for the assignment of reading in the textbook or exercises to be worked and when no attention is given to motivation or to offering study suggestions, students may find learning difficult. Then, too, the assignment may be given after the bell ending the class period has rung. Since attention usually dissolves once the bell rings, students often do not hear such assignments. Or if they hear it, they forget it. When their time for study arrives, they do not remember what they should do and they come to class unprepared. Giving as much thought to the assignment as to the plan of the lesson will pay off in student performance.

Basic causes of student difficulties in learning such as those pointed out in this section are significant; they give rise to symptomatic behavior. Without knowledge of the basic causes, a teacher may make the mistake of treating symptoms. Just as students come to understand mathematical concepts and principles when they have been embedded in a structure of mathematical theory, teachers come to understand student behavior by embedding this behavior in a structure of psychological theory. The theory permits explanation and offers hypotheses as to how behavior can be controlled and determined. Basically, this is the objective of teaching.

Thought questions

1   Suppose you have a student in your class who continually does not follow your directions as to assignments, passing in papers, and altering behavior that disturbs other students. What might be a cause of this unusual behavior? How could you test your hypothesis?

2   It has been stated that emotional factors may be a cause of learning difficulties. Can these be a result of learning difficulties? Explain.

3   Would you expect that a student whose family has moved to different residences several times during the school year—and, hence, the student has changed schools several times—would have difficulty in keeping abreast of the classwork? Explain.

4   Why might a school policy of grouping by ability, so that each group is expected to cover the same subject matter, be a basic cause of some students' difficulties? Why might ability grouping in which not all groups are expected to cover the same subject matter still be a cause of some students' difficulties?

5   All states have compulsory education laws that require adolescents of up to the age of 16 or 17 to attend school. Is this policy a basic cause of some students' difficulties in learning? Why?

6   Suppose you think that one of the basic causes listed in this section may be the cause of a particular student's inability to attain some objective you have. How would you test this conjecture?

7   One of your students often makes fun of other students when they make mistakes. He usually does not make mistakes. Why may he be doing this? How would you determine whether your explanations are correct?

8   There follow questions from tests and a reproduction of a student's answer to each. Identify the error the student made and offer one or more conjectures as to its cause. Then explain how you would test to be sure that the cause you stated is the actual cause.

    a   Solve:
$$x^2 = x$$
$$x^2 = x$$
$$x = 1$$

b   Solve:

$$\frac{5}{x} + 3 = \frac{17}{4}$$

$$\frac{5}{x} + 3 = \frac{17}{4}$$

$$20 + 3 = 17x$$

$$23 = 17x$$

$$\frac{23}{17} = x$$

c   Subtract:

$$\frac{2y}{y-1} - \frac{1}{y+1}$$

$$\frac{2y}{y-1} - \frac{1}{y+1} \quad (\text{LCD} = y^2 - 1)$$

$$\frac{2y(y+1)}{y^2-1} - \frac{y-1}{y^2-1}$$

$$\frac{2y^2 + 2y - y - 1}{y^2 - 1}$$

$$\frac{2y^2 + y - 1}{y^2 - 1}$$

d   The enrollment in Center City High School was 1,103 in 1968 and 1,324 in 1970. The enrollment in 1970 was what percent of the enrollment in 1968?

$$\begin{array}{r} .833 \quad = 83.3\% \\ 1{,}324\overline{\smash{)}1{,}103.000} \\ 1\,059\,2 \\ \hline 43\,80 \\ 39\,72 \\ \hline 4\,080 \\ 3\,972 \\ \hline \end{array}$$

$$\begin{array}{c} 1{,}103 \\ \hline 1{,}324 \end{array}$$

e   Expand:

$$(3n^2 - 5)^2$$

$$(3n^2 - 5)^2 = 9n^4 - 25$$

f   Prove the identity:

$$\frac{1 - \cos^2 x}{\sin x \cos x} = \tan x$$

$$\frac{1 - \cos^2 x}{\sin x \cos x} = \tan x$$

$$1 - \cos^2 x = \tan x \sin x \cos x$$

$$1 - \cos^2 x = \frac{\sin x}{\cos x} \times \sin x \cos x$$

$$1 - \cos^2 x = \sin^2 x$$

$$1 = \sin^2 x + \cos^2 x$$

g   Solve over R:

$$\tan \theta \cot \theta = \tan \theta$$

$$\tan \theta \cot \theta = \tan \theta$$

$$\tan \theta \cot \theta - \tan \theta = 0$$

$$\tan \theta (\cot \theta - 1) = 0$$

$$\tan \theta = 0$$

$\theta = 2\pi n, n \in Z$
$\cot \theta - 1 = 0$
$\cot \theta = 1$

$\theta = \dfrac{\pi}{4} + \pi n, n \in Z$

h   In a certain alloy, 0.2% of the alloy is zinc. What is the weight of zinc in 25 pounds of the alloy?

$$\begin{array}{r} 25 \\ .20 \\ \hline 5.00 \end{array}$$

i   The scale of a drawing of the floor plans of a house is 1:24. A room in the drawing has the dimensions 14 inches by 12 inches. What will be the dimensions of the room in the house once it is built?

$$\begin{array}{r} 14 \\ 24 \\ \hline 56 \\ 28 \\ \hline 336 \text{ feet long} \end{array} \qquad \begin{array}{r} 12 \\ 24 \\ \hline 48 \\ 24 \\ \hline 288 \text{ feet wide} \end{array}$$

j   Discuss the nature of the real 0's of the function $f(x) = 8x^4 - 16x^3 - 9x^2 + 20x - 4$. For each characteristic you list, tell how you know it is a characteristic of the 0's. (A rational 0 is 2. Rational approximations of irrational zeros are -1.2, 0.2, and 0.9.)
     One real 0 is 2 because $f(2) = 0$. There is a real 0 between -2 and -1 because $f(x)$ changes signs as it decreases from the value at -2 to the value at -1. This real 0 is irrational, since 2 is the only rational 0.

Diagnosing difficulties in using concepts

In speaking of using a concept, we assume that students have been taught it once but have not mastered it. They may forget all or part of it, or the concept may be vague or even incorrect in their minds. Among the kinds of difficulty students manifest in using concepts, experience shows that the following are common.

One is not being able to give the short or technical name for objects in a certain set, as not being able to call a line segment determined by the vertex of a triangle and the midpoint of the opposite side a *median*. If the cause of a student's difficulty is inability to remember the technical name, he or she will have to be reminded what the name is. Exemplification moves may be used in which either medians are drawn from other vertices and the student is asked to give a name to these or the student is asked to draw one or more medians of a given triangle.

A second kind of difficulty is inability to state the meaning of the term designating a particular concept. A student may be unable to tell what the term *tens digit* means, for example. This difficulty is the opposite of the first. A version of not being able to say what a term means is not being able to give a definition of the term.

A definition move or a necessary and sufficient condition move should be effective. This move can be elicited from other students by means of an appropriate question. The teacher will have to check to see that the student comprehends the language being used. Exemplification moves are useful for this.

A third kind of difficulty is inability to remember one or more conditions necessary for an object to be denoted by the designating term. For example, a student may not remember that, if a relation has two members with the same first components but different second components, it is not a function. As a consequence, the student may think some relations are functions that are not. The student has to be reminded of the necessary condition.

A fourth kind of difficulty is inability to remember a condition sufficient for an object to be denoted by the term designating the concept. For example, a student may not remember that if an angle is an acute angle, it is an oblique angle. The remedy is like that for not remembering a necessary condition; the student has to be reminded of the sufficient condition.

Not being able to give or recognize an example is a fifth kind of difficulty. For instance, a student may not recognize that "6" in "164" is the tens digit. This differs from the first difficulty in that a characterization is given in the first but the student is unable to assign the short or technical name. In the fifth kind of difficulty an example is given but the student does not recognize it as an example.

One may hypothesize that a cause of the fifth difficulty is not knowing or remembering a sufficient condition. The student who does not recognize "6" in "164" as the tens digit may not know that being in the second position to the left from the decimal point, printed or understood, is sufficient for being a tens digit. This is inability to classify. The teacher may initiate a move of sufficient condition by a question such as "How can we tell if a digit is a tens digit?" Exemplification moves can be used to reinforce the concept.

Misclassifying in either of two ways is another kind of difficulty. One way is to misclassify a nonexample as an example, as when a student calls a drawing of a hyperbola a parabola. The other is to misclassify an example as a nonexample, as when a student says xy is not a polynomial of degree 2. Misclassifying is to be contrasted with not being able to classify at all.

Misclassifying can be traced to not knowing or not remembering necessary or sufficient conditions. A student who misclassifies a nonexample as an example probably does not at the time know a necessary condition. The necessary condition restricts the set of objects denoted by the concept; not knowing the necessary condition disposes the student to include in the set objects that are excluded by the necessary condition. A student who misclassifies an example as a nonexample probably does not know a sufficient condition. The sufficient condition admits objects to the set denoted by the concept; not knowing the sufficient condition disposes the student to exclude objects that should be in the set.

In errors of misclassifying, a teacher has first to identify the kind of misclassification manifested. The teacher can then test to see whether the student knows the appropriate condition. The teacher might ask, "How do we tell whether or not something is a ——?" (where the blank is filled with a name that designates the concept). If the student does not know, a move of necessary or sufficient condition can be used.

Sometimes students can classify correctly but cannot justify, cannot tell why their classification is correct. For example, a student may correctly recognize 236 in $2,832 \div 12 = 236$ as the quotient but be unable to say why this is the quotient. In such cases, one possible cause is that the student guessed correctly but does not really know. To test this conjecture, similar division problems can be given expressed in a form different from that of the one first considered. A student who is erratic in classification probably guessed correctly the first time. In this case, the teacher will have to design a strategy of moves that enable him or her to infer whether the student has acquired the concept. The student who classifies correctly every time has a nonverbal concept. The teacher will have to help such students identify the sufficient conditions.

The last kind of difficulty we shall discuss is inability to deduce useful information from a concept. For example, in attempting to prove that the diagonals of a rhombus are perpendicular, a student may be unable to prove the theorem because he or she cannot prove that triangles ABE and ADE (see Figure 9.1), or another analogous pair are congruent. The student cannot prove these triangles congruent because he or she cannot deduce from the hypothesis $ABCD$ is a rhombus that $\overline{AB} \cong \overline{AD}$. This kind of difficulty is harder to cope with. It is probably correlated negatively with intelligence—that is, the less bright the student is, the more of this kind of difficulty he or she will experience. It is hard to offer methodological suggestions of a general nature to help a teacher help students who have this difficulty. One example of how a teacher might proceed is illustrated in the following dialogue. The student is trying to prove the theorem stated in the paragraph above and is using a figure like that in Figure 9.1.

Figure 9.1

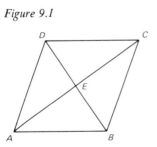

T Having trouble? What's the trouble?

S I can't prove it.

T I see you have a figure. How do you know it is the right figure?

S Well, it says the diagonals of a rhombus are perpendicular. So I drew a rhombus and the diagonals.

T O.K. So *ABCD* is a rhombus with diagonals $\overline{AC}$ and $\overline{DB}$. And you want to prove what?

S $\overline{AC}$ and $\overline{BD}$ are perpendicular.

T $\overline{AC}$ and $\overline{BD}$ perpendicular. Let's start with this and work backward. Suppose $\overline{AC}$ and $\overline{BD}$ are perpendicular. What would be true of angles *AED* and *AEB*?

S They'd be right angles.

T Yes, and hence congruent. Right? How can we prove two angles congruent?

S Corresponding parts of congruent triangles.

T Such as which triangles?

S *ABE* and *ADE*.

T And how could you prove these congruent?

S *SAS*, *ASA*, or *SSS*. I tried all these and they wouldn't work.

T Really? Let's see what we know. For these triangles, $\overline{AE}$ is common. What else? (*Student does not answer.*) Well, what looks congruent? That should give us a hunch.

S $\overline{AD}$ and $\overline{AB}$.

T Yes. Anything else?

S This angle and that one (*pointing to angles* AED *and* AEB).

T Go ahead. What else?

S This angle and that angle (*pointing to angles* ADE *and* ABE) and $\overline{DE}$ and $\overline{BE}$. But I couldn't prove it.

T I look at your figure, and it looks like a parallelogram. Is it?

S Yeah.

T How do you know? Why did you draw it like a parallelogram?

S It's a rhombus.

T O.K., so it's a rhombus. How do you know it's a parallelogram? (*Student does not answer immediately.*) What is a rhombus?

S A—ah—a rhombus is a parallelogram.

T A rhombus is a parallelogram. Is every parallelogram a rhombus? (*Student does not answer. The teacher waits a bit and then draws a parallelogram that is not a rhombus.*) Is this a rhombus? It's a parallelogram.

S No.

T Why not?

S The sides are not equal—I mean congruent.

T O.K. The sides aren't congruent. So for a parallelogram to be a rhombus, the sides have to be congruent. And if we know that a figure is a rhombus, what do we know about it?

S   It's a parallelogram.

T   Yes. And what else?

S   The sides are congruent.

T   So if $ABCD$ is a rhombus, what do we know about $\overline{AB}$ and $\overline{AD}$?

S   They're congruent.

T   Right. Now we've got two pairs of corresponding sides congruent. Do we know that $\overline{BE}$ and $\overline{DE}$ are congruent? (*The student does not reply.*) You said that rhombus $ABCD$ was a what?

S   Parallelogram.

T   What do you know about the diagonals of a parallelogram? We proved a theorem about the diagonals of a parallelogram. Remember? What do we know about the diagonals of a parallelogram?

S   They bisect each other.

T   Great! So what do you know about $\overline{BE}$ and $\overline{DE}$?

S   They're congruent.

T   Sure. They're congruent. Do you think you can prove the triangles congruent now?

S   I guess so. Thanks.

Here is a case in which evidently the student had the concept of a rhombus for he drew the correct figure, but he had difficulty drawing useful conclusions from the concept. Outside the context of drawing the figure, he had difficulty in realizing that if $ABCD$ is a rhombus it is a parallelogram and all its sides are congruent. Why he had this difficulty is hard to say. But it was up to the teacher to help him see what conclusions are possible. This the teacher did by focusing on the concept of a rhombus and asking leading questions to direct the student's thinking. Being able to ask such questions is a skill every teacher should try to develop. The skill is developed by practice.

Thought questions

1   Student A does not know what the term *median* means but knows what the longer expression "line segment from the vertex of a triangle to the midpoint of the opposite side" means. Student B thinks the term *median* means the midpoint of a side of a triangle. Which lack of knowledge is more serious? Why?

2   Explain why remedial teaching of concepts depends on the results of diagnosis.

3   Why is it useful for a teacher to know kinds of difficulties students have in using concepts?

4   Suppose a student cannot do the following. What kind of a difficulty might the student have?
    a   Uses the term *projection* correctly to denote projections but cannot tell what a projection is.
    b   On being asked to give an example of a ratio to help another student acquire this concept, cannot do it.

   c On being asked to give an example of an exponent, cites 2 in 2*x*.

   d After finding out that $AC = BC$ in triangle ABC, cannot tell what kind of triangle ABC is.

   e Cannot answer the question : What is the name of a line that intersects a circle in just one point ?

   f Cannot answer the question : How can we tell whether a digit in a measurement is significant ?

5 For each of the difficulties described in question 4, determine a strategy for remedial teaching.

Diagnosing difficulties in learning and using principles

When the difficulties students have in using principles are analyzed, it appears that there are common causes. It is well for a teacher to know these; they become conjectures as various difficulties are indentified. The conjectures then can be tested for the particular case.

If students do not have the concepts that are to be used to develop a principle as a new item of knowledge, they will have trouble comprehending the principle. Imagine a teacher who is teaching how to judge the accuracy of a measurement by saying, "One way to judge is to find the percent of error." A student who has no concept of percent will get little meaning from the teacher's statement. And if the teacher continues to use this concept in the development without checking to see that the students know what a percent is, the students will not comprehend the principle the teacher hopes they will attain.

Lack of basic concepts is a potential cause of difficulty in learning principles taught by guided discovery as it is in learning by exposition. Suppose a teacher in a basic mathematics course intends to teach the generalization that a circle can be circumscribed about every regular polygon with which the students are familiar—equilateral triangle, square, pentagon, hexagon, and octagon. She tells one group of students to draw squares, another group to draw equilateral triangles, a third group to draw regular pentagons, and so on. She then tells all the students to draw the diagonals of the polygons and use the intersection of these as a center to attempt to circumscribe a circle about the polygon. She finds that some students have drawn no figure. She might conjecture that the students do not know what a regular pentagon is. If the students have drawn regular polygons but have not drawn the diagonals, she might conjecture that they do not know what a diagonal is. If the cause of the difficulty is not having certain concepts, the teacher will have to review these or reteach them or use equivalent designations before discovery can proceed.

In teaching by guided discovery, particularly when inductive discovery is used, there are two common causes of students' inability to make a discovery. One is inaccuracy in computation or in algebraic operations. Imagine an algebra teacher who is trying to teach the principle that if $x < y$, then $x + z < y + z$ by an inductive discovery strategy. She has started with $2 < 9$ and has suggested that the students add such rational numbers as 5, -5, -1, 15, $\frac{1}{2}$, $-\frac{1}{2}$, and -50 to both sides of the inequality. The student who is inaccurate in adding rationals is unlikely to detect a pattern. It will appear that he or she has some counterexamples to a possible generalization. Many teachers testify to the hazard of inductive strategies when students are inaccurate in computations or algebraic operations.

Another cause of difficulty when an inductive discovery strategy is used is the inability of a student to decide what factors are relevant and consequent inability to abstract the pattern. A question such as "Do you suppose there is a relation between these two ——?" will direct attention to the relevant factors.

Some students who do not understand a principle will memorize it. They can state the principle but cannot tell what it means and cannot apply it. The teacher who takes into consideration only ability to state a principle will not realize the cause of difficulty. Memorizing may give students a feeling of security or it may have proved rewarding in previous classes where applications of generalizations were not stressed.

Many such students are eager to learn; their effort to memorize a principle largely meaningless to them is an indication of this. Some of them may not know how to study, how to find out what a principle stated in a textbook means. Some may be insecure and fearful of asking questions in class or seeking help from the teacher. The teacher who realizes the tendency of such students to memorize without comprehension can point out this tendency and suggest ways they can determine what a principle means— look up definitions of terms used in the principle, try to think of instances, ask the teacher to clarify the principle, or ask other students for help.

Students commonly have difficulty in applying principles. A student may know a principle and be able to state it correctly. He or she may also comprehend it, as shown by ability to paraphrase it or give instances of it, yet given a problem to which the principle is relevant not be able to apply it to solve the problem. Application is basically deduction. On deciding which principle is relevant, the principle is conjoined with data given in the problem and the valid conclusion is drawn. The principle is thus applied.

One cause of a student's inability to apply a principle is not knowing the principle in the first place. A student who cannot convert inches to centimeters may not know the relation between them. A student may not be able to prove that a circle can be circumscribed around each regular polygon because he or she does not know the properties of a regular polygon. It seems obvious that if not knowing some item of knowledge, a concept, a singular statement, or a principle is the cause of a student's difficulty, he or she will have to be taught or retaught the item.

Whether a principle has been taught by guided discovery or by exposition, a student who does not get the principle clearly in mind will have trouble applying it. Such students may forget necessary conditions, as that in computing the product of two radicals it is necessary that they have the same index. Or students may know the principle for finding the volume of a rectangular solid but not remember that all the dimensions must be in the same unit of measure if the volume is reported in cubic units of that measure. Students may then merely find the product of the dimensions given, irrespective of their units or measure, and report the volume in cubic units of one of the dimensions.

A student who does not have clearly in mind what a principle says and what it does not say may think that the converse or inverse holds. Consider a student who is somewhat confused about the principle that two angles that are right angles are congruent. This student may think that since in the figure he is considering two angles are congruent and look like right angles then they are right angles. When asked how he knows the angles are right angles, he says "because they are congruent." Or he may think that two angles that are not right angles are not congruent. A student who has not clearly in mind what cancellation applies to and what it does not apply to may overgeneralize and cancel any two symbols that are the same irrespective of where they appear. An analogous statement may be said for transposition, if this principle is taught.

Suppose a student knows what a principle means, as evidenced by ability to paraphrase it and give some instances, yet in a particular problem for which the student knows that the principle is relevant cannot draw a conclusion using the principle and the data of the problem. Perhaps the student has forgotten the given data. If not, then for some reason the student apparently sees no relation between the principle to be applied and the data. This ability is harder to treat than others are. Perhaps using the *modus ponens* model will enable the student to perceive the implication.

Finally, consider students who both comprehend a principle and can apply it when they know it is relevant yet given a problem for which they are not told which principle or principles are relevant cannot solve the problem. The following excerpt from a paraphrase of a classroom dialogue illustrates this. The algebra class had been taught a principle that had been called *cross-multiplication:*

If $\frac{x}{y} = \frac{u}{v}$, then $xv = yu$ provided $y \neq 0$ and $v \neq 0$.

The students were solving equations that were instances of the hypothesis of this principle. One equation was

$$\frac{18y}{1,592} = \frac{21y + 48}{1,592}$$

It was probably included in the textbook to encourage the students to analyze a problem before immediately applying the principle just taught. One student had solved the equation by applying the cross-multiplication principle and had obtained the root. In walking around the room as the students were working on the exercises, the teacher observed this student's solution and realized that it was not elegant.

1 T I see you solved that hard equation correctly. But I see an easier way to solve it than you used. Take a look at the given equation. Is there something you can do to the equation before you cross-multiply? (*The student does not respond.*) Suppose you could get rid of the 1,592's. Would it then be easier to solve the equation?

2 S Yeah.

3 T What operation could you perform on both sides of the equation to get rid of the 1,592? (*The student indicates that he does not know.*) Look at the left side of the equation. What does this mean?

4 S 18y divided by 1,592.

5 T Right. What's the inverse of division?

6 S Multiplication?

7 T Sure, but you don't seem very certain about it. Sure, multiplication is the inverse of division. Now do you remember the principle we learned about using inverse operations to get us out of trouble?

8 S Multiply both sides by 1,592?

9 T O.K. Try it. (*The student performs the operation correctly and derives* $18y = 21y + 48$.) Great! That equation is easier to solve than the given one, isn't it? What would you do?

10 S Transpose the 21y.

11 T Well, O.K. Why not factor the right side? What would you get if you did that? (*The student factors the right side as* $3(7y + 16)$.) Now what can you do to both sides?

12 S Divide by 3. (*Divides and derives* $6y = 7y + 16$.)

13 T Good. Now what? You can solve that, can't you?

14 S Yeah.

15 T See? You want to study an equation before you go to work on it right away. You can often see an easy way to solve it. You solved the equation all right, but you did some unnecessary work. Had some big multiplications, didn't you? If you had thought a bit about the equation, you might have seen the easy way. That's why equations like that are put in the book—to make you think. Class, would you like to see the neat way he solved number 28? (*The teacher has the student put his solution on the chalkboard and explain it.*)

In utterance 7, the teacher cued the student as to what principle was relevant, since it appeared that he did not know. The student's immediate application of it indicated that he understood it once he knew that it was relevant. Similarly, in utterance 11, the teacher implied the relevance of another principle. Again, the student immediately applied the principle correctly. This warranted that the teacher infer that the student knew the principle and could apply it. The pedagogical challenge then became one of deciding how to help the student determine when a principle is relevant in the solution of a problem.

Let us review the argument in this section: if the teacher is aware of some of the causes of students' difficulties in learning and using principles, he has some ready conjectures. These can be tested to see if one of them is the cause in a particular case. If it is, appropriate remedy can be provided.

Thought questions

1 If you think the cause of a student's difficulty is not knowing one or more concepts that are used in the principle, how could you test this conjecture?

2 If you think a student has memorized a principle without comprehending its meaning, how could you test this conjecture?

3 Suppose you decide that the cause of a student's difficulty is not being able to tell when a particular principle is relevant. How could you help this student?

4 Suppose you intend to teach the principle that every nonconstant linear function has an inverse by deductive discovery strategy. What are some difficulties you might anticipate some students would have in following the development? How could you test these conjectures?

5 In a combination of an inductive and deductive discovery strategy, some students are interested only in discovering the conclusion for the particular instance selected and are not disposed to think generally. Hence they do not sense the generality of the principle. How could you tell if this characterizes a particular student? How could you remedy this tendency?

6 A teacher who is teaching the relations between the parameters a and b in the equation of an ellipse $\left(\dfrac{x^2}{a^2} + \dfrac{y^2}{b^2} = 1\right)$ and the intercepts finds that the students do not follow the deductive development. Suggest some causes that explain the students' trouble. How could the teacher test each of these conjectures?

7 Questions 7–10 pertain to the dialogue on page 224. In utterance 10, the student designated an operation as transposition. Evidently the teacher accepted this designation. Some mathematics teachers do not teach this concept because they believe it encourages "symbol pushing" without understanding—that is, knowing the mathematical operation on which the rewriting of symbols is based. They claim that some students "transpose" when there is no operation to justify the transposition. What do you think about this issue?

8 In utterance 5, the teacher asked, "What's the inverse of division?" She might have asked the questions asked in utterance 7. Then if the student did not respond, she could have asked the former question. Do you think her sequence was the better one? Which sequence do you think is the better? Why?

9 In utterance 11, the teacher was quite directive in the question she asked. Should she have asked a sequence of questions that would have allowed the student to discover the further simplification of the equation?

10 In utterance 15, the teacher asked the class if they would like to see the elegant solution developed by the student with whom she had been working. She then had the student write his solution on the chalkboard. On what grounds can this action of the teacher be defended? On what grounds can the action be attacked as unwise?

Diagnosing difficulties in solving verbal problems

Teachers become poignantly aware of students' difficulties when the students cannot solve verbal problems. This may be because the teachers think that if the students cannot solve the verbal problems that are in the textbook, they will not be able to solve problems encountered in a nonacademic context. However, a student's inability to solve the conventional verbal problems that appear in textbooks does not necessarily predict his inability to cope with the mathematics involved in problems that he or she faces or will face in the nonacademic world. The verbal problems presented to the student in the mathematics classroom are different from those that arise outside the classroom. In a sense the verbal problems are not "real." They do not arise from situations in which students are intimately involved; rather, they are imposed on them with no more than an academic context to give them significance. They are preformulated with only data that are necessary and sufficiently presented. Reading ability is heavily weighted. A narrow range of value judgments is involved. Without the context in which a real problem is embedded that gives meaning and significance to the problem, it is understandable that verbal problems in the mathematics class may present difficulties for some students.

Yet students in mathematics classes are expected to be able to solve verbal problems. This is justifiable. The problems indicate some of the relevance of the mathematical theory. They provide opportunity for applying concepts, singular statements, principles, and values and thus enhance the understanding of these items of subject matter. Moreover, they provide an opportunity for the teacher to teach skills of problem-solving. This will be discussed in Chapter 10. Since solving verbal problems is regarded as the capstone of formal mathematical study by many teachers, it is worthwhile considering the difficulties students commonly have with this kind of intellectual activity.

Since a knowledge of concepts, singular statements, and principles is necessary for comprehension and solution of verbal problems, any student who does not know what certain terms mean, who does not know certain so-called mathematical facts, or who does not know principles that relate these will have trouble solving verbal problems. What we have previously said about diagnosing students' difficulties in using concepts and principles is relevant in discussing corresponding difficulties in solving verbal problems.

Lack of knowledge of concepts will manifest itself when a student reads a problem and cannot comprehend it. If the teacher thinks that the student has difficulty comprehending what he or she reads, the teacher may ask the student to read the problem aloud. It is likely that any word over which a student stumbles while reading will have little if any meaning. By using some of the moves in teaching a concept, the teacher can check to see whether such a term has any meaning to the student. If not, the teacher will have to teach the concept that the term designates.

After students have read the problem, the teacher can ask them to state it in their own words. Inability to do this, even if they have pronounced the words correctly, probably indicates that they do not comprehend. The teacher may have to read the problem with the students, checking to see that they know what important terms mean. The teacher should be sure students know what is given and what the problem asks them to find. Students may then be asked whether they know any mathematical principle that relates what is given to what is asked for.

Lack of knowledge of principles will manifest itself when the student does not know the principle that can be used to interpret the relation or relations on which the problem is based. For example, in facing a problem such as

The sum of the two digits of a two-digit number is 7. If 26 is subtracted from the number, the result is twice the unit's digit. Find the two-digit number.

if the student does not know that the number can be expressed as $10t + u$ where t is the tens digit and u the units digit, he or she cannot set up an equation to solve the problem. Similarly if students do not know how profit is computed as a function of the cost, they will not be able to solve problems based on this function. It seems obvious that in such cases the teacher will have to remind students of the principle, assuming they know it but do not realize it is relevant. Or the teacher immediately will have to take time to teach the principle.

On occasion, students know a principle but are not able to apply it in a particular problem. This is often the case when the problem requires variables and the formation of an equation to solve it. Students may not know what quantity to represent by a variable. Or if they know this, they may not be able to set up an equation or equations describing the relations on which the problem is based. In the latter case, one technique is often helpful. Once the students show that they comprehend the problem, they are advised to guess an answer. If the guess is correct as determined by obtaining a true statement when checking, the problem is solved. If the guess is not correct, as determined by obtaining a false statement when checking, students are told to replace it by a variable and solve the resulting equation. As one example, consider the problem,

A plane takes off from an airport and flies East at an average ground speed of 340 miles per hour. One half-hour later a second plane takes off from the airport and flies East at an average ground speed of 420 miles per hour. How long after it takes off will it overtake the first plane?

Suppose the student guesses one hour. (It really makes little difference what the guess is.) Then when the second plane overtakes the first, the two planes will have traveled the same distance. Hence

$$420 \times 1 = 340 \times (1 + \tfrac{1}{2})$$
$$420 = 510$$

It is obvious that the last statement is not true. Hence the guessed answer, 1, is replaced by a variable, say t, and the equation $420t = 340 \times (t + \tfrac{1}{2})$ is solved.

This method may appear easier because students are dealing only with numbers. Of course, they still have to know the relation basic to the problem, in the case of the problem above that between distance, rate, and time. Once students have experience with this method, they should find that it is about as easy to guess a variable as an answer as it is to guess a constant. Hence they ultimately come to use the more elegant method.

Another cause of error manifested as inability to solve verbal problems is not checking that the answer satisfies the conditions of the problem. Hence, a mistake in solving an equation or using the wrong open equation is not discovered. A less-exact but useful check is the reasonableness of the answer. If an answer is unreasonable—the speed of an automobile appears to be 1,400 miles per hour, the price of a dress in a store comes out to be 32 cents, or the enrollment in a school seems to be 486.5 students—the students should realize that an error was made in solving the problem. Although such a check is useful, it depends on the students' ability to judge the reasonableness of an answer. If students' experience is restricted—they have never lived on a farm, have made few purchases in a store, or have heard little about taxes—they will find it impossible to judge the reasonableness of answers to problems involving such relations or situations. The teacher should try to formulate problems based on situations with which they have experience. Mathematics is sufficiently abstract that this should be possible.

Another difficulty some students have is attempting to apply a principle where it is not relevant. This is often the result of their having only a vague notion of the principle—for example, not knowing the domain over which it holds. Thus students may try to apply the Pythagorean theorem to an oblique triangle because they do not know or have forgotten that it is restricted to right triangles. Or they will say that $a^2 + b^2$ is not factorable because they did not learn that the principles used to factor other polynomials are restricted to polynomials over the integers. In cases like these, the teacher can patiently reteach the principle, stressing the domain over which it holds.

Finally, a cause of some student difficulty in solving verbal or other kinds of problem is unawareness of the nature of a problem. A necessary condition of a problem is temporary blocking of the methods usually employed to arrive at a solution. The student has to think, entertain hypotheses as to how the problem may be solved, and test these hypotheses. Without the temporary blocking and ensuing deliberation, the problem is an exercise; it requires only application of a principle or concept the student has been told is relevant and is more in the nature of practice than problem-solving.

If students have had experience chiefly with exercises, and little experience with problems, it is understandable that they will find it difficult to tolerate the period of temporary blocking of their habitual responses. They will manifest their frustration typically by ceasing to think about the problem or by making such remarks as, "We haven't had any problems like this" or "I can't do this one." The teacher should point out that it is expected they will experience blocking; the problem was formulated in order to produce this. They need to be reassured that their psychological state is natural and the way to relieve it is to think. The teacher can be supportive and express confidence that their thinking will enable them to solve the problem.

Indicating things they might think about rather than telling them how to solve the problem will be of more lasting value, even though at the time the students may not appreciate this.

Arranging problems in a sequence of increasing difficulty to challenge students yet not overwhelm them is a sound principle. It holds both in initial and in remedial teaching. Following this principle will not completely eliminate students' difficulties in solving verbal problems, but it will make the period of indecision less threatening and more readily tolerated.

Thought questions

There follow what you might expect to find on the papers of some students as you work with them during supervised study while they are attempting to solve problems. In each case, the problem is stated above the student's attempt to solve it. Consider each case and tell how you would diagnose the student's difficulty. Assume you determine the cause of his difficulty. Tell what you would then do.

1   Mr. Dobrowski gets about 14 miles to a gallon of gasoline when he drives his automobile. Mr. Crill gets about 21 miles to a gallon. What is the ratio of Mr. Dobrowski's mileage to that of Mr. Crill?

Student A:
14   21

Student B:
$$\frac{21}{14} = \frac{3}{2}$$

2   Last year our school collected $152.60 for the Red Cross. This year we collected $202.84. What is the percent of increase in the amount of money collected this year over the amount collected last year?

Student A:
$$\frac{.752}{202.84)\overline{152.60000}} = 75.2\%$$
```
          141 988
          _____
           10 6120
           10 1420
           _____
              47000
              40568
```

Student B:

```
$202.84
$152.60
_____
$ 50.24
```

```
               .247      about 25%
202.84)50.2400
       40 568
       _____
        9 6720
        8 1136
        _____
        1 55840
        1 41988
```

Student C:

$$
\begin{array}{r}
202.84 \\
152.60 \\
\hline
50.24
\end{array}
$$

$$
\begin{array}{r}
.32\% \\
152.50)\overline{50.2400} \\
45\ 750 \\
\hline
4\ 4900 \\
3\ 0500
\end{array}
$$

3   Mrs. Moskowitz runs a machine and earns $2.07 per hundred for finishing pieces of metal on her machine. One week she finished 7,260 pieces. How much did she earn to the nearest cent?

$$
\begin{array}{r}
7,260 \\
2.07 \\
\hline
50820 \\
0000 \\
14520 \\
\hline
\$15028.20
\end{array}
$$

4   The Robertses can buy some furniture priced at $450 by paying $45 down and twelve monthly payments of $40 each. They can also borrow $400 from the credit union at Mr. Roberts' company and pay $33.33 each month for twelve months and 1 percent interest a month on the unpaid balance. Which is the better plan? How much money will they save by using the better plan?

$$
\begin{array}{r}
450 \\
45 \\
\hline
405
\end{array}
\qquad
\begin{array}{r}
40 \\
12 \\
\hline
80 \\
40 \\
\hline
480
\end{array}
\qquad
\begin{array}{r}
33.33 \\
12 \\
\hline
66\ 66 \\
333\ 3 \\
\hline
399.96
\end{array}
$$

5   The sum of four consecutive positive integers is 162. Find the integers.

$$
\begin{array}{r}
24 \\
25 \\
26 \\
27 \\
\hline
102
\end{array}
\quad
\begin{array}{r}
50 \\
51 \\
52 \\
53 \\
\hline
256
\end{array}
\quad
\begin{array}{r}
35 \\
36 \\
37 \\
38 \\
\hline
146
\end{array}
\quad
\begin{array}{r}
37 \\
38 \\
39 \\
40 \\
\hline
154
\end{array}
\quad
\begin{array}{r}
40 \\
41 \\
42 \\
43 \\
\hline
166
\end{array}
\quad
\begin{array}{r}
39 \\
40 \\
41 \\
42 \\
\hline
162
\end{array}
$$

The integers are 39, 40, 41, and 42.

6   At a summer camp a hiker started walking down a trail at an average speed of 3 miles per hour. A half-hour later another hiker left and followed the same trail. The second hiker walked at an average speed of 4 miles per hour. How long after he left did he overtake the first hiker?

Student A:

Let t = time of second hiker

$4t$ = distance of second hiker

$t + \frac{1}{2}$ = time of first hiker

$3t + \frac{1}{2}$ = distance of first hiker

$4t = 3t + \frac{1}{2}$

$4t - 3t = \frac{1}{2}$

$t = \frac{1}{2}$

Student B:

$3x \quad \frac{1}{2}x \quad 4x$

$4 - 3 = 1$

7   A man has $5,000 invested, part at 4 percent and the rest at 6 percent. The income from the two investments is $220 a year. How much does the man have invested at each rate?

Student A: Let x = amount invested at 4 percent   (4 percent = .04)
5000 − x = amount invested at 6 percent   (6 percent = .06)
$.04x = .06 \times 5000 - x$
$\qquad = 300.00 - x$
$.04x + x = 300$
$\qquad 1.04x = 300$
$\qquad\quad x = 288.46$ at 4 percent
$\qquad\qquad 4711.54$ at 6 percent

```
              288.46
        1.04)300.00
              208
              920
              832
              880
              832
              480
              416
              640
              624
              160
              104
```

```
  5000.00
   288.46
  4711.54
```

Student B: Let x = amount invested at 4 percent
5000 − x = amount invested at 6 percent
$4x$ = income from the 4 percent amount
$6(5000 - x)$ = income from the 6 percent
$4x + 6(5000 - x) = 220$
$4x + 30000 - 6x = 220$
$\qquad 4x - 6x = 220 - 30000$
$\qquad\quad -2x = -29780$
$\qquad\qquad x = 14890$

8   A tinsmith has been asked to make a tray of a rectangular piece of copper 6 inches longer than it is wide. The tinsmith decides to cut out a 1-inch square from each of the corners, fold up the sides, and solder them in place. When he does this, he finds that the volume of the tray is 72 cubic inches. Find the length and width of the sheet of copper.

Let x = width
Then $x + 6$ = length
$\qquad x(x + 6) = 72$
$\qquad x^2 + 6x = 72$
$\qquad x^2 + 6x - 72 = 0$
$(x + 12)(x - 6) = 0$

$x + 12 = 0$ $\qquad\qquad x - 6 = 0$
$\qquad x = -12$ width $\qquad\quad x = 6$ width
$-12 + 6 = -6$ length $\qquad 6 + 6 = 12$ length

Guidelines for remedial instruction

As we have pointed out in previous sections, the purpose of diagnosis is to find the cause of a student's difficulties so that subsequent teaching can be directed at removing the cause. Often diagnosis and remedial teaching go hand in hand, the teaching serving as a test of the hypothesis as to the cause of the difficulty.

Base remedial teaching on diagnosis

Different causes usually will require different treatments for individual students. If the cause is that students do not know certain concepts, these will have to be taught by moves that have been discussed in the chapter on the teaching of concepts. If the cause is a temporary emotional disturbance, patience and empathy on the part of the teacher may be all that is necessary. If the cause seems to be inability to remember certain mathematical "facts," the teacher may be able to think of some mnemonic device to enable the student to remember.

Not only for a particular student will different causes usually require different treatments, but for different students the same hypothesized cause (irregularity in attendance or inaccuracy in computations, for example) may require different treatments. This is because behind each cause there are causes of the cause. Suppose the teacher identifies the cause of a student's difficulty as not knowing the meaning of certain symbols. It is possible to ask why he does not know their meaning. If the answer is that he is not interested in mathematics and does not expend the effort necessary to learn the meaning of the symbols, it is then possible to inquire why he lacks this interest.

It is advisable to consider each case unique. Reasoning by analogy (as the cause of Tommy's mistakes seems to be the same as that of Ann's mistakes; what I did to help Ann may also help Tommy) should be regarded as conjecture with respect to remedial teaching. If a conjecture is unsubstantiated, the teacher should not be stubborn in continuing with it or blame the student for its lack of success; factors affecting two students are not the same for each. Diagnosis must be extended and remediation determined by the amplified evidence.

Finally, remedial teaching will have to be modified in light of new evidence as to its success. During the teaching, a student may show that one of the causes of his difficulty has been largely eliminated. For example, he now knows what an inscribed angle of a circle is but still does not know the relation between such an angle and the arc of the circle it determines. The teacher then has to focus on teaching this relation, has to be flexible, adapting instruction as needs become apparent. Effective remedial teaching is based on continual diagnosis and is modified in terms of this diagnosis.

Provide motivation

Ausubel (1968) has pointed out that what is generally regarded as achievement motivation in formal education is by no means a unitary or homogenous drive. It has at least three components. One of these is what Ausubel identifies as a cognitive drive—the need and desire for acquiring and using knowledge as ends in themselves. This is task-oriented in that the motive for engaging in it resides in the task itself. The reward, the attainment of the knowledge, is also related to the task. For example, a student may learn mathematics because he expects to use it later.

A second component, as Ausubel has indicated, is not task-oriented. It is related to the ego. Psychologists tell us that each person has an image of himself—notions of what his strengths and weaknesses are, what he thinks is important in life, what others think of him, how successful he thinks he is; this is his self-esteem. His self-image is his ego. Whatever enhances his ego, he finds satisfying; whatever diminishes it, he finds dissatisfying and threatening. He seeks more of the former and tries to avoid the latter. Ausubel terms this component *ego-enhancing*. When we say "Success is its own motivation," we support thereby Ausubel's statement (p. 365) that "The causal relation between motivation and learning is typically reciprocal rather than unidirectional." Ausubel believes that normally ego-enhancement is the strongest motivation available during a student's formal education, particularly during the periods of secondary education.

The third component is neither task-oriented nor primarily ego-enhancing. It is oriented toward the approval of some person or group with which the student identifies. The student is motivated to do the things he believes will elevate his status in the eyes of these individuals. Ausubel terms this component *affiliative*. This third component explains the behavior of a student who could do well in mathematics but deliberately does poorly because in his peer group this is the thing to do. It also explains the good performance of a student who says he dislikes mathematics but wants to satisfy the wishes of parents who expect him to do well.

Teachers may be able to utilize the cognitive component of motivation by pointing out the utility of the knowledge or skill that is the subject of the instruction. They may be able to excite students' intellectual curiosity. They may be able to form exercises more interesting than those in the textbook. They may be able to relate the items of mathematics to a hobby or other student interest. Some teachers have found that inviting a speaker from the nonacademic realm to talk to the class about uses of mathematics and the importance of the subject will produce some motivation, temporary though it may be.

The general implication of ego-enhancement is that the teacher should try to provide experiences for students having difficulty that do not unnecessarily diminish their ego. However, it may be necessary to make some students think realistically about their potentialities lest they develop false images of themselves and think they cannot be successful in mathematics when they can or that they can be successful when it is unlikely that they can be.

More specifically, the theory would seem to imply that teachers should set expectations for students that are commensurate with intellectual aptitude. The ego of a student of low intellectual aptitude—one who does not abstract readily, is not facile in deductive reasoning, has a meager reservoir of concepts, has difficulty interpreting sentences—will be beaten down if the teacher expects him to learn mathematics as readily as students who have average intellectual aptitude. Unrealistic expectations may induce anxiety, withdrawal into indifference or irregularity of attendance, or aggression, direct (blaming or otherwise attacking the teacher verbally) or displaced (annoying other students).

Further, the theory would imply that making invidious comparisons between students having trouble and those not ("The other students try; you don't"; "You make more mistakes in one period than the other students make in a week"; "Your sister always did so well in mathematics that I can't understand why you have so much trouble") will lower a student's self-image unnecessarily. Similarly, stigmatizing students having difficulty by placing them in a group that is regarded, overtly or covertly, as inferior is usually not conducive to improvement. If the students accept the stigma and incorporate it in their self-image, they are not inclined to exert much effort to learn mathematics, for they become convinced that they cannot learn. When a teacher says "You could do O.K. if only you would try," it is quite logical for the student not to try. If he did and did not succeed, he would dispel the teacher's image of him. The smart thing to do is not to try and thereby retain the teacher's somewhat positive image. If the students reject the stigma, the counterproductive behavior of withdrawal or aggression may become evident.

In contrast, supportive behavior by teachers will sustain or enhance ego. Praise where students realize that it is merited is supportive. So is an optimistic attitude: "You haven't learned how to add rational expressions *yet*, but you will." (The emphasis on *yet* gives the sense of "I have confidence that you will learn how to do this before long.") "Are you aware that you are not making the mistakes that you were making last week?" If the latter support is used, it would be well for the teacher to be specific and definite in naming the mistakes the student is no longer making.

It is likely that a student's ego will not be damaged if the teacher can establish the attitude that the remedial teaching is an opportunity for learning rather than a penalty for not having learned. The attitude might be that everyone makes mistakes and acquires misunderstanding. The important thing is to have a chance to eliminate these. And if a student can see that taking advantage of the opportunity does eliminate these, it is conceivable that self-esteem will be enhanced.

In childhood, the affiliative component of motivation is directed toward adults—parents and the teacher. In adolescence, the component is normally directed increasingly to peers. In middle-class groups, both adults and the peer group value academic achievement. The teacher can trade on this component of motivation. In lower-class groups and in so-called culturally deprived minority groups, little value is placed on academic achievement. For students in these groups, the affiliative component of motivation may actually work against success in remedial teaching. From a practical standpoint, the teacher will have to try whatever component of motivation proves effective and work to reduce the influence of affiliative motivation if this is in the wrong direction.

Encourage the student to plan the remedial treatment

Brueckner and Bond (1955) recommend that students should help formulate remedial treatment. This can be defended on two grounds. First, it is educational. One of the concomitants of education should be the disposition to try continually to improve understanding and skills and, in addition, to acquire the skill of self-diagnosis and self-prescription to implement this disposition. Participating with a teacher in deciding what treatment is appropriate will initially force students to consider, as did the teacher, the nature of their mistakes and misunderstanding. This will lead to conjecture as to their cause. And this, in turn, leads to judgment about what remedial work is appropriate. Repeated sharing of thoughts, with increasing responsibility on the student to be his own self-evaluator, should build insight and skill in this significant aspect of education.

The second ground for encouragement of students to participate in formulating remedial treatment is enhanced motivation. Whether this should be regarded as within the cognitive component or within the ego-enhancement component is unclear. If the student actively participates in deciding what to do about clearing up difficulties because he thinks this will enhance the teacher's regard for him, it is affiliative. The classification is of less importance than the explanation of the effectiveness of the procedure. When the student has a say in determining treatment, he will have a stronger inclination to follow it. His ego is involved. If he fails, it is a greater threat to his ego than if he fails in a treatment prescribed only by the teacher. And if he is successful, his ego is enhanced, and he is ready for further experiences of this kind.

Establish priorities in remediation

Some causes of difficulty are more significant than others because they are more basic. They are causes of other causes. For example, if a student is not understanding what is being taught because he does not know what certain symbols mean (does not have the concepts that the symbols designate), and it is found that he cannot see well enough to follow the explanations given in the textbook or on the chalkboard, treatment of the latter should have priority over the former. If he is inaccurate in ordinary computations in arithmetic, treatment of this should come before treatment of inaccuracies in operations with rational (signed) numbers. If he is irregular in attendance, this behavior has to be altered along with or even before the treatment of its cause is instituted. Little can be done to remove the cause of a student's not knowing how to reduce a common fraction to a decimal, and vice versa, unless he is present for the teacher to talk to him.

Some teachers believe that a student who has a negative attitude toward mathematics or toward school should have this attitude treated before attempt is made to rectify misunderstanding about mathematics. This relative priority cannot be justified in all cases. Although negative attitudes may be the cause of poor achievement, they may also be the effect. If the teacher can provide remediation that results in the student becoming aware of better understanding, making higher scores on tests especially designed to assess his progress, being able to answer questions in class, or being able to explain the mathematics to other students who also are having trouble, this may well change his attitude toward the subject.

A similar view is held concerning the relation between motivation and learning—namely, that motivation should precede an attempt to reteach a concept, principle, or algorithm that a student does not understand. Yet as Ausubel points out, motivation is not an indispensable condition of learning (unless one *defines* learning such that motivation is a necessary condition). Success in learning may be both the result and the cause of motivation. Provided the teacher can get the student to respond favorably to his conversation (which the student might be disposed to because he is polite or because he regards himself in an authoritative relation with the teacher), the teacher might be able to help him. If the student is convinced that the instruction is of benefit to him, his motivation may change and he will be more receptive to similar instruction in the future and for reasons grounded more in the task than in the social relations. Of course, if the teacher is not able to get the student to remain in his vicinity or even to listen to what he is saying, such behavior should have precedence over the student's disabilities in mathematics.

Generally speaking, physical disabilities that cause academic disability and are remediable should have priority over other causes. The same can be said for emotional disturbances. It is noteworthy that in schools where many students come to school hungry, they are given breakfast before they go to classes. Similarly, students who have severe emotional disturbances are often kept out of classes so a counselor can talk to them.

The principle of prerequisite knowledge can be used to determine priority in providing remedial teaching. Concepts are the most basic items of cognitive knowledge. Conceptual confusion will echo in the learning of other kinds of subject matter. Hence clarification of concepts should ordinarily have priority over other kinds of remedial teaching. Skills that are prerequisite to other skills should have priority when decisions as to where to begin are made.

A caveat should be expressed. Many students have difficulty in mathematics because they are weak in fundamentals. They are so weak that repeated remedial teaching on the fundamentals is necessary. This may have to be repeated by one teacher or by teachers in successive courses. Were each teacher to use the principle of prerequisite knowledge in ordering the remedial teaching, the student might turn off: "I get the same old stuff in every course."

If the teacher decides that the student's interest is waning for this reason, he would be well advised to turn temporarily to less basic remedies until the student's interest and motivation are restored.

Thought questions

1 Why must the treatment of learning disabilities be based on a diagnosis?

2 Suggest how a teacher can find time for remedial teaching.

3 What agencies other than the school might be able to participate in diagnosis and remedy?

4 Describe a hypothetical case in which a teacher might have to lower a student's self-image as part of a remedy.

5 A teacher once said that as a matter of principle it should be possible for a teacher to find something nice to say about any student. Is this realistic?

6 Do you agree that as students progress through school, they should be held increasingly responsible for their own diagnosis and remedy? Defend your judgment.

7 In the flyleaf of Ausubel's book *Educational Psychology: A Cognitive View*, there is this statement: "If I had to reduce all of educational psychology to just one principle, I would say this: The most important single factor influencing learning is what the learner already knows. Ascertain this and teach him accordingly." Do you agree with this? Defend your judgment. How is this related to diagnosis?

Self-test on the competencies

1 State possible causes of a student's difficulties in learning.
   a What are possible causes of a student's difficulties in learning mathematics?
   b What are some categories into which possible causes of a student's difficulties in learning mathematics may be classified? Within each of the categories name more specific causes.

2 Identify the kind of difficulty a student has in using concepts, using principles, and solving verbal problems. What kind of difficulty does each student manifest in the following cases?

   a **T** What do we call a polygon all of whose vertices are on a circle?
      S A polygon in a circle?

   b **T** Terry can tell us what a prime number is, can't you Terry?
      S No I can't.

   c **T** Who can give Tom an example of a quadratic equation?
      S $x + y = 16$.

   d **T** What do we know about the relation between the length of chords and their distances from the center of the circle?
      S The longer the chord, the farther it is from the center of the circle.

   e **S_1** But how do you know triangle *ABC* is congruent to triangle *BEF*?
      S_2 Their angles are respectively equal.

   f **T** Yes. You're right. An ellipse is not a function. But why isn't it a function? (*The student does not answer.*)

g S Isn't it true that every polynomial equation of odd degree has at least one real root?

   T Not necessarily.

h T Now that you have graphed several instances of $ax^2 + bx + c = 0$, what can you say about the relation between values of a and the graph? (*Several students see no relation.*)

i T Look around the room, and give us an example of two skew lines.

   S I don't see any skew lines in the room.

j T You say that 25/4 is a proper fraction. Why is it a proper fraction?

   S Because the numerator is larger than the denominator.

k T For two sets to be identical, what is necessary?

   S Beats me.

l T What happens if we divide both sides of an inequality by a negative number?

   S The inequality is reversed.

   T Right. So what follows from $14 < -2x$ if we divide both sides by -2?

   S $-7 < x$.

m T What conclusion can you draw from the statement: If a line is perpendicular to a radius of a circle at the intersection of the radius and the circle, it is tangent to the circle?

   S If a line is tangent to a circle, it is perpendicular to the radius determined by the point of contact.

n T How can you tell if a function is a periodic function?

   S If it repeats itself.

o T Ed claims that a in $ax = b$ is not a coefficient. Do you agree with him?

   S Yes.

p T Take the proposition: no A is B. Does it follow that no B is A?

   S No. The converse of a proposition doesn't follow.

q T Two airplanes left the same airport and flew in the same direction. When one overtakes the other, what do we know?

   S That the faster plane has overtaken the slower plane.

r T How much antifreeze will have to be added to 5 gallons of a 25 percent solution of antifreeze and water to raise it to a 40 percent solution? If you add x gallons, how many gallons will you have?

   S I guess I don't know.

   T It would be $5 + x$, wouldn't it? Now if the 5 gallons of a mixture of antifreeze and water was 25 percent antifreeze, how many gallons of antifreeze would be in the 5 gallons?

   S Is it possible to figure it out?

   T Sure. 25 percent of 5 gallons is what?

   S I never could do percent.

   T Well, let's do this one. 25 percent is what decimal fraction?

   S I told you I never could do percent.

   T 25 percent is 25 one-hundredths. So 25 one-hundredths of 5 is what? (*The student does not answer.*) What operation would you use to find the answer?

   S Multiply?

   T So multiply, and what do you get?

   S 1.24.

T What does that mean?

S Why do we have to do problems like this?

3 Form and test conjectures as to the cause of the difficulties stated in competency 2. For each of the cases in competency 2, state a conjecture as to the cause of the student's difficulty. Explain how you would test to see whether your conjecture is correct.

4 Having accepted a conjecture concerning the cause of a difficulty, provide remedial teaching.
For each of the probable conjectures you stated for competency 3, describe teaching that you might carry out to remedy the difficulty.

References

Ausubel, David P. *Education Psychology: A Cognitive View*, New York: Holt, Rinehart and Winston, 1968. Ch. 10.

Betts, E. A. *Foundations of Reading Instruction*. New York: American Book Company, 1946.

Blair, Glenn M., R. Stewart Jones, and Ray H. Simpson. *Educational Psychology*, 2nd ed. New York: Macmillan, 1962. Ch. 12.

Brueckner, Leo J., and Guy L. Bond. *The Diagnosis and Treatment of Learning Difficulties*. New York: Appleton-Century-Crofts, 1955. Chs. 1–5, 8, 9, and 13.

Dewey, John. *How We Think*. Boston: Heath, 1933. Ch. 7.

National Council of Teachers of Mathematics. *The Learning of Mathematics: Its Theory and Practice*, Twenty-First Yearbook. Washington, D. C.: National Council of Teachers of Mathematics, 1953. Ch. 8.

National Society for the Study of Education. *Educational Diagnosis*, Thirty-Fourth Yearbook. Chicago: The National Society for the Study of Education, 1935.
———. *The Education of Exceptional Children*, Forty-Ninth Yearbook. Chicago: University of Chicago Press, 1950. Part II, Ch. 3.

Office of the Superintendent of Public Instruction of the State of Illinois. *Teaching About Drug Abuse*. Springfield, Ill.: Office of the Superintendent of Public Instruction, 1972.

Lankford, Jr., Francis G. "What Can a Teacher Learn About a Pupil's Thinking Through Oral Interviews?" *The Arithmetic Teacher*, 21 (1974), 26–32.

10

Teaching problem-solving

This chapter is designed to help you become a better teacher of problem-solving. To facilitate the discussion in this chapter and to provide insight into the problem-solving process, we suggest that the following three problems be considered. Try to solve them.

1 How many squares are contained in a standard 8×8 checkerboard? The answer is not 64 squares! There are actually over 200 squares in an 8×8 checkerboard.

2 Imagine a row of one thousand lockers, all closed, and a line of one thousand men. Suppose the first man passes by and opens every locker. The second man now passes by and closes every other locker, starting with the second locker. The third man goes along and changes the state of every third locker (if it is open, he shuts it and vice versa). Suppose the fourth man in passing by changes the state of every fourth locker. This process continues until all one thousand men have passed by all the lockers. Which lockers are open in the end?

3 Construct an equilateral triangle given a median of one inch and using only a compass and straightedge.

At the conclusion of this chapter, you should be able to demonstrate the following competencies:

1 State conditions under which a given question is a problem

2 Generate problems from a given hypothetical teaching situation in which the mathematical context and the mathematical maturity of the students are specified

3 Generate a problem for a specified student population from a given situation

4 Generate or find problems that are recreational or stem from mathematical curiosities

5 State maxims for helping students solve problems

6 Indicate how the maxims would be applied to a specific problem you could present to students

7 Use the maxims in an actual teaching situation

What is a problem?

To help develop a definition of the term *problem*, consider the following questions:

Why is it difficult (that is, why is it a problem) for many five-year-old children to tell time?

Why is telling time not difficult (that is, not a problem) for an adult?

Why is it unlikely that Albert Einstein was ever concerned about kicking field goals? That is, why is it unlikely that kicking field goals ever posed a problem for Albert Einstein?

Why is it likely that kicking field goals would be of concern (that is, pose a problem) for a high school sophomore trying to make the varsity football team as a placekicker?

Most individuals would agree that a problem consists of a question to be answered. However, most observers would also agree that not every question to be resolved constitutes a problem. For example, consider the question "What time is it?" Surely this is a problem for many five-year-old children. Most children of this age are interested in telling time and yet few can indicate it simply by glancing at a clock. It is difficult for them because their lack of knowledge and experience has not yielded to them a systematic procedure for telling time. On the other hand, an adult's knowledge and experience has provided an algorithmic procedure for telling time at a glance. Thus, one consideration as to whether a question is a problem depends on the knowledge that a given individual possesses. Knowledge varies from individual to individual. For one person, a question may be answered through the use of a routine procedure. For another, the same question may require great deliberation if knowledge does not offer a procedure for answering the question.

Consider, for example, the question of finding the first ten prime numbers. For the readers of this text, the question does not represent a challenge. For a youngster in the fourth grade, however, it represents a question requiring considerable experimentation and deliberation. We shall stipulate, then, that *for a question to be a problem, it must present a challenge that cannot be resolved by some routine procedure known to the student.* It follows, then, that a question may be a problem for one student and not for another student.

There is another condition that must be satisfied if a question is to present a problem, however. Why is it unlikely that kicking field goals was ever a problem for Albert Einstein? In all likelihood, Einstein was not proficient in kicking field goals. But because for a variety of reasons kicking field goals did not interest him; it did not represent a problem. That is, a question may represent a challenge, but if the challenge is not accepted then in a real sense the question is not a problem.

The value of i^i, for example, may not be known to the reader and perhaps the reader is not sure how to begin evaluating this expression. Does finding the value of i^i represent a problem to the reader? It does only to the extent that the reader is interested in evaluating i^i. There may be a challenge to find the value of i^i, but if the challenge is not accepted then the question is not a problem. *A challenging question becomes a problem to an individual only to the extent that the individual accepts the challenge.* It follows, then, that for a question to be a problem the student must be motivated to answer it. (For ease of discussion, the term *problem* will in subsequent sections refer to challenging questions that have been presented in such a way that students accept the challenge.)

The definition of a problem presented here is consistent with other definitions in educational literature. In many cases, a problem is described as some sort of block before a goal. The position we take here is that the block does not constitute a problem unless the student is motivated to overcome it and attain the goal. The educational significance of this distinction is that, if a question is to constitute a problem, it must be presented in a way that fosters acceptance of challenge. Students will be more inclined to accept challenges presented by a teacher who radiates enthusiasm for solving problems and who reinforces students in their problem-solving efforts. It is unlikely that challenges will be accepted when students perceive the challenge as beyond their intellectual grasp.

Having defined *problem*, what is meant by *problem-solving?* Very simply, problem-solving is the process of accepting a challenge and striving to resolve it. The teaching of problem-solving, then, is the action by which a teacher encourages students to accept challenging questions and guides them in their resolution. In contrast to the chapters on the teaching of concepts and generalizations—products—this chapter deals with the teaching of a process— an intellectual skill. Solving problems requires students to engage in a process and hopefully to become skillful in selecting and identifying relevant conditions and concepts, searching for appropriate generalizations, formulating plans, and employing previously acquired skills. Teachers present problems because it is through problem-solving that students can practice and integrate previously learned concepts, generalizations, and skills and because it is important for students to practice processing information.

Thought questions

1   Does telling time meet both conditions for being a problem for most five-year-old children?

2   When is it likely that a challenging question will not represent a problem for a particular student? Can you identify such a case from your own experience as a mathematics student?

3   Differentiate problems, problem-solving, and the teaching of problem-solving.

4   Is it possible for a question to completely overwhelm a student (so that the student has not the least notion how to begin) and still be a problem? Justify your answer.

5   Why is finding the first eight pairs of twin primes (primes having a difference of two) not a problem for someone who knows how to construct the sieve of Erastosthenes?

6   Can you differentiate between what many textbooks call exercises and what we have termed probems? For a second-year algebra student well-honed in the use of the quadratic formula, does solving the following equation for x constitute an exercise or a problem?

$$x^2(y - 2) + x(y + 3) + y^2 - 3 = 0$$

7   Can you think of two reasons why determining the value of i^i would not be a problem for some mathematics students?

8   Which of the following questions do you consider to have the potential to be problems for eighth-grade students? For twelfth-grade students in an advanced mathematics class? You may wish to place conditions on your responses.

  a   Why is the product of two positive rational numbers, each less than one, always less than unity?

  b   What is the greatest area of a rectangular region that can be enclosed by 300 feet of fence?

  c   What is the sum of the first one thousand positive integers? The first one thousand positive odd integers?

  d   What is the ratio of the area of an equilateral triangle to the area of a square having the same perimeter?

  e   In dividing one rational number by another rational number we can always use the shortcut, "Invert the divisor and multiply." Why?

  f   What number multiplied by itself yields the product -16?

  g   An item marked $16.95 is to be marked down 10 percent. What is the new selling price?

9   What actions would you expect a teacher to be engaged in when helping students solve problems? From your experience as a mathematics student, does it appear that mathematics teachers tend to emphasize problem-solving as a primary instructional goal?

10   In the preceding section, problem-solving was categorized as an intellectual skill. What moves discussed in Chapter 8 could be appropriately used in teaching problem-solving?

Importance of teaching problem–solving

Most mathematics educators believe problem-solving is an important instructional activity. The belief is usually predicated on one of two supporting arguments. The first involves the researchable hypothesis that teaching students to solve problems enables them to become more analytic in making decisions in life. The second argument focuses on the value judgment that problems and problem-solving are of paramount importance in learning mathematics. Let us briefly consider these two positions relative to the importance of teaching problem-solving in school mathematics.

Every individual in our society is faced with making decisions. Some are trivial while others, such as the selection of a career, can have far-reaching effects. In making intelligent decisions, people must have the ability to think rationally and objectively. This involves defining clearly the problem to be solved, gathering relevant information, analyzing the information, and being aware of and evaluating the anticipated outcomes. Historically, one of the aims of teaching mathematics has been to help students think rationally and objectively. Because of its very nature, studying mathematics can provide experiences in gathering and analyzing information and making deductions from this established knowledge. Can the study of mathematics contribute to the overall aim of producing better thinkers? The evidence is not conclusive. It is difficult to evaluate people who are adept at making decisions.

To consider the second argument, let us review the opinions of various mathematicians relative to the importance that problems play in learning mathematics. In 1963 the Cambridge Conference on School Mathematics, composed of prominent mathematicians, scientists, and educators, projected the mathematical needs of the United States in the remainder of the twentieth century and proposed a curriculum for meeting them. The report, entitled *Goals for School Mathematics*, stated (p. 28): "...the construction of problem sequences is one of the largest and most urgent tasks in curriculum development." Further attesting to the interest of the mathematics community in problem-solving is the fact that the International Commission on Mathematical Instruction selected the role of problems in the development of student mathematical activity as one of three topics for discussion at the 1966 International Congress of Mathematicians in Moscow, U. S. S. R. The U. S. Conference Board of the Mathematical Sciences completed a report to this International Commission that contained views of leading mathematicians on problem-solving in teaching mathematics. Included in this report are the following statements.

We regard problem-solving as the basic mathematical activity. Other mathematical activities such as generalization, abstraction, theory building, and concept formation are based on problem-solving [p. 130].

Mathematics seems inconceivable without problems [p. 135].

There is, however, another more important role for problems in the high school curriculum and that is to motivate the subject matter not only for those who have a special interest in mathematics and a special aptitude for it, but for all students [p. 113].

Such statements attest to the importance that many mathematicians place on problems in the learning of mathematics. If teachers subscribe to its importance, then it can be argued that considerations should be given to the teaching of problem-solving skills.

Thought questions

1 To what extent should schools be accountable for producing effective thinkers?

2 Explain your position on the importance of problems in the teaching of mathematics.

3 What kind of evidence is needed to support the first argument concerning the importance of teaching problem-solving?

4 Construct an argument that supports the teaching of problem-solving and is based on the importance of problems in learning mathematics.

What we know about problem-solving

A review of the educational literature dealing with problem-solving indicates that psychologists and educators have studied problem-solving in a variety of contexts. Reviews and discussions of this research (Cronbach, 1954), (Biehler, 1974), (De Cecco, 1968), and (McDonald, 1965) indicate that the following general conclusions seem warranted.

1 Problem-solving is impeded when the problem-solver is anxious, threatened, or confused as to the nature of the problem and its solution.

2 Specific procedures for solving problems tend to improve an individual's ability to solve similar problems but tend to inhibit resolution of problems that require a "new" approach.

3 Encouragement of alternate solutions can contribute to more creative problem-solving behavior.

4 The successful problem-solver tends to formulate hypotheses and test them.

5 When an individual understands a principle and has had an opportunity to practice its recognition and employment in a variety of situations, then that individual is able to "transfer" knowledge of the principle in subsequent problem situations.

Biehler (1974) offers the following general suggestions on how to teach students to solve problems. Teachers should: make students aware of how they are solving problems, make sure that students have the necessary prerequisites for working a problem, encourage an atmosphere conducive to free inquiry and the expression of ideas, set an example as an intuitive thinker, and keep in mind that students have individual differences in problem-solving ability.

Although evidence is inconclusive, there are indications that students improve in their ability to solve mathematics problems when they are made aware of *both* general and task-specific problem-solving maxims and when they have opportunity to practice using these maxims (Wilson, 1967). However, research in high school geometry classrooms indicates that less than 3 percent of classroom time spent on problem-solving is given to discussing a method for solving a problem and that only 7 percent of classroom time spent on problem-solving is given to discussing student solutions (Stilwell, 1967). In light of these findings in geometry classrooms, where it is likely that students have many opportunities to solve problems, it is doubtful that many mathematics teachers emphasize general and specific problem-solving maxims or that they encourage students to formulate intelligent guesses and test their conjectures.

Polya in his classic work *How to Solve It* (1957) sets forth maxims that can be used in solving problems. Kilpatrick (1969) makes the following observation with reference to Polya's maxims:

> Modern interest in heuristic—the study of the methods and rules of discovery and invention—is due principally to Polya (1957, 1962, 1965), who has set forth maxims for problem-solving which, he postulates, correspond to mental actions. Evidence for the validity of Polya's observations on the problem-solving process has come most strikingly from work on computer simulation of human behavior. Programmers have found that the incorporation of general heuristic rules, such as working backward or using a diagram, not only makes problem-solving more economical, but it also results in performance by the computer that closely resembles the behavior of human subjects struggling with similar problems.

In the following section we shall present, discuss, and illustrate maxims that can be used in teaching problem-solving. These maxims were influenced by the work of Polya and reflect the research summarized above.

Maxims for teaching problem-solving

The following maxims can serve as guidelines for teachers in helping students solve problems. The teacher's task in relation to the maxims is twofold: first, he should use them to help students solve problems; second, he should make students explicitly aware of the maxims and help students incorporate them into their problem-solving behavior.

1 Make sure students understand the problem

It is difficult for students to remain interested in a problem if they do not understand it. In general, people lose interest in subjects they do not understand. The person who understands little of the theory of music composition is unlikely to sustain interest in analyzing symphonic music. Likewise, the spectator who has a meager understanding of rugby will probably not maintain an interest in it without development of a better understanding of the game.

Similarly, if students do not understand a question that has been presented to them, it is likely that the question will not represent a problem to them. Students must understand a question sufficiently well that the answer appears to them to be within their intellectual grasp. Only then is it a problem. If the resolution of a problem appears to be beyond a student's intellectual abilities, then he or she is unlikely to pursue a solution.

Students sometimes feel that answering a question is beyond their intellectual abilities, when the solution to the question is actually attainable. A teacher should assume the responsibility for ensuring that students recognize when resolution of a question is within their intellectual reach. If students are to realize that an answer is attainable, it is imperative that they understand exactly what the question asks for. The following questions can serve as guidelines.

1a Do the students understand the meaning of the terms in the problem? To solve the third problem at the beginning of this chapter, students must be knowledgeable about equilateral triangles and medians of triangles. Are there any terms in the first two problems that need clarifying?

1b Do the students take into consideration all the relevant information? Recognizing the information given in a problem is essential for generating and gathering relevant knowledge. Many students are not successful problem-solvers because they fail to identify the given conditions of a problem. Symptomatic of this difficulty is the statement, "I couldn't even get started."

Sometimes students are unable to solve problems because they are not using all the given information. They may have analyzed part of the given completely, but if they have overlooked some of the given conditions, they may be oblivious to information necessary to solve the problem. Suppose, for example, students are asked to determine the nature of the quadrilateral formed by joining the successive midpoints of the sides of an isosceles trapezoid. If the students ignore the fact that the trapezoid is isosceles, then their analysis will lead them to the conclusion that the quadrilateral is a parallelogram. While this conclusion is true, it is incomplete. If the solver considers the given condition that the trapezoid is isosceles, then analysis will lead to the discovery that the quadrilateral is not only a parallelogram but also a rhombus.

1c Can the students indicate what the problem is asking them to find? Evidence indicating that students understand a problem includes their ability to identify the nature of the answer. Does the answer call for a number (as in the checkerboard problem), a set of elements (as in the locker problem), or a constructed figure (as in the equilateral triangle problem)? The answer may consist of a graph, an equation, or some other mathematical entity. It is important that students know the nature of the solution if they are to realize when they have finished the problem.

Knowing the nature of the answer can also provide direction as students begin to formulate strategy for solutions. For example, in the locker problem the solution consists of a set of locker numbers. If students understand this, then one strategy they might employ is to identify elements in this set, hoping thus to find a pattern enabling them to predict other elements. Generally speaking, when a solution to a problem constitutes a set, it is useful to generate elements of the set in the hope that they will allow hunches with respect to generating remaining elements.

While ability to understand the nature of the solution does not always ensure that a viable strategy will be identified, some problems can be simplified by recognizing the nature of the solution. Students should be encouraged to state the kind of mathematical entity that constitutes a solution and try to surmise how this mathematical entity can be generated.

1d   Can the students state the problem in their own words? If appropriate, can the students explain the problem in terms of a sketch? If students can indicate they know the meaning of all the terms stated in a problem and can identify the given information and the nature of the required solution and additionally can express the problem in their own words, then the teacher has a substantial basis for assuming that the problem is understood.

Thought questions

1   Are questions 1a–1d similar in any way to the moves in teaching generalizations? Discuss.

2   Consider the equilateral triangle problem at the beginning of the chapter. Suppose students say they do not understand the problem. Discuss how you could employ maxims 1a–1d to help them.

3   Suppose a student is confronted by the following problem:

> An Earth satellite traces out an elliptical path as it revolves around the Earth. The eccentricity of this path is .20, one focus is the center of the earth, and the major axis of the orbit is 10,000 miles. If the mean diameter of the earth is 8,000 miles, what are the greatest and least distances the satellite is from the Earth?

What terms might you review to help the student? What information in the problem is given? Draw a sketch that you might expect a student to draw to illustrate the problem.

4   Consider the nature of the solutions to the following two problems:
a   Which numbers have exactly four divisors (including one and the number itself)?
b   Given two points in plane E, what is the set of points in E that can serve as a vertex of a $50°$ angle whose rays pass through the two given points?
In problem a, what is the nature of the solution? Does this suggest a strategy for solving this problem? In what way is the solution to problem b similar to the solution of problem a? In what way could the strategies for solving these be analogous?

5   This problem asks the solver to find a probability: If three dice are thrown simultaneously, what is the probability that at least one 5 will come up? What then, is a probability? Does it have an upper bound and a lower bound? How could answers to these two questions be of use to students solving the problem?

6 Consider the following problem: A student has nine coins consisting of only nickels, dimes, and quarters. She has at least one coin of each denomination. The exchange value of the nine coins is $1.35. Determine the number of each type of coin the student possesses. From the given information we can establish two equations:

$$n + d + q = 9$$
$$5n + 10d + 25q = 135$$

Solving the first equation for q and substituting this value into the second equation we obtain: $n = (18 - 3d)/4$. At this point the solver may be stymied by having two unknowns in one equation. What are the conditions of the problem that allow a unique solution to be determined? Which maxim is illustrated here?

7 Consider the following problem: What whole numbers can be represented geometrically by a triangular array of dots, where the configurations form equilateral triangles and the dots are equally spaced? The first triangular number is one. What is the nature of the solution to this problem? How can students use this knowledge to formulate a strategy?

2 *Help students gather relevant thought material to assist in creating a plan*

To solve problems, it is essential that the problem-solver identify information that is relevant for attaining a solution. Unsuccessful problem-solving attempts result often from the inadequacy of the information derived from the given conditions. It is necessary not only to establish that which is given in a problem but also to recognize implications from the given—that is, the relations that follow from the given information (and sometimes the assumed solution). The recognition of these relations is one method of obtaining relevant thought material. Another method is to consider simpler but related questions, perhaps incorporating some of but not all the conditions of the problem. Relevant information may also be obtained by recognizing analogous problems and using solution methods that have been successful in solutions to such related problems. Problem-solvers are sometimes blocked in attaining solutions because they persist in gathering relevant thought material from a restrictive point of view. In such cases the solvers need to "break the set" and search for a new source of relevant information. We discuss and illustrate each of these techniques in the following pages.

2a Assist the students in gathering information by having them analyze the given conditions (and sometimes the assumed solution). It is important for teachers to encourage students once all the given conditions have been identified, to generate all the information that can be derived from them. This information should be obtained even if some of the derivations appear not to be applicable in attaining a solution. A teacher may recognize which information is useful and which is irrelevant. The student grappling with the problem, however, needs to gather this information and then determine how much of it will be the most productive in solving a problem. Students need practice in obtaining information and determining what subset of this knowledge is most likely to be relevant.

The teacher who discourages students from deriving information that the teacher knows is irrelevant to the solution can produce at least three undesirable results. The first is that students can become discouraged in trying to obtain information and, hence, resort to guessing what is on the teacher's mind in order to gain approval (we discussed this as defensive behavior in Chapter 2). A second undesirable effect is that students are prevented from deciding for themselves which information is relevant. Third, the teacher may stifle a potentially unique and insightful student solution.

Let us determine what deductions we can make from the given information in the problem of the equilateral triangle posed at the outset of this chapter. What are the given conditions? We are given a median of an equilateral triangle, and we are to use a straightedge and a compass to construct an equilateral triangle. What do we know about the median? The median of any triangle bisects the side to which it is drawn. We also know that the three medians of any triangle are concurrent at a point that divides the length of the median into a ratio of 2:1. Furthermore, the medians of an equilateral triangle satisfy these additional conditions:

1 Each is perpendicular to the side to which it is drawn (an altitude).

2 Each is an angle bisector.

3 The three medians are congruent.

In addition, we know that an equilateral triangle has three congruent sides and three congruent angles. Hence, each angle has a measure of 60.

We also know that by using a straightedge and compass we can perform the following constructions:

1 Line segments and angles can be constructed congruent to given line segments and angles.

2 Angles and line segments can be bisected.

3 Perpendiculars can be constructed to a given line from a point on or off the line.

4 Certain special angles such as angles of 90°, 45°, 60°, and 30° can be constructed.

Which of the information above is needed to solve the problem?

To answer this question it is helpful to consider the problem solved and see what information can be obtained from analyzing the assumed solution. For example, suppose we consider the equilateral triangle problem as solved in Figures 10.1 and 10.2. From our examination of the given, we can further deduce that triangles ABD and CBD are both 30°-60°-90° triangles (Figure 10.1). Does this analysis help solve the problem? Can a 30°-60°-90° triangle be constructed, given one of the legs? Which of the basic constructions would be used?

Figure 10.1

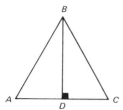

Let us now analyze the problem by using Figure 10.2, in which the three medians are concurrent at point *O*. From a certain geometric theorem we know that

$$\frac{BO}{OD} = \frac{AO}{OF} = \frac{CO}{OE} = \frac{2}{1}$$

We have also established that $\overline{BD} \cong \overline{AF} \cong \overline{CE}$. Do these considerations enable us to find the lengths of segments $\overline{BO}$, $\overline{AO}$, and $\overline{CO}$? How? If $m \sphericalangle FAC = m \sphericalangle ECA = 30$ could we find the measure of $\sphericalangle AOC$? Would $\sphericalangle AOC$ be congruent to angles $\sphericalangle AOB$ and $\sphericalangle COB$? Can we, using only a straightedge and compass, construct angles equal in measure to angles AOC, AOB, and BOC? Can you now devise a second plan, different from the first, for solving this problem?

Notice that the plan to solve the equilateral triangle problem by the second method involves knowledge different from what is used in the first plan. What information is useful in creating the second plan but not needed for the first plan of solution (and vice versa)? Why does this suggest that teachers should be open to students' suggestions and cautious in telling them what information will be relevant in solving a problem?

The strategy of deriving information from both the given and an assumed solution is a powerful method of attacking problems. It is particularly appropriate in solving geometry problems. The reader may wonder where one stops obtaining information from the given and starts analyzing an assumed solution. Actually both of these analyses occur jointly, each reinforcing the other. It is through their interplay that one obtains needed information.

Figure 10.2

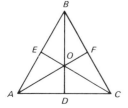

To illustrate this strategy in another context, consider the following problem:

> Two parabolas have the same focus on the y-axis. Their vertices are also on the y-axis and on opposite sides of the focus (but not necessarily the same distance from 'it). Show that the curves intersect at right angles.

Our first step is to try to understand the problem by drawing a sketch (maxim 1d). The general equation of a parabola whose axis is the y-axis is given by the equation $(x - 0)^2 = 4p(y - k)$, where p is the undirected distance from the focus to the vertex of the parabola. The coordinates of the vertex of this parabola are $(0, k)$. Hence, the equation of parabola 1 in Figure 10.3 is

$$x^2 = -4p_1(y - k_1)$$

(Why?) The equation of parabola 2 in Figure 10.3 is

$$x^2 = 4p_2(y - k_2)$$

(Why?) Now let us examine the conclusion of the problem. That the curves intersect at right angles implies that the tangents to these curves at the points of intersection are perpendicular. It follows, then, that the product of the slopes of the tangent lines at a given point of intersection is -1. The question now becomes "How can we establish the product of the slopes of these lines is -1?" To answer this, we must find the slopes of the tangent lines.

This suggests that the solver should return to the equations for each parabola derived from the given information and determine their slopes at the points of intersection. The points of intersection can be found algebraically and the slopes at these points can be determined from the first derivatives of the curves and an algebraic substitution. By differentiation and substitution, we obtain the following expressions.

Slope of first parabola at point A (Figure 10.3) $= -\sqrt{\dfrac{p_2(k_1 - k_2)}{p_1(p_1 + p_2)}}$

Slope of second parabola at point B (Figure 10.3) $= +\sqrt{\dfrac{p_1(k_1 - k_2)}{p_2(p_1 + p_2)}}$

Multiplying these expressions and simplifying, we obtain

$$-\frac{k_1 - k_2}{p_1 + p_2}$$

The solver might now be stymied. How is it that this expression can equal -1? Have we used all our given information? No. We have not made use of the fact that the parabolas share a common focus. How does this enable us to complete the problem?

Figure 10.3

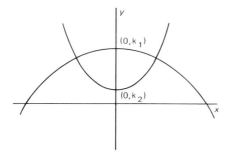

Information can be solicited from students in a number of ways. Slower students can be called on to give the more obvious implications or to agree with information volunteered by other students. The teacher may accept a statement from one student and then call on another to verify or deny the implication. After obtaining relevant information the teacher should guard against telling students outright which information should be used or discarded. It is important that students decide these matters themselves though they should not be left in complete quandary.

Thought questions

1 In obtaining information from the given conditions of a problem, students can use definitions and theorems. Which of the information obtained from the equilateral triangle problem follows from definitions? From theorems?

2 What information would you expect students to derive from the given information in question 3, page 248? Develop a series of questions that you might use to elicit this.

3 Consider the following problem for junior high school students: The mean value of 10 houses on a block is $20,000. The median value of the houses is $17,500. If the most expensive house undergoes some improvements that increase its value by $5,000, then what are the new mean and median values of the 10 houses? What information would you expect students to derive from the information given in this problem? Develop a series of questions that you might use to elicit this.

4 What maxims were illustrated in the discussion of the problem involving the two parabolas intersecting at right angles?

5 Consider question 4b on page 248. You may have determined that the desired set of points lies on the arc of a circle and the arc's reflection about the line connecting the two given points. Consider now the problem of constructing this arc. One way to analyze the problem is to assume it has been solved and from the resulting sketch determine the relations that enable the construction to be performed from the given conditions. A sketch of the assumed solution might be drawn as illustrated in Figure 10.4 where $\overline{AB}$ is the given segment and C is an arbitrary point on the desired major arc AB of circle O. Now "work backward" and determine the relation between angle C and angles OAB and OBA. Does this relation enable you to construct circle O using $\overline{AB}$ and the measure of angle C?

6 In maxim 1c, we suggested that knowing the nature of the solution can facilitate the formulation of a plan to solve the problem. As we mentioned earlier, the solution to

Figure 10.4

the locker problem consists of a set of locker numbers. Hence one possible way of solving this problem is to generate elements in the solution set. This strategy requires the determination of the first few lockers that will remain open. The identification of these lockers may assist in predicting which other lockers will remain open. The chart in Figure 10.5 presents the final state of the first twenty lockers after the first twenty men have passed. Using the chart, determine the four lockers (of the first twenty) that will remain open. From this information predict which of the remaining lockers will also be open after all one thousand men have passed.

7 Construct a sequence of questions and considerations that you could present to students to guide their understanding of the nature of the solution to the locker problem. In what way could these questions also assist the students in devising a plan for solving the problem? In attempting to have students systematically identify elements of the solution set, would you advocate the construction of a chart similar to the one displayed in Figure 10.5?

Figure 10.5

Lockers

	1	2	3	4	5	6	7	8	9	10	11	12	13	14	15	16	17	18	19	20
Man 1	O	O	O	O	O	O	O	O	O	O	O	O	O	O	O	O	O	O	O	O
Man 2		C		C		C		C		C		C		C		C		C		C
Man 3			C			O			C			O			C			O		
Man 4				O				O				C				O				O
Man 5					C					O					O					C
Man 6						C						O						C		
Man 7							C							O						
Man 8								C								C				
Man 9									O									O		
Man 10										C										O
Man 11											C									
Man 12												C								
Man 13													C							
Man 14														C						
Man 15															C					
Man 16																O				
Man 17																	C			
Man 18																		C		
Man 19																			C	
Man 20																				C

Figure 10.6

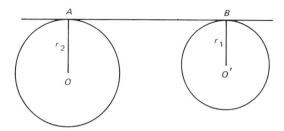

2b Help students obtain information by analyzing an analogous problem. Sometimes the analysis used to solve one problem can serve as the basis for analyzing another problem. Some problems are sufficiently similar that this is feasible. To illustrate how the method of finding the solution to one problem can assist in solving another problem, turn to a geometric setting. Through analysis we shall present a solution to the problem of constructing an external tangent to two noncongruent circles. We shall then present a dialogue in which a teacher helps students solve an analogous problem of constructing an internal tangent to two noncongruent circles.

Consider first the problem of constructing a common external tangent to two noncongruent circles. Figure 10.6 depicts a common external tangent. From certain theorems, we know that $\overline{AO} \perp \overline{AB}$ and $\overline{O'B} \perp \overline{AB}$, where A and B are points of tangency. Analysis and insight will lead us to construct a line segment parallel to $\overline{AB}$ through point O', forming rectangle $ABO'C$ (see Figure 10.7). (Why is $ABO'C$ a rectangle?) $\overline{CO'}$ will be tangent to a circle with center O and a radius of length $r_2 - r_1$. (Why does $\overline{CO} = r_2 - r_1$?) If we could find point C given only the two original circles, we could then determine point A and, hence, point B. How? The problem is now reduced to finding point C. We must draw a circle with center O having radius $r_2 - r_1$. A tangent from point O' to this circle will determine point C and, hence, point A. Point B can be located either by erecting a perpendicular to $\overline{CO'}$ at O' or by erecting a perpendicular to $\overline{OA}$ at point A.

Figure 10.7

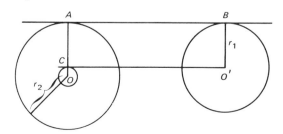

Thus, to construct a common external tangent to two noncongruent circles, we can proceed as follows:

1 Construct a circle concentric to the larger circle (circle O) with radius $r_2 - r_1$, where r_2 signifies the length of the radius of the larger circle.

2 From the center of the smaller circle (O') construct a tangent to the circle of radius $r_2 - r_1$. Call this point of tangency point C.

3 Draw $\overrightarrow{OC}$. Label the intersection of $\overrightarrow{OC}$ and circle O point A. Point A is a point of tangency.

4 Construct a perpendicular to $\overrightarrow{OA}$ at point A. This perpendicular is the desired common external tangent.

Let us now assume that students in the dialogue below have learned how to construct a common external tangent to two circles using the procedure just discussed. The teacher presents the analogous problem of constructing a common internal tangent to two noncongruent circles:

1	T	Do you folks remember how we constructed a common external tangent to two circles? I believe we discussed it yesterday.
2	S$_s$	(*In unison.*) Yes.
3	T	O.K. Today I would like us to explore the problem of constructing a common internal tangent.
4	S$_1$	Ugh!
5	T	Do any of you remember what a common internal tangent is? S$_2$?
6	S$_2$	Yeah. It's a line that just barely touches the circle in two points.
7	T	Well, let's be a little more precise.
8	S$_2$	Well, it just touches . . . oh, I mean tangent to each circle.
9	T	Anything else? S$_3$?
10	S$_3$	I think it must cross the line of centers—you know, the line from one center to another.
11	T	Right. Otherwise it would be a common external tangent. O.K. Could someone draw a sketch of what our construction should look like when we solve the problem? S$_3$?
		(*S$_3$ goes to chalkboard and draws a diagram similar to Figure 10.8.*)

Figure 10.8

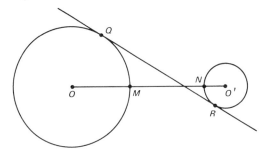

12	T	Good. O.K. Can anyone tell us how to construct the internal tangent. S_4?

13	S_4	Well, you just have to bisect the line segment between the circles. Here, let me show you. (*Goes to chalkboard.*) Bisect segment $\overline{MN}$. That gives point P here.

14	T	That's interesting. Then what?

15	S_4	Well, just construct tangents from point M to the circles—like $\overleftrightarrow{PQ}$ and $\overleftrightarrow{PR}$.

16	T	How do you know the tangents will form a straight line?

17	S_5	Oh, we could prove that, I'm sure.

18	T	Maybe so. How do the rest of you like this proposed solution?

19	S_6	Looks great, man. Easy. That's the most important thing!

20	S_7	I don't think it will work. I mean, like, it seemed to work in that case but how about if the circles are not congruent?

21	T	Would that make a difference?

22	S_7	Yes. I think so. (*Class investigates this and concludes that the suggested method works only in the case of congruent circles.*)

23	T	Well, then we still have the same problem facing us.

24	S_6	Crap!!

25	T	(*Frowns at S_6.*) Let's focus on the essential aspects of constructing the common external tangent. What was special about that construction?

26	S_8	Oh, the construction of the concentric circle.

27	T	Yes. I suppose that was important. What is the radius of that circle? Does anyone remember?

28	S_9	Yeah. The radius was the difference of the two radii of the given circles.

29	T	Right. Do you suppose that could give us any hint on what to do? Could anybody make a guess?

30	S_{10}	Maybe it's the sum. I mean maybe you make a new concentric circle having a radius equal to the sum of the radii of the two given radii.

31	T	Gee, that's a thought. What do you suppose we should do then?

32	S_{10}	I'm not sure.

33	T	How did we proceed in constructing the common external tangent?

34	S_{11}	We constructed that rectangle.

35	S_{12}	We could construct a rectangle here too.

36	T	I believe we're coming up with some good ideas. How would we construct the rectangle?

37	S_{12}	Mm . . . I'm not sure.

38   **S₁₃**   I think I've got it. In the other construction, we made a tangent from O' to the new circle. (*Goes to the board and draws Figure* 10.9.)

Figure 10.9

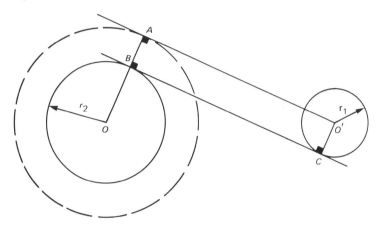

39   **T**   And what is the radius of this new circle?

40   **S₁₃**   Well, this time it's $r_1 + r_2$. O.K.? Then this tangent gives us point A. Now, just like before, draw $\overline{OA}$. This gives us point B.

41   **T**   Good. How do we find the other point of tangency, then?

42   **S₁₄**   Well, before, we said we could construct a perpendicular to $\overline{OA}$ at B or a perpendicular to $\overline{O'A}$ at O'.

43   **T**   Nicely done. You people have analyzed this problem very well.

In this dialogue, what use did the students make of the technique of constructing a common external tangent? How likely do you think it is that students would have solved the problem without using the analogous problem of constructing a common external tangent? In which utterances did the teacher use maxim 1? Do you think it is probable that most students understood the problem from the teacher's presentation? A solution was suggested by S₄. The teacher "played dumb" (see utterance 18) and neither approved nor disapproved the suggestion. Do you think the teacher's technique was effective? Hypothesize what you would do had students in general agreed that the proposed solution works in cases for noncongruent circles. Look at Figure 10.8 drawn by S₃. How might this diagram have influenced S₄ in formulating a plan for attacking the problem? If you were presenting this problem to students, would you have provided more or less assistance to them?

Another way of using the analogous problem technique is to consider simpler but related questions relevant to the problem. Let us return to the

Figure 10.10

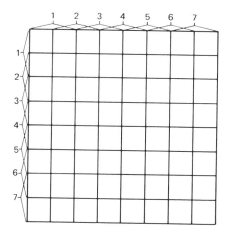

checkerboard problem. At first it would appear that an 8 × 8 checkerboard contains only sixty-four squares. On further consideration, however, it becomes apparent that a checkerboard contains more squares than sixty-four. How many more? Consider some simpler but related questions. What are the dimensions of the other squares in the checkerboard? Clearly there are squares of dimensions 2 × 2 and 3 × 3. The teacher can ask for the number of 2 × 2 squares in the checkerboard and, through questioning, help students realize that there are forty-nine. This can be deduced from analysis of Figure 10.10. Having resolved that there are forty-nine 2 × 2 squares, we can consider another related question: "How many 3 × 3 squares are there?" Teachers should encourage students to venture a guess, which can then be verified or refuted by directly counting the total number of squares. By counting, we can verify that there are thirty-six 3 × 3 squares. At this point it would be helpful to organize the information into a table similar to the one in Figure 10.11. From these entries, a pattern can be recognized and verified by direct count.

Figure 10.11

Size of squares	Number of squares
1 × 1	64
2 × 2	49
3 × 3	36
4 × 4	?
5 × 5	?
6 × 6	?
7 × 7	?
8 × 8	?

Thought questions

1   Determine a plan that junior high school students could devise to solve the following problems:

   a   Given a globe, a tape measure, and the fact that the circumference of the Earth is approximately 25,000 miles, find the approximate distance from Chicago to Hong Kong.

   b   Given a yardstick (and a sunny day) determine the height of any given flagpole.

   c   Given a simple balance, weights, an empty envelope, and loose paperclips, find the number of paperclips in a sealed envelope.

   In what way are these problems analogous? What mathematical principle can be used to solve them all?

2   Why can proving $\sqrt{2}$ is irrational serve as an analogous problem for proving $\sqrt{5}$ is irrational? Explain. How can the student who is faced with the problem of proving that $\sqrt{5}$ is irrational obtain a hunch from his previous proof that $\sqrt{2}$ is irrational?

3   If students were expected to determine the length of a cube's diagonal, given an edge e, what analogous problem would you expect them to identify?

4   Consider question 4b on page 248 and the analysis of it in question 5 on page 253. Suppose now the problem were changed so that the given angle is $110°$. How would the analysis of the previous problem assist in analyzing this problem?

5   Here is a well-known puzzle, sometimes referred to as The Tower Problem:

   > On one of three posts there rests a stack of five graduated disks arranged in order from the largest to the smallest with the largest disk on the bottom (see Figure 10.12). What is the minimum number of moves it will take to reassemble the stack of graduated disks to one of the other empty posts? (A move consists of moving a disk from one post to another post in such a way that a larger disk is never placed on top of a smaller disk. That is, the disks on any one of the posts at any particular time must always be arranged in order with the largest disk on the bottom.)

   Describe a series of simpler questions by which a student might solve this. Could this procedure (considering simpler questions) lead one to determine the number of minimum moves needed to reassemble a stack of n disks?

6   To determine the center of gravity of a tetrahedron, what simpler analogous problem could be useful? (For an interesting discussion of this question, see *How to Solve It* by George Polya, pp. 38–42.)

Figure 10.12

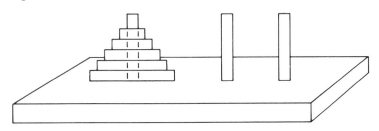

Figure 10.13

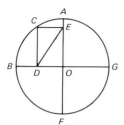

2c *When students have become discouraged by pursuing an unproductive approach, help them view the problem from a different perspective.* Sometimes problems are not solved because the solver is unable to "break a set" toward a particular approach to solving a problem. He or she may have derived a wealth of information from the given and perhaps much of the knowledge is relevant. The way in which this information is used may not be fruitful, however. The solver who persists in such an attack is likely to become discouraged and give up. Consider the following problem.

Circle O is a unit circle with perpendicular diameters $\overline{AF}$ and $\overline{BG}$ (see Figure 10.13). Point C is any point on arc AB of circle O. $\overline{CE}$ is parallel to diameter $\overline{BG}$ and $\overline{CD}$ is parallel to diameter $\overline{AF}$. What is the length of $\overline{DE}$? We challenge the reader to solve this problem before reading the next paragraph.

It is highly probable that from the given information you have established that angle C is a right angle. If your approach to finding the length of $\overline{DE}$ was based on applying the Pythagorean theorem to triangle CED or EOD, it is likely that your attempt was unsuccessful. Considering the given information, such an approach seems quite reasonable, but at some point the solver must recognize that the use of the Pythagorean theorem is not fruitful. One must search for an alternate plan. Rather than trying to use triangles CED and EOD, consider quadrilateral $CEOD$. You may have observed that it is a rectangle. Why? What do we know about rectangles and, in particular, about their diagonals? Using these considerations, see if you can determine why $DE = 1$.

For the solver who had become discouraged in attacking the preceding problem with the Pythagorean theorem, it was necessary to take a different perspective. Sometimes analyzing a problem from a different point of view can be achieved by setting it aside and returning to it at a later time. This is not to say that problems should be abandoned every time a person realizes frustration in attempting to find a solution.

Here is another problem for which a second look facilitates a solution:

Imagine two bicycle riders A and B 50 miles apart, pedaling toward one another at speeds of 10 and 15 miles per hour, respectively. A "superbee" starts from A and flies to B and then back to A and then again to B and so on. The "superbee" continues this oscillation at a speed of 40 miles per hour until A and B collide. How far does the "superbee" travel in flying between the two riders?

The following dialogue portrays a teacher leading a discussion on this problem. Notice that the teacher encourages students to view the problem from a different perspective.

1	T	O.K. Now that we have had S_1, S_2, and S_3 act out the super bee problem, I think we all understand what we have here. What is it we want to find, S_4?
2	S_4	The total distance the bee flies before the collision. By the way I assume the bee is crushed in the wreck.
3	T	Maybe so, but remember that any bee that can turn around instantaneously may be able to escape from relatively slow-moving bicycles! O.K., so we need to find the bee's total distance. Any ideas?
4	S_5	Let's first get the distance for his first trip.
5	T	How do we do that?
6	S_5	It's just 50 miles.
7	S_1	No, it isn't. The riders are closer than 50 miles when the bee finishes his first trip, so he had to go less than 50 miles.
8	T	Do you agree with S_1, S_5?
9	S_5	Yeah, she's right. I forgot B was moving in.
10	T	How would we calculate the length of the first trip?
11	S_2	Well, the bee and B go 50 miles between them.
12	S_7	But how fast? They go at different speeds.
13	T	How did we do the problem when the airplanes were flying toward one another?
14	S_3	We combined the speeds! So B's 15 plus the bee's 40 makes 55 miles per hour.
15	T	How does that help?
16	S_5	Well, at 55 miles per hour we can use $T = D/R$ and get $T = 50/55$, which is a little less than one hour.
17	T	Then what?
18	S_8	Then the distance the bee travels will be that number times 40.
19	T	O.K. Let's figure that out (*calculates these figures with some help from students*). Now what?
20	S_2	Now the bee goes back toward A!
21	S_3	The combined speed now is 50 miles per hour. And the distance is ...
22	T	What's the matter, S_3?
23	S_3	This is going to get messy and this is only the second trip.
24	T	Why?

25	S₃	Well, *A* has moved in already and keeps moving in.
26	T	We handled that a minute ago.
27	S₈	But this time it's worse and it's going to keep getting that way.
28	S₉	The bee is going to make dozens of trips. We can't figure that out!
29	S₅	I'll bet if we do a few, we'll see a pattern.
30	T	That's a good idea. We could do three or four trips.
31	S₁	There must be an easier way.
32	T	Why?
33	S₁	I just think so.
34	T	Well, we have a plan to fall back on but it does look treacherous. Let's stop a minute and see if we can come up with another plan. Any ideas?
35	S₁₀	How about if we changed the numbers around to make it easier?
36	S₁₁	It's not the numbers that make it hard! 50, 10, and 15 are easy enough.
37	T	How have we considered this problem so far? I mean, which part have we looked at?
38	S₆	The bee's part, mostly.
39	T	Right. How else could we look at it?
40	S₅	You mean from the rider's part?
41	T	Possibly. We know how fast they go, don't we?
42	S₁₂	They go 10 and 15—that's 25 miles per hour.
43	T	How does that help? Do we know anything else?
44	S₈	They go 50 miles.
45	S₆	Oh, no—50 miles—25 miles per hour. That's 2 hours traveling time!
46	T	And?
47	S₄	Yeah. Then the bee goes for 2 hours too.
48	T	So?
49	S₂	Now it's easy. The bee flies 80 miles!

Judging from the teacher's statement in utterance 1, several students were assigned roles for illustrating the problem. In what way is the teacher using a modification of maxim 1? To provide assistance in answering the question posed by S₇ in utterance 12, the teacher asked the class to consider how they solved problems involving airplanes. What maxim does the teacher appear to be using in utterance 13?

If you were teaching the "superbee" problem, how would you encourage students to consider the riders rather than the bee? In which utterance did the teacher seem to encourage a view of the problem from a different perspective? In your opinion, should the teacher have encouraged students to calculate some distances (see utterances 29 and 30) before changing directions?

In general, does the teacher seem to be direct or indirect with the students? Base your answer on utterances 5, 10, 17, 30, 34, 39, and 46. How well do you think the teacher conducted the episode?

Problem-solvers should be wary of abandoning quickly an approach to a solution if they are convinced that the approach is well founded. Problems by definition are not easy to solve and, hence, necessarily require persistence as well as insight. In the "superbee" problem there was a method alternative to the tedious one originally suggested. This was fortunate, because the alternate method allowed the problem to be resolved rather quickly. Some problems require long and involved calculations, however. Such methods should not always be abandoned in the search for more elegant solutions.

Thought questions

1   What factors would you consider when deciding whether to give a student a hint to help break a set?

2   Suppose a student is confronted with the following problem:

> Given an equilateral triangle, prove that the sum of the distances to the sides from any point inside the triangle is a constant. That is, if $\overline{AB} \cong \overline{BC} \cong \overline{CA}$ and P is any point, then prove $PE + PD + PF$ is a constant (see Figure 10.14).

Some students are unable to solve this problem because of their persistence on using the Pythagorean theorem, which is not productive. The problem can be solved by taking a different perspective by using the concept of area. Can you solve this problem by considering the area of the equilateral triangle and the area of triangles PAB, PBC, and PCA? Show that $AG = PE + PD + PF$. Use this information to solve the problem. What questions could be posed to help students break their set if they use the Pythagorean theorem?

3   One way to approach a probability problem from a different perspective is to first determine the probability of a failure rather than the probability of a success. Consider the "birthday problem":

> What is the probability in a given class of twenty-four students that at least two students will have birthdays on the same month and the same day of the month (but not necessarily in the same year)?

Figure 10.14

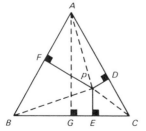

To calculate the desired probability directly is a formidable and confusing task. (Try it!) Consider the problem from a different perspective: what is the probability that twenty-four students have birthdays on different days? Once this has been determined, how can the desired probability be found?

4   Make up a problem of your own that illustrates the point made in question 3.

5   Try to solve the following puzzle without referring to the hint given below it:

> A commuter is in the habit of arriving at his suburban station each evening exactly at 5:00 o'clock. His wife is always waiting for him with the car. She also arrives at the station each day at exactly 5:00 o'clock. One day he takes an earlier train, arriving at the station at 4:00 o'clock. The weather is pleasant, so instead of telephoning home he starts to walk along the route always taken by his wife. They meet somewhere on the way. He gets into the car and they drive home, arriving 10 minutes earlier than usual. Assuming that the wife always drives at a constant speed and never varies her route, can you determine how long the husband walked before he was picked up?

If you have attempted to solve this problem by considering the situation from the husband's perspective—by using the data in reference to the commuter's activities— it is likely that you have been unsuccessful. A more fruitful approach is to view the problem from the wife's perspective—the time that she is (or is not) gone from home. Solve this problem and then outline a series of questions a teacher might use to help students who persisted on solving the problem from the husband's perspective.

3   Provide students with an atmosphere conducive to solving a problem

Making sure a student understands a problem and has obtained all the relevant information does not ensure that the student will solve the problem. The resolution of a problem requires a certain degree of insight that must come from intellectual effort. The teacher cannot provide this insight but can provide an atmosphere conducive to the student's focus of creative abilities to solve the problem. A teacher may encourage students in their efforts to solve a problem by indicating to them that their plan of attack is viable and by providing them with sufficient time to investigate the problem. By recognizing that a problem is difficult and by not penalizing students for making nonproductive attacks, a teacher can encourage students in a positive manner with statements such as "That's a start—keep going," "That might work—try it and see," and "This one gave me a hard time also—take your time."

You may at times wish to give students hints, particularly students who are frustrated and discouraged from pursuit of nonproductive plans of attack. When students are discouraged to the point of quitting, neither their self-concepts nor their attitudes toward mathematics are enhanced. Students do not mature, either mathematically or socially, when they are driven to despair. (A word of caution: a teacher must be careful not to squelch insightful approaches that at first glance appear to be nonproductive.)

Teachers should also help students formulate and test conjectures. Forming and testing them has been shown to be a productive problem-solving strategy (Kilpatrick, 1967). Students should be encouraged to guess and then verify, reject, or modify the conjecture. This type of activity is often employed by mathematicians and mathematics teachers in solving problems. Unfortunately, as teachers we frequently conceal our false starts and dead ends from students and give the impression that we solve problems by behaving in a completely deductive mode. This impression is misleading and can discourage students, who should realize that we employ the same problem-solving maxims and searching procedures that they have been encouraged to use.

Encouragement to formulate and test conjectures and follow hunches can lead students to find more than one solution to a problem. This can provide a teacher the opportunity to illustrate the power of mathematics and perhaps alleviate pressure on students who believe that they must find *the* correct way of solving a problem. By definition, a problem ensures that the solver has some interest in attaining a solution. Teaching problem-solving requires that a teacher capitalize on this. After helping students understand the problem and gather relevant thought material and after providing them with encouragement and sufficient time, a teacher must then wait for the student to produce his or her own solution.

Thought questions

1   Discuss how maxims 2a–2c could serve as the basis for giving a hint to a student who has been unsuccessful in solving a problem. You may include examples in your discussion.

2   React to each of these statements, made by mathematics teachers.

> If no one in the class can solve a problem after working on it for a few days, I always work through a solution with the class. Any problem that is worth a student's time should be explained.

> I never explain a problem that no one in the class can work. I'll give hints, but if no one is interested enough to work it out, I'm not going to just give the answer away.

> I assign at least one challenging problem on every test. This is a good way to separate the A students from the B students.

3   Suppose you have a student who is approaching a problem in a way that you know will lead eventually to a solution. You also know, however, that the approach taken by this student is quite long and extremely difficult and that there are a number of more efficient methods. Under what circumstances would you encourage this student to change approaches? Justify your answer.

4   *Once students have obtained a solution, encourage them to reflect on the problem and the means of solution*

After a solution to a problem has been obtained, it is both enjoyable and instructive for students to reflect on their efforts. The student attempting to solve a problem experiences a certain degree of tension. Once a solution has been obtained (or, at least, once the student is confident that a solution has been obtained) the tension is replaced by a feeling of triumph. Student's who through intellectual processes overcome blocks to solutions have a most rewarding experience.

A teacher can reinforce triumphant feeling by providing students the opportunity to bask in accomplishment. Additional mathematical understanding of a problem can be promoted by capitalizing on the positive attitudes, by encouraging students to verify solutions obtained by inductive processes, search for alternate means of attaining a solution, and investigate questions related to the problem. Consider each of the following strategies for capitalizing on student accomplishment.

4a If possible have students verify solutions that have not been established deductively. When the solution to a problem has been established through deductive means, the verification of the solution is implicit in the deductive process. For example, in discovering a procedure to construct an equilateral triangle, given the median, one uses information deduced from given information and subsequent analysis. These deductions, at least in part, justify the procedure used to complete the desired construction. The solution to a problem by inductive means, however, goes without verification, although it may be quite plausible and acceptable to students. We shall examine a problem whose solution is obtained inductively and then discuss how the solution can be established deductively.

In Polya's book *How to Solve It* (1957, p. 23), there is an interesting problem that can be stated as follows:

Inscribe a square in a given triangle. Two vertices of the square should be on the base of the triangle, the other two vertices of the square on the other two sides of the triangle, one on each.

The reader is encouraged to solve this problem before reading further. The final construction should result in a figure similar to that in Figure 10.15.

The solution to this problem is difficult unless one considers solving a simpler but related problem: can a square be constructed so that two of its vertices are on one side of the triangle and its third vertex is on another side of the triangle, with no restrictions on the location of the fourth vertex of the square? Several such squares are illustrated in Figure 10.16. What can be observed about vertices *D*, *E*, and *F* in relation to vertex *A* of the triangle? Several constructions involving different triangles may convince the reader that points *D*, *E*, and *F* are collinear with point *A*. This should suggest a procedure for solving the original problem.

Figure 10.15

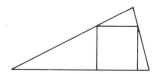

Figure 10.16

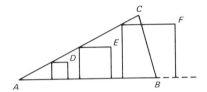

This solution is predicated on the conjecture, established inductively, that points D, E, and F and all such fourth vertices of constructed squares are collinear with a respective vertex of the given triangle. Can this conjecture be verified? It is sufficient to establish the collinearity of any two fourth vertices M and T (see Figure 10.17) with vertex A of the given triangle ABC. In general, what strategies can we employ to show that three points are collinear? Two strategies might be employed from coordinate geometry: the slope and the distance formulas. We shall employ the concept of slope in our discussion and leave to the reader the development of a verification involving distance.

To use coordinate geometry, we must assign coordinates to the vertices of triangle ABC in Figure 10.17. It seems appropriate to place A at the origin and $\overrightarrow{AB}$ on the positive x-axis. Assigning the coordinates of K as (a, O) and assuming that square $KLMN$ has a side of length b, what are the coordinates of L, M, and N? Assigning the coordinates of R as (c, O) and assuming that square $RSTU$ has a side of length d, what are the coordinates of S, T, and U? Using the concept of slope, what relation must be established to verify the collinearity of A, M, and T? We leave the verification of this relation to the reader. Do not forget that points A, N, and U are known to be collinear.

Consider a verification of the solution of the locker problem. The solution was obtained through inductive means by observing the changes in the first twenty lockers. By direct computation it had been established that lockers 1, 4, 9, and 16 would remain open. This pattern suggested that only lockers whose numbers are perfect squares would remain open. To verify this solution by direct computation would be a formidable exercise. Let us examine a deductive argument for it.

The state of a locker will be changed by any man whose number is a divisor of the number of the locker. Since the first man will open every locker, it follows that only the lockers with numbers that have an odd number of divisors will be open after the one-thousandth man has passed. Why? The question then becomes: "Which locker numbers have an odd number of divisors?" or "Which integers from 1 to 1,000 inclusive have an odd number of integral divisors?" Is it the case, then, that perfect squares and only perfect squares have an odd number of divisors?

Figure 10.17

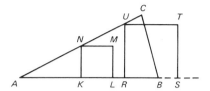

Suppose n is some integer from 1 to 1,000 inclusive. We are assured that there exist two numbers p_1 and q_1 (not necessarily different) such that $p_1q_1 = n$. Why? If n is prime, then p_1 and q_1 are the only divisors and in fact, are 1 and n. Suppose n is not prime. Then there exists another number p_2 different from 1 and n such that n divided by p_2 results in an integer, say q_2. Thus p_2 and q_2 are both divisors of n. How, then, can a number n have an odd number of divisors when seemingly the divisors p_i and q_i come in pairs? The answer lies in the fact that the pair of divisors p_i and q_i may not be distinct—that is, p_i may equal q_i. In such a case, n has an odd number of divisors, since p_i and q_i represent the same divisor. To illustrate this argument, consider the number 36 and its divisors. As can be seen in Figure 10.18, the divisors of 36 can be paired so that the product of each pair is 36. The elements of these pairs are distinct except when one of the divisors is 6. Thus 36 has an odd number of divisors. The reader may wish to formalize the above argument in a more rigorous way.

The solution to a problem sometimes leads the solver to a mathematical generalization. Indeed, the teacher's purpose in presenting a particular problem to students is sometimes to make students aware either explicitly or implicitly of a mathematical generalization. The generalization evolving from the locker problem might be phrased as follows:

A positive integer has an odd number of integral divisors if and only if it is a perfect square.

When problems are presented for the purpose of establishing mathematical generalizations, then the teacher is in effect teaching a discovery lesson.

Figure 10.18

Pairs of divisors whose product is 36	Number of distinct divisors
1,36	2
2,18	2
3,12	2
4,9	2
6,6	1

The reader may rightfully infer that problem-solving ventures are at times discovery lessons.

4b   Encourage students to seek and present alternate ways of solving a problem. A teacher should be receptive to students discovering alternate methods of solving a problem. It is easy to focus on a single method of solution to the exclusion of other approaches. The teacher who ceases to be receptive to alternate methods may stifle creativity and may even do students the disservice of suggesting that alternate methods of solution are invalid. By encouraging students to present original methods, the teacher gains an opportunity to illustrate mathematical interrelationships and, at the same time, promote mathematical self-concepts.

Sometimes students originate a variety of ways to solve a problem through their own cleverness. They enjoy presenting original means of attaining solutions, especially when their approaches are more elegant than those of their classmates or even those of the teacher. Teachers should not be defensive about their own techniques for solving problems. Rather, teachers should praise and encourage students for their cleverness and perhaps take pride in the fact that they have provided students with an opportunity to make such a discovery. If alternate means of solving a problem do not appear in initial presentations, then teachers can encourage students to uncover different approaches by asking them to refocus their attention on a different aspect of the problem.

In an earlier section of this chapter (see Figures 10.1 and 10.2) two different analyses were presented, each leading to the resolution of the equilateral triangle problem. One of the analyses focused on the construction of a 30°-60°-90° right triangle while the other was based on the concurrency of the medians and the angles of intersection of the medians at their point of concurrency. Let us examine still another method of attack by focusing our attention on yet a different aspect of the problem.

It has been established that OD represents one-third the length of $\overline{BD}$ and AO and OC are two-thirds the length of the given median (see Figure 10.19). On the basis of this information and the fact that the given median $\overline{BD}$ is perpendicular to the line containing base $\overline{AC}$, students can

Figure 10.19

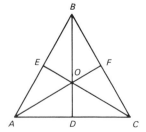

construct segment $\overline{OD}$. Students may now realize that from point O arcs can be constructed to determine points A and C. How? By encouraging students to pursue this analysis, the teacher provides the format for development of an additional method of solution.

Another problem that lends itself to a variety of analyses is the following:

> Generate Pythagorean triples a, b, and c such that $a^2 + b^2 = c^2$, values for a are consecutive odd integers, and b and c are consecutive integers.

The reader may recognize that 3, 4, and 5 and 5, 12, and 13 satisfy the conditions of the problem. Upon further trial-and-error calculations, one might discover that 7, 24, and 25 and 9, 40, and 41 also satisfy the stated requirements. It becomes apparent that at some point the generating of these triples must rely on a systematic approach rather than a system of hit-and-miss calculations. By organizing these established triples as shown in Figure 10.20, students can conjecture various ways of generating other triples. That is, the first Pythagorean triple is 3, 4, and 5, the second triple is 5, 12, and 13, and so on. The reader may now wish to discover ways of predicting other desired triples.

The prediction of the a values is easy ($a = 2n + 1$). Prediction of the b and c values, however, requires more extensive analysis and greater insight. Since the difference between each b value increases by consecutive multiples of 4, the relation $b_n = b_{n-1} + 4n$ can be formulated. For example, $b_5 = b_4 + (4 \times 5)$. That is, $b_5 = 40 + 20$, or $b_5 = 60$ and, hence, $c_5 = 61$. Further analysis will yield other expressions for b, including:

1 $b_n = \dfrac{a_n^2 - 1}{2}$, for example, $b_4 = \dfrac{a_4^2 - 1}{2}$ or $b_4 = \dfrac{9^2 - 1}{2} = 40$

2 $b_n = n(2n + 2)$, for example, $b_3 = 3(2(3) + 2) = 24$

3 $b_n = b_{n-1} + a_{n-1} + a_n$, for example, $b_5 = b_4 + a_4 + a_5$ or $b_5 = 40 + 9 + 11 = 60$

Since the difference between any b_n and the corresponding c_n value is stipulated to be 1, the relationships presented in 1, 2, and 3 can be restated, using the expression $c_n = b_n + 1$.

Figure 10.20

Number of Pythagorean triple	a	b	c
$n = 1$	3	4	5
$n = 2$	5	12	13
$n = 3$	7	24	25
$n = 4$	9	40	41
$n = 5$	11	?	?

Each expression in the display represents an alternate way of generating the Pythagorean triples. Each of the relationships for b_n stems from a different analysis of the data. Students enjoy searching and finding these and other expressions that allow one to predict other desired Pythagorean triples.

4c Challenge students to investigate variations of the given problem. You can stimulate students' mathematical curiosity by presenting a challenging question stemming from a given problem. By varying certain conditions of a problem, you can generate additional problems for students to investigate. For example, once students have solved the checkerboard problem, they could be presented with these variations: (1) how many squares are contained in an $n \times n$ checkerboard? (2) how many cubes are contained in a cube of dimensions $8 \times 8 \times 8$? Students who have solved the original checkerboard problem should be quick to realize that the answer to the first variation is not n^2 and that the answer to the second variation is not $8 \times 8 \times 8$ (or 512) cubes. Why? A teacher may wish to leave these challenges for students to ponder and return to at a later time. This is often an effective way of promoting interest—that is, presenting a challenge for students to consider outside class.

As in the case of the checkerboard problem, other problems can be varied by changing the setting from one of two dimensions to one of three dimensions. A second illustration of this is challenging students to find the equation describing the set of points in space equidistant from two given points, once they have discovered the equation of a line in a plane that is equidistant from two given points. In a similar way, students who have discovered the 2×2 identity matrix for multiplication can then be challenged to find the 3×3 identity matrix for multiplication.

The variations given above were obtained by changing the dimensional setting of the problem. Other variations to a problem can be generated by modifying other aspects of it, such as the given or required conditions. The equilateral triangle problem can be varied by asking students to construct an isosceles triangle given the median to the base and one of the other medians. A further variation, but more complex, would be to construct a scalene triangle given its three medians. We presented another example of variation when we discussed the construction of a common external tangent to two noncongruent circles. The variation that could be presented to students in this case is the analogous problem of constructing a common internal tangent to two noncongruent circles. Variations of given problems frequently result in analogous problems that can sometimes be solved by an analysis similar to the one used to solve the original problem.

Thought questions

1   In solving the Pythagorean triple problem (see discussion accompanying Figure 10.20), a student observes that $b_n = (a_n^2 - 1)/2$ and $a_n = 2n + 1$. How could he or she verify the observation with a deductive argument?

Figure 10.21

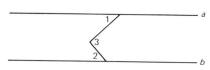

Given: $\overset{\leftrightarrow}{a} \parallel \overset{\leftrightarrow}{b}$
To prove: $m\sphericalangle3 = m\sphericalangle1 + m\sphericalangle2$

2 Identify three alternate ways of solving the problem in Figure 10.21.

3 Two different analyses of the equilateral triangle problem were presented, accompanying Figures 10.1 and 10.2. A third analysis was given, accompanying Figure 10.19. State which analysis can be used to solve the following variation of the equilateral triangle problem: Construct an isosceles triangle given the median to the base and either of the other two medians.

4 Suppose a seventh- or eighth-grade student is wrestling with the problem of determining the product of two negative numbers—for example, -5×-7. Assuming the student is not aware of the rule for multiplying two negative numbers, by what alternate ways might he or she approach this problem?

5 Suppose students have been investigating the speed at which a player can throw a baseball. What variations to this problem could the teacher present?

6 Create a two-dimensional variation and a three-dimensional variation of the following problem: Identify the points in a plane that are a given distance from a given point and equally distant from a pair of intersecting lines. In what ways are these variations analogous to the original problem?

7 Identify some algebra problem with which you are familiar and give several variations of it.

8 What benefits can students derive from classroom discussions that look back over a problem and the various means used to solve it?

Making students aware of maxims

Previously we stated that maxims 1–4 (and their submaxims) can be used to help students solve problems. We also stated that a teacher should be concerned with getting students to incorporate these maxims into their behavior as they solve problems on their own. One way a teacher can do this is to make students aware of the maxims by overtly referring to them as problems are solved with students. That is, a teacher helping students solve problems should frequently employ the ideas embodied in the maxims. Questions and statements similar to the following should characterize the teacher's interactions with students in problem-solving ventures:

1 Let's see if you really understand this. Can you restate this problem in your own words?

2 Can you and did you draw a sketch?

3 What will the answer be like? Does this give us any help?

4   Let's make a list of everything we know so far.

5   Let's assume for a minute that the problem is solved and try to work back from there.

6   Have we done anything like this before?

7   Let's try another approach.

8   Why don't you come back to this problem later and take a fresh look at it?

9   Make a guess: it's free!

10   Do you have a hunch?

11   That's a possibility. Let's see what it does.

12   Don't get discouraged. This is a tough problem!
     Don't expect to get it right away. I sure didn't.

13   That's good! Let's see why it works out that way.

14   That's one way to do it. See if you can find another way.

15   Well, we've solved that problem. Now what would happen if ———?
     Would your plan still work?

Polya (1957, p. 5) also speaks directly to this point.

> If the teacher wishes to develop in his students the mental operations which correspond to the questions and suggestions of our list, he puts these questions and suggestions to the students as often as he can do so naturally. Moreover, when the teacher solves a problem before the class, he should dramatize his ideas a little and he should put to himself the same questions which he uses when helping the students. Thanks to such guidance, the student will eventually discover the right use of these questions and suggestions, and doing so he will acquire something that is more important than the knowledge of any particular mathematical fact.

If one of the goals of teaching is that students become adept in the process of problem-solving, then it is appropriate for teachers to stress and value the procedures students use. In many cases the actual product (or answer) to a problem can be of secondary importance. The fact that a student realizes that there are exactly 204 squares on a checkerboard is not nearly as important as being able to use the process for solving this problem in future problem contexts. This suggests that students should be encouraged to reflect on their means of solving a problem and that alternate procedures in obtaining a solution are valued. In general, teachers and students spend little time and effort in looking back at problems after a solution has been attained—that is, in using maxim 4.

Another consideration in teaching problem-solving is centered on the amount of time a teacher should devote to problem-solving activities. The amount of class time spent on solving and discussing problems and the ways that problems are assigned vary from teacher to teacher. Some teachers prefer to assign several problems and allow students a specified period in which to solve them and then devote particular class meetings to examining the problems and their solutions. Some teachers using this procedure design or construct problems to accompany and amplify units of work or chapters in the textbooks being studied. Other teachers assign problems on a regular schedule by including problems in daily assignments or by posting sets of problems at regular intervals. Teachers sometimes use problems that are posted or assigned along with homework exercises as a way for students to earn extra credit.

The extent to which a teacher provides opportunities to solve problems is a reflection of the value that the teacher places on the importance of problem-solving behavior. Some teachers are unwilling to interrupt a regular schedule of following a given text to engage in presenting and discussing problems. Unless these teachers can justify a given problem in terms of mainstream curricula, they are not likely to present and discuss problems. This is a value judgment determined by a teacher's own preferences.

Unfortunately, teachers miss many opportunities to present curricula as problems because of an urge to complete a predetermined number of pages in a given year. Also unrecognized by some teachers is the extent to which everyday classroom questions can be dealt with in a problem-solving mode. (We shall discuss this situation in greater detail in a later section of this chapter.) Teachers must determine their priorities—that is, what is valued for a given class—and from this basis decide what, if any, problem-solving experience will be presented to students.

Still another consideration of great importance in teaching problem-solving is the attitude of the teacher. The teacher must be an enthusiast of adventure in mathematics. Curiosity is of utmost importance. Questions such as "I wonder if?" "Do you suppose?" "Is it possible that?" and "How could we find out?" typify the teacher who has an air of intellectual curiosity, an attitude that can be contagious to students.

Teachers must act. This calls for puzzled expressions, smiles, and other body language intended to heighten the excitement of making mathematical discoveries. Sometimes a teacher must play the role of one who is also searching for a solution to a problem. This was manifested in the dialogue on the construction of the common internal tangent on pages 256–258. A teacher can also play the skeptic—guiding students and yet being aloof with respect to telling them how to solve a problem. Similarly, the teacher in the "super-bee" problem episode posed questions to guide the students in their thinking. The teaching of problem-solving is not easy. It is difficult to keep students interested and not let them get discouraged to the point of giving up and yet at the same time not provide so many hints that obtaining a solution ceases to represent a real challenge.

Finally, the teacher must be able to provide the spark of enthusiasm to motivate students to solve problems. At various places in this text we have discussed motivation. Many of the techniques for providing motivation discussed earlier apply to the teaching of problem-solving. In addition, because of the nature of problem-solving, Polya (1965, p. 105) suggests what he calls *best motivation* for teaching problem-solving.

> The best motivation is the student's interest in his task. Yet there are other motivations which should not be neglected. Let me recommend here just one little practical trick. Before the students do a problem, let them *guess the result*, or a part of the result. The boy who expresses an opinion commits himself; his prestige and self-esteem depend a little on the outcome, he is impatient to know whether his guess will turn out right or not, and so he will be actively interested in his task and in the work of the class—he will not fall asleep or misbehave.

Effective teachers of problem-solving use many teaching skills. They have the task of helping students solve problems and also of helping them incorporate strategies for solving problems into their own behavior. To realize this aim, a teacher must present problems to students in a way that encourages them to accept the challenge inherent in a problem and to form and test hypotheses on how the problem can be resolved. This requires careful planning and reacting to students in a most artistic way.

Thought questions

1 Identify the maxims to which each of the questions posed at the beginning of this section seem to refer. Match the question with the intended maxim.

2 Identify arguments for and against using problems as a vehicle for giving students extra credit or giving them credit to substitute for neglected daily assignments or unsatisfactory test scores. State and defend your position on this issue.

Generating problems to present to students

Problems can come from a variety of sources. Many can be developed from the textbook content being studied while others can involve model situations from life outside the classroom. Still others can be found by exploring various mathematical curiosities or recreational puzzles. We shall give examples and sources of these types of problem.

Problems developed from basic content

One way of generating problems is to present basic content as a problem-solving venture. For example, you might challenge your students to find the identity matrix for multiplication of 2×2 or 3×3 matrices (see discovery lesson 5 in Chapter 7). Another example would be to have students determine the relation between the sum (or product) of the roots of a quadratic equation and the coefficients of the equation (see discovery lesson 11). Students could also be asked to find the measure of an angle formed by two chords (or secants) in terms of the measures of the intercepted arcs (see discovery lesson 12).

Figure 10.22

When problems are presented whose solutions are mathematical principles the result is in essence a discovery lesson. When problems as illustrated in the previous paragraph are presented to students, the students may attack them by either an inductive or a deductive strategy. Students expected to identify various properties of a parallelogram (or some other geometric figure) may make inferences by making direct measurements of such figures (see discovery lesson 2) or by deducing the desired properties (see discovery lesson 9).

Not all problems involving basic content have solutions that are mathematical principles. The solutions to some problems are singular statements, as illustrated by the following problems:

1   Suppose you wish to enclose a rectangular area with 100 feet of fence so that its area is maximized. The rectangular area is already bordered on one side by a wall, the remaining three sides to be enclosed by fence. What dimensions of this lot will maximize its area?

2   Approximate the $\sqrt{3}$ using the binomial expansion. (Assume students have used the binomial expansion with integral exponents.)

3   Given that $\overline{AB}$ and $\overline{DC}$ are congruent and perpendicular to $\overline{BC}$, prove that $\angle A \cong \angle D$, using no theorems based on the parallel postulate (see Figure 10.22). Can it be proved that angles A and D are right angles without using the parallel postulate or any theorems derived from this postulate?

4   Points *A–H* represent fractional numbers in order on the number line. The number represented by *C* is multiplied by the number represented by *E* and the product is known to be represented by one of the other points *A*, *B*, *D*, *F*, *G*, or *H*. Which of these points must represent the product of *C* and *E*? (See Figure 10.23.)

Figure 10.23

These and other, similar problems emphasize content basic to school mathematics curricula. Such problems can be found in textbooks, in periodic publications such as *The Mathematics Teacher* and *The Mathematics Student Journal*, and in various mathematics contests. (References of compilations of contest problems and other problems are given at the end of this chapter.) Solving such problems reinforces the student's knowledge of basic mathematical concepts and principles and requires the student to apply this knowledge at a rather complex level of understanding. Such applications of his knowledge enable him to appréciate interrelationships in mathematics.

Problems generated by the technique of variation

We have all observed the phenomena of stimulating classroom discussions that seem to be an extension to the main point a teacher was making. Such discussions can be the result of a teacher skillfully asking questions such as "What happens if?" in discussing a given item of knowledge. In maxim 4c, we discussed the technique of variation as a means of generating problems from a given problem. This technique can also be applied to generate problems from expository or discovery lessons dealing with basic content. Students can be challenged to consider variations of a given generalization, such as its converse, or other generalizations obtained by changing the hypothesis of the given generalization. Consider, for example, students who have just discovered the graph of the equation,

$$|x| + |y| = n$$

where n is a positive real number. They might then be asked to consider the analogous problem of graphing a similar but different equation,

$$|x| + y = n$$

where n is a positive real number. Clearly, other variations could be made also.

Geometry is a branch of mathematics in which variation can be used effectively to generate problems. Once a theorem such as

> If a line is parallel to one side of a triangle and intersects the other two sides in distinct points, then it cuts off segments which are proportional to these sides.

has been discussed, then the problem of considering its converse can be posed. Although the converse of this theorem is true, students are sometimes surprised to learn that the converse of every theorem is not always true.

An interesting and different type of variation for students to consider is the problem of proving generalizations without the parallel postulate or any of its derivatives. Students are surprised that many of the theorems they use are predicated on this postulate. They are also surprised at the amount of knowledge that can be developed by using theorems and postulates not based on the parallel postulate.

Teachers should not feel that it is always their responsibility to initiate variation. Students themselves often provide the necessary "spark" by asking "What happens if?" or similar questions. These situations must not be overlooked as potential problem-solving episodes. The exploration of interesting conjectures requires that the teacher have a commanding knowledge of mathematics. Those who are not well grounded are likely to consider questions such as the following as troublesome and hence avoid resolving them in a problem-solving mode.

> **Student** I remember we said that, if a series converges, then its sequence of terms must converge to 0, like $1 + \frac{1}{2} + \frac{1}{4} + \frac{1}{8} + \frac{1}{16} \ldots$. But what if the terms converge to 0? Does that mean the series converges?

This is not to say that you must know the path that every question will take. You will have to make decisions, however, as to the amount of time that should be spent in problem-solving excursions. The question above may warrant a good deal of class time for discussion and resolution. The question below can probably best be dealt with quickly, however, recognizing that the student would appear to have a conflict but realizing that the "conflict" arises because of the misuse of the general principle,

$$\sqrt{a}\,\sqrt{b} = \sqrt{ab} \text{ where } a, b, >0$$

> **Student** I'm confused. You said that $\sqrt{-1}$ times $\sqrt{-1} = -1$. But if I take $\sqrt{-1}$ times $\sqrt{-1}$, I get $\sqrt{+1}$, which is $+1$. Why don't we get the same result?

A teacher must use discretion in deciding whether it is best to handle a student's question quickly or to use the question as a problem-solving episode. The decision will be based in part on the level of the students, the teacher's perception of their interest in the question, and the mathematical significance of the situation.

Problems oriented toward life situations

One of the arguments for studying mathematics is its usefulness in solving practical problems. Teachers can promote the practical value in studying mathematics by presenting students with problems from life situations. For example, some students are interested in determining how fast they can throw a baseball. The solution to this problem necessitates that students calculate the time it takes to throw a baseball a given distance. Attaining a solution, then, requires observations from an experimental setting. Other variations of interest are determining the speed at which an individual can run or walk a given distance or the speed at which a creek is flowing. Another problem of interest to junior high school students and also requiring empirical evidence is the determination of the approximate value of one's thumb if it were solid gold. References at the end of this chapter provide a source of problems requiring empirical investigations in a laboratory-like setting.

Some teachers of general mathematics classes have had success in generating a series of problems starting from questions of social or economic interest. Questions such as "How much does it cost to own and operate a car?" "How would you design a house?" and "Do you save money in the long run by buying a sewing machine and making your own clothes?" can provide the basis for problem-solving experiences. The investigation of these questions can involve individuals or the entire class for a few days or longer. Consider, for example, how the question "How would you design a house?" could develop into an entire unit of work based on social and economic concerns. Students could begin by drawing rough floorplans of their present house, listing its advantages and disadvantages for their family, and then sketching a floorplan of another dwelling that suits better their needs and desires while still meeting certain practical restrictions. Restrictions on the size of the house and the dimensions of the interior can lead to direct measurements of existing rooms and houses and into scale drawings constructed with simple drafting instruments. Just how far a teacher should develop this unit would depend on the interest of the class and the teacher's ability to capitalize on it. In a unit such as this, additional questions such as "How much will a house like this cost?" are likely to arise. Such questions can lead to the investigation of the cost of different types of dwellings in relation to the number of enclosed square feet, the cost of furniture, carrying charges, the amount of storage space needed, mortgages, down payments, monthly payments, real estate commissions, insurance, taxes, and maintenance. These topics allow invitation of "outside experts" to class and field trips to construction sites and business establishments. Each of these topics has the potential of spawning further questions and problems for investigation.

While it may be clear that a great deal of mathematics can be involved in the investigation of social and economic questions, it is not clear why such units seem to work in some general mathematics classes and for some teachers but not for others. Part of the answer may lie in our definition of a problem. In addition to being a challenge that cannot be resolved by some routine procedure, the problem must be accepted by the student as a challenge. If the social and economic questions and topics mentioned above stem from and are accepted by students, then it is likely that they will put forth substantial effort in answering them and receive mathematical and social benefits from the unit. It is unlikely, however, that students will be interested in social and economic questions that they perceive as being forced on them by the teacher, especially if the teacher represents a social class with different needs and values. In such instances it may be best to set the stage and probe for social and economic topics and questions and then capitalize on the students' concerns. This demands that a teacher be open to suggestions from students and willing to incorporate them into the curriculum.

The potential of investigating social and economic questions has been indicated in research reported by Travers (1967) and Keil (1965). Travers found that ninth-grade male students show a strong preference for answering questions from social-economic situations as opposed to mechanical-scientific or abstract settings. Keil found that ability to solve textbook problems improves when students are given experience in writing and solving problems they have generated for themselves.

Many political and economic decisions are based on analysis of data obtained from empirical investigations. Suppose a farmer, for example, has to decide how to apportion 200 acres of land between two crops *a* and *b*. Assume further that he wishes to base his decision on some sort of mathematical analysis. In accordance with this desire, the farmer might determine the cost per acre of producing and estimate the expected market price for selling each crop. Once these determinations have been made, the problem might then be described as follows:

> A farmer has 200 acres of land to be planted in two crops *a* and *b*. No more than 150 acres of land can be planted in crop *a*. The expected income from *a* is $300 per acre and the expected income from *b* is $260 per acre. The farmer's cost for seed for crop *a* is $60 per acre and for crop *b* it is $100 per acre. Crop *a* requires an average of 15 hours of labor per acre at $2.80 per hour. Crop *b* requires an average of 10 hours of labor per acre at $2.50 per hour. How many acres of each crop should be planted if the farmer wants to maximize potential profit?

The problem can now be solved by the algebraic technique of linear programming, a technique useable by first- or second-year algebra students.

A teacher can capitalize on many life situations to develop mathematics problems. It is hoped that students will develop their abilities to make decisions based on rational grounds. It would seem that solving problems involving life situations would contribute to the development of this ability.

Recreational problems and mathematical curiosities

Mathematics has been a source of intriguing intellectual problems for centuries. Teachers, students, scholars, and others have been challenged to solve problems that are mathematical in nature. Illustrations of some of these are given below. You may be familiar with them or variations of them.

1 Find the whole number represented by each of the letters in the following addition problem:

       SEND
     + MORE

      MONEY

2 A man died and left his estate to his three sons, divided as follows. To my eldest son, I leave one-third of my land. To my second son, I leave one-third of the remaining acres. To my youngest son, I

leave one-third of the acres still remaining. The remaining eight acres I leave to whichever of my sons is clever enough to determine from this information the total acres in my estate and the number of acres I have just assigned to him and his brothers. Can you determine the size of the man's estate and the apportionments given in the will?

The following problem (Copi, 1968, p. 31) is one of many logic problems students find of interest. See if you can solve it.

3   Benno Torelli, genial host at Hamtramck's most exclusive nightclub, was shot and killed by a racketeer gang because he fell behind in his protection payments. After considerable effort on the part of the police, five men were brought before the District Attorney, who asked them what they had to say for themselves. Each man made three statements, two true and one false. Their statements were:

Lefty   I did not kill Torelli. I never owned a revolver. Spike did it.

Red   I did not kill Torelli. I never owned a revolver. The other guys are all passing the buck.

Dopey   I am innocent. I never saw Butch before. Spike is guilty.

Spike   I am innocent. Butch is the guilty man. Lefty lied when he said I did it.

Butch   I did not kill Torelli. Red is the guilty man. Dopey and I are old pals.

Whodunnit?

Many students are interested in a mathematical curiosity sometimes called the "birthday problem." The problem can be presented to students in the form of a question such as:

We have twenty-four students in this room. What is the probability that at least two have birthdays in the same month and on the same day of the month (but not necessarily the same year)?

Students are usually astounded to discover that the odds are approximately even that at least two people of twenty-four will have the same birthday.

Another form of mathematical curiosity is fallacy. One fallacy is the proof that every triangle is isosceles. Consider a given scalene triangle *ABC*.

Figure 10.24

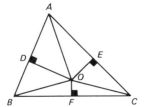

Let us examine the fallacy that establishes that $AB = AC$ (see Figure 10.24). Suppose the perpendicular bisector of side $\overline{BC}$ and the bisector of angle A intersect at point O. From point O, perpendiculars are constructed to $\overline{AB}$ and $\overline{AC}$. Consider, now, the following statements.

$$AO = AO$$
$$OD = OE$$
$$\therefore \quad \triangle ADO \cong \triangle AEO$$
$$\therefore \quad AD = AE$$
$$BO = OC$$
$$\therefore \quad \triangle BDO \cong \triangle CEO$$
$$\therefore \quad DB = CE$$
$$\therefore \quad AB = AC, \text{ or } \triangle ABC \text{ is now isosceles}$$

Can you find the fallacy?

Another well-known fallacy of interest to algebra students is the argument that claims to establish $2 = 1$. Study the following steps to determine the logical error in the argument. Let x and y be any two nonzero real numbers such that $x = y$.

If $x = y$, then $x^2 = xy$.
Therefore $x^2 - y^2 = xy - y^2$ and $(x + y)(x - y) = y(x - y)$.
Hence, $x + y = y$.
Since $x = y$, then by substitution $2y = y$.
Since y is a nonzero real number, it follows that $2 = 1$!

Mathematical puzzles and curiosities should be viewed by teachers and students as interesting activities. Puzzles and curiosities are often useful to teachers in maintaining student interest in mathematics and, in some cases, averting potential discipline problems. Teachers should not feel apologetic for occasionally presenting them to students. Some problems, such as the fallacies, emphasize mathematical principles. Others are mainly exercises in logical thinking. The presentation of recreational problems may emphasize basic content and also provide students with a stimulating break from routine classroom activities.

Students are often stimulated by short mathematical contests that pit them against the teacher or other students in nonthreatening situations and in a context in which they perceive they have a competitive position. The game of "21" is an example. In this, two contestants begin at zero and take turns in advancing along a number line (or adding to a pile of tokens) in "jumps" of one, two, or three. A player must move forward in each turn. The first player to reach twenty-one wins. This dialogue could represent one such game:

T   We have three or four minutes left, Student$_1$. Do you think you have devised a plan to beat me in 21?

S$_1$ I think so.

T   Go ahead.

S₁   No, you go first!

T   All right. I'll take 3.

S₁   I'll take 2 more and get 5.

T   I'll take 3 and get 8.

S₂   Take 5 and get 13, S₁.

S₁   I can't. That's not allowed. I'll take 1 and get 9.

T   Right. I'll take 1 and get 10.

S₁   I'll take 1 and get 11.

T   I'll take 2 and get 13.

S₁   (*Beginning to look concerned.*) I'll take 2 and get 15.

T   I think you're in trouble now. I'll take 2 again and get 17.

S₁   I'll take 3 and get . . . No, I'll take 1 and get 18 (*frowns*).

T   Then I'll take 3 and get 21 (*wins*).

S₁   *Damn*!

T   That was a good game, S₁. I think you're on the road to devising a plan. You knew that you were in trouble three or four moves before the end; that's a good sign. S₃, how about you? Have you solved this puzzle?

After students have solved the problem of winning at "21," the game can easily be changed to a game of "50" or "100," using moves of varying size. These games can be analyzed as analogous problems.

By reading the literature, attending professional meetings, and sharing notes with colleagues, you will come into contact with many problems of various types. References for additional problems are listed at the end of this chapter. We suggest that you compile a list of various types of problems to provide opportunities to illustrate various mathematical concepts and principles, help students realize the importance of mathematics in their lives, and provide motivation for learning mathematics.

Thought questions

1   Identify a mathematical principle and discuss how you would present it to students as a problem-solving experience.

2   On page 277, we gave four examples of problems whose solutions require the use of basic mathematical knowledge. Identify the level of student for which you think each question could represent a problem. Identify the basic content (the mathematical concepts and principles) used in the resolution of each of the four questions.

3   Graph the equations $|x| + y = 1$ and $|x| + y = 2$. Assume that you have guided students in discovering the pattern for graphs of equations of the form $|x| + |y| = n$ where n is a positive real number. (This lesson was discussed in Chapter 7.)

Outline how you would guide these students in the problem of discovering the graphs of these equations. What is the pattern for graphs of equations of the form $|x| + y = n$, where n is a positive real number?

4   In addition to $|x| + y = n$, where n is a positive real number, what other variations of the basic equation $|x| + |y| = n$, where n is a positive real number, can be considered?

5   In the preceding section, a student initiates a variation by asking whether the converse of the theorem "If a series converges then the sequence of its terms must converge to zero" is true. How could you, as a teacher, react to this student in a problem-solving mode?

6   Suppose your students have discovered the Pythagorean identity $\sin^2 x + \cos^2 x = 1$ (see Chapter 7, lessons 7 [page 155] and 10 [page 159]). What variations could be undertaken to develop other trigonometric identities?

7   Often problems about life situations involve proportions. Discuss and illustrate how proportions can be used in answering the question "How far is it from Chicago to Hong Kong?"

8   State a problem involving a life situation that can be solved using proportions.

9   Suppose the family of a student in your general mathematics class is considering buying a freezer, renting a frozen-food locker, or using the freezer in their own refrigerator. What mathematical problems could be developed from this situation?

10   Linear programming is a technique usable by first- and second-year algebra students. Use it to answer the question concerning the farmer apportioning his 200 acres (on page 281). What concepts, principles, and skills do students use in linear programming?

11   State a problem involving a life situation that can be solved with linear programming.

12   What hints would you give students to help them find the isosceles triangle and the $2 = 1$ fallacies on pages 282–283.

13   Give an example of a situation in which a mathematical puzzle or curiosity could be used to avert a potential classroom disturbance.

14   Sometimes games can be used to promote the study of various mathematical topics. For example, the problem of winning at Nim can be analyzed by using the binary numeration system. Identify a game that can be used to promote a problem-solving experience.

Developing problem–solving episodes from student questions

Teachers do not have to rely on specific problems to engender problem-solving behavior. Questions that students ask and teachers pose often have this potential. By encouraging students to search for answers, the teacher can foster problem-solving. One might even claim that the development of ability to resolve questions, mathematical or nonmathematical, can best be promoted by dealing with daily questions in the context of a problem-solving venture.

Students are often confused about the equation of the *x*-axis, for example. When this happens, teachers can help them by having them examine an analogous situation. The following dialogue illustrates a teacher's strategy in dealing with this situation (see Figure 10.25):

Figure 10.25

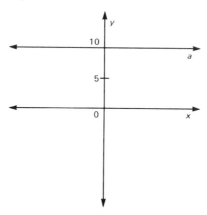

S   I forgot the equation of the *x*-axis. What is it?

T   What is the equation of line *a*? (*Points to a line* a.)

S   It's $y = 10$.

T   How do you know?

S   Because *y* is always 10.

T   O.K. What is the value of *y* at any point on the *x*-axis?

S   Zero. Oh, then the equation of the *x*-axis must be $y = 0$.

T   Exactly.

An alternative strategy would be for the teacher to remind the student that the equation of the *x*-axis is $y = 0$. Which strategy would be the most effective?

Similarly, beginning algebra students may become confused in solving an equation such as $2(x - 4)/5 = 6$. To alleviate such confusion, the teacher might enumerate a procedure for solving the equation, but the teacher could react this way instead:

S   I have the equation $2(x - 4)/5 = 6$. But I don't know what to do first.

T   Look at the entire equation. What must be the value of the numerator on the left side?

S   The entire numerator has to equal 30, since it has to be divided by 5 and give 6.

T   Can you write a new equation from what you just said?

S $2(x - 4) = 30$.

T (*Writes this on the board.*) Good. Can you now tell me what the value of the expression inside the parentheses should be?

S 15, because 2 × 15 = 30.

T What equation can you write now?

S $x - 4 = 15$. Then $x = 19$.

T (*Writes both of these equations on the board.*)
O.K. Now let's look back at the original equation and the three equations you generated. Can you analyze your work and tell what you could do to carry out each step?

What prescriptions will be identified in the student's analysis? Which maxim does the teacher seem to be using? Do you think this approach would be effective?

Sometimes students forget mathematical relations. Teachers can help them reconstruct forgotten knowledge by helping them realize how it is related to knowledge they have not forgotten. Suppose they cannot recall the trigonometric identity $\tan^2 x + 1 = \sec^2 x$, $x \neq \pi/2 + \pi n$, $n \in Z$. It is likely that students will remember the basic Pythagorean identity $\sin^2 x + \cos^2 x = 1$. By asking leading questions, the teacher can help students realize that the forgotten knowledge can be established by dividing each member of the basic Pythagorean identity by $\cos^2 x$, given the restriction on x.

Similarly, students may forget whether a permutation of ten objects taken three at a time ($_{10}P_3$) is calculated by the expression $10!/3!$ or by $10!/7!$. Students will most likely remember that a combination of ten objects taken three at a time is calculated by the expression $10!/7!3!$. This is usually easier to remember, because both of the factorial factors appear in the denominator and hence a choice is not required. The teacher can help students decide the correct expression for $_{10}P_3$ by using relation $_{10}C_3 = 10!/7!3!$ and the realization that each combination containing three objects can be arranged $3!$ ways. Hence the number of permutations can be expressed as $(10!/7!3!) \times 3!$, or $10!/7!$.

These and other situations can occur in the context of classroom discussion. Teachers should be alert for opportunities to engage students in problem-solving episodes, particularly when they have provided the initiative. The teacher whose philosophy of teaching is permeated by a problem-solving approach has many opportunities to enter into mathematical discussions with students that also provide a context for evaluation of their depth of understanding.

Thought questions

1 Consider the problem-solving episodes in the preceding section. In each the teacher could have responded directly by telling students the correct answer. Do you think taking the time to engage students in a problem-solving exchange will help them recall and apply the knowledge in question? Why?

Figure 10.26

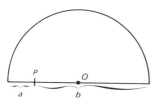

2   Discuss how a mathematics teacher could generate a problem-solving episode in responding to the following situations. Write a brief dialogue indicating how this might be done.

a   An average seventh-grade student asks: "Why do we always move the second row over in multiplying problems like 34 × 276?"

b   Ninth-grade algebra students familiar with the laws of exponents for non-negative integral exponents are confused when asked to evaluate 5^{-2}.

c   A second-year algebra student, familiar with synthetic division, asks: "If I do my synthetic division by -3 and the remainder is 0, is the root of the equation 3 or -3?"

d   A twelfth-grade advanced mathematics student has forgotten the formula for the area of an equilateral triangle given the length of one side.

e   A beginning algebra student is unsure whether to express "x less than y" as $x - y$ or $y - x$ or in some other way.

3   Suppose a geometry student is undecided how to construct a mean proportional to two given segments a and b. The student has begun by constructing a semicircle whose diameter is $a + b$ (see Figure 10.26) but is confused on whether to construct a perpendicular at O (the center of the semicircle) or at P, the point of division between the two given segments. What questions might a teacher ask to help the student resolve the indecision? In particular, what maxims might be used? Write a brief dialogue illustrating how the question could be resolved in a problem-solving context.

Self-test on the competencies

1   State conditions under which a given question is a problem.
Under what conditions (age and ability of student and so on) would the following questions be a problem?

a   What are the dimensions of a rectangle if its perimeter is 56 feet and its area is 192 square feet?

b   The sum and product of the roots of a quadratic equation are $-\frac{7}{2}$ and -15, respectively. Find a quadratic equation with roots that satisfy these conditions.

2   Generate problem(s) from a given hypothetical teaching situation in which the mathematical context and the mathematical maturity of the students are specified. Illustrate how you could generate a problem-solving episode from the following situations.

a   In an average eighth-grade mathematics class, students are investigating properties of polygons of more than four sides.

b   In a senior advanced mathematics class, a student cannot evaluate cosecant 270°.

3 Generate a problem for a specified student population from a given situation.

  a What problem might evolve for junior high school students from a situation in which a student is considering which if any of several newspaper routes to accept?

  b What problem might evolve for senior advanced mathematics students investigating the distance a projectile will travel after being launched from some device?

4 Generate (or find) problems that are recreational or stem from mathematical curiosities.

  Give an example of a mathematical puzzle or curiosity that could become the basis for a problem for junior high school students or advanced high school students.

5 State the maxims for helping students solve problems.

  State or paraphrase the four major maxims and their submaxims.

6 Indicate how the maxims would be applied to a specific problem you could present to students.

  Write a series of questions you could ask in helping students investigate the following problems. Identify the maxim that each of your questions reflects. Include questions designed to help students examine variations.

  a How many diagonals does a twenty-sided convex polygon have? Assume you are working with junior high school students.

  b Construct a circle tangent to a given line and containing two given points. Assume you are working with high school geometry students.

7 Use the maxims in an actual teaching situation.

  If a teaching situation can be arranged, identify a problem appropriate for your students and develop a series of questions keyed to the maxims. Present your proposed lesson to your instructor for suggestions, teach it, and analyze your effectiveness.

References

Andree, Richard V. *Selections from Modern Abstract Algebra*. New York: Holt, Rinehart and Winston, 1958.

Ashlock, Robert B., and Wayne L. Herman. Jr. *Current Research in Elementary School Mathematics*. New York: Macmillan, 1970. Pp. 193–234 and 477–485.

Biehler, Robert F. *Psychology Applied to Teaching*, 2nd ed. Boston: Houghton Mifflin, 1974.

Brownell, William A. "Problem-solving." *The Psychology of Learning*, Forty-first Yearbook of The National Society for the Study of Education, Part II. Chicago: University of Chicago Press, 1942.

———, and Gordon Hendrickson. "How Children Learn Information, Concepts, and Generalizations." *Learning and Instruction*, Forty-ninth Yearbook of The National Society for the Study of Education, Part I. Chicago: University of Chicago Press, 1950.

Conference Board of the Mathematical Sciences. *The Role of Axiomatics and Problem-Solving in Mathematics*. Boston: Ginn, 1966.

Copi, Irving M. *An Introduction to Logic*, 3rd ed. New York: Macmillan, 1968.

Cronbach, Lee J. *Educational Psychology*. New York: Harcourt Brace Jovanovich, 1954.

———. "The Meaning of Problems." *Arithmetic*, Supplementary Educational Monographs, No. 66. Chicago: University of Chicago Press, 1948.

DeCecco, John P. *The Psychology of Learning and Instruction: Education Psychology.* Englewood Cliffs, N. J.: Prentice-Hall, 1968. Pp. 428-477.

Dewey, John. *How We Think.* Boston: Heath, 1933.

Educational Services, Inc. *Goals for School Mathematics,* Report of the Cambridge Conference on School Mathematics. Boston: Houghton Mifflin, 1963.

Gardner, Martin. *The Scientific American Book of Mathematical Puzzles and Diversions.* New York: Simon and Schuster, 1959.

Henderson, Kenneth B., and Robert E. Pingry. "Problem-Solving in Mathematics." *The Learning of Mathematics: Its Theory and Practice,* Twenty-First Yearbook of The National Council of Teachers of Mathematics. Washington, D. C.: The Council, 1953.

Johnson, Donovan, and Gerald R. Rising. *Guidelines for Teaching Mathematics.* Belmont, Calif.: Wadsworth, 1969. Pp. 104-125 and 426-427.

Keil, Gloria Emilie. "Writing and Solving Original Problems as a Means of Improving Verbal Arithmetic Problem Solving Ability." Ph.D. dissertation. Bloomington: Indiana University, 1964.

Kidd, Kenneth P. "Measuring the Speed of a Baseball." *School Science and Mathematics,* 66 (1966), 360-364.

Kilpatrick, Jeremy. "Analyzing the Solution of Word Problems in Mathematics: An Exploratory Study." Ph.D. dissertation. Stanford, Calif.: Stanford University, 1967.

———. "Problem-solving and Creative Behavior in Mathematics." *Studies in Mathematics,* Vol. 19: *Reviews of Recent Research in Mathematics Education,* ed. by James W. Wilson and L. Ray Carry. Palo Alto, Calif.: School Mathematics Study Group, 1969.

Kinsella, John J. "Problem-solving." *The Teaching of Secondary School Mathematics,* Thirty-Third Yearbook of the National Council of the Teachers of Mathematics. Washington, D. C.: The Council, 1970.

McDonald, Fredrick J. *Educational Psychology,* 2nd ed. Belmont, Calif.: Wadsworth, 1965.

Pollak, H. O. "Applications of Mathematics." *Mathematics Education,* Sixty-ninth Yearbook of The National Society for the Study of Education, Part I. Chicago: University of Chicago Press, 1970.

Polya, George. *Mathematical Discovery: On Understanding, Learning, and Teaching Problem-Solving.* New York: Wiley, 1962 (vol. 1), 1968 (vol. 2).

———. *How to Solve It,* 2nd ed. Garden City, N. Y.: Doubleday, 1957.

Rising, Gerald A., and Richard A. Wiesen, eds. *Mathematics in the Secondary School Classroom: Selected Readings.* New York: T. Y. Crowell, 1972.

Stilwell, Merele Eugene. "The Development and Analysis of a Category System for Systematic Observation of Teacher-Pupil Interaction During Geometry Problem-solving Activity." Ph.D. dissertation. Ithaca, New York: Cornell University, 1967.

Travers, Kenneth J. "A Test of Pupil Preference for Problem-Solving Situations in Junior High School Mathematics." *Journal of Experimental Education,* 35 (Summer 1967), 9-18.

Wertheimer, Max. *Productive Thinking,* enlarged ed., ed. by Michael Wertheimer. New York: Harper & Row, 1959.

Wilson, James William. "Generality of Heuristics as an Instructional Variable." Ph.D. dissertation. Stanford, Calif.: Stanford University, 1967.

Problems and puzzles

Bell, Max S. *Studies in Mathematics*, Vol. 16: *Some Uses of Mathematics: A Source Book for Teachers and Students of School Mathematics*. Palo Alto, Calif.: School Mathematics Study Group, 1967.

Boethm, George A. W., and the Editors of Fortune Magazine, eds. *The New World of Mathematics*. New York: Dial Press, 1959.

Brandes, Louis Grant. *Geometry Can Be Fun*. Portland, Me.: J. Weston Walch, 1958.

————. *Yes, Math Can Be Fun!* Portland, Me.: J. Weston Walch, 1960.

Charosh, Mannes, ed. *Mathematical Challenges*. Washington, D. C.: The National Council of Teachers of Mathematics, 1965.

Dorrie, Heinrich. *100 Great Problems of Elementary Mathematics*. New York: Dover, 1965.

Irland, M. J., and E. E. Ensign. "An Experiment in Automobile-Stopping Distances." *School Science and Mathematics*, 46 (1946), 267–271.

Kidd, Kenneth P., Shirley S. Meyers, and David M. Cilley. *The Laboratory Approach to Mathematics*. Chicago: Science Research Associates, 1970. Pp. 59–90 and 197–267.

Montgomery, G. G. "What Does It Cost to Own and Operate an Automobile?" *The Mathematics Teacher*, 35 (1942), 15–17.

National Aeronautics and Space Administration. *Space Mathematics: A Resource for Teachers*. Washington, D. C.: U. S. Government Printing Office, 1972.

National Council of Teachers of Mathematics. "Hints for Problem-solving." Booklet 17, *More Topics in Mathematics for Elementary School Teachers*. Thirtieth Yearbook. Washington, D. C.: The Council, 1969.

————. *Enrichment Mathematics for High School*. Twenty-Eighth Yearbook. Washington, D. C.: The Council, 1963.

————. *Enrichment Mathematics for the Grades*. Twenty-Seventh Yearbook. Washington, D. C.: The Council, 1963. Pp. 211–220 and 359–368.

Polya, George, and Jeremy Kilpatrick. "The Stanford University Competitive Examination in Mathematics." *The American Mathematical Monthly*, 80 (1973), 627–640.

Posamentier, Alfred S., and Charles T. Salkind. *Challenging Problems in Geometry: 1, 2*. New York: Macmillan, 1970.

Rapaport, Elvira, trans. *Hungarian Problem Book*, Vols. 11 and 12, *The New Mathematics Library*. New York: Singer, 1963.

Salkind, Charles T., ed. *The MAA Problem Book II*, Vol. 17, *The New Mathematics Library*. New York: Singer, 1966.

————, ed. *The Contest Problem Book*, Vol. 5, *The New Mathematics Library*. New York: Singer, 1961.

Schaaf, William L. *Recreational Mathematics: A Guide to the Literature*, 3rd ed. Washington, D. C.: The National Council of Teachers of Mathematics, 1963.

School Mathematics Study Group. *Studies in Mathematics*, Vol. 18: *Puzzle Problems and Games Project, Final Report*. Palo Alto, Calif.: School Mathematics Study Group, 1968.

11

Teaching an understanding of proof

S tudents bring a concept of proof to their first courses in mathematics in the secondary school. It is likely that they have not been taught this concept directly but that they have heard the terms *proof* and *prove* used in various contexts and have acquired their concepts by abstracting from these contexts. Their concepts are vague but pertain to supplying evidence and reasons to warrant the belief that a proposition is true or false. It is doubtful they have considered how much evidence is necessary and how tight reasoning should be. Their criterion of proof is generally idiosyncratic: "If I am convinced, the proposition has been proved."

As students progress through a sequence of mathematics courses, their teachers seek the development of a concept of proof appropriate for mathematics and an appreciation of rigor appropriate to their level of sophistication. They also seek to teach them how to follow and evaluate proofs of mathematical propositions and to improve their skill in giving such proofs. It is true that students learn about proof incidentally and concomitantly in the context of learning mathematical principles, provided teachers justify some principles by proving them. Learning about proof can be maximized when teachers accept it as an explicit objective and pursue it as diligently as they pursue other teaching objectives.

In this chapter we shall offer some suggestions of how teachers can help students understand the nature of mathematical proof, and follow and evaluate proofs. We shall begin with a brief review of the nature of proof, stressing deduction. We then turn to how a junior high school teacher can increase student appreciation of the deductive reasoning basic to mathematical proof. Next we discuss development of skill in giving proofs in which planning is central. We follow this with a discussion of strategies of proof. We conclude the chapter with a section on how mathematics teachers can provide students with insight as to how a mathematician might create a body of mathematics.

At the conclusion of this chapter, you should be able to demonstrate the following competencies:

1 Point out the functions of proof in mathematics

2 Tell how a junior high school mathematics teacher can begin to develop an intuition of proof

3 Describe various strategies of proof

4 Tell how a senior high school mathematics teacher can give students an experience in building a simple mathematical structure

Proof in the context of high school mathematics

Students are empiricists, and this is the result of past experience in which they have dealt only with empirical propositions established—"proved"—by adducing observable evidence or by listening to the testimony of authorities. Even when deductive reasoning is used, students tend to regard premises as empirical propositions.

That students have a concept of proof is evident from their responses to questions such as "Why?" "How do you know?" or "What makes you think so?" They realize that such questions require evidence or reasons to prove that the assertion that led to them is true. In the first mathematics courses, the teacher must attempt to sharpen the vague and intuitive concepts of proof that students have. In later courses, the teacher must restrict the concept of proof to that of giving a deductive argument in which all the reasons are true and the conclusion follows necessarily from the reasons. In its broad sense, we shall mean by *proof* all the ways in which confidence in the truth or falsity of a proposition is acquired. Hence, proof is like justification, as we discussed it in Chapter 6.

In this broad sense, proof becomes appropriate when there is uncertainty or doubt and a concomitant desire to remove it. Proof is a social transaction, involving a person (the prover), an audience (the person or persons who need to be convinced), and an argument (the means the prover uses to convince the audience). Usually the prover and the audience are different persons, as when a mathematician seeks to convince colleagues that a particular proposition necessarily follows from other propositions. But the prover and the audience may be the same person, as when a mathematician first works out alone a proposition as an implication of other propositions or when a person convinces himself that the repairs he made on an auto-mobile removed the malfunction.

The existence of uncertainty or doubt is necessary to make proof significant, something other than a game. This becomes evident when we consider situations in which doubt does not exist. A person who has a pain in the jaw needs no proof of pain. But that person may ask for proof that the pain is caused by an abscessed tooth. When it was still believed that the Earth is flat, scholars who asserted the contrary were expected to offer proof. A desire to remove uncertainty or doubt is also necessary to make proof significant. This becomes evident when a person admits uncertainty as to whether a particular proposition is true or false, but also indicates no desire to find out. Such a person would probably pay no attention were a proof attempted, but might appear attentive out of desire not to be regarded as impolite.

There are implications of these conditions for the mathematics teacher. If there is no doubt in the students' minds that a mathematical proposition is true, giving a deductive proof will not strengthen their belief. Students who have been using the formula $A = 1/2ab$ to find the area of a triangle will be no further assured that this is the correct formula if it is proved in a geometry class. Assuming that the students in a second algebra course have the concept of a theorem, labeling some mathematical proposition as a theorem is enough to convince them that it is true. They realize that it has been proved to be true; otherwise it would not be called a theorem. Proving it for them will not increase their confidence that it is true. As Exner and Rosskopf (1970, p. 197) point out, "If the sole motive for proving statements is to create belief in them, then one might well question the value of proving the theorem about the congruence of vertical angles, since few people are any more convinced by the proof than they were without it." Hendrix (1961, p. 516) supports this contention: "Those responsible for mathematics education have never been on tenable ground when holding forth increased certainty and intellectual security as goals to be achieved through deductive proof alone."

If students are so uninterested in mathematics that they do not care whether a statement is true or false, they will not become involved in proofs that establish truth-values. For students like this, the first task of the teacher has to be development of an interest in mathematics in general and proof in particular. Otherwise, proving statements will be a trivial game. They will engage in it if the teacher employs sanctions against them for not engaging, but it will have little meaning to them.

If "Now we *really* know that the statement is true" is not a sufficient justification for convincing students of the necessity of proof, what other justification is there? As students gain mathematical knowledge, it is possible to raise the question of the relationships of items of knowledge—in other words, to begin to organize knowledge. What statements can be deduced from others? Do some hold over an extensive domain like the rationals or the reals? Are the definitions precise enough to reason from them with confidence? As students are led to consider these questions, they become aware of the structure of mathematics.

Proof shows the relation between a statement that is the object of proof and other statements, which may be axioms or theorems. The statement is shown to be a consequence or implication of other statements. Thus proof helps students see how a mathematical structure is built—which statements are assumed, which are easily deduced from these and hence are near the base of the structure, and which are more remote deductions and hence farther from the base.

Some teachers have found it helpful to portray a mathematical structure by means of a tree diagram. Starting with some theorem, they get the class to identify all the axioms and theorems used to prove the theorem. Then they repeat this analysis for each theorem used, continuing until only axioms and definitions are left. Many students enjoy making this kind of analysis and are able from it to appreciate the nature of mathematics.

Kinds of proof

Considering proof in its broad sense as a gaining of assurance concerning the truth-value of a proposition or the wisdom of an action, we can identify four ways by which assurance is gained. One is by personal experience. If a student states that there is a fire in a downtown store and someone asks, "How do you know?" the student's statement that he has just driven past the store and seen the flames is considered proof of the existence of the fire. Such assurance assumes the student's veracity. A questioner who has doubts can drive past the store and verify the report. Such observations would prove the assertion true or false.

When personal experience is not available, we may be willing to accept the judgment of an authority. Thus students are willing to consider statements in a textbook to be true because they believe that the author has expertise in the subject and would not knowingly state false propositions. Similarly, if the mathematics teacher or the author of the textbook states that a proposition is a theorem, most students are willing to believe that it is. A proof that it is a theorem does not materially enhance their confidence.

A third way by which confidence in the truth of a proposition is gained is by induction. If all the investigated instances of a generalization are true, we are reasonably confident that the generalization is true. If we find a counterexample, then we know that the generalization is not a universal. If we find some counterexamples but not many, we may accept the generalization while indicating its logic by qualifiers such as "generally speaking," "in most cases," "with some exceptions," or "probably." Before students learn how to prove a statement by a deductive argument, proof or justification by instances is convincing. It is used frequently by teachers.

The fourth way by which assurance of the truth of a statement is obtained is by valid deductive argument. If it can be shown that a statement follows necessarily, by using accepted laws of logic, from other statements known to be true, our confidence in the truth of the statement is enhanced. Thus when the Internal Revenue Service states that a single person whose income is $1,700 or more must file an individual income tax return and you are single and earned $2,800 last year, you are quite confident that you must file an individual income tax return.

It is this latter kind of proof that predominates in mathematics. In fact, when *proof* is used in a mathematical context, it is this kind of proof that is meant. It is the principle of formal implication, often referred to as the "if-then principle." Certain statements, namely axioms and postulates, are accepted as the premises—the "if's." The conclusions that follow by use of the principle of formal implication—the "then's"—must also be accepted. It is then possible to use these as premises to deduce whatever they and other premises imply. A structure of propositions is then developed in which validity rather than conformance to reality is the test of assurance.

We are now in a position to offer a definition of a *proof* in the context of mathematics. An argument is a proof if and only if it satisfies two conditions: (1) all the premises (or reasons) are true and (2) the argument is valid.

Thought questions

1   How would an elementary school student prove that the subtraction of one number from a larger number can be checked by addition?

2   Why does measuring, an operation taught in elementary school, reinforce belief that statements are proved by observable evidence?

3   How would an elementary school teacher prove that addition is commutative?

4   Why are junior high school students more familiar with induction than with deduction for establishing the truth of a statement?

5   Why is induction—generalizing from a sample—invalid reasoning?

6   What assumption or assumptions have to be accepted for induction to be valid?

7   It has been said that personal experience for judging the truth of a principle is convincing but not reliable. Give evidence supporting this contention. Under what conditions would the contention not hold?

Developing an intuition about proof

Long before students are introduced to formal proof, they can acquire an intuition about proof. In fact, they have some sort of an intuition by the time they enter junior high school, evident from their appropriate responses to questions such as "Why?", "How do you know?", or "What makes you think so?" They realize that these questions require supplying evidence or reasons that the assertion that led to the question is true.

Students have frequently given and heard deductive arguments both in and outside school. This is evident by their generally correct use of logical connectors that signal that a reason is to follow, such as

because	if
provided that	suppose that (in the sense of assume)
since	for (in the sense of because)
assuming that	inasmuch as
as shown by	as indicated by
follows from	in view of the fact that
for the reason that	given

and logical connectors that signal that a conclusion is to follow, such as

therefore	hence
so (in the sense of hence)	then (in the sense of hence)
proves that	shows that
consequently	conclude that
you can see that	allows us to infer that
implies	it is obvious that
it follows that	leads me to believe that
suggests that	we can deduce that
indicates that	entails
convinces that	justifies a belief that

supported by the statements signaled as reasons. Moreover, they have appraised such arguments long before they have acquired the concepts of valid and invalid arguments. The mathematics teacher can build on this foundation.

One of the best ways for a teacher to introduce and promote deductive proof is to ask "Why?" "How do we know that?" or any similar question that requires either evidence or one or more reasons as an answer. These are good questions, for they force students to relate the statement at issue with other knowledge that they have and see the logical connections. Not all answers to such questions will be satisfactory, as is illustrated in the following classroom dialogue. The eighth-grade class is discussing how to solve for the unknown in a proportion. The particular proportion is $x/16 = 20/24$.

1 **T**   How do we know we can do that? (*Derive* $24x = 320$.) S_1?

2 **S_1**   Crossmultiply.

3 **T**   That's not a reason; it's a description of what we did. How do we know that we can crossmultiply? That's what we want to know. Who knows? (*Calling on another student.*) Yes?

4 **S_2**   That's what the book says. That's the way they do it.

5 **T**   Oh, come on! That's not a good reason. How do the authors of our textbook know that this is a permissible operation? S_3?

6 **S₃** Equals multiplied by equals?

7 **T** O.K. That's why we can crossmultiply. But I'll bet not everyone knows what we multiplied both sides of the equation by. It's a bit subtle. What did we multiply both sides of the equation by? Tell us, S_3.

8 **S₃** By the product of the denominators.

9 **T** Yes. Good! How about coming to the board and showing how this is done. Some of us may not follow.

10 **S₃** $\left(\right.$ *Comes to the board and writes*

$$16 \times 24 \times \frac{x}{16} = \frac{20}{24} \times 16 \times 24.\left.\right)$$

The 16's cancel and the 24's cancel.

$\left(\right.$ *Draws lines through* 16 *and* 24 *as follows:*

$$\not{16} \times 24 \times \frac{x}{\not{16}} = \frac{20}{\not{24}} \times 16 \times \not{24}.\left.\right)$$

And 20 times 16 is 320. (*Writes* $24x = 320$.)

11 **T** O.K. Everybody see that? One more question. Why can we cancel the 16's and the 24's? Yes (*indicating* S_4)?

12 **S₄** Equals divided by equals?

13 **T** Equals divided by equals? What equals are divided by what equals? (*Silences several students who have their hands up.*) No, let's let S_4 reason this out. What equals are divided by what equals?

14 **S₄** 16 equals 16 and 24 equals 24. You divide.

15 **T** I think you're confused. When we apply the principle of equals divided by equals, we always have an equation, and we divide both sides of the equation—since it is an equation, the two sides are equal; they're equals—by the same number. S_3 didn't divide both sides of the equation by either 16 or 24, did she? Did she? No. Who knows why we can cancel the 16's and the 24's? Yes (*indicating* S_3)?

16 **S₃** Reducing to lower terms.

17 **T** Sure. Look. (*Writes on the board.*) Here's what we have:

$$16 \times 24 \times \frac{x}{16} = \frac{20}{24} \times 16 \times 24$$

$$\frac{16 \times 24 \times x}{16} = \frac{20 \times 16 \times 24}{24}$$

$$\frac{\not{16} \times 24 \times x}{\not{16}} = \frac{20 \times 16 \times \not{24}}{\not{24}}$$

$$24x = 20 \times 16$$

$$24x = 320$$

We reduced this fraction (*pointing to the left number of the equation*) by dividing numerator and denominator by what? By 16, and this fraction (*pointing to the right member of the equation*) by dividing numerator and denominator by what? By 24. Do you understand, S_4? (S_4 *nods.*) Now one more step. How do we solve $24x = 320$ for x? Now we are ready for your principle, S_4. How do we do it? (S_4 *appears hesitant to answer.*) What did you tell us a bit ago?

18   **S₄**   Divide both sides by 24?

19   **T**   And how do we know we can do that? What's the principle you stated a bit ago? Now's the time.

20   **S₄**   Equals divided by equals?

21   **T**   Equals divided by equals give equals. Since $24x = 320$, if we divide both sides by 24, we have $24x$ divided by 24 gives x and 320 divided by 24 gives (*does the division*) $13\frac{1}{3}$. So (*writes*) $x = 13\frac{1}{3}$. Any questions? Think you can solve any proportion now?

Once students have acquired a concept of a variable, the teacher can further extend their intuition about deductive proof. The teacher can offer a generalization as a conjecture and ask students whether they think it is true of all the members in the domain over which the generalization is made. For example, they can be asked whether they think the sum of any three rational numbers is exactly one rational number. It is likely that they will say "Yes." They can then be asked why they think so. One student may pick three rational numbers and by adding them show that their sum is unique. The teacher can then admit that the sum is unique *for that particular trio* and then ask how they know that this will be true for any trio of rational numbers. Exhibiting other trios may strengthen the belief a bit but will not dispose of the question that the teacher can continue to ask: "But is it true of all trios of numbers? You have only shown that it is true of certain trios."

If a student challenges the teacher to find a counterexample or otherwise prove that the sum is not a unique rational number, the teacher can point out that inability to do this may only reflect lack of knowledge; an unperceived counterexample may exist. Argument from ignorance is never support for a proposition.

It may seem, then, that some student will offer a deductive argument, such as

> Well, we know that the sum of any two rational numbers is just one rational number because of the closure principle for addition. Then if you find the sum of that sum and any other rational number, this new sum will be just one rational number for the same reason—that is, the closure principle for addition.

This constitutes a proof, and the teacher will have to admit that now we can be sure that the sum of any and hence all trios of rational numbers is exactly one rational number.

The teacher then can show how variables can be used in the argument—let x, y, and z be any three rational numbers. We know that $x + y$ is a unique rational number. (Why?) We also know that $(x + y) + z$ is a unique rational number. (Why?) Therefore, for any rational numbers $x, y,$ and $z, x + y + z$ is a unique rational number.

Easy proofs of simple theorems should serve informally to develop a feeling for deductive proof—certain propositions we assume to be true imply others we then must accept as true. The reasoning is quite natural and fits the model with which the students are familiar. Should the teacher later choose to use the two-column format for proofs (a format of doubtful value, restricted to high school mathematics, that students have to abandon when they enroll in college courses) the transformation is easy. Actually, proofs in the form of paragraphs are more natural and easier for students to construct; they resemble the way people talk in presenting arguments. In such proofs, the teacher can insist on reasons for assertions as easily as in the two-column model.

Thought questions

1   State some nonmathematical situations in which elementary school students probably have used or experienced deductive reasoning.

2   Examine some arithmetic textbooks used in elementary school and find examples of informal, deductive proof.

3   What are some advantages of the two-column format for proofs? What are some disadvantages?

4   The following questions pertain to the dialogue in this section. Do you agree with what the teacher said in utterance 3? Is it consistent with utterances 7 and 17 in accepting what the student said in utterances 6 and 16, respectively?

5   Explain how using a description like *crossmultiply* correctly might mask lack of understanding. Might this also be true when "equals multiplied by equals" is used? Why?

6   Do you approve of the teacher's asking in utterance 7 for elaboration on the application of the uniqueness principle for multiplication? Was this needless?

7   In utterance 10, the student referred to the operation of canceling. Did he give a reason or a description?

8   Some teachers oppose using the term *cancel* because it refers to different operations. What is your attitude toward using this term?

9   In utterance 17, the teacher developed a sequence of equivalent equations without exploring how each was deduced from the previous one. It is possible that some students did not follow the development. How could the teacher have ascertained whether the students understood the development without asking such questions as "Do you understand?" or "Is this clear?"

10   In utterance 21, the teacher asks "Any questions?" Teachers frequently ask this. Suppose the students say "no" or ask no questions. What inferences are possible? How might the teacher ascertain whether the students really understand?

Teaching principles of logic

Some mathematicians believe that formal logic *per se* should not be taught. Proofs should be given, and the students will learn intuitively the principles of logic that are used. Hilton (1971, p. 390) says, "I believe that there should be rather little of such explicit, overt appeal to logic and that, in the main, the student should acquire respect and appreciation of sound reasoning through practice rather than through learning explicit rules of logical inference and being trained to apply them." Individuals on this side of the issue believe that it is not primarily the appreciation of logical structure that attracts students to mathematics but rather the substance of mathematical concepts and principles. Too much concern for the logical structure of arguments may serve to make some students believe that it is the form rather than the substance of an argument that is important.

Other mathematicians believe that there is good reason for teaching formal logic. They point out that without some rules of inference there is no way to settle differences of opinion over whether an argument is a non sequitur. Exner (1971, p. 395) makes this point: "If the student has no criteria for making such judgments, the correctness of his proofs is a function of the judgment of his teacher at the moment." Certainly it is true that judgment has to be used in deciding how much logic to teach. But without it, the only recourse to judgments about the adequacy of a proof is intuition. Unfortunately, not everyone intuits the same thing.

In countering the contention that the teaching of principles of logic may distract students from the mathematical substance of the propositions being proved, individuals who favor teaching some principles of logic say that if this undesirable distraction occurs, it is probably the result of bad teaching; any teacher is capable of losing perspective. But if the principles of logic taught are regarded as means for understanding the arguments presented and are not regarded as ends in themselves, they should enhance the student's intellectual development and offer the potential of transfer to nonmathematical arguments.

One finds that it is not high school mathematics teachers who oppose teaching some principles of logic but research mathematicians. The high school teachers who have taught principles of logic to their students in connection with the elucidation of proof seem to be satisfied with the results. In fact, in professional journals there are more reports of success in these ventures than of failures. It is possible to infer from this that teachers realize the desirability of supplying this kind of knowledge. Also, it may be that mathematicians as high school students were able informally to pick up the knowledge of logic they needed, but this should not be taken as indication that the majority of high school students will be able to do this. The latter opinion may have been reflected in the recommendation of The Cambridge Conference on School Mathematics (1963, p. 39), whose participants were professional mathematicians and mathematics educators:

> While extensive formal study of logic in the elementary grades is not favored by most mathematicians, it is hardly possible to do anything in the direction of mathematical proofs without the vocabulary of logic and explicit recognition of the inference schemes. The feasibility of such study has already been demonstrated by classroom experimentation.

If one wants understanding from the majority of students, it is best deliberately to teach for this rather than to take the chance that they will acquire understanding as a concomitant of skill. It seems desirable to teach the concepts and principles of logic that will enable students to understand deductive reasoning. They should at least know the necessary and sufficient conditions for drawing a deduction, (that the reasons have to be true and the reasoning valid). In addition, they should become aware of the various strategies of proof available to them as they plan a proof of a proposition. We shall turn to these in a later section.

Thought questions

1 What concepts of logic should be taught if students are to understand mathematical proofs?

2 What principles of logic should be taught to provide an understanding of the arguments presented in proofs?

3 What are the advantages of teaching truth tables for the simple logical relations of negation, conjunction, disjunction, and implication? What are the disadvantages?

4 Should Venn diagrams be taught as a technique for determining the validity of inferences in the predicate calculus? Why?

5 List the principles of logic taught in five algebra textbooks.

6 List the principles of logic taught in five geometry textbooks.

Teaching about the nature of proof

Once students have an intuition about deductive arguments that convince people that a particular statement follows from other statements—that is, is true if the other statements are true—the teacher can sharpen this concept by a deliberate study and analysis of formal proof.

Basic knowledge

Students should learn early the distinction between truth and validity. Truth, or lack of truth (falsity), is a property of statements; it is not a property of arguments. That is, if we are speaking carefully we may characterize a statement but not an argument as true or false.

The truth values *true* and *false* are assigned to statements (propositions) according to certain rules. For empirical statements, the rule is to assign the truth value *true* to each statement that is a correct description or report of what, in fact, is the case, and to assign the truth value *false* to every statement that is an incorrect description or report of what, in fact, is the case. For analytic statements, the rule is to assign the truth value *true* to each axiom or postulate and to each statement that follows from an axiom or postulate by the principle of formal implication, and to assign the truth value *false* to any statement that is a contradiction of a true statement or is otherwise inconsistent with true statements.

Validity, or lack of validity (invalidity) is a property of argument forms and of instances of these forms—that is, of particular arguments. It is not a property of statements. If we are speaking carefully, we may characterize an argument form or an argument as valid or invalid but not a statement as valid or invalid.

People do not always speak carefully. Characterization of an argument as "false reasoning" can be interpreted as meaning invalid reasoning or invalid argumentation. And the locutions "valid conclusion" or "invalid conclusion" can be regarded as elliptical expressions for the conclusion of a valid argument and the conclusion of an invalid argument, respectively. Not infrequently one has to *infer* what a person means.

It is most helpful to define *validity* in terms of argument forms (patterns). Once we have identified valid argument forms, every instance (or particular argument) of these forms will be a valid argument. Similarly, once we have identified invalid argument forms, every instance (or particular argument) of these forms will be invalid.

The form of an argument may be obtained by replacing the particular statements in the argument by variables such as p, q, and r. The domain of each variable is the set of statements. Thus the following argument

If $P(x)$ is a polynomial over the integers and $P(a) = 0$, then a is a zero of $P(x)$. The polynomial $P(x) = x^3 - 4x^2 + x + 6$ is over the integers and $P(2) = 0$. Therefore, 2 is a zero of $x^3 - 4x^2 + x + 6$.

has the form

If p and q, then r. p and q. Therefore, r.

Similarly, the argument

If a quadrilateral has two sides congruent and parallel, it is a parallelogram. Hence, if a quadrilateral is a parallelogram, it has two sides congruent and parallel.

has the form

If p, then q. Hence if q, then p.

We now give a definition of a *valid argument form*. If it is impossible for the conclusion of an argument form to be false when the premises are true, the argument form is *valid*. If it is possible for the conclusion to be false when the premises are true, the argument form is *invalid*. When we say it is impossible for the conclusion to be false when the premises are true, we mean that it is not possible to find an instance of the argument form such that the premises are true and the conclusion is false. Proof of this can be given by using truth tables.

We know the first form of argument above is a valid form because it is an instance of a principle of formal implication often designated as *modus ponens*, or affirming the antecedent. We know that the second form is invalid, though both statements in the argument are true, because we can find an instance of the form in which the premise is true but the conclusion is false:

> If a quadrilateral is a square, it is a rectangle. Hence, if a quadrilateral is a rectangle, it is a square.

We can regard this as a counterexample of the argument form. A counterexample of an argument form proves that the form is invalid.

Notice in the following dialogue how the teacher uses a counterexample to point out the fallacy in a student's reasoning. The context is a geometry course in which the class is discussing a particular exercise assigned as homework.

T   What makes you think these two triangles are not similar? They look similar to me.

S   They aren't equilateral.

T   I agree. So what?

S   Well . . .

T   Quote us a theorem.

S   If two triangles are equilateral, they are similar.

T   I don't follow your reasoning. Sure, that's a theorem. But how does that prove the triangles are not similar?

S   Well, you know, if the triangles are equilateral, then they are similar. But the triangles aren't equilateral, so they aren't similar.

T   Ah, yes. Your reasoning is like this, isn't it? If today is a Tuesday, our geometry class meets. That's true, isn't it? Today isn't Tuesday. Right? Therefore our class isn't meeting. Right? Right?

S   No.

T   Then there is something wrong with your reasoning. I used the pattern you used and the conclusion wasn't true. See, here's your pattern (*writes on the chalkboard*):

If ———, then . . . . . .
Not ———.
∴ not . . . . . .

Anything that fits this pattern is bad reasoning. The conclusion just doesn't follow from the two reasons. (*Labels the first two forms as reasons and the last as conclusion.*)

Let us summarize the salient principles that students should learn about proof by deduction. Deductive arguments are valid or invalid. Validity is a relation within an argument; it is determined by the relation between the truth of the premises and the conclusion. Every argument is an instance of an argument form. If it is not possible to find an instance of an argument form in which the premises are true and the conclusion is false, the argument form is valid; otherwise, it is invalid. Every instance of a valid argument form is valid, and every instance of an invalid argument form is invalid.

When we know that an argument is valid, we know *from that property alone* nothing about the truth of the premises or conclusion of the argument. All we know is that *if* the premises are true, then the conclusion is true. If the premises of an argument are true and the argument is valid, the conclusion is true and the argument is a proof of the conclusion.

Suggestions for teaching

In addition to teaching this basic knowledge, other things seem desirable for teachers to do. Students should be given ample experience in proving propositions. This is a skill, and, as we pointed out in Chapter 8, practice under guided supervision is necessary for acquiring skills. Almost all geometry but few algebra textbooks provide a large number of exercises for such practice. Traditionally, exercises in algebra are intended for practice in applying principles rather than proving them. Hence a teacher who wants to continue to stress proof after the first study of formal proof will have to design separate exercises.

Students should not be required to memorize proofs of theorems. The theorems are the focus. The purposes of the proofs are to teach principles of proof and develop skills in proof. Hence the proofs of particular theorems are less important than general outcomes. Now and then, it is well for teachers to trace the proof of a theorem back to axioms and definitions. This can be done by a tree diagram. Such experiences help students appreciate the structure of mathematics.

The teacher should detect invalid reasoning. Ideally, students themselves should identify such lapses, but if they cannot, the teacher must.

Thought questions

1   Why is the following argument invalid?

> Mr. X, the famous scientist, says that gasoline is less dense than water. Therefore, gasoline is less dense than water.

2   Why is the following argument invalid?

> The graph of $y = 2x^2 + 4$ is a parabola.
> The graph of $y = -2x^2 - 5$ is a parabola.
> The graph of $y = 0.25x^2 + 10.6$ is a parabola.
> The graph of $y = x^2$ is a parabola.
> Therefore, for all values of a and b, the graph of $y = ax^2 + b$ is a parabola.

3   Why are the arguments in questions 1 and 2, though invalid, still plausible?

4   On occasion, the inability to find a counterexample of a generalization is taken as proof that the generalization is true. Why is this invalid reasoning?

5   Many students think that the only theorems in mathematics are labeled "theorems." They do not realize that many of the propositions that they prove as exercises are theorems and can be used as reasons in the proofs of other propositions. Propose some explanations of how this might come about in geometry classes.

6   Pick a theorem in a geometry textbook and develop a tree diagram showing the theorems, postulates, and definitions of which it is a consequence.

Teaching strategies of proof

Experience has shown that there are individual differences in how quickly students learn to give satisfactory proofs more involved than giving one or two reasons. The teacher can help slower students by pointing out various strategies available for proving a statement. These become possible plans for proving a proposition. Once students learn these and have practiced them, they can become more resourceful. We discuss next some strategies that can be used to prove statements. Each is a valid argument form. Hence any instance (or particular argument) of a strategy will be valid.

Modus ponens

Suppose a student asserts that there are no real roots of the equation $x^2 - 4x + 5 = 0$ while another student challenges this statement. How can the first student prove that the assertion is correct? One strategy would be to solve the equation and examine the roots. But a more elegant strategy is to cite the theorem—if the value of the discriminant ($b^2 - 4ac$) is less than zero, the roots are not real numbers—and then show that the value of the discriminant of $x^2 - 4x + 5$ is less than zero. Therefore, it follows necessarily that the roots are not real numbers.

The form of this argument can be determined by replacing the particular statements in the reasons and conclusion by variables, thereby obtaining:

If p, then q	$p \Rightarrow q$	Theorem
p	p	Second reason
$\therefore q$	$\therefore q$	Conclusion

This valid argument form is frequently used to prove an assertion. It is known as *modus ponens*, the Latin name ascribed to it by logicians in the middle ages. Since the premises (or reasons) in the particular argument about the nature of the roots of $x^2 - 4x + 5 = 0$ are true and the argument is valid, the conclusion is true and the assertion is proved.

To employ *modus ponens* as a strategy for proving an assertion, one tries to find a true conditional (a proposition of the form "if p, then q") whose conclusion (the value of q in the conditional) is the assertion to be proved. If such a conditional can be found, one then establishes that the hypothesis of the conditional (the value of p in "if p, then q") is true. One can then assert the conclusion, thus proving it.

As an example of *modus ponens* as a strategy, suppose a draftsman wants to draw a tangent to a circle at a given point on the circle. He draws a radius of the circle to that point and a line through the point and the center of the circle and then constructs a perpendicular to that line at the point on the circle. Now suppose someone questions that the second line is actually tangent to the circle. The draftsman wishes to prove that the line is tangent to the circle. He searches for a theorem of the form "if p, then q" such that "the line is tangent to the circle" is the value of q. One theorem that satisfies these conditions is: If a line is perpendicular to a radius of a circle at the intersection of the radius and the circle, it is tangent to the circle at that point. The draftsman then calls attention to his particular construction of a perpendicular to the line determined by the point on the circle and the center of the circle, pointing out if necessary that a subset of this line is a radius of the circle. He can then assert that the line is tangent to the circle, since he is using a valid argument form.

This strategy of *modus ponens* is learned easily by students, probably because they use it so frequently in their reasoning. They need to realize that it may not be effective for proving some statements but represents one possible approach. It is equally applicable when the proposition to be proved—the value of q in "if p, then q"—is a compound proposition, a conjunction or disjunction, or even another conditional.

The deduction theorem

Suppose a student wants to prove the conditional: If two angles of a triangle are unequal, the greater side lies opposite the greater angle. The advice textbooks usually give is to take the hypothesis as the "given" and prove the conclusion. Examples of such proofs are given, and the students find it easy to imitate the model and thus prove conditionals. But it is doubtful that they understand the logic of such proofs.

The proof of a conditional using the strategy described above is based on the deduction theorem of symbolic logic, first proved by Tarski. The deduction theorem may be stated as follows: If from one or more true statements and an assumption p, it is possible to deduce q, then it is possible to deduce $p \Rightarrow q$ from the true statements alone.

Consider as an example of the application of the deduction theorem the proof of the theorem: If two angles of a triangle are congruent to two angles of another triangle, then the third angles are congruent. This is a conditional of the form $p \Rightarrow q$, where p is the hypothesis "two angles of a triangle are congruent to two angles of another triangle" and q is the conclusion "the third angles are congruent." The proof proceeds by assuming the hypothesis. In the conventional language of high school textbooks, this is characterized as "given." From this and the relevant theorems and postulates, the conclusion (the third angles are congruent) is deduced. The deduction theorem then allows the conditional that was the object of proof to be deduced.

The advice usually given for proving a conditional $p \Rightarrow q$ is good as far as it goes, but it does not go far enough. Students typically end their proofs with the deduction of the conclusion q, having taken p as given. The final step, having deduced q, should be to conclude $p \Rightarrow q$. It is the latter that is the proposition to be proved and not q.

Some teachers prefer to teach their students to say "assume p" rather than "given p." They believe that this locution makes the application of the deduction theorem more apparent. These teachers also insist that the final step in the proof be the assertion of the conditional that is the object of proof.

Suppose one wants to prove as an example of the use of the deduction theorem

The angles opposite the congruent sides of an isosceles triangle are congruent.

This proposition is equivalent to the following conditional,

If a triangle is isosceles, the angles opposite the congruent sides are congruent.

A figure for the proposition appears in Figure 11.1. We assume that $\triangle ABC$ is isosceles. It follows from the definition of an isosceles triangle that two sides are congruent, say, $\overline{AB} \cong \overline{AC}$. We shall prove $\triangle ABC$ congruent to itself. We already know that $\overline{AB} \cong \overline{AC}$. $\angle A$ is congruent to itself. Therefore $\triangle ABC \cong \triangle ACB$ by two sides and the included angle. Hence $\angle B \cong \angle C$, since they are corresponding parts of congruent figures. Therefore, by the deduction theorem, if a triangle is isosceles then the angles opposite the congruent sides are congruent.

The deduction theorem can be used to prove a biconditional $(p \Rightarrow q) \Leftrightarrow (q \Rightarrow p)$. An example of a biconditional is

Two arcs of a circle are equal in measure if and only if the chords determined by them are equal in measure.

A biconditional (an "if and only if" statement) is equivalent to the conjunction of its two conditionals. Thus

$$[(p \Rightarrow q) \Leftrightarrow (q \Rightarrow p)] \Leftrightarrow [(p \Rightarrow q) \text{ and } (q \Rightarrow p)]$$

Hence a biconditional can be proved by two applications of the deduction theorem, one for each of the conditionals.

Figure 11.1

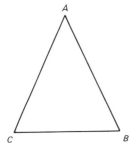

In proving conditionals, or propositions that can be stated as conditionals, many textbooks use the "given-to prove" format and teachers tend to follow it. Students are taught to write the conditions of the hypothesis of the conditional as the "given" and the condition or conditions of the conclusion as "to prove." For example, to prove the proposition,

If the slopes of two lines are equal, the lines are parallel,

the students are taught to write:

Given: Two lines $\overleftrightarrow{AB}$ and $\overleftrightarrow{CD}$ whose slopes are equal

To prove: $\overleftrightarrow{AB}$ and $\overleftrightarrow{CD}$ are parallel.

The disadvantage of this format is that students (and in some cases teachers) miss the logic of the proof. This condition has to be proved (deduced) but the actual object of proof is the conditional; the proof of the conclusion is a means to that end. By focusing on the conclusion, the student's attention is directed away from the conditional.

To enable students to follow the logic of the proof of a conditional, it would be better to make the argument explicit. What is to be proved is the conditional. To do this, we assume the hypothesis and deduce the conclusion. Deducing the conclusion allows us to infer the conditional. Hence the first statement in the proof should be "Assume ———" with whatever the condition or conditions of the hypothesis written in the blank. The conclusion of the conditional is then deduced. The final statement in the proof should be the conditional itself preceded by some linguistic signal such as "therefore" to indicate that it is a conclusion. This will then fulfill the condition of a proof that the final statement be the proposition to be proved.

This format suggested is just as easy to teach as the misleading "given-to prove" format. The logic of the proof of a conditional by use of the deduction theorem can be explained to the students with the role of the deduction theorem clearly stated. The format can be explained and repeatedly illustrated. With practice, students should readily be able to master it. Additionally, they will understand the logic of this strategy, which is so frequently used in mathematics.

The transitivity of implication

The relation of implication is transitive. That is,

$$[(p \Rightarrow q) \,\&\, (q \Rightarrow r)] \Rightarrow (p \Rightarrow r)$$

Expressed in "if-then" language, this is

If p then q, and if q then r; therefore, if p then r.

This transitivity relation is a strategy for proving propositions. It is the basis of the advice some mathematics teachers give their students. They recommend that students focus on the proposition they want to prove and then find a condition which, if proved, implies the proposition. Then they look for a condition which, if proved, implies the first condition. The analysis continues until a condition is found that is known to be true. Then the proof is made by beginning with the last condition and proceeding to the proposition that was to be proved in the first place.

In the following dialogue, the teacher employs analysis to help the students plan a proof of the theorem: The bisectors of the base angles of an isosceles triangle intersect the opposite sides so as to form two pairs of congruent line segments.

1　**T**　So how can you prove it? Who has an idea? (*No student responds.*) Let's see. (*Draws the Figure 11.2 on the chalkboard.*) What do we want to prove? S_1?

2　**S_1**　$\overline{BD}$ is congruent to $\overline{CE}$ and $\overline{AD}$ is congruent to $\overline{AE}$.

3　**T**　All right. And what do we have given?

4　**S_1**　Triangle *ABC* is isosceles and $\overline{BE}$ bisects angle *B* and $\overline{DC}$ bisects angle *C*.

5　**T**　O.K. Now we're ready. (*Refers to an inattentive student.*) Tom's ready, too, aren't you, Tom? Who has an idea as to how we can prove it? (*No student responds.*) Well, let's take it a step at a time. Take $\overline{BD}$ and $\overline{CE}$. You can prove these congruent if you can prove what? S_2.

6　**S_2**　They're corresponding parts of congruent triangles.

7　**T**　Now we're going. Got an idea about what triangles? What triangles look congruent?

8　**S_2**　Triangles. Put a letter where the lines, ah . . . where $\overline{DC}$ and $\overline{BE}$ intersect. (*The teacher writes F at this point.*) Triangles *BFD* and *CFE*.

9　**T**　Yeah. O.K. And we can prove these triangles congruent if we can prove what? (*Nods to a student.*)

10　**S_3**　SAS or ASA.

11　**T**　All right. Let's try SAS. I see two congruent angles. Do you? (*Points to a student.*)

Figure 11.2

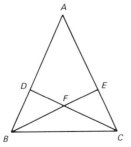

12	S_4	Angles *DFB* and *EFC*.

13 **T**   That's the pair. Why are they congruent?

14 S_5 Vertical angles.

15 **T**   O.K. We've got the pair of angles. That means we'll have to prove what else if we are using SAS? S_6.

16 S_6 You can't prove those triangles congruent.

17 **T**   No? How do you know?

18 S_6 Well, angles *DBF* and *ECF* are congruent. But you can't prove a pair of sides congruent. $\overline{BD}$ and $\overline{CE}$ are what you're trying to prove congruent, and you can't prove $\overline{BF}$ and $\overline{CF}$ congruent to get ASA.

19 **T**   But we were trying to get SAS.

20 S_6 To get SAS with the vertical angles you'd have to prove $\overline{BF}$ and $\overline{CF}$ congruent. And you can't.

21 **T**   So let's look for a different pair of triangles. Got a candidate?

22 S_6 Triangles *BCD* and *CBE*.

23 **T**   How can you prove they're congruent?

24 S_6 Angles *B* and *C* are congruent; they're the base angles of the isosceles triangle. Angles *EBC* and *DCB* are congruent because they're halves of the congruent base angles. And $\overline{BC}$ is common. So the triangles are congruent by ASA.

25 **T**   Wow! That came pretty fast. Let's go over it again. (*Meticulously reviews the steps S_6 stated, asking the class to justify each assertion.*) O.K. That gives us $\overline{BD}$ and $\overline{CE}$ congruent and we're half done. How do we prove $\overline{AD}$ and $\overline{AE}$ congruent? Yes, I know you know how, S_6, but let's ask someone else.

26 S_7 (*To S_6.*) How do you do it?

27 **T**   Let's ask someone else. We can prove these congruent if we can show what? S_8?

28 S_8 Triangles *BEA* and *CDA* congruent?

29 **T**   Yes, that would do it. But isn't there an easier way? (*S_8 does not respond.*) S_9.

30 S_9 $\overline{AB}$ and $\overline{AC}$ are congruent; the triangle was given isosceles. $\overline{BD}$ and $\overline{CE}$ are congruent; we just proved that. Subtract these, you know, *BD* and *AB* from *CE* from *AC*, and you get $\overline{AD}$ congruent to $\overline{AE}$.

31 **T**   Look's good. Let's write it out. (*Writes statements of equivalence and shows the operation explicitly.*) But, mind you, we haven't given a proof, have we? All we have done is shown how a proof can be made. Now let's write the proof. No, I'll tell you: each of you take a piece of paper and write the proof. If you need some help, raise your hand.

The strategy based on the transitivity of implication is usually used along with the strategy of proving a conditional. The transitivity property can be extended to develop as long a chain of implications as is necessary to prove any theorem that lends itself to this strategy.

Counterexample

This strategy has been discussed in previous chapters. It is useful for dis-
proving a generalization. For example, let $p(x)$ be a generalization pur-
porting to hold over a set A that is the domain of x. Hence for some $a \in A$,
$p(a)$ is a singular statement obtained by replacing the variable x in the
generalization by the constant a. As a convention in symbolic logic,
$\sim p(a)$ designates the negation of $p(a)$. Using this notation, the argument
form for the counterexample strategy is the following:

> For all $x \in A, p(x)$.
> $a \in A$ and $\sim p(a)$.
> $\therefore$ for all $x \in A, \sim p(x)$.
> That is, the generalization, for all $x \in A, p(x)$, is false.

Let us illustrate the use of the strategy of counterexample. Suppose a
student asserts that every parabola is the graph of a function. Another
student can display a parabola whose axis is parallel to the x-axis and
point out that this is not the graph of a function. Hence, the generalization
stated by the first student is false.

The contrapositive

A general strategy for proving a proposition is to prove an equivalent
proposition. Two propositions are equivalent if and only if each implies
the other. In other words, p and q are equivalent if and only if $p \Rightarrow q$ and
$q \Rightarrow p$.
   Every conditional $p \Rightarrow q$ has a contrapositive $\sim q \Rightarrow \sim p$. Notice that the
contrapositive of a conditional is formed by exchanging the hypothesis
and conclusion and negating both. Thus the contrapositive of

> If two points have the same x-coordinate, they lie on the same per-
> pendicular to the x-axis.

is

> If two points do not lie on the same perpendicular to the x-axis, they
> do not have the same x-coordinate.

A proposition and its contrapositive are equivalent. Hence a student
who experiences difficulty proving a given proposition may be able to
prove its contrapositive. Then, since the two propositions are equivalent,
the given proposition follows necessarily from its contrapositive.
   Many conditionals contain a conjunction of conditions in either the
hypothesis or the conclusion. Thus the conditional

> If a line is parallel to one side of a triangle and bisects another side,
> it bisects the third side.

has a conjunction of two conditions in the hypothesis. The conjunction of conditions in a hypothesis is more subtle in other conditionals. The conditional

If a line intersects two parallel lines, the alternate interior angles are congruent.

is essentially a conditional whose hypothesis is a conjunction of two conditions:

If two lines are parallel and another line intersects them, the alternate interior angles are congruent.

In case a conditional has a hypothesis that is a conjunction of conditions, more than one contrapositive can be formed. These are formed by interchanging the conclusion and any one of the conjuncts in the hypothesis and negating both propositions interchanged. Each of the possible contrapositives is equivalent to the given conditional. If the hypothesis is a conjunction of three conditions, a number of contrapositives are possible:

$$(p \,\&\, q \,\&\, r \Rightarrow s) \Leftrightarrow (\sim s \,\&\, q \,\&\, r \Rightarrow \sim p) \Leftrightarrow (p \,\&\, \sim s \,\&\, r \Rightarrow \sim q) \Leftrightarrow$$
$$(p \,\&\, q \,\&\, \sim s \Rightarrow \sim r) \Leftrightarrow (\sim s \Leftrightarrow \sim(p \,\&\, q \,\&\, r))$$

All these contrapositives are equivalent. Any one can be used to prove any other.

Suppose a student wishes to prove the proposition: If two lines are cut by a transversal so that the alternate interior angles are congruent, the lines are parallel. The indirect proof given in some textbooks is hard for some students to follow. But the proof of a contrapositive is easy. Form the contrapositive: If two nonparallel lines are cut by a transversal, the alternate interior angles are not congruent. This conditional can be proved by the strategy of the deduction theorem; the hypothesis is assumed and the conclusion is deduced. Thus if the lines are not parallel, they will intersect. Then a triangle will be formed, of which two sides are subsets of the nonparallel lines and the third is the subset of the transversal between the nonparallel lines. Hence one of the alternate interior angles will be an exterior angle of the triangle and hence greater than the other alternate interior angle, which will be an angle of the triangle nonadjacent to the exterior angle. By the deduction theorem, the contrapositive is proved. Its equivalent proposition, the one given to be proved, necessarily follows.

Indirect proof

Indirect proof is a powerful strategy in that it can be used to prove any proposition. Unfortunately, the reasoning for it is subtle and hence not easily understood by students. Students sometimes say, "How come you'll let me assume that the proposition is false, but you won't let me assume that it is true?" Students learn how to use indirect proof by imitation and practice, but some are not convinced that it is sound reasoning.

The strategy begins by assuming the negation of the proposition to be proved. Suppose we wish to prove a proposition p. We assume its negation, namely, $\sim p$. Then we prove that $\sim p$ leads to a contradiction, for example, $r \ \& \ \sim r$ (which is necessarily false). That is, we prove $\sim p \Rightarrow (r \ \& \ \sim r)$. From the contrapositive of this conditional we prove the negation of the negation of the proposition to be proved. That is, we show that $\sim (r \ \& \ \sim r) \Rightarrow \sim \sim p$. The negation of the negation of the proposition to be proved implies the truth of the proposition to be proved. That is, $\sim \sim p \Rightarrow p$.

Students often have difficulty with such proofs. To use indirect proof, students have to know how to negate a proposition. In the case of a conditional $p \Rightarrow q$, a negation is $\sim (p \Rightarrow q)$. This is not a useful negation. However, one negation of $(p \Rightarrow q) \Leftrightarrow \sim (p \ \& \ \sim q)$ is $\sim (p \Rightarrow q) \Leftrightarrow (p \ \& \ \sim q)$. Hence $p \ \& \ \sim q$ is a negation of the conditional $p \Rightarrow q$. It is a useful negation and the one students can be taught.

A special form of indirect proof is *reductio ad absurdum*. It is based on the argument form $\sim \sim p \Leftrightarrow p$—that is, the negation of the negation of a proposition implies the truth of the proposition.

One reason indirect proof is difficult for some students is that teachers treat this topic only casually. One teacher said, "I present one indirect proof and discuss the logic of indirect proof. But it is hard for the students to understand, so I don't do anything more with it." Under such conditions students will not master the strategy of indirect proof. It is true that it is hard but it is also important. It should be a challenge to mathematics teachers that their students understand it and become competent in its use. Careful explanation and much practice will enable students to use it.

Proof by cases

Suppose a student has the problem of proving that if a and b are real numbers, then $|a + b| \leq |a| + |b|$. One way of doing this is to consider the cases

$a \geq 0$ and $b \geq 0$

$a < 0$ and $b > 0$

$a < 0$ and $b < 0$

This is a partition of the set of rational numbers. Hence when each of these cases has been proved, the proposition has been proved for the given domain.

This strategy of proof by cases is based on a valid argument form. (The symbol "$\vee$" means "or.")

1   $p \Rightarrow (q \vee r \vee s)$

2   $[(q \Rightarrow t) \ \& \ (r \Rightarrow t) \ \& \ (s \Rightarrow t)] \Rightarrow [(q \vee r \vee s) \Rightarrow t]$

3   $\therefore \ p \Rightarrow t$

Conditional 1 represents the partition of the set into the cases. Conditional 2 is the argument form for the proof of each case implying the proof of the partition. Conditional 3 follows from the other two conditionals by transitivity.

An example of the use of this strategy in geometry is the proof of the theorem:

> The degree measure of an angle inscribed in a circle is one-half the degree measure of its intercepted arc.

The three cases are represented in Figure 11.3. The proposition is proved for each of these three cases. Since these are a partition, the theorem follows by the argument form above.

Figure 11.3

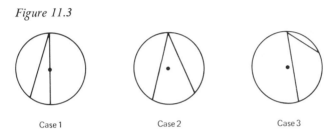

Case 1   Case 2   Case 3

Mathematical induction

The term *mathematical induction* is misleading, for this strategy of proof is deductive. The principle (theorem) of mathematical induction holds over the positive integers (Z^+). Suppose that a student thinks that a property holds for every positive integer n. If this student can prove that the property holds for $n = 1$ and prove that whenever it holds for $n \geq 1$ it also holds for $n + 1$, it follows that it holds for every positive integer n. In an abbreviated argument form, the principle of mathematical induction may be stated as follows:

$$[\exists k \in Z^+, p(k) \ \& \ \forall n \geq k \in Z^+, p(n) \Rightarrow p(n + 1)] \Rightarrow \forall n \geq k \in Z^+, p(n)$$

In this form, $p(n)$ stands for a proposition—for example, the nth positive odd integer is $2n - 1$.

It can be seen that the principle of mathematical induction is a conditional whose hypothesis is a conjunction. Hence when this principle is applied for proving a particular proposition (for example, the sum of the first n odd positive integers is n^2), the strategy of *modus ponens* is used. Each conjunct (or condition) in the hypothesis is proved, and the conclusion follows by *modus ponens*.

In the case of the proposition stated above, we show that the sum of the first positive odd integer is 1^2. Then we show that for all $n \geq 1$, if the sum of the n positive odd integers is n^2, the sum of $n + 1$ positive odd integers is $(n + 1)^2$. Then we can infer that for every positive odd integer n the sum of the first n positive odd integers is n^2.

The argument form of the principle of mathematical induction stated above is general. That is, instead of $p(n)$ being true for $n = 1$, this condition in the hypothesis is stated as $p(n)$ being true for $n = k$, where k is a particular, though unspecified, positive integer. Hence, in this form, the principle covers cases such as the proof of

> The sum of the degree measures of the interior angles of a convex polygon of n sides is $(n - 2)$ 180

where the smallest value of n is 3.

Mathematical induction is easier for students to understand when it is related to *modus ponens*, with which they should be quite familiar. Additionally, teachers find that analogy helps make the principle of mathematical induction reasonable. Suppose, for example, an infinite number of dominoes stood up on end. If it can be shown that any domino pushed over will knock the next over, then a particular domino pushed over will cause every domino after it to fall over. Or suppose a ladder with an infinite number of rungs, and that we are able to get on the first rung, and further, that if we are able to get on any rung we are able to climb to the next rung. Then it follows that we can climb to any, and hence every, rung on the ladder. Suppose, however, that for some reason we are unable to get to the first rung of the ladder but can get to the sixteenth rung. Since it is the case that once we get on any rung we can climb to the next rung higher up, then it follows that we can climb to any rung from the sixteenth on up.

Understanding the various strategies of proof and skill in using them are objectives in teaching about proof. Understanding is based on knowledge of concepts and principles. Skill is based on knowledge of understanding and sufficient practice. It is well to recall what was said in the chapters about the teaching of concepts, principles, and skills. Students will have to be given a concept of each strategy to be able to identify it and develop it when appropriate. Advice for applying a strategy can be phrased as prescriptions. Then practice can be given to develop speed and accuracy. Following the suggestions offered in Chapter 8, practice should be motivated. It should be spaced adequately so students do not forget what they have learned. Feedback should be provided so students know whether what they do is right or wrong. Reinforcement can encourage correct responses.

Thought questions

1   Another name for *modus ponens* is *detaching the hypothesis*. Why is the latter an appropriate term?

2   What will have to be proved to use *modus ponens* with the following theorem? If two parallel line segments have congruent projections on the *x*-axis, the line segments are congruent.

3   If a teacher uses the deduction theorem strategy to prove

$$ax^2 + bx + c = 0 \ \& \ a \neq 0 \Rightarrow x = \frac{-b \pm \sqrt{b^2 - 4ac}}{2a}$$

what is assumed? What is the last step in the proof?

4   Locus theorems are biconditionals. One such theorem is: The locus of points equidistant from two parallel planes is a plane parallel to the given planes and midway between them. State the theorem given as an example as a biconditional. State the plan of proof using the deduction theorem.

5   Questions 5–9 refer to the dialogue on pages 310–311. Using the figure the teacher drew, suppose you want to prove $\overleftrightarrow{DE}$ is parallel to $\overleftrightarrow{BC}$. Present an analysis (or plan of proof) based on the transitivity of implication.

6   In utterance 8, a student suggests two triangles that cannot be proved congruent. Should the teacher have told the students that these triangles cannot be proved congruent and saved class time? Why?

7   In utterance 25, the teacher refuses to let S_6 answer. Should he have done this? Why?

8   The teacher accepted an unfruitful hypothesis offered by a student in utterance 9 but not in utterance 29. Should he have been consistent and accepted the suggestion in utterance 29, allowing the students to discover for themselves that it was not efficient? Defend your answer.

9   At the end of utterance 31, the teacher changed his mind and asked each student to write the proof. Why was this decision wise?

10   In some geometry textbooks, students are asked only to prove that certain propositions are true. Should there be exercises in which students are asked to disprove certain propositions? If so, how could this be done?

11   State a contrapositive of each of the following:
   a   If two points have the same abscissa, they lie on the same line parallel to the y-axis.
   b   Two triangles are similar, provided they are congruent.
   c   If two right triangles have the hypotenuse and a leg of one congruent to the hypotenuse and leg of another, the two right triangles are congruent.
   d   If a diameter is perpendicular to a chord, it bisects the chord.
   e   If a plane is perpendicular to a radius of a sphere at its endpoint on the sphere, it is tangent to the sphere.

12   Prove by truth tables that a conditional and its contrapositive are equivalent.

13   To prove indirectly the theorem "Lines that have the same slope are parallel," what is assumed?

14   By indirect proof, prove that at a point on a line there is only one perpendicular to the line.

15   Prove the extended law of transitivity: $a_0 = a_1$, & $a_1 = a_2$, & $a_2 = a_3$, & ..., & $a_{n-1} = a_n \Rightarrow a_0 = a_n$. You may assume that $a_0 = a_1$ & $a_1 = a_2 \Rightarrow a_0 = a_2$.

16   Prove $\sum_{n=1}^{n} a_n = \frac{n(n \pm 1)}{2}$, $a \in Z^+$.

17   Prove the generalized law of exponents: $a^{x_1} a^{x_2} \cdots a^{x_n} = a^{x_1 + x_2 + \cdots + x_n}$. You may assume that $a^{x_1} a^{x_2} = a^{x_1 + x_2}$.

18   Look up the proof of the law of cosines in a trigonometry book or some other book that contains a discussion of circular functions. Tell how the strategy of proof by cases is employed in this proof.

19   Assume that the following two theorems have been proved:

The angles opposite the congruent sides of an isosceles triangle are congruent.

If two sides of a triangle are unequal, then the angle opposite the longer side is larger than the angle opposite the shorter side.

Use the strategies of proof by cases and indirect proof to prove the following theorem:

If two angles of a triangle are unequal, then the side opposite the larger angle is longer than the side opposite the smaller angle.

How much rigor?

Rigor is a property of proof; every proof is more or less rigorous. As far as the unsophisticated is concerned, rigor is also related to persuasion. Up to a point, the more rigorous an argument is, the more convincing it is; beyond that point an increase in rigor is considered unnecessary and becomes uninteresting. Students are not excited about proving that a line segment has just one midpoint or that there is just one additive identity. Professional mathematicians are concerned about such proofs, of course, not so much because the proofs convince them of the truth of propositions they have used for some time but rather because the proofs fill gaps in the structure they are creating.

Something similar can be said about axioms. Unsophisticated high school students are not particularly bothered by a strong set of axioms, a set of axioms some of which can be deduced from others. Nor are they bothered by an incomplete set of axioms—for example, geometry axioms that do not contain axioms about the betweenness relation. But once they become more sophisticated, they will appreciate the role of weakness and completeness of a set of axioms.

The goal of the mathematics teacher is to accept the unsophistication of students relative to rigor and to attempt to enhance their appreciation of it while under guidance. This appreciation has to be acquired gradually, by discovery rather than by exposition. Students will first have to be convinced of the need for tightness in reasoning before they will be really willing to learn how this can be attained.

An implication of the foregoing is that algebra should not be taught prescriptively where the only justification is pragmatic—the procedure results in the right answer—and then geometry taught as a sequence of proofs. Under such policy, it is no wonder that students emerge from high school mathematics believing that it is only in geometry that propositions are proved; in algebra one learns to apply principles that are taken for granted. As we pointed out in a previous section, junior high school teachers can introduce a concern for rigor by asking "Why?" and "How do we know this is true?" and "How do we know that we can do that?" *Modus ponens* and instantiation are used repeatedly and teachers can call attention to the forms of these inferences.

Simple proofs can be introduced in the first algebra course. For example, students can find counterexamples of false generalizations to prove their falsity. They can prove that the product of three rational numbers is a rational number, from their knowledge that the product of two rational numbers is a rational number. They can prove the righthand distributivity of multiplication over addition from the lefthand distributivity, or vice versa, depending on which is taken as the axiom. And when they study polynomials, they can readily follow the more involved proof of the product of binomials theorem. They can prove the extension of the law of positive integral exponents in multiplication to three factors $(x^m x^n x^p)$ from their knowledge of the law for two factors. When they come to study linear functions, they can prove that the slope of a linear function is constant. Simple invalid arguments such as "proving" $2 = 1$ are both interesting and potentially instructive. If the algebra teacher is alert for the opportunities for simple proofs, the students will develop understanding and appreciation of proof and will find the more formal proofs in later courses in mathematics less forbidding.

In geometry, it is well for the teacher to avoid proofs of theorems that appear obvious to students. They see no need for such proofs; they are not sophisticated enough mathematically to appreciate them. Presenting such proofs only decreases their interest in the subject.

When students present proofs, they can be led to see that every asserted statement must be an assumption, an axiom, a theorem or the conclusion of a valid inference whose premises are based on these. If the latter is implicit, reasons for its assertion have to be given. The proof is complete if there is no non sequitur. Only simple principles of logic need be used, leaving the more involved principles for college courses.

The rigor of proofs of some theorems of geometry given in textbooks can be increased if the teacher wishes to do so. For example, if the textbook does not give the postulate,

> If a line through a vertex of a triangle is between the two sides of the angle at this vertex, it intersects the opposite side between its endpoints.

when the theorem about the bisector of the vertex angle of an isosceles triangle bisecting the opposite side is proved, the teacher can ask the students how they know that the bisector of the vertex angle will intersect the opposite side. Should students try to argue from a drawing, the teacher can remind them that observation is not accepted as a "rule of the game of proof." If some say that if the line is straight and passes through the vertex between the sides of the vertex angle then "it just has to intersect the opposite side," the teacher can patiently repeat the question, "How do you know?" The ensuing discussion should lead to how postulates are identified and why they need to be made explicit.

A rigorous proof of the theorem,

The diagonals of a parallelogram bisect each other.

would first prove that the diagonals intersect. Few textbooks include this in the proof, yet it is easy to prove. (How?) The teacher can point to the lack of rigor, assuming it exists, and append a proof to that given in the textbook.

There usually are other gaps in rigor in textbook proofs, gaps that can be plugged relatively easily. The teacher can encourage students to detect them and fill them by proof. Even if this is not possible, the students will gain an appreciation of rigor.

Learning to think like a mathematician

As important as the teaching of proof is, if this were the only aspect taught, students would miss a full appreciation of how mathematicians think. As mathematicians contemplate the objects with which they work, they get hunches or conjectures about relations among the objects. For example, a mathematician observes that the trisectors of the angles of a triangle drawn with a protractor form a triangle that appears to be equilateral. She draws another triangle of a different shape and confirms this observation within the limits of the accuracy of measurement. She then has a hunch that this is true for every triangle but cannot be sure and so attempts to prove the conjecture. It may be that she flounders for a while, trying strategies that do not yield proof. But the mathematician perseveres and is finally able to give a proof that identifies a property of all triangles. The proof has embedded the property in the structure of Euclidean geometry.

Students who attempt to prove propositions asserted in exercises learn something about how mathematicians work as they try various strategies until they temporarily abandon the attempt to prove the proposition or hit on a strategy that enables them to prove it. But the proposition has been asserted for them in the first place. Where did it come from? How did the person who conceived of it get the hunch even before it was proved? Unless students gain some experience in making conjectures, they will miss this important aspect of how mathematicians think. Conjecturing, which many research mathematicians say is by far the most extensive and difficult part of mathematical activity, is completely missed if only proof is stressed.

Teachers who want to give students insight into how mathematicians operate, should provide opportunities for them to consider ideas and play with mathematical objects. Then they can experience flashes of insight, formation of conjectures, some right and some wrong, and attempts to show that these are consequences of other propositions in the structure of mathematics they are investigating. In such ventures, the meaning of proof is enhanced and so is appreciation of structure.

In the 1930's, Harold Fawcett, teaching at the University High School at Ohio State University, experimented with students in his geometry classes by asking them to build their own structures of geometry. After discussing what appeared to be true about the relations between points, lines, and planes, he directed the students to accept some of the statements they had made as postulates to see what they could deduce from them. They had to hypothesize propositions by induction over triangles, sets of parallel and perpendicular lines and planes, polygons, and any other geometric objects of which they conceived. Then they had to try to prove these propositions. Because there was no textbook, the proofs could not conform to "the way the textbook did it." They had to be convincing deductive arguments. The students defined terms as needed and added postulates where necessary.

Fawcett's course was called "The Nature of Proof," betokening its liberal conception. Fawcett continually directed student's attention to patterns of thinking that prevail in mathematics and elsewhere. For example, the class considered The Declaration of Independence, a deductive argument beginning with "We hold these truths as self-evident." "These truths" are analogous to postulates and proceed to justifications of charges against George III. They also considered the persuasive arguments in advertising and their logicality. The students in the University High School—a school dedicated to experimentation in curriculum and methods—wrote an account and appraisal of their experiences, which was published as a book entitled *Were We Guinea Pigs?* They decided that they had been guinea pigs but considered their school experiences worthwhile. Of particular significance, so they reported, was their experience in the nature of proof. They were satisfied that they learned geometry and how to think deductively.

Building minigeometric structures

Teachers do not have to elaborate as comprehensively as Fawcett did to give students experience in building geometric structures. It is possible to provide this experience by means of one or more simple units.

Suppose a geometry course has begun in the usual way through a textbook discussion of the topics on points, lines, angles, and triangles. Theorems are proved and the students gain some insight about the nature of proof. Then when the topics of parallelism and perpendicularity are approached, the teacher can conduct discussion leading to a definition of *parallel lines* and *perpendicular lines*. The teacher can draw a line intersecting two parallel lines and a line intersecting two intersecting lines and solicit conjectures about what appears to characterize the figures—congruency, for example. Other lines can be drawn—parallel, perpendicular,

Figure 11.4

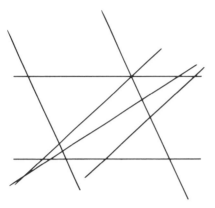

and intersecting but not perpendicular, as illustrated in Figure 11.4. Additional conjectures can be entertained.

Textbooks can then be dispensed with; students can be discouraged from referring to them. The teacher can do as Fawcett did: tell the students to pick a small, proper subset of the conjectures and consider them as postulates. Better yet, each student can select a set so that there will be many unique structures. Then each student can determine what his or her postulates imply—what can be deduced from them. Each will have to form conjectures and test them by deductive proof.

Since students will have acquired the concepts of parallelogram, diagonal, rectangle, and square in their previous courses, they will probably employ them in developing their structures. The teacher can encourage the students to conceive of other geometric objects to facilitate development of their structures and to name them. Thus, what are conventionally defined as alternate interior and exterior angles, corresponding angles, rhombi, bisectors of angles or sides, and altitudes will be conceived by some students. If other students find the concepts useful, they can accept them and place them in their own structures, proving theorems about them.

The proofs that are given will have to be evaluated somewhat differently than those experienced before this exercise. It is conceivable that such queries as "Is the reason you gave for this assertion one of your postulates or is it a theorem in your structure?" "How do you define this?" or "Aren't you assuming something that you haven't proved?" will push students naturally toward greater rigor. The evaluations will more closely approximate evaluations of proofs made by mathematicians as they assess structures.

Teachers can also ask particular students whether one or more of their postulates can be proved a consequence of others. If this is possible, the proofs can be exhibited to the class, thus encouraging other students to assess their own postulates. By this inquiry, they can get a feeling for the desirability of independence. Other topics that lend themselves to a similar approach are circles, prisms, cylinders, and spheres. Ministructures can be developed for each of these.

The teacher who illustrates how different geometries can be developed can get the students to conceive of space as the union of the boundaries of a circle and its interior. Lines, then, become finite in length, and not all nonparallel lines intersect. The teacher can do the same with the surface of a sphere, where parallelism does not exist. Some properties are analogous to those of Euclidean geometry, but others are not. Thus students can be introduced to and gain an appreciation of non-Euclidean geometry.

Teachers whose students have developed ministructures are enthusiastic about the experience. They report similar enthusiasm from most of the students, who become involved in mathematics by developing their own structures and discussing them with the other students. As might be expected, some students conjecture and prove many "theorems"; others do not do as well. But all learn something about how a mathematician develops a mathematical structure.

Some teachers may fear that geometry classes will miss significant subject matter if such activities are introduced. Such fears seem groundless. Once an activity has been completed, textbooks can be brought out. Each student can compare his or her structure with the subject matter in the textbook. Teachers who have used such activity say that private language—idiosyncratic definitions—is readily abandoned in favor of conventional language. Students are pleased to find in the textbooks some of the "theorems" they have proved. They are also gratified when they find they have proved "theorems" not in the textbook.

Self-test on the competencies

1 Point out the functions of proof in mathematics.
   Which of the following are functions?
   a Facilitate the assignment of truth values to mathematical propositions.
   b Determine whether a given proposition is a consequence of a set of postulates and definitions.
   c Form a conjecture by induction.
   d Establish the empirical truth of statements.

2 Tell how a junior high school mathematics teacher can begin to develop an intuition of proof.
   a Give examples to support the conjecture that students have some conception of what it means to prove a statement is true or false by the time they enter junior high school.
   b State things a junior high school mathematics teacher can do to extend the intuition of the nature of proof that students have when they enter junior high school.
   c How can a junior high school mathematics teacher convince a student that a particular argument is invalid?

3 Describe various strategies of proof.
   Name seven strategies of proof and describe how a person would use each.

4 Tell how a senior high school mathematics teacher can give students an experience in building a simple mathematical structure.

Tell how a teacher could give students an experience in developing a mini-geometric structure in a finite geometry such as nine-point geometry.

What should be the major learning outcomes of an experience in building a minigeometry?

References

Exner, Robert M. "Should Mathematical Logic Be Taught Formally in Mathematics Classes? Pro." *The Mathematics Teacher*, 64 (1971), 388 and 394–401.

———, and Myron F. Rosskopf. *Logic in Elementary Mathematics*. New York: McGraw-Hill, 1959.

———. "Proof." *The Teaching of Secondary School Mathematics*, Thirty-Third Yearbook of the National Council of Teachers of Mathematics. Washington, D. C.: The National Council of Teachers of Mathematics, 1970. Ch. 8.

Fawcett, Harold P. *The Nature of Proof*, Thirteenth Yearbook of the National Council of Teachers of Mathematics. Washington, D. C.: National Council of Teachers of Mathematics, 1938.

Goals for School Mathematics, Report of the Cambridge Conference on School Mathematics. Boston: Houghton Mifflin, 1963.

Hallerberg, Arthur E. "A Form of Proof." *The Mathematics Teacher*, 64 (1971), 203–214.

Hendrix, Gertrude. "The Psychological Appeal of Deductive Proof." *The Mathematics Teacher*, 54 (1961), 515–520.

Hilton, Peter J. "Should Mathematical Logic Be Taught Formally in Mathematics Classes? Con." *The Mathematics Teacher*, 64 (1971), 389–394.

Klingler, Donn L. "Structuring a Proof." *The Mathematics Teacher*, 62 (1964), 200–202.

Mathematics in General Education, Report of the Committee on the Function of Mathematics in General Education. New York: Appleton-Century-Crofts, 1940. Ch. 9.

Robinson, Edith. "Strategies of Proof," *The Mathematics Teacher*, 61 (1963), 531–534.

Smith, Eugene P., and Kenneth B. Henderson. "Proof." *The Growth of Mathematical Ideas: Grades K–12*, Twenty-Fourth Yearbook of the National Council of Teachers of Mathematics. Washington, D. C.: The National Council of Teachers of Mathematics, 1959. Ch. 4.

Smith, Stanley A. "What Does a Proof Really Prove?" *The Mathematics Teacher*, 61 (1968), 483–484.

12

Teaching slow learners

We shall begin this chapter by describing behaviors that slow learners often emit in the mathematics classroom and offer conjectures to account for such behaviors. We shall offer suggestions for working with these students together with mathematical activities that can be used in teaching them.

At the conclusion of this chapter, you should be able to demonstrate the following competencies:

1 Characterize behavior common to many slow learners and offer reasons why they occur

2 Suggest guidelines for working with slow learners

3 Describe programs, games, activities, and units that can be used in teaching mathematics to slow learners

Difficulties associated with teaching slow learners

Students who have had difficulty in learning mathematics are likely to have negative attitudes toward it and be convinced that they cannot understand or do anything of a mathematical nature. Seeing themselves as mathematical failures, they are prime candidates for all the defensive behavior discussed in Chapter 2. In some cases, these students switch from defensive tactics such as day dreaming, excessive questioning, and guessing. They become hostile, cut class, refuse to work, annoy other students, and lash out with disruptive behavior such as jostling each other, making obscene gestures, throwing objects, or making remarks like

I don't understand any of this junk.

You're confusing me as usual.

I hate these stupid fractions. What good are they anyway?

If Phil makes one more smart remark, I'm gonna bust him right here!

I'm not gonna do it. You can't make me.

I don't do homework.

Some crud stole my paper.

While such actions are not exclusive to students unsuccessful with mathematics, they are more likely to be employed by students who perceive the mathematics classroom as a hostile environment. Disruptive behavior can occur in any classroom, from any student, when the teacher is seen as a weak or incompetent manager. When students are hostile toward mathematics and the teacher is also unable to maintain control, then the classroom is almost certain to become a chaotic scene comprised of a frustrated teacher shouting ineffectual commands and amused students enjoying the teacher's plight and seeking additional means of disruption.

Some students who are slow in learning mathematics turn up in algebra and geometry classes. Often in the minority, sometimes under pressure from home to succeed in college preparatory courses, they usually employ defensive rather than disruptive behavior. On the other hand, the majority of students in classes labeled "general," "fundamental," or "basic" mathematics and in "slow" sections of junior high school courses are slow learners of mathematics and are prone to exhibit disruptive as well as defensive behavior. This coupled with the tendency of many administrators to place inexperienced, ineffectual, or unprepared teachers in such teaching situations has contributed to the unsavory reputation attached to courses for the unsuccessful mathematics student.

Some students who have difficulty in learning mathematics come from home environments that handicap their performance in school. The families of some students disparage schools and belittle intellectual endeavor. Rather than encourage their children to succeed in school and set their sights on gainful occupations, apathetic parents often implicitly promote actions designed "just to get by." Other parents place intense pressure on their offspring to attain academic success. Some students of such parents react by deliberately making poor grades; others strive to reach goals that are beyond their intellectual capabilities.

The expectations set for students are likely to influence academic accomplishments significantly. Students are sensitive to the expectations of their parents, peers, and teachers when setting personal goals. The relation of teachers' expectations to student achievement has been investigated by a number of researchers. A notable study by Rosenthal and Jacobson (1968) reported significant gains in the intelligence scores of randomly selected children whose teachers had been told to expect unusual intellectual growth during the school year. This study has been severely criticized (Thorndike, 1968), but it raises some interesting questions about the influence that teachers' expectations have on student achievement.

Other students who are slow learners of mathematics may have interests or abilities that partially explain their substandard academic performance. Students who perceive mathematics as irrelevant to their needs are likely to be uninterested. Many pupils lack the maturity to be concerned about their future needs and show interest only in things that have utility for the present. Some students may be slow in learning mathematics because of their need to base their thinking on physical referents. They have difficulty dealing with the abstract symbolism of formal mathematics. Schulz (1972, p. 5) speaks to this point in the National Council of Teachers of Mathematics Thirty-Fifth Yearbook, *The Slow Learner in Mathematics:*

> In one sense, achievement is a testimony to an insidious sorting and rewarding process that prizes head orientation over hand orientation, or verbal skills and style over physical skills and style. In such a value system, the slow learner is often a loser, for in many cases his primary learning style is one of physicalization—confrontation with the immediate environment on a physical basis. While the importance of visual and action-based mathematical experiences has been hypothesized on a neurological basis for all children, tactile experiences with objects and events are indispensable to the learner who has no other effective input channel. To form concepts and work mathematical problems, he needs the physical input provided by such manipulative materials as fraction pieces, Dienes blocks, geoboards, puzzles, games, machine calculators, and in fact the entire mathematics laboratory.

This author also states that slow learners are apt to have deficient language-symbolic systems, restricted reading and listening comprehension, and weak conceptual and factual backgrounds. In addition, these students are likely to have difficulty using abstract symbols, generalizing, ordering, analyzing, and maintaining a verbal thought sequence.

Another source of difficulty in teaching slow learners is the teacher. In all likelihood the mathematics teacher was not a slow learner of mathematics. His or her attitude derives from positive learning experiences. It is doubtful that teachers of general or basic mathematics courses were ever students in such classes or that they had a great deal of difficulty in learning mathematical concepts, generalizations, and skills. Teachers of mathematics are prone to view the subject as precise and logical and, therefore, meaningful, whereas, slow learners often view it as complex, confusing, and arbitrary. This divergence of views is in itself enough to cause the teacher to become frustrated and discouraged with students' limited progress. Compounding the problem is the fact that the teacher is likely to value and reward neatness and conscientiousness in assignments, proper care of curriculum materials, punctuality, and adequate work preparation. On the other hand, slow students are less likely to be concerned with such matters that do not directly relate to their needs.

Another source of problems is in the content being taught. Slow students studying algebra and geometry may be trying to master content at a pace beyond their intellectual capability. Students in mathematics courses labeled "general," "basic," or "fundamental" often deal with content commonly taught in the elementary grades. These students are "tired of this same old arithmetic" (or perhaps tired of not being able to succeed with it) or embarrassed to be studying elementary school material. Their teacher, trained to teach higher mathematics, may also find arithmetic topics unstimulating. Students are quick to perceive that a teacher is uninterested in the subject or unsympathetic to their learning problems. A teacher who conveys such attitudes reinforces and nurtures apathetic behavior.

In the following section, we shall discuss guidelines to alleviate some of these difficulties.

Thought questions

1   What are some reasons that cause school administrators to assign classes comprised of slow learners to inexperienced or minimally prepared teachers?

2   React to the following policy statement by a secondary school principal. "I try not to assign a beginning mathematics teacher more than one basic or remedial mathematics class. Whenever possible, I assign a beginning teacher as an assistant to one of my strongest, most experienced teachers in one of their remedial classes. Sometimes this causes me to assign a beginning mathematics teacher as an assistant in a science or language class. This policy almost always costs the new teacher his preparation period. However, I feel that the lessons a new teacher gains from being an assistant to an effective teacher more than make up for the inconvenience of losing a planning period."

3   Why will an algebra or geometry teacher have difficulty motivating a student to learn the subject if this student appears to be interested only in things of immediate utility?

4   Consider an algorithm for performing long division. Discuss how a mathematics teacher and a slow learning student could have widely differing perceptions as to the meaning of the steps required in this procedure.

5   How is it that parent and teacher expectations can encourage some students to work diligently and others to despair?

6   In view of your mathematical background and values, what difficulties do you perceive encountering when teaching mathematics to slow learners?

7   Consider the following exchange between two junior high school mathematics teachers and discuss the relative merits of each position.

T_1 Next week I'm going to start a unit on probability in my slow section. I think my students will find this an interesting change of pace.

T_2 How can you justify taking the time to teach such material when those kids can hardly compute with whole numbers, fractions, or decimals?

Suggestions for teaching mathematics to slow learners

Teaching mathematics to slow learners is difficult, but teachers should not use this as an excuse to put forth less than best effort. Students need to acquire a certain degree of mathematical literacy and are entitled to a willing teacher, even when teaching conditions are far from ideal. To ignore students who are uninterested in learning mathematics on the grounds that "Well they don't care anyway, so why should I beat my brains out trying to teach them mathematics?" is to shirk professional obligation. Students, especially slow learners, are not generally mature individuals. Teachers must lead and encourage them to acquire mathematical literacy and to develop their potential to think quantitatively.

In addition to the question of professionalism, there are pragmatic concerns in allowing students not to participate in classroom activities. Students who are allowed to "go their own way" tend to disrupt classes when left unoccupied for long periods of time. The teacher who permits students to withdraw from classroom activity may gain momentary relief but is sure to sow the seeds of disaster in ensuing months.

Furthermore, a teacher accomplishes little by expressing anger at a student's inability to learn. This is not to say that teachers should never express displeasure with a student performance. But anger should be directed at the product of the student's efforts (or lack of effort), never at the student's innate worth or ability. Physicians do not heal patients by chastising their condition. Similarly, teachers do not facilitate learning by criticizing students' ability (or inability) to learn. In relation to this point, Schulz (1972, p. 2) states, "Ironically schools may be the only treatment centers that blame the patient rather than the treatment when things go wrong."

Teachers are not always to be held accountable when students are unsuccessful in learning subject matter. Lawyers, psychologists, and others in the helping professions cannot always be blamed when their services fail to meet with success for a client. Sometimes circumstances prevent even the best treatment from resulting in desirable outcomes. A lawyer may lose a case or a patient may not be cured, not because the lawyer or doctor is incompetent but because the treatment is not sufficient to overcome the difficulty or because the advice of the professional is not heeded. Similarly, a teacher's strategy may represent the best that one can reasonably expect but it may not suffice for observable student progress. A teacher's merit should be based not solely on results gathered from test scores but also on the seeming appropriateness of classroom techniques.

It is not difficult to offer advice for teaching mathematics to slow learners. Chapters in methods textbooks and articles in pedagogical periodicals offer a wealth of practical advice. Maxims such as

Keep the students involved in activities and classroom discussions.

Use a variety of activities within each class period.

Keep the units of work short.

Relate the mathematics being studied to life situations.

Set specific objectives for each lesson.

Keep the reading difficulty of the materials students use at an appropriate level.

Use a variety of manipulative and audio-visual materials to maintain interest and provide meaning for abstract symbols.

Be patient and refrain from sarcasm or embarrassment to students.

are appropriate as guidelines for teaching students who have experienced difficulty in learning mathematics. Each maxim is intended to help teachers overcome the learning problems of slow learners. They do not strike at the heart of the difficulty, however. A teacher's frustrations in working with slow learners usually stems from one of two basic concerns. First in the mind of the teacher, especially a beginning teacher, is classroom management. Real learning seldom occurs in chaotic classroom situations. A teacher can use a variety of activities—keep units short, relate mathematics to life situations, and follow other maxims stated above—but if students are inattentive, disruptive, and show lack of respect, then they will have no real impact on learning. Of course, maintaining control without excessive tension is not something that can be achieved in isolation from other classroom techniques. We suggest, then, a second basic concern in teaching slow learners—namely, providing the students with continued successful learning experiences. A classroom that is under control yet has unsuccessful students does little to contribute to intellectual development.

We turn our attention now to suggestions for effective and forceful classroom teaching for slow learners and for providing them with successful learning experiences in mathematics.

Project yourself as a forceful, confident, and concerned leader

In any teaching situation, but particularly in classes dominated by unsuccessful students who are apathetic or antagonistic, it is imperative that the teacher establish order immediately and then maintain it. An organized and controlled learning environment provides a calm and unharried teacher, specific assignments, and an orderly atmosphere in which to work and ask questions. This type of secure environment can pave the way for successful experiences that are so essential for the slow-learning student.

Establishing such an atmosphere must not be done by belittling students with sarcastic or maligning remarks. Respect is an integral part of the desirable learning situation, but it is not obtained through weakness and permissiveness. It is cruel to permit chaotic classrooms in which students have little idea of what their role is to be and spend valuable time groping for the limits of acceptable behavior. It is cruel to the teacher, also, for the teacher will become discouraged and frustrated and begin to direct anger and frustration at the students. Usually, a vicious circle develops, as the students become less likely to respect the teacher and, hence, become more disruptive in lieu of ill-defined limits of acceptable classroom behavior. This can occur in any classroom but is more likely to occur when students lack the initial motivation to learn.

In discussing the nature of a desirable classroom atmosphere and the related problem of discipline, David Ausubel discusses what he calls *democratic discipline*. To Ausubel (1968, p. 460) democratic discipline is

> as rational, nonarbitrary, and bilateral as possible. It provides explanations, permits discussion and invites the participation of children in the setting and enforcement of standards whenever they are qualified to do so. Above all it implies respect for the dignity of the individual, makes its primary appeal to self-controls, and avoids exaggerated emphasis on status differences and barriers between free communication. Hence, it repudiates harsh, abusive, and vindictive forms of punishment, and the use of sarcasm, ridicule, and intimidation.

Distortions of *democratic discipline* appear under the guise of permissiveness toward student behavior. Disruption is not conducive to learning; it is in fact detrimental to any really democratic classroom. For this reason, misconduct must be dealt with firmly and forcefully to maintain the dignity of teacher and students. In reference to this point, Ausubel (1968, p. 462) writes

> When such misconduct occurs, pupils have to be unambiguously informed that it will not be tolerated and that any repetition of the same behavior will be punished. This action does not preclude in any way either an earnest attempt to discover why the misbehavior occurred, or suitable preventive measures aimed at correcting the underlying causes. But, by the same token, the mere fact that a pupil has a valid psychological reason for misbehaving does not mean that he is thereby absolved from moral accountability or rendered no longer subject to punishment.

The teacher who decides to establish and maintain rigid rules governing classroom behavior should make them explicit, explain why they have been established, and enforce them consistently. It may be effective to assist slow learners in learning these rules by providing reminders. For example, the teacher who insists students be recognized before answering or asking questions can, during the first few weeks of the term, be careful to direct questions to specific students and to use directives such as "Let me see the hands of those that know the answer to this next question" or "If anyone has a question, remember to wait until I call on you." Such reminders can prevent the teacher from awkward positions of wanting to acknowledge correct responses while having to reject the manner in which the response was given.

Specific behavior that will ensure an orderly classroom for every teacher has not and probably cannot be prescribed. Assigning seats, requiring recognition before speaking, requiring late and absence permits, and taking immediate disciplinary action for each instance of misbehavior can be employed successfully by some teachers and yet fail to result in controlled and orderly classrooms for others. Some teachers hand out a list of rules on the first day of class—no candy, food, or gum-chewing. Others react to each situation as it occurs. Each procedure is as successful as the teacher makes it.

Although specific prescriptions cannot be given for creating an orderly classroom atmosphere, some general attributes are characteristic of forceful teachers:

Knowing each student by name

Knowing students' academic and social backgrounds

Determining and manipulating seating arrangements

Planning lessons and having necessary teaching aids at hand

Moving around the classroom while lecturing, questioning, or helping students

Being alert to potential disturbance and distraction, and taking immediate and direct nonverbal or verbal action to stop undesirable activity

Refraining from sarcasm

Speaking to or calling on every student during each class period

Frequently asking students questions and coming back to those who respond incorrectly with other, perhaps easier, questions

Demanding the attention of students when speaking to the class

While this list is clearly not exhaustive, it represents some ways a teacher can project force and concern. The essence of establishing order in a classroom, however, is not so much what the teacher says as it is how the teacher says it and the actions taken. It is not the specific rule or the size or gender of the teacher that generates order and respect from students. It is the expression on the teacher's face, the tone of voice, and confidence and consistency that establish and maintain order. Students are quick to ascertain ill-defined and inconsistent limits of acceptable behavior. They make their judgments primarily from their perception of the teacher's verbal and written directives.

The teacher who begins a year projecting a forceful posture can at option relax the conditions later. This option may be exercised when student achievement is satisfactory and hostility and apathy have abated. Extending the limits of behavior can lead to a more relaxed classroom atmosphere, which may be of value, but the teacher who begins the year as a permissive manager of frequent disruption will find it extremely difficult to change to strict management once the classroom atmosphere has become detrimental to learning. The unfortunate situation of seeking and failing to establish and maintain control after things have gotten out of hand occurs in the classrooms of many inexperienced teachers.

The book *Don't Smile Until Christmas* is a collection of essays by first-year teachers reflecting the problems they encountered in their initial year of teaching. Kevin Ryan, the editor, comments on the problem caused by the teacher idealism. Most of the teachers were disappointed in themselves and their students with regard to development of free and open classrooms. Ryan observes (1970, p. 180):

> While some beginning teachers thrive on the exercise of authority, many beginners do not see the necessity of assuming classroom leadership. What is more, they do not want to. They don't want to be authority figures. They don't want to impose themselves on their students. They don't want to be feared. They wish to rule by love and sweet reason. They want a free, honest relationship with their students. They are ready to respect their students' right and dignity, and they expect their students to respect theirs. They don't want their relationship with students to be based on pre-existing codes of behavior between students and teachers. They chose teaching because they wanted to be recognized as human beings. They don't want to be like the aloof, formal, cold teachers they remember from high school. However, their students don't know this—and some wouldn't care.

In Ryan's view, idealism and students' expectations conflict. The beginning teacher often fails to achieve stability until his or her idealism is tempered by the frustrations and disappointments of experience. In summarizing, Ryan (p. 181) draws the following conclusion:

> In the first year of teaching, then, we witness the sad counterpoise of two sets of attitudes on how the teacher should act. The students are looking for strong personalities and leadership. The beginning teacher, however, seeks a more gentle leadership style. For some few teachers, this works. For the legions, it fails.

Ryan's comments are made in relation to the first-year teacher but they are especially relevant for the teacher of slow learners.

We have tried to establish the advisability of developing and maintaining an orderly classroom environment. In general, this can be done by setting reasonable and definite limitations for behavior, enforcing rules consistently, listening carefully and respectfully to every student, requiring students to listen respectfully to each other, speaking to or giving personal attention to each student every day, informing students of their academic responsibilities and making these requirements attainable, and planning each class session so that time is occupied with productive activity.

Provide activities that students can do successfully

Slow learners need to have successful experiences; they need to get correct answers. This is particularly true for students dominated by fear of failure or hostility. Students must begin to get correct answers frequently and consistently before they will listen attentively to logical explanations and seek to increase their mathematical understanding. They need confidence and encouragement more than they need to know the basis for particular procedures. For example, getting slow students initially to obtain correct answers to questions involving the subtraction of integers using the prescriptive principle "Change the sign of the second one and then combine the resulting numbers" is likely to reduce tension and generate more confidence than is justification of this principle.

One might draw the analogy to a person with a severe medical problem. Doctors may treat symptoms to enable the patient to achieve stability. Once this has been done then treatment can begin for the causes of the problem. Similarly, when students are uninterested in mathematics, treatment dictates the generation of correct answers. This entails prescriptive principles designed to accomplish specific tasks. The immediate concern is not with understanding but with successful completion of a task. The student who meets with genuine success may be more amenable to explanations designed to justify algorithms. The student who is drowning in failure needs desperately to obtain many right answers. If the teacher does not take action to help, the student is likely to take desperate measures on his or her own: cheating, disrupting class, or retreating into an impenetrable shell. After tension has been abated and the student has gained confidence, the teacher can ask the student to investigate the procedures that have led to the correct answers in order to promote understanding. How far to promote such understanding depends on the teacher's judgment of the significance and difficulty of the mathematics, the student's ability to attain the understanding, the time required, and the value the teacher places on understanding.

When tests are given, it is important that students believe they have a reasonable chance to succeed. Classroom tests should be designed so that every student is virtually assured of getting the majority of the items correct. Returning papers to students with scores of 20, 30, or 40 percent is a devastating event and serves only to reconfirm their feelings of inadequacy and frustration with mathematics (regardless of the grade). Asking a number of formidable questions under the pressure of a testing situation often results in incorrect and incomplete answers. Such questions usually reinforce slow students' negative feelings about mathematics and their ability to do mathematics. For students who have difficulty with mathematics, it is advisable to pose difficult questions in contexts in which they have ample time to work and opportunity to solicit assistance. In such a context, students can learn from mistakes without being penalized for every error.

One way of helping students be successful is to provide them with the specific objectives for a given unit of instruction. Seeing that the instructional program and the corresponding evaluation instruments are based on objectives can lead to the security of knowing what is expected of them. Objectives represent learnable knowledge to students. When the evaluation instruments are clearly related to stated objectives, instruction and evaluation have a higher degree of validity in the eyes of the students. Furthermore, the teacher is less likely to be viewed as engaging in trickery, purposely devising questions to confuse students. Objectives can be profitably used in any classroom, but they are especially helpful for slow learners. The student who knows what is expected and realizes that he or she can demonstrate mastery of objectives is more able to relax, take pride in accomplishment, and be receptive to more detailed analysis of mathematics.

When students attain objectives or perform in ways that are pleasing to the teacher, it is important that genuine praise or some other form of reward be given. It is important that such credit be given to the student's performance, not to the student, however. The importance of this distinction cannot be overemphasized. The student who infers that he or she is a good person because he or she does good work is likely to feel unworthy when told that his or her performance is substandard. In fact, it is highly probable that slow learners have long been drawing self-debasing conclusions as a result of their previous academic performance. A teacher may say "No, that answer is not correct" or state forcefully "That type of behavior is discourteous and will not be permitted in this room." By choice of words, gestures, and facial expressions, teachers can and should direct remarks to the student's product, not to the student. Students should be explicitly informed when their intellectual product or their social behavior is unacceptable or inappropriate. This is not the same as indicating that the student himself is not acceptable. Teachers sometimes err when they utter reprimands such as, "Mary, you are wrong" or "Jack, you were terrible and very discourteous." Statements of this type attack students' egos and trigger defensive (perhaps disruptive) behavior. Indicating displeasure over performance is psychologically different from expressing displeasure with the individual giving the performance. To reprimand a performance allows the teacher to encourage the student and provide direction and guidance so that the performance can be improved objectively without explicitly involving individual personalities.

The teacher must be careful not to equate the worth of an individual with academic ability or performance. A student with a higher degree of intelligence as measured by some standardized instrument is not necessarily better than one who is unfortunately less intelligent. It is imperative that teachers maintain and upgrade the dignity of all students, regardless of whether they can perform specific mathematical tasks. Such acceptance may not be easy for mathematics teachers generally successful in their study of mathematics. Teachers should not be blind to the fact that many worthy adults attained mathematical competence late in life or engage in pursuits that do not require them to work problems involving fractions, decimals, percent, or the quadratic formula. To imply that a student is unworthy or will never amount to much on the basis of performance in mathematics is wrong and can only have negative effects on behavior.

Having successful experiences, particularly getting correct answers, is perhaps the best medicine for students who see themselves as mathematical failures. Success tends to reduce fear, hostility, and apathy and provides excellent background for reducing disruptive and defensive behavior. Success builds pride and positive outlook and serves as motivation of continued achievement.

Thought questions

1   In Chapter 2, we gave a number of general maxims for establishing and maintaining control in the classroom. These can be stated as follows : use nonverbal techniques to thwart potential disturbance, refrain from confrontation in the classroom, take action appropriate to the deed, refrain from administering group punishment, and be consistent in taking disciplinary action. Are these maxims appropriate for slow learners ? Discuss your answer. Are these maxims consistent with the advice presented in this chapter ? Discuss your answer.

2   What factors in home environment should a teacher consider before assigning homework ? What implications follow from your answer ?

3   In the preceding section we took the position that praise or reproof should be directed at a student's performance, not at the student directly. React to this contention.

4   In many schools awards are given during commencement exercises, some for personal or intangible qualities such as good citizenship. Should academically slow students receive just as much consideration for such awards ? Do they ?

5   Construct or find a list of the types of behavior that a mathematically literate adult should be able to exhibit. Which should be objectives for slow-learning students in a junior high school mathematics course ?

6   Why is it difficult for a teacher to become a forceful leader after operating a classroom in a permissive manner ?

7   Discuss the merits and drawbacks to each of the two methods of establishing the mode of behavior expected in a classroom :
    a   On the first day of class, distribute or post a set of rules and procedures governing behavior in class.
    b   React to each situation calmly and decisively as it occurs.

Helping slow learners in heterogeneous classes

Sometimes slow learners are assigned to pre-algebra, algebra, or geometry courses designed for students of average and above-average ability. Such assignments often come about as a result of parental or social pressure on the students to take college preparatory courses. Slow learners in courses designed for able students are severely handicapped in trying to compete with their classmates. Teachers must be particularly sensitive to their plight and assist them to improve the academic quality of their work and their feelings of worth.

Earlier in this chapter we discussed the importance of involving slow learners in classroom activities and discussions. Slow learners who are allowed to become only passively involved in classroom activities are likely candidates for failure, dropping out, or poor discipline. The difficulty associated with keeping slow learners involved is compounded in hetero-geneous classes because it is easy to neglect reluctant students in favor of the more talented ones. Teachers must make special effort to communicate with these students, either during or after class and even perhaps about nonacademic matters. Extra effort should be made to encourage the students, make sure that assignments are clear to them, and provide them with tutorial assistance whenever possible. Sometimes this assistance can be channeled through peers by assigning other, more able students to work with them. Daily assignments can include review exercises. Perhaps even more than other students, slow learners need to experience distributed practice if they are to thwart forgetting. Sometimes review exercises can be given in a differentiated assignment:

> For tomorrow try the odd-numbered exercises through 29 on page 136. Be sure to check your answers with those given at the back of the text. For the second part of the assignment, try the challenging prob-lems at the bottom of page 137 or work the review exercises on page 120.

In the subsequent class meeting, presentation of completed homework can benefit every student.

Teachers must sometimes provide slow learners with additional practice, particularly on fundamental skills. Supplemental exercises can be obtained from additional textbooks. It may be advisable to set additional practice in contexts that suggest opportunity rather than chores. The differentiated assignment in the paragraph above is one such context. Practice may also be made to sound novel. For example, consider the diagram in Figure 12.1. Practice in adding integers can be obtained by performing the indicated operations. The same design or variations of it can provide practice in all the fundamental operations on the integers as well as various polynomial expressions.

Figure 12.1

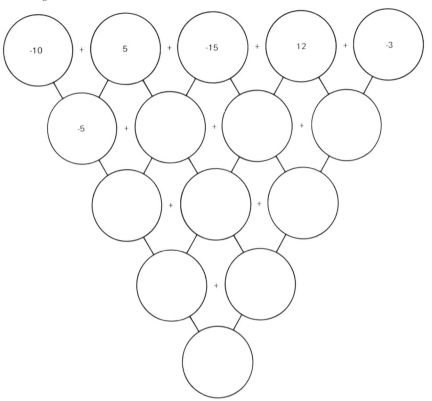

When teachers confer with parents of a slow learner enrolled in an algebra or geometry course, it is advantageous first to ascertain the parents' position. If they are convinced that their child must pursue college preparatory courses, little is likely to be gained by expressing concern over inadequate intellectual ability of the student. Teachers should inform parents of the difficulties students encounter and inform them (if it is true) that in light of the situation a passing grade is indeed a significant accomplishment. Rather than initiating suggestions concerning a tutor or transfer to another mathematics course, teachers will be wise to point out positive measures being taken to help students and then wait for the parents to solicit opinions concerning a tutor or the appropriateness of a particular mathematics course for their children. This is not to imply that teachers should refrain from pointing out actions students may be taking that interfere with learning. If a student is cutting class or refusing to work or pay attention, parents should be informed of this in a forthright manner. It is also the teacher's place to predict likelihood of a student's success in advanced and more difficult courses.

Thought questions

1 React to the contention that the most important measures a teacher can take to help slow learners in heterogeneous classes are actions that help such students feel important and involved in class activities.

2 What are the potential benefits of a teacher's identification of a slow learner's talents in fields other than mathematics?

3 In addition to advantages presented in this section, what can be realized from giving a differentiated homework assignment? Are there any disadvantages?

4 What options are available in regard to averaging test scores to determine a student's grade? How can these options be used to encourage and help slow learners in heterogeneous classes?

5 What criteria would you use to select a student to provide tutorial assistance to a slow learner in a heterogeneous class?

6 What rationalizations might parents give to explain a child's difficulty in learning mathematics? How might a teacher respond to these rationalizations?

7 The directions below could accompany an "extra practice" assignment in a junior high school mathematics class.

> Consider the "scrambled square" in Figure 12.2. Cut out the sixteen small squares and reassemble them into another 4 × 4 square so that all the adjacent numerals match. For example, 15 percent matches $\frac{3}{20}$, since 15 percent $= \frac{3}{20}$. (The four squares having only two numerals are the four corner pieces.)

Construct another scrambled square that could provide extra practice for slow learners in a regular eighth-grade mathematics class. Construct a scrambled square that could provide practice for slow learners in an algebra class. How could the scrambled square be used in a geometry class?

8 Assume that you are nearing completion of a geometry unit on areas of polygons and circular regions. Design a worksheet for additional practice that could be given to a slow learner in your class. The worksheet should require the student to use formulas for calculating areas of triangles, rectangles, parallelograms, trapezoids, and circles. The worksheet should require practice in a somewhat novel setting.

Figure 12.2

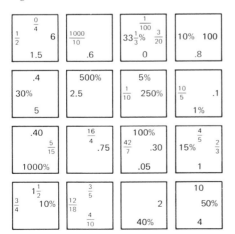

Ability grouping

In high school, students generally have the option of selecting mathematics courses that best reflect their interests and graduation requirements. In junior high school, however, they are usually assigned to specific classes. In some junior high schools, assignments are made on the basis of academic records and standardized test scores. This practice is often referred to as *ability grouping*. When classes of slow learners are formed by ability grouping, the range of mathematical competence within any given class should be reduced in comparison to the range in heterogeneous classes. Classes labeled "basic," "fundamental," "slow," "accelerated," or "advanced" are usually the result of ability grouping. Some mathematics teachers favor it because it permits them to select and sequence a common core of subject matter and to use strategies appropriate for the majority of students. Others oppose it on the grounds that it is detrimental to students assigned to the lowest levels. Some of these issues are raised and discussed in the following dialogue:

T_1 I wish we didn't use ability grouping in our junior high mathematics classes.

T_2 Why?

T_1 Well, first of all, it tends to concentrate in one class students who are discipline problems. Half the kids in my fourth-period class are basically discipline problems. I can't turn my back on them for one minute. I don't like having to spend half my time as a policeman.

T_2 O.K., but most of the kids in your fourth-period class would probably flunk if they had to do regular eighth-grade work. You know that. They don't have the background or the ability. When you have them all together, you can at least teach them what they are capable of learning.

T_1 I think we sell some of these kids short. Sure, their backgrounds are weak. They probably goofed off last year and the year before. But many are smarter than they let on. I think a lot of them could rise to the challenge if they were in regular classes.

T_2 But would they?

T_1 That's partly up to us. Right now they all look around and seem to say "This is a class for stupids. I'm stupid in math, so why try?" I think a lot of them resent being branded in this way.

T_2 That sounds O.K. at first, but how do you think most of them will feel when they're placed in a class that's too tough for them? They still get branded when they make the lowest marks in the class.

T_1 I don't know if that's always the case. As long as a grade is passing, many kids can accept it, especially if they feel adequate as a person regardless of their test scores.

These teachers typify others in their opinions of ability grouping. A teacher's position is usually predicated on certain assumptions. The questions on page 341 focus on some of these.

Thought questions

1   Identify the major points made by teachers 1 and 2 regarding the advisability of using ability grouping for classes of junior high school mathematics. Which teacher do you side with? Why? Are the points made by teachers 1 and 2 valid in regard to high school mathematics courses? Discuss your answer.

2   Identify some additional points regarding the advantages and disadvantages of ability grouping for students who are slow learners of mathematics.

3   Teacher 1 began the argument by mentioning some concerns about classroom management. Based on the other remarks, do you think this teacher was concerned primarily with discipline problems? Justify your answer.

4   How could teacher 2 argue that ability grouping can help slow learners build positive self-concepts?

Mathematics programs for slow learners

Mathematics curricula for slow learners in grades 7–12 have received considerable attention from national, state, and local curriculum committees since the middle of the 1960's. Courses of study have been outlined, special editions of textbooks have been published, and a variety of teaching aids have been introduced into mathematics courses for unsuccessful students. We shall describe some of these innovations and approaches. References about the programs are provided at the conclusion of this chapter, should the reader be interested in additional information.

Each of the following programs is designed to deal with some of the problems slow learners have in learning mathematics. Each attempts to provide them with content that is interesting, significant, and within their intellectual grasp. Various provisions are also made to compensate for lack of reading ability and to provide realistic or physical referents. The number and variety of curricula for slow students indicate many ways to structure mathematics programs. Some of the following programs have been tested experimentally with positive results. Others have only the testimony of the teachers, students, or administrators involved in their development and implementation. However, it should be emphasized that important though it may be, a curriculum itself cannot guarantee a classroom atmosphere that promotes success. The teacher is the prime mover in establishing and maintaining the classroom atmosphere. Any curriculum for slow learners, no matter how well conceived, will fail to produce intended results if it is administered by a teacher who cannot establish and maintain order, diagnose difficulties, and provide students with successful learning experiences.

SMSG program

As a result of a conference and an exploratory experiment, the School Mathematics Study Group (SMSG) published a junior high school mathematics program for students who had been extremely unsuccessful in mathematics in elementary school. This program is published under the title

Secondary School Mathematics—Special Edition and consists of eighteen units of work for students in grades 7 and 8. Titles of the units reflect the fact that this curriculum is similar to the program for students capable of college work. Some of these titles are structuring space, number theory, probability, rational numbers, the integers, equations, and functions. Distinctive features are organization in worksheets and avoidance of tiresome calculations. Students are provided with tables for all calculations. The material is produced in a large, bound volume whose pages can be removed and easily reproduced. Each unit is subdivided into lessons of one or more pages in length. The teacher can reproduce and distribute these each day. The teacher's guide provides extensive suggestions for meeting many of the difficulties students have with content. Oral exercises are frequently used to ensure student success with exercises. The amount of reading material is kept to a minimum, and the reading level is designed for students reading below the seventh grade. Each unit contains self-tests for the students' edification, and a practice test helps them prepare for the final unit examination. Research into this program indicated that students using these materials were successful in learning the content and that there was a significant improvement in their attitude toward mathematics.

SMSG has also produced a beginning algebra program for students of average and slightly below-average mathematical ability. The content normally presented in first-year algebra was spread throughout a two-year course of study. The SMSG textbooks for these courses present the content at a slower pace, pay careful attention to recalling related arithmetic concepts, generalizations, and skills, and provide a larger amount of practice exercises than textbooks designed for a one-year course in algebra. A similar program has also been developed for junior high school students. Begle (1973, p. 210), in discussing these materials, writes:

> We chose junior high school students, seventh and ninth graders, who were between the 25th and the 50th percentile with respect to previous mathematics achievement. We gave these students two years to cover what more capable students covered in one year. The below-average seventh graders did almost as well on a final test as an above-average control group. The below-average ninth-grade students actually outperformed the above-average control group.

Partly as a result of these findings, a number of commercial publishers have produced algebra textbooks similar to the SMSG volumes. The commercial textbooks are intended for average and below-average students taking their first course in algebra over a two-year period.

The results of this project and the subsequent production of commercial textbooks are encouraging developments. Many students with average and slightly below-average ability in mathematics are pressured by peers or parents into taking first-year algebra. They often encounter serious difficulty with first-year algebra when it is taught over a one-year period. Allowing them to cover in two years what is normally presented in one may prevent some of them from developing negative attitudes toward themselves and toward any mathematics they may subsequently encounter.

UICSM programs

The University of Illinois Committee on School Mathematics (UICSM) has produced two courses of study for low achievers in junior high school. *Stretchers and Shrinkers* is the title of the text for a course covering addition, subtraction, multiplication, and division of whole numbers and rational numbers and selected topics such as number theory and percent. The textbook is a radical departure from the traditional textbook or workbook, however. The year's work consists of completing four paperbound workbooks written extensively in a cartoon format. The cartoons present a cast of characters who work in various settings using machines that either stretch or shrink rods or sticks. The operations of stretching and shrinking are tantamount to multiplying and dividing whole numbers. The cast of characters includes representatives from various social and ethnic groups who work together to solve problems. The cartoons are relatively easy to read and incorporate a modest amount of humor and social message. A page from one of the student's workbooks is given in Figure 12.3. The five machines illustrated in Figure 12.3 represent multiplication by five—that is, changing a one-foot stick to a five-foot stick. Other machines (shrinkers) represent division. By hooking machines together, operations involving rational numbers can be represented.

UICSM's second course for low-achieving junior high school students is entitled *Motion Geometry*. This course is also contained in four workbooks. The mathematics involves basic motions in the plane such as translations, reflections about a line, and rotations about a point. Symmetry is treated as both line and turn symmetry. These topics are treated in such a way that a high degree of student interest can be maintained. The reading is easy and some of the material is cartoon.

A basic reason why these geometry materials have met with success is that the low-achieving student does not view the mathematics as remedial. The texts call for the use of tracing paper so that students can determine whether various figures are congruent or a given figure has line or turn symmetry. With the use of tracing paper, students can decide whether two figures are slide congruent (one figure can be superimposed on another by a translation) or two figures are flip congruent (one figure can be superimposed on another by a reflection about a line) or the figures are turn congruent (superpositions can be obtained by rotation). Students are involved in extensive physical activity by virtue of tracing figures and manipulating the tracings in appropriate ways.

Figure 12.3

From Peter G. Braunfeld, *Stretchers and Shrinkers, Book 1, The Theory of Stretching Machines* (New York: Harper & Row, 1969), p. 31. Reprinted by permission of the University of Illinois Press.

A program based on performance objectives

From 1963 through 1971 the school system of Baltimore County, Maryland, sponsored a series of summer workshops to create a program appropriate for slow learners. The program in mathematics for grades 7 through 11 is titled *Basic Education in Mathematics*. The teacher's guide for each grade level contains a comprehensive set of behavioral objectives for each topic. The topics in the curriculum and the mathematical competencies specified were significantly influenced by the National Council of Teacher of Mathematics "Second Report of the Commission on Post-War Plans" (1945). The topics include numbers, operations and algorithms, measurement, probability and statistics, graphing, algebra, and geometry. Walbesser's (1972, pp. 78–81) nine action verbs ("name," "identify," "demonstrate," "construct," "describe," "state the rule," "apply the rule," "interpret," "order," "distinguish") were used in constructing the performance objectives for each topic at each grade level. In addition to the objectives, each course guide lists activities for teachers to use in helping students reach the objectives. Suggested evaluation procedures to test student achievement are also included.

In addition to following the guide, teachers are encouraged to divide each class period into bands of time ranging from five to twenty-five minutes. A typical class period includes three bands. First, a class may begin with a five-to-ten-minute drill, review, or puzzle designed to maintain a skill or arouse curiosity. The second segment of class activity, usually lasting from twenty to twenty-five minutes, is directed at the topic being studied. Students are engaged in instructional activities to help them reach the performance objectives. The final band often features individualized student activity. Students may choose to work on some recreational puzzle or obtain help with an individual difficulty, perhaps by using a set of drill and practice activity cards. A number of the mathematical games and activities used in this project have been published in an appendix in the National Council of Teachers of Mathematics Thirty-Fifth Yearbook. The program has not been evaluated by a formal research study, but informal evaluations and reactions to the project by teachers, supervisory personnel, and educators have been favorable.

A laboratory-based program

Many schools have turned toward a laboratory approach to teaching students unsuccessful in learning mathematics. In a laboratory setting students can take surveys and analyze data, use desk calculators, operate filmstrip equipment or slide projectors for drills, measure and manipulate physical objects, and do exercises or solve problems. It is possible for an entire class to be actively involved in a laboratory project, but the majority of mathematics laboratory activities are carried out by small groups of two or three students or by individuals. In addition to audiovisual equipment and standard measuring devices, many mathematics laboratories have physical equipment such as geoboards and Cuisenaire rods, activity cards for using these aids, tangram puzzles, commercial and homemade games involving mathematics, dice, logical and multibase blocks, balances, and prepacked sets of worksheets for sequential skill development.

The teacher's responsibility in a mathematics laboratory is to provide appropriate activities, equipment, and instructions for students. The teacher's role is to diagnose students' needs and provide guidance and assistance as they attempt to follow directions and solve problems. References for using laboratory activities are provided at the conclusion of this chapter.

Thought questions

1   Obtain a copy of a recently published mathematics textbook for very low achievers in junior high school. Compare the features of this textbook with those incorporated in the projects discussed in the preceding section.

2   Discuss how each of the programs described in the preceding section attempts to meet the problems associated with teaching slow learners.

Supplementary materials for slow learners

In this section we shall present specific games, activities, and units of work. Most will emphasize basic computation, a problem for many slow learners. The materials are of minimal reading level and are likely to be novel and interesting. An ingenious teacher can create additional materials for use with slow learners. Activities illustrated below and others can be created without the use of special equipment such as calculators, computer terminals, or special textbooks. In creating games, activities, and various other units, a teacher must decide what mathematics is deemed important. The selection of content for slow learners is probably best based on the principle of utility in nonacademic life. Various lists of mathematical content based on this and other practical considerations have been given by mathematics educators. The most recent list is that of Edwards, Nichols, and Sharpe (1972, pp. 671–677). Once a teacher has selected content, activities can be devised.

References for many of the games and activities mentioned in this section along with suggestions for developing other materials are given at the close of the chapter.

Games

Games can be used for introducing or reviewing content or for recreation. In some cases the same game can be used at different times in all these ways. It is important, however, that the intended purpose of a game be identified by teacher and students. When a game is used for introducing material, the teacher may wish to modify the rules as the game progresses.

The teacher should be in complete control of the direction of the game and thus able to stop it to make comments relative to the subject matter being explored. In games designed to introduce content, winning and losing should be de-emphasized, since the teacher may wish to ask a difficult or "impossible" question and take advantage of student difficulties to analyze the mathematics. In games of this nature, students should not be penalized for errors.

When a game is used to review or provide drill, it is important that students understand all the rules and procedures. It is appropriate to a-ward team or individual points for correct responses. There should be ample opportunities for every student to participate successfully in the game. In using a game as drill, the teacher must be wary of stopping and delaying the game for explanations concerning errors that occur. Some explanation may be necessary when students have misconceptions, but in general lengthy discussions serve only to sacrifice interest in the game. Incorrect answers should be corrected calmly and quickly with emphasis on moving ahead and subsequent questions. It is an excellent idea for teachers to have easy questions at their fingertips for extremely slow or nervous students and for erring students who need to regain points.

When a game is played for enjoyment, the classroom atmosphere can be more relaxed than usual. Teachers may not need to dominate the pro-ceedings or be as strict in controlling student enthusiasm as may be needed in games used for introduction or review. Since games used for recreation are likely to generate enthusiasm and a certain degree of spontaneity, they should be used at the end of a class period. Students particularly enjoy games in which they can challenge the teacher. Winning such a challenge can be an exhilarating experience for a slow learner. Unlike most games used for introduction of content and many games used for drill, recreational games can be played by individual students or by a group of students receiving little supervision. Students who become especially skillful in rec-reational games should be recognized by the teacher.

The commercial game "Stocks and Bonds" can introduce basic pro-ceedings of the stock market. In this game students buy and sell stocks in various companies as the market fluctuates. Students are required to perform a large number of arithmetic operations, and the teacher can provide practice in computation with a game whose primary purpose is entertain-ment in the context of purchasing and trading securities.

An interesting game for two to four participants that incorporates review and practice in dividing is called "The Remainder Game." The playing surface can be a checkerboard or any array of squares on which a path leads to some goal (see Figure 12.4).

Play begins with one player rolling a die (or dice) or by drawing a numbered card and moving a token a number of spaces equal to the re-mainder obtained by dividing the number on his present space on the board by the number on the die or card. For example, a player whose token is on the space numbered 10 will not advance if he throws a 1, 2, or 5. On

Figure 12.4

7 ↗	21	48	60	50	100	47	12	36	5 ↘
10	0 ↗	5	9	48	58	68	20	7 ↘	17
13	12	3 ↗	25	32	48	121	75 ↘	11	18
14	10	11	12 ↗	18	24	5 ↘	13	12	415
15	411	10	10	6 ↗	2 ↘	1	41	17	510
618	511	7	7	21	G	8	51	18	111
215	311	6	4	19 ↖	3 ↙	7	65	115	112
114	13	4	5 ↖	2	6	4	3 ↙	110	310
16	19	1 ↖	4	22	90	87	16	9 ↙	417
8	6 ↖	40	1	0	95	90	85	75	8 ↙

↑
Start

the other hand, a throw of 4 will permit him to move his token two spaces. Players can challenge an opponent's move. If the challenge is upheld, the move is taken back. If the challenge is not sustained, the challenger must move his token backward two spaces. The numbers on the playing surface can be varied. Variations can also be made in the set of divisors and in the rules. For example, it can be stipulated that, in order to reach the goal, the remainder matching the exact number of spaces needed to go out must be obtained. It can also be stipulated that any division by a single-digit divisor must be carried out mentally. This game can be played with numeration systems other than base 10.

A review of mathematics topics can be conducted with a large group of students using games patterned after popular sports. For example, a series of review questions could be constructed with each assigned a difficulty rating of from one to four. Students could be divided into opposing baseball teams and take turns answering questions. A batting order for each team could be determined, with each batter given the option of trying for a single, double, triple, or homerun. The teacher would choose a question with a difficulty of one for a student attempting a single, a question with a difficulty rating of two for a student vying for a double, and so on. A missed question would constitute an out. Additional variations could also be introduced. For example, students could create some of the questions in the game, and the team in the field might be responsible for answering correctly any questions missed by a batter. An incorrect response from a member of the team in the field could constitute an error.

Review activities similar to the baseball game could be patterned after football and basketball contests. Review activities for the entire class can also be conducted in games patterned after "Password" or "Concentration." Commercial games designed to review basic computational facts and operations can be purchased and used with small groups of students. Some of these are mathematical versions of such well-known games as "Scrabble," "Bingo," and "Gin Rummy." Commercial games designed for small groups of mathematics students are usually viewed by students as more recreational than material review. These games are often limited to the arithmetic content typically found in standard fourth-, fifth-, and sixth-grade textbooks.

A modified form of "Twenty Questions" can require that questions be posed by a "panel of experts," a small group of four or five students at the front of the room. The teacher gives the remainder of the class a term denoting a mathematical concept or principle. The panel tries to ascertain the unknown concept or principle by asking questions of the class. In almost every case questions by the experts should be answered by "yes" or "no." Examples of items for the panel to discover are parallelogram, angle bisector, common denominator, the product of two negative numbers as a positive number, and division of two fractions by inverting the divisor and multiplying. If the panel obtains no acceptable form of the desired answer in twenty questions (or some other specified number), they are replaced with another panel and another item of knowledge is chosen. On certain items the teacher may wish to give the panel a hint by identifying the nature of the knowledge in question.

Another format for review begins with the numbering of the seating spaces in the room following a particular pattern. The teacher calls on students to answer previously constructed questions by drawing a seat number out of a collection of numbered objects. If the student answers correctly, no change in the seating arrangement is made. If the student's answer is incorrect, she or he must leave her or his seat to occupy the seat with the largest number. This allows other students to move to the seat with the next lower number. Following this procedure, the student in seat number 1 at the conclusion of the contest is the winner. It is advisable to designate seat numbers other than 1 as winning positions. This keeps students alert, since everyone is always reasonably close to a winning space. Since this game has individual winners, it is easy to award prizes or privileges.

Activities and special lessons

Sometimes interest in mathematics can be generated through special demonstration lessons or activities that are departures from daily routine. Such lessons may be desirable simply because they provide variety and can serve to motivate learning. In general, activities should be selected for their interest to slow learners, their capability for understanding the mathematics in the activity, and the potential utility of the activity for promoting the investigation of additional mathematics.

Computational curiosities and shortcuts can provide several interesting lessons. One involves a "lightning method" of adding sums of five three-digit numbers. The technique is illustrated in the dialogue below:

T   I have discovered a lightning-fast method of adding sums of five three-digit numbers. I want to show it to you and see if you can figure out how it works. You can use it to amaze some of your friends.

S₁   Can we pick the five numbers or do you?

T   You get to pick three of them. I choose the others. You can pick your three numbers all at once and then I pick mine, or we can take turns, you first. Which way would you like to do it?

S₂   Let us pick two of our numbers first. Is that O.K.?

T   Yes. S₃, pick two numbers.

S₃   647 and 792.

T   (*Writes these on the board vertically.*) Fine. Now I'll supply these two numbers. (*Very quickly writes* 207 *and* 352 *on the board under the other numbers.*) S₄, give us a fifth addend.

S₄   849.

T   (*Writes this down.*) The sum is 2,847. Check that, please.

S₅   Hey it works! How did you do that?

The demonstration could continue with the teacher performing other similar "lightning additions" on sets of two-, four-, or five-digit addends. The only requirement is that all the addends have the same number of digits and that there be an odd number of addends, the teacher supplying one less than half the numbers to be combined. The key to performing the additions rapidly is in forming "complementary" addends to those supplied by the students. In the illustration above, the two numbers supplied by the teacher were designed to pair with the two three-digit numbers given by the students, so that each pair of addends totaled 999 ($792 + 207 = 999$ and $647 + 352 = 999$). The sum of the first four addends is 1,998 or $2,000 - 2$. The mental arithmetic performed by the teacher is now reduced to adding 1998 to the fifth addend. This is easily performed by subtracting 2 from whatever number is given by the students and annexing a 2 in the thousands place (providing five three-digit numbers are added). The procedure for performing "lightning additions" with four- or five-digit addends is analogous to the one just described.

Instructional activities that enable students to practice a skill in a novel context are often a welcome alternative. Practicing the plotting of ordered pairs can be an interesting activity when the line segments joining specified sets of ordered pairs form figures or pictures. The following set of ordered pairs forms a picture graph of an automobile when the points are joined, in the order presented, by line segments:

(1,1) (0,1) (0,3) (3,4) (6,4) (7,3) (9,3) (9.5,2.5) (9,2) (9,1) (8,1) (7.5,0) (6.5,0) (7,1) (3,1) (2.5,0) (1.5,0) (1,1)

The designation of the ordered pairs comprising a picture graph need not be the exclusive domain of the teacher. Students enjoy and are often very creative in this enterprise. After a picture graph has been developed, the teacher can have students determine how the elements of each ordered pair should be changed in order to translate (slide) or flip (reflect about a line) the picture to another location in the plane. For example, the picture graph of the automobile could be translated to the second quadrant by appropriately changing the x-values of the coordinates. The graph could also be reflected about the y-axis by leaving the y-values unchanged and taking the negative of each of the original x-values. The students can examine the "effects" of these two motions (the direction the car would appear to be moving and its position on the x-axis). From these observations, other graphs can be drawn and then translated or reflected about a line.

Laboratory activities

Another type of instructional activity places the burden of investigation and discovery primarily in the hands of the students. In recent years the term *laboratory activities* has been applied to assignments that provide small groups or individual students with some type of direction to follow and questions designed to ask them to reflect on given mathematical experiences. An example is finding distances between cities on a globe. The "activity card" or "laboratory worksheet" tells the students to obtain a globe, a string, and a yardstick. The first few steps followed by the students ask them to establish the relation between inches and miles on their particular globe. This could be done by measuring the length of the equator with the string and the yardstick and using the fact that the Earth is very nearly spherical with a circumference of approximately 25,000 miles. Students could be asked to look up this fact or deduce it from a distance given as the radius of the Earth. Having established a relation of perhaps 27.5 inches for 25,000 miles, the students could then be directed to use ratio for converting the inch measurements they can make between various locations on the globe. This laboratory activity presupposes that students are reasonably skilled in setting up and solving proportions.

Many other laboratory experiences can be based on ratio and proportion. Another consists of predicting the number of pennies in a sealed envelope. In addition to the sealed envelope, students are provided with an empty envelope, a few pennies, a balance, and a set of weights. They must determine the weight of the sealed envelope, the weight of an empty envelope, and the weight of a few pennies in order to establish the proportion needed to solve the problem. Other similar problems are to determine the number of paper clips in an envelope or the number of beans in a jar. Such activities promote group work in which students can work in teams to predict unknown quantities. In some cases, rewards can be given to the team with the most accurate result. The reward might be the number of pennies in the envelope. Still other problems solved by proportion are determining in miles per hour how far a person can walk, run, or ride a bicycle, how fast a baseball can be thrown, and how fast a stream is flowing. In each a stopwatch is needed to measure time. Knowing the relevant time and distance, students can solve a simple proportion problem to obtain the desired answer in miles per hour. Slow learners usually enjoy solving such problems because the work is related to their interests and provides them the opportunity to be physically active while gathering data and solving the problem.

Many of the activities mentioned above and a substantial number of additional laboratory exercises for students are described in *The Laboratory Approach to Mathematics* by Kidd, Meyers, and Cilley (1970). This is a comprehensive treatment of the laboratory method of teaching mathematics and should be consulted by teachers planning to use it.

Sometimes activities for slow learners can be centered on various manipulative devices. The geoboard is excellent for lessons exploring and reinforcing mathematical concepts and generalizations. A geoboard can easily be constructed by uniformly distributing a square array of pegs (or nails) over a flat surface (see Figure 12.5). Rubber bands are stretched and anchored across the pegs, forming plane geometric shapes. Using the horizontal or vertical distance between any two pegs as a unit of distance, the area of a square such as *FGHI* in Figure 12.5 as a unit of area, and the Pythagorean theorem, students can find perimeters and areas of regular and irregular figures—for example, polygon *JKLMNOP* in Figure 12.5. Students can also be asked to construct figures of specified length, area, or perimeter. The reader may wish to pause and contemplate how to construct a square of area 2 on the geoboard.

A geoboard is inexpensive and lends itself to dozens of independent explorations. Activity cards directing students to construct shapes or find

Figure 12.5

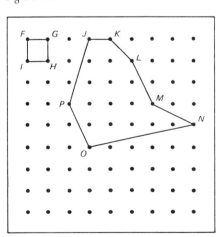

areas, perimeters, and lengths can be created by the teacher or purchased commercially. The following questions and activities are examples of investigations that students can conduct with this device:

Compute the probability of a dart hitting inside a specified area of the geoboard or in one of two given regions.

Construct a triangle of area 3.

Construct a trapezoid of area 5.

Construct rectangles and squares with the same area. Compare their perimeters.

Is it possible to construct a square of area 3 on the geoboard? Of area 5? Of area 8?

There are many activities that students can pursue that require no special equipment. Paper and pencil are all that is needed for students to work crossword puzzles using terminology from mathematics or crossnumber puzzles that require numerals to be placed in the puzzle spaces. Crossnumber puzzles can provide practice for arithmetic and algebraic skills. A number of crossnumber puzzle workbooks are available, but many students enjoy designing their own versions. In fact, it is likely that students will be more interested in creating their own crossnumber puzzles or solving some posed by other students than in working always on puzzles supplied by the teacher.

Units

Mathematics lessons can be constructed around many topics and themes. Building a unit of work around worldly topics of concern to students can help slow learners maintain interest and see the need for mathematical literacy. Jobs, other economic concerns, and sports can provide the basis for developing certain mathematical concepts and skills.

Many students have or are contemplating part-time employment in retail shops or in services. Teachers can capitalize on student interest in after-school or weekend employment by constructing activities involving particular jobs students are likely to hold. Students can employ mathematical knowledge in contemplating ways to spend or save their earnings. In addition to using mathematically related tasks that employers may require such as making change and estimating or computing bills, teachers can have students work with hourly rates, social security and income tax withholding, overtime, employee discounts, taxes, shipping charges, carrying charges, discounts, and interest rates.

Since the mathematics connected with most sports tends to be computational, units constructed around them can provide distributed practice in skills involving the four basic operations with whole numbers and decimals. Rather than massing lessons involving sports into a one-, two-, or three-week period, teachers should consider short units based on particular sports when they are in season. Let us consider some mathematical activities that can be generated from baseball and basketball.

For most baseball players the most vital statistic is a batting average, the three-place decimal computed by dividing the number of base hits obtained by the number of times the player was charged with a time at bat. After demonstrating how a batting average is obtained and discussing its importance in determining a player's value to a team, the teacher can have students compute batting averages of popular professional players. During the baseball season, current data on professional players can be obtained from the newspapers. Batting averages for members of the school team or some local teams can also be calculated.

The position or standing of a team in a league is determined from its winning percentage: the number of victories divided by the number of games played, the quotient being expressed to three decimal places. Given their won-lost records, students can be asked to order by rank a number of teams.

Other statistics commonly figured include a pitcher's winning percentage, a pitcher's earned run average, a batter's slugging percentage, and a player's fielding percentage. After illustrating the computation of these statistics and discussing their significance, assignments in them can allow students to practice computational skills in sports-related contexts. The following questions and activities could be suitable for a series of eighth- or ninth-grade mathematics lessons.

Given a list of players or teams and their appropriate statistics, determine various averages and percentages (see Figure 12.6).

Given the dimensions and seating capacities of various stadiums, students can make scale drawings of the playing fields and answer questions concerning distances and attendances. Some sample questions are given below:

What is the average distance from home plate to the left-field fence in each of the National League parks?

In which park or parks is the centerfield fence farther from home plate than the length of a football field?

Which playing fields appear to be symmetrical?

When the Atlanta Braves play to a full house, how much money do they collect from the sale of tickets if the average ticket is $2.50?

The total home attendance of the St. Louis Cardinals last year for eighty games was 1,200,000 spectators. What was the average attendance for the games? If the average cost of a ticket was $2.75 how much income did the Cardinals receive last year? Did all this money represent profit?

Figure 12.6

Batting records (Fill in the missing figures)

Player	Games	AB	R	H	BB	Avg.
D'Angelo	36	120	45	40	12	?
Washington	28	80	19	24	9	?
Thomas	35	125	49	?	15	.310

Pitching records (Determine each pitcher's winning percentage and earned-run average)

Player	IP	ER	SO	BB	W	L	Pct.	ERA
Evans	50	5	48	16	5	0	?	?
Wilson	40	8	23	4	3	1	?	?

Team standings (Find the missing data)

Team	W	L	Pct.
Southwest High	12	?	.800
Parker Tech	11	4	?
Central High	8	8	?
Carroll High	3	12	?

During the basketball season, mathematics teachers can capitalize on interest in this sport by having students participate in the following activities:

Using encyclopedias students can look up various historical facts and rules concerning the game. They can research the game's origin, inventor, and popularity. The required dimensions of a basketball court, backboards, baskets, and ball itself can be found. Students may be surprised to find that the diameter of the rim is almost large enough to permit two basketballs to pass through at the same time.

Students can make a scale drawing of the school's basketball court.

Students can be asked to calculate the shooting and free-throw percentages for players on the school teams. The figures for calculations can be obtained from the coach or from students appointed to gather data while watching home games.

A bulletin board display of the school teams can be kept current by a group of students. Team statistics and current newspaper clippings can be posted.

After examining the statistics for one of the school's teams, students can be asked to give reasons why the coach may choose to use some players who do not have high score averages. It can be pointed out that some players make their contributions to the team with their defensive ability or with their ability to obtain rebounds. Another player may earn his place on the team because of his ability to lead the team and make accurate passes to set up scores for other players.

Determining scores and team totals in bowling and track requires students to pay careful attention to scoring procedures and to calculate with fractional numbers. In bowling, the scoring for any given frame can depend on a bowler's performance in subsequent frames. In team bowling, handicaps have to be determined by the use of a fractional constant. In track, fractional points must be awarded in the event of ties. Ties rarely occur in running events, but they appear frequently in field events such as high jump and the pole vault. Activities for mathematics classes stemming from bowling and track could include scoring of hypothetical or actual games and meets.

Most sports have a wealth of statistics, records, and facts that can be gathered and analyzed. Probably the best single periodical source of statistical information for professional baseball, basketball, football, and hockey is *The Sporting News*. A unit based on graphs can use various displays that appear in newspapers and magazines. Students can obtain meaning from various published graphs and reports and evaluate claims by commercial and government concerns. One possible series of activities for a beginning unit on graphing is described below:

At the completion of a unit on graphs students should be able to:
1   Read and answer questions about bar, line, and figure graphs that appear in newspapers and magazines
2   Make frequency tables from graphs found in newspapers and magazines or from data given in class
3   Construct a bar, line, or figure graph from a frequency table or from another graph

The teacher could begin the unit by distributing copies of graphs taken from a local newspaper article or a magazine of interest to the students. Once the teacher believes the students have competence in reading and interpreting the graphs, data can be presented from which other graphs can be constructed. Discussions about frequency tables and other statistical notions would be appropriate. Following the construction of different kinds of graphs from given data, the teacher might ask each student to construct a graph on a topic of the student's choice.

An extensive treatment of different kinds of graphs could include the development of such concepts as mode, median, average, and percentile. Data for graphs could be obtained from sports, economics, politics, and field trips to businesses, shops, and so on. Students can go on fact-finding missions to obtain data.

One source of hundreds of excellent ideas, games, activities, and projects is the group of booklets produced for the Central Iowa Low

Achiever Mathematics Project (CILAMP) under the auspices of a U. S. Office of Education grant and available at cost through the ERIC Document Reproduction Service (EDRS) on microfiche and in a "hard" copy. Another extensive set of curriculum materials, produced under the Federal Elementary and Secondary Education Act, are the booklets produced in West Palm Beach, Florida, by Foley et al. These are also available through EDRS and in a commercial version under the title *Individualizing Mathematics*.

Thought questions

1   In working with slow learners, why is it sometimes advisable to play recreational games near the end of a class period?

2   Obtain a textbook designed for slow learners, select a chapter in it, and make a list of words that would be used in playing the game of "Password."

3   Using the same chapter, write a set of questions that could be used to play baseball as described on page 348.

4   In making the playing surface for "Remainder," what set of numbers would make it impossible for students to advance a token with a single die? Does this mean that these numbers should not be used on the playing surface?

5   Describe an activity that would involve ratio and proportion in the context of kitchen recipes.

6   Discuss the advantages and disadvantages of the following types of laboratory activity for slow learners:
    a   Activities that give the students step-by-step procedures for using equipment and answering questions. A list of the necessary equipment is provided along with diagrams for all the written instructions.
    b   Activities that pose a question for students to resolve. Students must formulate their own workable plan, obtain the teacher's approval, and take the steps necessary to arrive at a solution. The teacher may provide clarification, answers, and some assistance.
    Examples of questions that could be answered in *a* or *b* include: How high is the campus flagpole? The ceiling of the gym? How fast can you run 50 yards? How many drops of water would be needed to fill this room? Find the cost of wall-to-wall carpet for this room. Is it safer to travel by car or by plane?

7   Do some of the geoboard activites mentioned in this chapter. Create three additional activities or questions for use with a geoboard. They should be geared for the slow learner.

8   Develop a dialogue illustrating the "lightning method" of addition with seven four-digit addends.

9   The following question could be posed for slow learners familiar with the lightning method of addition:

    Suppose you are trying to impress a friend with your speed in adding five four-digit numbers. Your friend has selected the numbers 3,162, 5,193, and 6,182. What remaining numbers could you select and what will the sum be?

    Design other similar questions relating to the lightning method. Why might it be advantageous for slow learners to impress their friends with this computation gimmick?

10   Describe activities involving translations and reflections that slow learners might use with picture graphs.

11   In determining the number of pennies in a sealed envelope, must the weights used with the balance be standard weights? Discuss your answer.

12   How are ratio and proportion used in determining the number of pennies in a sealed envelope?

13   In the discussion concerning the use of sports for generating mathematics lessons we cited a number of sports-related statistics as being useful in getting students to practice computational skills. We mentioned that teachers should point out the significance of each statistic as well as demonstrate the necessary computation procedures. Why was this recommendation made? Do you agree with it?

14   What arithmetic skills are involved in computing a baseball player's batting average?

15   Create a list of activities for slow learners that centers on football and its statistics. Your list might include average yards gained per carry for a halfback and the quarterback's pass-completion percentage. Where might data for the activities be obtained?

16   In mathematics the terms *average* and *percentage* refer to different concepts. In sports, these terms are often used interchangeably. Compare and contrast the meanings associated with these terms. How much of a distinction would you make for slow learners? Justify your position.

17   Suppose you are teaching a series of lessons based on a particular sport to a class of slow learners in grade 9. The boys seem quite interested in the material, but many of the girls are uninterested and disdainful. What could you do to kindle their interest in the unit? What are some topics that could serve as the basis of a series of mathematics lessons of interest primarily to adolescent girls?

18   Construct a quiz appropriate for slow learners completing the unit on graphs described in this chapter. It should be based on the objectives stated at the beginning of the unit and should include questions requiring different levels of cognition.

Self-test on the competencies

1   Characterize behaviors common to many slow learners and offer reasons why they occur.
    Identify characteristics of slow learners that generally differentiate them from average and above-average students and provide a plausible explanation why some students develop these characteristics.

2   Suggest guidelines for working with slow learners.
    State guidelines for working with slow learners and suggest techniques that can be used to achieve them.

3   Describe programs, games, activities, and units that can be used in teaching mathematics to slow learners.

    a   Select two curriculum projects described in this chapter and discuss how they can help teachers deal with some of the problems associated with teaching slow-learning students.

    b   Select a game, an activity, and one of the proposed units and dicuss how these also can help teachers deal with some of the problems associated with teaching slow-learning students.

References

Ausubel, David P. *Educational Psychology, A Cognitive View.* New York: Holt, Rinehart and Winston, 1968. Chs. 7 and 13.

Bassler, Otto C., and John R. Kolb. *Learning to Teach Secondary School Mathematics.* Scranton: Intext Educational Publishers, 1971. Ch. 17.

Begle, E. G. "Some Lessons Learned by SMSG." *The Mathematics Teacher*, 66 (1973), 207–214.

Braunfeld, Peter, Clyde Dilley, and Walter Rucker. "A New UICSM Approach to Fractions for the Junior High School." *The Mathematics Teacher*, 60 (1967), 215–221.

Braunfeld, Peter, and Martin Wolfe. "Fractions for Low Achievers (Stretchers and Shrinkers)." *The Arithmetic Teacher*, 13 (1966), 647–655.

Chandler, Arnold M. "Mathematics and the Low Achiever." *The Arithmetic Teacher*, 17 (1970), 196–198.

Commission on Post-War Plans. "The Second Report of the Commission on Post-War Plans." *The Mathematics Teacher*, 36 (1945), 195–221.

Edwards, E. L., Jr., Eugene Nichols, and Glyn H. Sharpe. "Mathematical Competencies and Skills Essential for Enlightened Citizens." *The Mathematics Teacher*, 65 (1972), 671–677.

Esposito, Dominick. "Homogeneous and Heterogeneous Ability Grouping: Principal Findings and Implications for Evaluating and Designing More Effective Educational Environments." *Review of Educational Research*, 43 (1973), 163–179.

Findley, Warren G., and Miriam M. Bryan. *Ability Grouping: 1970 Status, Impact and Alternatives.* Athens, Ga.: Center for Educational Improvement, University of Georgia, 1971.

Garf, David. "Some Techniques in Handling a Slow Class in Elementary Algebra." *The Mathematics Teacher*, 65 (1972), 591–594.

Gibb, E. Glenadine. "Mathematics in Baseball." *The Mathematics Teacher*, 45 (1952), 35–36.

Ginott, Hiam G. *Between Parent and Child.* New York: Macmillan, Chs. 1–5. 1965.

Greenholtz, Sarah. "Successful Practices in Teaching Mathematics to Low Achievers in Senior High School." *The Mathematics Teacher*, 60 (1967), 329–335.

———, and Mildred Keiffer. "Never Underestimate the Inner-City Child." *The Mathematics Teacher*, 63 (1970), 587–595.

———. "What's New in Teaching Slow Learners in Junior High School?" *The Mathematics Teacher*, 57 (1964), 522–528.

Holton, Boyd. "Motivation and General Math Students." *The Mathematics Teacher*, 57 (1964), 20–25.

Johnson, Donovan A., Gerald R. Rising. *Guidelines for Teaching Mathematics.* Belmont, Calif.: Wadsworth, 1972. Ch. 20.

Kidd, Kenneth P., Shirley Meyers, and David M. Cilley. *The Laboratory Approach to Mathematics.* Chicago: Science Research Associates, 1970.

National Council of Teachers of Mathematics, *The Slow Learner in Mathematics*, Thirty-Fifth Yearbook. Washington D. C.: The Council, 1972.

Pikaart, Len, and James W. Wilson. "The Research Literature." *The Slow Learner in Mathematics*, National Council of Teachers of Mathematics Thirty-Fifth Yearbook. Washington, D. C.: The Council, 1972. Ch. 2.

Rosenthal, Robert, and Lenore F. Jacobson. "Teacher Expectations for the Disadvantaged." *Scientific American*, 218 (1968), 19–22.

Ryan, Kevin, ed. *Don't Smile Until Christmas*. Chicago: University of Chicago Press, 1970.

Schulz, Richard W. "Characteristics and Needs of the Slow Learner." *The Slow Learner in Mathematics*, National Council of Teachers of Mathematics Thirty-Fifth Yearbook. Washington, D. C.: The Council, 1972. Ch. 1.

Sobel, Max. *Teaching General Mathematics*. Englewood Cliffs, N. J.: Prentice-Hall, 1967.

Thorndike, R. L. "Review of Pygmalion in the Classroom." *American Educational Research Journal*, 5 (1968), 708–711.

Travers, Kenneth J., John W. LeDuc, and Garth E. Runion. *Teaching Resources For Low-Achieving Mathematics Classes*. Columbus, Ohio: ERIC Information Analysis Center for Science and Mathematics Education, 1971. Contains extensive bibliography.

Walbesser, Henry H., and Heather L. Carter. "Behavioral Objectives." *The Slow Learner in Mathematics*, National Council of Teachers of Mathematics Thirty-Fifth Yearbook. Washington, D. C.: The Council, 1972. Ch. 3.

Wells, David W., and Albert P. Shulte. "An Example of Planning for Low Achievers." *The Teaching of Secondary School Mathematics*, National Council of Teachers of Mathematics Thirty-Third Yearbook. Washington, D. C.: The Council, 1970.

Mathematics curriculum projects for the slow learner

In addition to the projects listed here, the National Council of Teachers of Mathematics Thirty-Fifth Yearbook (pp. 345–401) contains reports and references to approximately thirty other mathematics projects for the slow learner. References below to *The Slow Learner* are to this work.

Brant, Vincent. "Mathematics for Basic Education (Grades 7–11)." *The Slow Learner*.

DeVenney, William S. "SMSG Programs for Low-Achieving Junior High School Students." *The Slow Learner*.

———. *Final Report on an Experiment with Junior High School Very Low Achievers in Mathematics*, SMSG Report No. 7. Stanford: School Mathematics Study Group, 1969.

Herriot, Sarah T. *The Slow Learner Project: The Secondary School "Slow Learner" in Mathematics*, SMSG Report No. 5. Stanford: School Mathematics Study Group, 1967.

Mendelsohn, Melvin. "Computer-Assisted Instruction in New York City." *The Slow Learner*.

Scott, Jessie L. "Chicago's Attempts to Meet the Needs of the Inner-City Child via Math Labs." *The Slow Learner*.

Units and courses of study

Activities in Mathematics—First Course (Patterns, Numbers, Measurement, Probability). Donovan A. Johnson et al. Available from Scott, Foresman, 1971.

Activities in Mathematics—Second Course (Graphs, Statistics, Proportions, Geometry). Donovan A. Johnson et al. Available from Scott, Foresman, 1971.

Haines, Margaret. "Modular Arithmetic." *The Arithmetic Teacher*, 9 (1962), 122–126.

Individualizing Mathematics (Skills and Patterns Series—Patterns and Discovery Series). Jack Foley et al. Available from Addison-Wesley, 1970, 1971.

Lingo, Margaret. "Some Family Finance Topics for Seventh- and Eighth-Grade Math." *The Mathematics Teacher*, 51 (1958), 128–130.

Lyda, W. J., and Margaret D. Taylor. "Facilitating an Understanding of the Decimal Numeration System Through Modular Arithmetic." *The Arithmetic Teacher*, 11 (1964), 101–103.

Motion Geometry (Book 1—Slides, Flips and Turns; Book 2—Congruence; Book 3—Symmetry; Book 4—Constructions, Area, and Similarity). Jo McKeeby Phillips and Russell E. Zwoyer. New York: Harper & Row, 1969.

National Council of Teachers of Mathematics. *Experiences in Mathematical Ideas.* Washington, D. C.: The Council. Vols. 1 and 2.

———. *Experiences in Mathematical Discovery.* Washington, D. C.: The Council. Units 1–9.

Stretchers and Shrinkers (Book 1—The Theory of Stretching Machines; Book 2—Advanced Topics in Stretching and Shrinking; Book 3—The Theory of Fractions; Book 4—Decimals). Peter G. Braunfeld, O. Robert Brown, Jr., and L. Rowland Genise. New York: Harper & Row, 1969.

The following units of study are available from ERIC Document Reproduction Service (EDRS). They may be ordered from

Leasco Information Products. Inc.
4827 Rugby Ave.
Bethesda, Maryland   20014
Phone: (303) 657-3316

by using a six-digit number with an ED prefix. They are available in Microfiche (MF) or paperback (HC). Microfiche copies are relatively inexpensive (usually less than one dollar). Paperback copies vary in cost according to the number of pages. Current price listings are available from the vendor.

Basic Mathematics I for the Secondary Schools by Charles T. McCarthy. Board of Education City of Chicago. ED   001   913. 157 pp.

Central Iowa Low Achiever Mathematics Project (CILAMP) Materials:
   Math in Sports. ED   025   432. 67 pp.
   A List of "Gimmicks" for Use With Junior High School Students. ED   018   389. 97 pp.
   Measurement. ED   025   431. 88 pp.
   ESP. ED   025   437. 64 pp.
   Low-Achiever Motivational Project. ED   025   433. 145 pp.

ESEA Title III Project Mathematics by Jack L. Foley et al., West Palm Beach, Florida:

   Action with Fractions, Addition, and Subtraction. ED   020   897. 34 pp.
   Action with Fractions Is Contained in Division. ED   024   565. 15 pp.
   Action with Whole Numbers. ED   020   896. 59 pp.
   Angles, Measures. ED   020   895. 35 pp.
   Curves, Vertices, Knots, and Such. ED   020   894. 65 pp.

Divisibility Tests. ED   020   893. 34 pp.
Events and Chance. ED   021   732. 15 pp.
Ideas from Number Theory. ED   020   891. 45 pp.
Integers, Addition, and Subtraction. ED   021   727. 23 pp.
Maneuvers on a Geoboard, ED   020   887. 23 pp.
The Math Go-round, A Unit of Mathasborg. ED   020   888. 29 pp.
Metric Geometry, Concepts of Area and Measure. ED   020   892. 37 pp.
Metric Geometry, Linear Measure. ED   020   890. 49 pp.
Modulo Seven. ED   021   730. 16 pp.
Numeration Systems, Past and Present. ED   021   729. 26 pp.
Patterns, Particulars and Guesses. ED   021   725. 25 pp.
Per Cent Fractions. ED   020   886. 38 pp.
Sets, Subsets, and Operations. ED   020   885. 37 pp.
Similarity. ED   021   731. 53 pp.
Square Roots, Right Triangles. ED   021   728. 30 pp.
Volume and Surface Area. ED   020   889. 30 pp.

Reports available through EDRS

Herriot, Sarah T. *The Slow Learner Project: The Secondary School "Slow Learner" in Mathematics.* SMSG Report No. 5. Palo Alto: School Mathematics Study Group, 1967. ED   021   755. 168 pp.

Layer, Nathan. *Learning Laboratory to Teach Basic Skills in a Culturally Deprived Area (Final Report).* Miami: Booker T. Washington Junior-Senior High School, 1968. ED   033   186. 33 pp.

Richmond, Ruth K. *Instructional Guide for Basic Mathematics I, Grades 10 to 12.* Los Angeles: 1966. ED   016   623. 34 pp.

Small, Dwain E., et al. *The Problems of Under Achievement and Low Achievement in Mathematics Education.* Gainesville, Fla.: University of Florida, 1966. ED   010   535. 88 pp.

Woodby, L. G., ed. *The Low Achiever in Mathematics.* ED   030   678. Only MF available. 94 pp.

Books and articles on mathematics laboratories

Berger, Emil J., ed. "Devices for a Mathematics Laboratory." *The Mathematics Teacher,* **44** (1951), **45** (1952), and **46** (1953). All issues.
———. "Devices for the Mathematics Classroom." *The Mathematics Teacher,* **47** (1954), **48** (1955), and **49** (1956). All issues.

Davidson, Patricia S. "The Laboratory Approach." *The Slow Learner.* Contains a bibliography of 161 books, articles, journals, films, manipulative materials, activity cards, and computation kits.
———. "An Annotated Bibliography of Suggested Manipulative Devices." *The Arithmetic Teacher,* **15** (1968), 509–524.
———. "A Mathematics Laboratory—From Dream to Reality." *The Arithmetic Teacher,* **17** (1970), 105–110.

Greenes, Carole E., Robert E. Willcutt, and Mark A. Spikell. *Problem-Solving in the Mathematics Laboratory: How to Do It.* Boston: Prindle, Weber & Schmidt, 1972.

Kidd, Kenneth P., Shirley Meyers, and David M. Cilley. *The Laboratory Approach to Mathematics*. Chicago: Science Research Associates, 1970.

Reys, Robert E., and Thomas R. Post. *The Mathematics Laboratory: Theory to Practice*. Boston: Prindle, Weber & Schmidt, 1973.

Schaeffer, Anne W., and Albert H. Mathe. "Problem-Solving with Enthusiasm—The Mathematics Laboratory." *The Arithmetic Teacher*, 17 (1970), 7–14.

Sweet, Raymond. "Organizing a Mathematics Laboratory." *The Mathematics Teacher*, 60 (1967), 117–120.

Activities and games for teaching mathematics

"Activities, Games, and Applications." Thomas E. Rowan and William G. McKenzie. *The Slow Learner*. Appendix A.

Brandes, Louis Grant. *4 The Math Wizard*. Portland, Me: J. Weston Walch, 1962.

Central Iowa Low Achiever Mathematics Project. Des Moines, Iowa. See EDRS listings under Units and Courses of Study.

Cutler, Ann, and McShane Rudolph trans. *The Trachtenberg Speed System of Mathematics*. New York: Doubleday, 1960.

Gorts, Jeannie. "Magic Square Patterns." *The Arithmetic Teacher*, 16 (1969), 314–316.

Hewitt, Frances. "4 × 4 Magic Squares." *The Arithmetic Teacher*, 9 (1962) 392–395.

Liedtke, Werner. "What Can You Do with a Geoboard?" *The Arithmetic Teacher*, 16 (1969), 491–493.

McCombs, Wayne E. "Four-by-Four Magic Square for the New Year." *The Arithmetic Teacher*, 17 (1970), 79–80.

Secret Codes. Washington, D.C.: National Council of Teachers of Mathematics, 1961.

Yates, William E. "The Trachtenberg System as a Motivational Device." *The Arithmetic Teacher*, 13 (1966), 677–678.

Many activities and games are available from a variety of commercial sources. Principal vendors are:

Creative Publications
P.O. Box 10328
Palo Alto, Calif.   94303

Midwest Publications Co., Inc.
P.O. Box 129
Troy, Mich.   48084

The Math Shop
5 Bridge St.
Watertown, Mass.   02172

We suggest that interested individuals write for catalogues. A sampling of such items follows:

A Cloudburst of Math Lab Experiments, Donald Buckeye, William Eubank, and John Ginther. Available from Midwest Publishing Company and The Math Shop.

Aftermath Series (*Books 1–4*). Dale Seymour, et al. Available from Creative Publications and The Math Shop.

Creative Constructions. Dale Seymour and Reuben Schadler. Available from Creative Publications and The Math Shop.

Crossnumber Puzzles (Books I and II). Available from Creative Publications and The Math Shop.

Daily Chores. Chuck Allen. Available from Creative Publications and The Math Shop.

Eureka (Challenges and Curiosities). Dale Seymour and Dick Gidley. Available from Creative Publications and The Math Shop.

Geoboard Geometry and Geoboard Activity Sheets. Available from Creative Publications and The Math Shop.

Graph Gallery. Pat Boyle. Available from Creative Publications and The Math Shop.

Math Activity Worksheet Masters. Mary Laycock and William T. Stokes. Available from Creative Publications and The Math Shop.

Mathimagination. Steve Marcy and Janis Marcy. Available from Creative Publications and The Math Shop.

Money Matters. Linda Silvey. Available from Creative Publications and The Math Shop.

Games for teaching mathematics

Block It! (Addition and multiplication combinations). Creative Publications, The Math Shop.

Bibliography of Recreational Mathematics, Washington, D. C.: National Council of Teachers of Mathematics. Vol. 1 (1965) and vol. 2 (1973).

Games and Aids for Teaching Math. Mikki Schreiner. Creative Publications, The Math Shop.

Mancala (A Game of Logic). Creative Publications, The Math Shop.

Number Sentence Games. Dale Seymour, Margaret Holla, and Nancy Collins. Creative Publications, The Math Shop.

Numble (Crossword Type Number Games). Creative Publications, The Math Shop.

Numo (Bingo-type Games Emphasizing Arithmetic Facts and Relationships). Kenneth Kidd. Midwest Publishing Co., The Math Shop.

Prime Drag (Prime and Composite Numbers). Creative Publications, The Math Shop.

Ranko (Ordering and Sequencing). Kenneth Kidd. Midwest Publishing Co., The Math Shop.

Tuf (Equations). Creative Publications, Sigma Scientific, The Math Shop.

Sports information

The Sporting News. 1212 N. Lindbergh Blvd., St. Louis, Missouri   63131

13

Teaching students of high ability

Professional journals and professional meetings make one aware of general concern for students of high ability in mathematics. The case for special attention to them is similar to that for special attention to students of low ability. Our national ethic requires that all students, regardless of physical or intellectual endowment, race, religion, or socio-economic background, have the right to education of optimal benefit to themselves and society. This philosophical position is often expressed by the phrase "equality of educational opportunity," where "equality" means not identical education but adaptation to ability and needs.

Moreover, society faces problems of wise use of natural resources, prevention and treatment of disease, management of economy, provision of food, treatment of waste, communication, and protection, and the solutions depend on science and technology. Basic to both, mathematics contains models that permit explanation and control of them. Research in mathematics leads to the development of new and more powerful models. We must cultivate human resources that promise advancement in applied and in pure mathematics. Students of high ability in mathematics represent such human resource.

We shall consider in this chapter what can be done for such students. We begin with a discussion of how to identify them, paying particular attention to characteristics that allow early identification. We turn then to special provisions, considering institutional provisions first. For example, special schools in some large cities teach the intellectually talented. Within other secondary schools, ability grouping and special curricula have been established. Special summer programs have been organized. Institutional arrangements are not always possible, however, particularly in small schools, and we turn to the second kind of special provision for students of high ability in mathematics: classes of small size. Finally, we consider the teacher vis-à-vis the student of high ability. How does a teacher cope with a student who may be much more able in mathematics than the teacher? What are some desirable characteristics of a teacher of high ability students? We shall attempt to answer these questions.

> At the conclusion of this chapter, you should be able to demonstrate the following competencies:
>
> 1 State characteristics of students who indicate high potential in mathematics
>
> 2 Suggest possible institutional arrangements to insure adequate education for students of high ability in mathematics
>
> 3 Offer suggestions for what a mathematics teacher of a few able students can do to adapt instruction for them

Identifying students of high ability

From one point of view a student of high ability is one who makes high grades. One difficulty with identifying students this way is that it may result in selecting some students who really do not have high potential. A teacher who sets low expectations will have many students of "high ability." A teacher whose tests reward only students who memorize readily and not those who understand and can apply knowledge to solve problems will find the wrong kind of student of "high ability." A teacher who is greatly impressed by politeness, diligence, conformance, attention, neatness, or regularity of attendance may also misjudge qualities of high potential.

Furthermore, students who actually have high potential but exhibit behavior problems and annoy the teacher, daydream, do not do all the drill problems, or show a distaste for school may be overlooked as mathematically able. Such characteristics may be symptoms of a bright student consciously or unconsciously manifesting frustration with monotonous routine, slow pace, and lack of challenge in the mathematics being taught. When such students are judged without further evidence as necessarily lacking in talent, many bright ones are missed.

Assuming that teachers set reasonable expectations, recognize a hierarchy of intellectual endeavor, and are perceptive in evaluation of students, the students who do well in their classes probably have high ability. It is possible to study them to ascertain the characteristics that distinguish them. These characteristics can be used as the bases of prognostic tests that identify students of high potential before teaching actually begins.

High-ability students have excellent memories, but this by itself is not a specific determiner of high potential in mathematics. Tests that assess only recall or recognition do not identify only students of high potential. Students of high ability are verbally facile. They have large vocabularies and readily understand what they read. They speak easily; their writing is cogent, logical, and insightful (though not necessarily grammatically correct). But tests of general intellectual aptitude, assessing what students have been given an opportunity to learn, not what has been deliberately taught, do not sort out only students who have special ability in mathematics. It is generally agreed that paper-and-pencil tests alone are not valid indicators of mathematical potential. They have to be supplemented by judgments of teachers who can observe students studying mathematics and can report on characteristics not readily amenable to measurement.

Students of high ability in mathematics are quick to learn. When they are sufficiently motivated, little clarification is necessary. They readily determine the meaning of symbols, sentences, and implications. They are also intuitive. They seem able to choose solutions that work. When asked why they have chosen particular methods, they appear not to have arrived at them deductively: "I just had a feeling that it ought to work," they say. They have a talent for viewing problems from new angles and developing hunches about how they can be solved. They have intellectual curiosity and persist in asking questions, particularly "why?" They manifest eagerness to investigate topics and relations out of the mainstream of the content of a course. They show a strong desire to understand and make sure they see relations between new knowledge and knowledge they already have. They continue the study of mathematics on their own, being often one or more chapters in the textbook ahead of the class or reading advanced texts borrowed from the library and adults.

The committee of the National Council of Teachers of Mathematics listed in *Program Provisions for the Mathematically Gifted Student in the Secondary School* the following observable characteristics of able students (1957, p. 20):

1 Are sincerely interested in mathematics and seem to have fun studying it

2 Are not satisfied with a minimum discussion of a topic but ask questions which indicate they are thinking ahead and are curious about what follows

3 See the relationships between different parts of their mathematics and think in terms of basic principles, not isolated examples

4 Show originality in their thinking and are not just regurgitating what they have been reading and hearing

5 Are able to express themselves clearly in well-organized logical form, both orally and in writing

6 Can work independently and carry through a job with a minimum of guidance, both in regularly assigned work and in individual special projects

In the interest of science education in keeping with the abilities of gifted students, Brandwein published (1955) the results of his ten-year study of 31 working scientists, from graduate students to researchers at the highest levels, 431 boys and girls who indicated they were interested in science as a career, 263 college freshmen who were the subjects of a study of the stability of science interests, 201 students who were subjects in a program to ascertain whether high ability can be predicted by tests, and 82 teachers with clearly established reputations for stimulating students of high ability. Brandwein's conclusions seem plausible when generalized to students of mathematics. Brandwein identified three factors, the inter-relationship of which characterizes gifted science students. One is what he called (p. 9) *genetic factors:* "They have a relationship to high intelligence and *may* have a *primary* basis in heredity." He identified in this category high verbal ability, both oral and written, high ability in mathematics, and adequate sensory and neuromuscular control. These factors appear to set limits to development. How close to these limits a student develops depends on environmental stimulation—that is, informal and formal education.

Genetic factors are not sufficient for high ability, however, as is in-dicated by individuals who possess them yet do not attain distinction in science. High ability is marked also by what Brandwein designates as *predisposing factors:* persistence, evidenced by willingness to spend time beyond the ordinary in accomplishing tasks, willingness to withstand discomfort (no lunch, no holidays, fatigue, strain, working even when beset with illness), and willingness to face failure. Another factor is what Brand-wein terms *questing:* general dissatisfaction with easy explanations. Authority and scholarship are not rejected, but neither are they accepted without ques-tion. Curiosity characterizes questing—asking "How?" and "Why?"—or, as Brandwein (p. 11) expresses these questions, the three perennials: What do we know? How do we know what we know? and How well do we know what we know? Persistence and questing, additional conditions necessary for talent, predispose students who already rank high in genetic factors to make maximum use of their talent.

The third factor Brandwein speaks of as the *activating factor*. In con-trast to the others, this is largely "outside" the student. It comprises oppor-tunities for advanced training and contact with an inspiring teacher. The activating factor calls the other two into play; in the popular idiom, it "turns students on." Brandwein's hypothesis is that all these factors are necessary; no one is sufficient. Their interaction becomes sufficient.

There is an erroneous belief that students exceptional in some respects are necessarily deficient in others, that intellectually talented students are weak physically. Leta Hollingworth (1929) found that gifted students tend to be well-proportioned, physically vigorous, and in good health. Another fallacious belief is that brilliant students are nervous or maladjusted. In fact, they associate readily with other students, and enjoy their company, and often attain positions of leadership. Geniuses in mathematics do not "burn themselves out" later in their academic careers or regress to mediocrity or psychosis. It is true that for each misconception one can find an individual whose characteristics support it, but as generalizations, the misconceptions are false. When talented students go wrong, it is the fault of environment rather than some law of nature offsetting brilliance with mediocrity in others.

Thought questions

1   Why is the grade in a mathematics course not necessarily a valid predictor in identifying students of high potential ? Why is the score on a general academic aptitude test (a so-called I.Q. test) not necessarily a valid predictor ?

2   Choose some test of general academic aptitude, analyze its items, and determine what abilities are assessed.

3   Suppose you were charged with developing a test to select students of high potential in mathematics. What items would you put in it ? For each of the various kinds of item you would use, write two items as examples.

4   Educational psychologists speak of underachievers, students whose actual performance in class is less than what would be expected from their scores on aptitude tests, and overacheivers, whose actual performance in class is higher than what would be expected from such scores. Suppose the score of an underachiever on a mathematical aptitude test ranks with the scores of students of high ability. Should this student be regarded as having high ability ? Suppose the score of an overachiever on the same test ranks below the scores of students of high ability. Should this student be regarded as having high ability ?

Institutional arrangements for students of high ability

Differential arrangements in school provide specialized attention to students of high ability in mathematics. These may be within a particular school, as when special classes are arranged, or within a school system, as in a special high school for academically talented students. We shall consider some of these institutional practices.

Ability grouping

The most common institutional practice for caring for students of high ability is to group them into classes of advanced subject matter and special methods of teaching. Selection of students is based typically on standardized tests and teacher judgment. Grade placement may be the same for these students as for students in regular classes while course content is altered to stimulate the more able students. Thus, in an algebra course in the ninth grade, for example, the content covered by ordinary students is covered more rapidly by the advanced ones, who also study additional topics.

This has the advantage of allowing students originally placed in special classes to transfer into regular classes if it is found that selection was in error or if the students decide that they do not enjoy instruction in the special classes.

In contrast to differentiating the mathematics courses while maintaining the same grade placement is the practice of accelerating the coverage of content by placing it earlier in the grades. Able students are thus identified in the elementary school and given an accelerated seventh-grade mathemathics course as their first course in junior high school. This prepares them for the first course in algebra in the eighth grade. In some schools, a second course in algebra is presented in the ninth grade and a geometry course combining two- and three-space geometry is presented in the tenth. In other schools, this order is reversed. But whichever order is used, the students in the regular courses follow it too. In the eleventh grade, there may be a one-semester course in trigonometry and another in college algebra or a one-year course in analysis that includes trigonometry and analytic geometry. For the twelfth grade, there may be calculus, elective courses in calculus, matrix algebra, finite mathematics, probability and statistics, or computer science.

A sequence of courses in mathematics intended for students of high ability has been developed by the Secondary School Mathematics Curriculum Improvement Study (SSMCIS). SSMCIS gathered distinguished mathematicians from various countries for conferences on the selection and sequence of subject matter for secondary school courses in mathematics. It became possible thus to draw on the experience of Belgium, France, Switzerland, and West Germany in experimental curriculum development. This group of consultants determined the broad outlines of a curriculum, and writers knowledgeable about mathematics and sensitive to the maturation of secondary school students wrote the text materials to implement the design developed by the consultants. These experimental text materials were subsequently tried in schools and revised in light of what was found. Howard Fehr (1968, p. 667), the director of SSMCIS, described the scope of the program of studies in secondary school mathematics:

> The number system of the cardinals, the integers, the rationals, the reals, and the complex; the structure of the group, the ring, the field, the ordered field, and the algebraic-geometric (or geometric-algebraic) structure of vector spaces and their linear algebra. In each of these structures one investigates the properties of the operations, the expressions and functions on the set of elements, the solution of sentences (equations, inequations, with absolute values, etc.), gradually developing these notions in a formal algebra of functions and formal solutions of sentences, once the real-number field has been obtained. Probability with statistical inference, the calculus, and elementary numerical analysis, provide a fitting and satisfying climax for the last years of secondary-school study.

The following two chapter sequences are examples of the implementation of this concept by SSMCIS for the first two courses in mathematics.

Course 1 Seventh Grade

1 Finite number systems, clock arithmetics, $(Z_m, +), (Z_m, \cdot)$

2 Sets and operations, operational systems $(Z_m, +, \cdot), (W, +, \cdot)$

3 Mappings, $W \to W$ and points to points, translations

4 Integers, addition, a group $(Z, +)$

5 Probability and statistics, relative frequency and graphs

6 Integers, multiplication, a ring $(Z, +, \cdot, <)$, dilations

7 Lattice points in a plane and $Z \times Z$

8 Sets and relations, equivalence, arrow diagrams

9 Transformations of the plane, reflections, translations, rotations

10 Segments, angles, measure, isometries, triangle sum of angles

11 Elementary number theory, divisibility, Euclid's algorism, factor-ization

12 Rational numbers, infinite decimals, a field $(Q, +, \cdot, <)$

13 Applications of rational numbers, ratio, proportion, percent, group of translations

14 Flow-charting mathematical processes (a review of all algorisms)

Course 2 Eighth Grade

1 Mass-point geometry, preparation for axiomatic methods.

2 Structure on sets of sets, power sets

3 Groups (a more formal study), groups of permutations

4 Affine plane geometry, first introduction to axiomatics, models

5 Descriptive statistics, notation, mean, standard deviation (variance)

6 Fields and real numbers, the real-number line

7 Coordinate geometry, from affine to the Euclidean plane, Pythgorean theorem, cosine, triangle inequalities, vectors

8 Real functions, algebra of functions, linear, quadratic, and linear systems of equations

9 Transformations in the plane, rigid motions, triangle congruence

10 Combinatorics, binomial theorem, probability

11 Space geometry, incidence, parallelism, perpendicularity

12 Introduction to trigonometry, acute angles (first quadrant)

13 Length, area, volume, the measure of point-sets

This project has produced textbooks for grades 7–12, teachers' commentaries, and supplementary student materials, all of which are available from Teachers College Press, Columbia University, New York.

Another curriculum development program for students of high ability is the Comprehensive School Mathematics Program (CSMP). It was instituted initially in an attempt to implement the ambitious proposals of the Cambridge Conference for teaching mathematics which was held in 1963. These were controversial; many educators doubted that they could be implemented in the forseeable future, but others were convinced of their soundness and wrote text materials for teaching the proposed topics.

A program of CSMP that has received attention is *Elements of Mathematics*, a set of texts for grades 7–12 for students in the top 15–20 percent of the school population and able to comprehend what they read. Large sections of the texts are not intended to be taught in the conventional teacher-directed mode. The students are expected to read several texts and consult with the teacher as needed.

In general, *Elements of Mathematics* (p. 8) aims at familiarizing students with "the mathematical problems, ideas, and theories that have at one time or another engaged the attention of serious mathematicians and serious users of mathematics . . . to bring the student as close as possible to the kinds of things that are of interest to contemporary mathematicians and contemporary users of mathematics." Implied as more specific goals are the following (p. 8):

1 Students should be familiar with, and, indeed, comfortable with, some of the basic ideas and techniques that are typical of modern mathematics. Similarly they should be familiar and comfortable with some of the basic language and notation of modern mathematics.

2 Students should be able to follow a mathematical argument; they should also have had experience in trying to invent and report such arguments themselves.

3 Students should have a familiarity with the axiomatic method in mathematics and have an appreciation of what this method does, and does not, assure. For example, students should be aware that a mathematical proof does not guarantee the "truth" of a given proposition, but does serve to show how this proposition is logically related to other propositions.

4 Students should have a familiarity with abstraction and its role in the development of a mathematical theory. They should be made aware of the power of apt abstractions as well as some of the ways in which mathematicians are led to such abstractions.

The books that form the basis of the curriculum are:

Book 0 *Intuitive Background*
Book 1 *Introductory Logic*
Book 2 *Logic and Sets*

Book 3   *Introduction to Fields*
Book 4   *Relations*
Book 5   *Functions*
Book 6   *Number Systems*
Book 7   *Real Analysis (Calculus of One Variable)*
Book 8   *Elements of Geometry*
Book 9   *Linear Algebra with Trigonometry*
Book 10   *Groups and Rings*
Book 11   *Finite Probability Spaces*
Book 12   *Introduction to Measure Theory*

An example of ability grouping that can be established in a school with a minimum of reorganization is described by Elder (1957). It is the practice of providing seminars for students of high ability in a junior high school. Students are selected by their scores on standardized tests, teachers' and counselors' reports and recommendations, physical fitness, emotional maturity, and "total behavior pattern as observed in a variety of situations" (p. 503). The selection is made by a committee of the principal, counselor, district psychologist, and department chairman. During selection, students meet several times with various members of the selection committee in order to obtain an understanding of the rationale and operation of the seminars. At these conferences further evidence is sought concerning each student's interest, curiosity, and quality of thinking. Parental consent is necessary before final selection is made.

The seminars contain no more than fifteen members. The students meet their classes as do the ordinary students but are released from two of their regular classes twice a week to meet in the seminars. They are responsible for all work missed during the periods in which they are excused from their regular classes. No textbook is used in the seminar and topics not in the regular courses are studied—for example, numeration systems other than the decimal, prime numbers, and groups. There is no predetermined or inflexible set of topics. The students select what they want to study and report what they learn to the other members of the seminar. Each is expected to write a paper summarizing his or her learning.

Elder reports (p. 504): "Not restrained or restricted by traditional outlines of study or exams, pupils continually amaze us with their 'discoveries.'" She also reports that the students enjoy the seminar, appreciating the informal atmosphere and the absence of pressure from tests and grades. Opportunity to "research" a topic of interest is sufficient motivation for sustained effort. No school grade or formal credit is awarded for the work in the seminar. The selection for membership in the seminar and the opportunity for self-directed study seem sufficient reward. The work of each student is evaluated informally during the course of the seminar, and each student shares in this evaluation.

Teachers of the regular classes also appreciate the seminars. During the two days each week when the members of the seminar are absent, they can spend additional class time on remediation without boring the abler students who do not need it. Moreover, they are pleased that the members of the seminar accept responsibility for making up work missed during their absences. Some teachers report that seminar members gained increased interest in the mathematics taught in the regular classes.

Fehr (1968) cautions that since students of high ability are facile with abstractions, there is a danger in presenting mathematics to them formally with its deductive nature emphasized. While they surely should understand this aspect of mathematics, their education in it should be through experiences in which they form and test hypotheses about the relations of the objects of their study. Fehr says (p. 669): "We court failure and revulsion on the part of good students if we adopt too early this unnatural and highly sophisticated axiomatic method of presenting all our mathematics."

Admission to college with advanced standing

Another form of acceleration is admission to college with advanced standing. That is, students are given college credit for high school mathematics courses.

Two studies were financed in 1952 by grants from the Ford Foundation—"General Education in School and College" (directed by Alan Blackmer of Phillips Academy) and "School and College Study of Admission with Advanced Standing" (directed by Gordon Chalmers of Kenyon College)—because of a belief that able students waste time in high school and the first two years of college because of excessive duplication of content. It was believed further that differentiation should be made in the high school courses so that able students could be kept with students their own age rather than sending them to college at a relatively young age. Implemented action of these beliefs would lead to courses in mathematics for high school equivalent to analogous courses ordinarily offered in college. The colleges too, would have to be convinced that the students who passed these courses had mastered the knowledge and skills presented to them.

A committee of mathematicians and secondary school teachers of mathematics ultimately planned a course for twelfth grade that covered the one year of analytic geometry and calculus typically offered in the first or second year of college. The College Entrance Examination Board prepared examinations to measure proficiency in the course. The grades of students who took the examination were reported to the colleges to which the students sought admission, and the colleges decided for which of their courses to allow student credit.

Were such a twelfth grade course in mathematics to be offered, the four years of mathematics ordinarily offered would have to be covered in three years. Schools would be able to do this by grouping and accelerated programs or by allowing able students to take more than one course in mathematics in one or more semesters a year.

Summer programs

When the National Science Foundation was financing programs for talented students in science and mathematics, several colleges developed courses and other activities offered during the traditional summer vacation. One of these, a summer mathematics camp, is described by Nichols (1960). The summer camp was publicized, applicants were screened by standardized test (an essay entitled "I Want to Attend the Math Camp—These Are My Reasons"), and recommendations were collected from the students' teachers and principals. Those selected studied in courses for four or five hours each day and carried on independent study as well. The courses, of varying numbers of weeks, covered programming the IBM 650, probability and statistics, advanced topics in algebra, and symbolic logic. All students took a six-week introduction to Russian. One group of students who had completed no more than the ninth grade but who had had at least one course in algebra took a two-week course in number theory. Another group of students who had completed no more than the eleventh grade and who had finished at least three years of college preparatory mathematics took a four-week course in this subject. Cultural and recreational activities were also arranged.

An institute was held for several summers at the University of Illinois at Urbana-Champaign. The students took two courses in mathematics, one in number theory, the other varying from summer to summer (probability and game theory, Boolean algebra, geometric transformations). Students also took a problems seminar devoted to thought-provoking, nonroutine problems of a variety of aspects chosen to illustrate techniques of problem-solving and mathematical discovery and intended to promote mathematical maturity. This seminar used many of the ideas and strategies of Polya, especially as presented in his book *Mathematical Discovery*. Students of unusually strong backgrounds in mathematics were excused from part of or all the regular course work and were assigned to senior faculty for independent tutorial study. The formal course work was supplemented by lectures on mathematical and vocational topics. Individual counseling about colleges and careers was provided for students who desired it.

Another summer program at St. Louis University presented two courses: the foundations of mathematics (the real number system using Peano's postulates) and fundamentals of numerical analysis (symbolic logic, electronic logic elements, switching circuits, the design of a binary adder, probability based on admissible number theory, and programming the IBM 610). Field trips were arranged to industries that used computers.

Other summer programs merely identified students of high ability in mathematics and allowed them to enroll in conventional summer college courses in mathematics. These students did as well as or better than many of the college students also enrolled in the courses. A variation of such programs for able students in high schools in cities and towns in which there also is a college dismisses them for some part of the school day.

Correspondence courses

Some small high schools cannot afford to offer special programs because of the small number of high-ability students. The school may then pay for correspondence courses in mathematics that the bright students take. Such courses are offered by many large universities. Able students work readily on their own and can complete such courses with a minimum of help by the school mathematics teacher.

Mathematics clubs

Many junior and senior high schools offer a mathematics club as part of the extracurricular program. In some cases any interested student may join; in other cases, restrictions allow what is discussed at meetings to be more advanced than what is studied in the regular courses. The clubs, under no expectations of covering a certain body of subject matter, can range widely and base interests on those of the participants. Students adopt projects or topics to investigate and report their findings to the other club members. In some cases computer programming is studied, and club work resembles that of a formal mathematics course. Opportunities for self-directed study provided can supplement the classroom mathematics. A school too small to offer a specialized program for able students may accommodate a mathematics club.

Contests and fairs

Some departments of mathematics encourage students to enter state, regional, or local mathematical contests, either as individual entrants or as school teams.

Students can be encouraged to enter these science fairs with exhibits or papers having to do with computers, linkages to perform some motion, polyhedrons of various materials, mechanical devices for performing certain mathematical operations, or miscellaneous research. All these activities generate interest and often result in tangible recognition. At the very least, preparation for the contests is a challenge to superior students.

Teachers who work with students in preparing for contests or fairs should be given released time or extra compensation, as are teachers who participate in the direction of interscholastic athletics, debate, and dramatic productions. Guiding a superior student takes much time. It is only fair that teachers who direct their study in mathematics over and beyond what they ordinarily do in their classes should be afforded some tangible recognition for this work.

Thought questions

1 Suppose a student shows promise in mathematics and the school has a special program for such students. The student resists being assigned to this program because he will not be with his close friends. Should the student be required to enroll in the program?

2 T_1 Yes, I favor ability grouping. Such grouping reduces the heterogeneity of background and ability, and you do more for students of varying competence in mathematics.

   T_2 But in ability grouping, children lose their individuality. They are regarded in terms of group characteristics instead of in terms of their own individual characteristics. Students in a group characterized as "high ability" do well just because the teacher expects them to do well. And students in a group characterized as "low ability" don't do well just because it is not possible for the teacher to conceive that they can do otherwise.

   T_1 This is not necessarily the case. If teachers so regard students, it is the fault of the teachers rather than the fault of the system.

   T_2 There is another bad feature of ability grouping. When you group students in terms of whatever is measured by so-called academic aptitude tests, you find that they are also grouped by ethnic and socioeconomic characteristics. So you have functional segregation in a school that is supposed to be nonsegregated.

   T_1 If you think you get viable integration simply by physical proximity, simply by having students of various minority groups sitting next to each other, either you are deluding yourself or you are taking a narrow view regarding integration.

   T_2 Studies show that where there is ability grouping, all groups are usually expected to learn the same things and are taught by the very same methods. So there is no adaptation of instruction to the groups of students of varying ability.

   T_1 Could be. But, again, this is no indictment of the system. It is an indictment of the practitioners of the system. Are you advocating that we give up Christianity simply because some people do not act in a Christian way toward others?

   Assess the worth of the arguments supporting and attacking ability grouping. With which teacher do you agree? What are advantages and disadvantages of ability grouping other than those mentioned by the two teachers?

3 Read some of the texts developed by the Secondary School Mathematics Curriculum Improvement Study (SSMCIS). What is your judgment about the content and presentation of the subject matter in the texts?

4 There are differences of opinion as to the wisdom of offering calculus in high school. State your judgment on this issue.

5 Visit a science fair and observe the mathematics projects exhibited. Which impress you? What ideas do you get for stimulating superior students in mathematics?

6 At one time, it was thought that the best way to provide for students of very great ability in mathematics was to accelerate their progress through secondary school so that they could enter college at an early age. Once there, they could be accelerated through college also, so they could finish a doctor's degree at age 20 or younger. This practice is no longer followed, although there is less rapid acceleration. Why was the practice abandoned?

Provisions in heterogeneous classes for students of high ability

Institutional arrangements are made for students of high ability just because it is difficult for the teacher of a heterogenous class to do much in the way of adapting instruction to students at the extremes of the normal distribution. To make sure that as many slow students as possible pass the course, a mathematics teacher will typically spend additional time with them to the neglect of superior students. The latter are consequently not challenged and may develop bad attitudes and poor work habits. Yet in many high schools, particularly small high schools, few if any institutional adaptations can be made for either the slow students or the superior ones. The classroom teacher has to adapt instruction as well as possible to make a contribution to both kinds of student. What can the teacher do for the students of high ability when mixed with other students in one class?

Special features of the textbook

Most textbooks have provisions for students of high ability. One is graded sets of exercises. Such texts contain a set of exercises of minimum application of concepts and principles as well as one or two other sets of challenging problems.

Another feature of many textbooks is optional topics beyond the minimum course. These are generally not assigned to the average students, but they can be assigned to students of high ability who can master them with little aid from the teacher.

Supplementary text materials

Even though a textbook may contain optional topics, there is usually not enough of these to enrich a course sufficiently for the superior students. The teacher will have to seek supplementary text material. One kind of supplementary material is conventional textbooks in mathematics that students can study on their own with a minimum of direction. Textbooks in abstract algebra, college geometry, finite mathematics, computer science, Boolean algebra, matrix algebra, linear programming, linear algebra, introduction to analysis, number theory, analytic geometry, calculus, vector analysis, and symbolic logic are possibilities.

Paperbacks on mathematics topics can also supplement course work. Some publishers have sets of booklets of low cost that students can purchase or that can be furnished them at no cost by the school. Dover Publications come from a house that reprints significant hardcover books. Not all these are appropriate for all high school students, but many are classics and within the comprehension of superior students. Blaisdell is another publisher, with a series entitled "Popular Lectures in Mathematics," among which are translations of significant lectures by Russian mathematicians. Heath has a similar series of more than fifteen booklets called "Topics in Mathematics." Many of these are also translations from Russian. Singer has a series, "New Mathematical Library," written by able mathematicians who have simplified the presentation of theory of many various subjects in mathematics. All such booklets are excellent enrichment devices.

Enrichment can also be provided in the form of books on popularized discussion of aspects of mathematics, ancillary publications on application, history, and philosophy of mathematics, and biographies of famous mathematicians. Following is a sample of such books:

Abbott, E. A. *Flatland*, 5th rev. ed. New York: Barnes & Noble, 1963.
Dantzig, Tobias. *Number: The Language of Science*, 4th rev. ed. New York: Macmillan, 1954.
Bell, Eric Temple. *Development of Mathematics*, 2nd ed. New York: McGraw-Hill, 1945.
———. *Mathematics: Queen and Servant of Science*. New York: McGraw-Hill, 1961.
———. *Men of Mathematics*. New York: McGraw-Hill, 1961.
Courant, Richard, and Herbert Robbins. *What Is Mathematics?* New York: Oxford University Press, 1941.
Cundy, H. Martyn, and A. P. Rollett. *Mathematical Models*, 2nd ed. New York: Oxford University Press, 1961.
Cutler, Ann, and Rudolph McShane. *The Trachtenberg Speed System of Basic Mathematics*. New York: Bantam, 1973.
Freebury, H. A. *A History of Mathematics*. New York: Macmillan, 1961.
Glenn, William H., and Donovan Johnson. *Exploring Mathematics on Your Own*. New York: Dover, 1972.
Glicksman, Abraham M. *Linear Programming and the Theory of Games*. New York: Wiley, 1963.
Hogben, Lancelot. *Mathematics for the Millions*. New York: Norton, 1968.
Jones, Burton W. *Modular Arithmetic*. New York: Blaisdell, 1964.
Kasner, Edward, and James R. Newman. *Mathematics and the Imagination*. New York: Simon & Schuster, 1963.
Keyser, Cassius J. *Thinking About Thinking*. New York: Dutton, 1926.
Kline, Morris. *Mathematics and the Physical World*. Garden City, N. Y.: Doubleday, 1969.
———. *Mathematics in Western Culture*. New York: Oxford University Press, 1953.
Langman, Harry. *Play Mathematics*. Hafner Publishing Company, 1962.
Meyers, Lester. *High-Speed Math Self-Taught*. New York: Pocket Books, 1967.
Newman, James R. *The World of Mathematics*. New York: Simon & Schuster, 1956–60. Vols. 1–4.
Reid, Constance. *From Zero to Infinity*. New York: T. Y. Crowell, 1965.
Ritow, Ira. *Capsule Calculus*. New York: Doubleday, 1962.
Sawyer, W. W. *Mathematician's Delight*, Baltimore: Pelican, 1943.
Schaaf, William L., ed. *Our Mathematical Heritage*. New York: Macmillan, 1966.
Sticker, Henry. *How to Calculate Quickly*. New York: Dover, 1955.

Turnbull, Herbert W. *The Great Mathematicians.* New York: New York University Press, 1961.

Vergara, William C. *Mathematics in Everyday Things.* New York: Harper & Row, 1959.

Waisman, Friedrich. *Introduction to Mathematical Thinking.* New York: Ungar 1951.

Williams, J. D. *The Compleat Strategyst*, rev. ed. New York: McGraw-Hill, 1965.

Teachers may also provide their own source of supplementary materials. Sources of ideas for such units are given in the two yearbooks of the National Council of Teachers of Mathematics: the twenty-seventh, *Enrichment Mathematics for the Grades* (this also contains suggestions for junior high schools), and the twenty-eighth, *Enrichment Mathematics for High School.* Another source of ideas is in the sections on special techniques and enrichment lessons in *Mathematics in the Secondary School Classroom: Selected Readings*, listed at the end of this chapter. These are collections of articles from professional journals for mathematics teachers. Most are reports of successful classroom practices.

It is an interesting and challenging experience to write units for able students. Not only do the units enrich the education of these students but the act of writing enriches the professional development of the teacher. One who has to express knowledge in writing so that it will be understood by others comes to know the subject better. One or two units written each year accumulate before long to a library of resource materials from which able students can select according to their interests.

Schools can subscribe to journals suitable for high school students or encourage students to subscribe to them. One of these is *The Mathematics Student Journal*, a publication of the National Council of Teachers of Mathematics. It presents short articles on problems and topics in mathematics as well as challenging problems to be solved. Some articles are written by students. It is generally well written and stimulating. Its articles propose and explicate original mathematical ideas, examine the mathematical basis for physical phenomena and sports, and discuss well-known mathematical topics and paradoxes such as linear programming, cyclic groups, transformational geometry, Zeno's paradox, and baseball arithmetic. Problems are posed by other readers as well as by the editors. Students

Figure 13.1

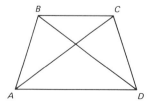

submitting correct solutions are credited in subsequent issues. Credit for solving certain problems is restricted to students in grades 9 and below. In the April 1973 issue, correct solutions to the following problem were credited to twenty-one students in a total of ten states.

Quadrilateral $ABCD$ has $AB = BC = CD$ and $AC = BD = AD$. Find the measure of angle ABC.

Acceleration within program of studies

We have based our descriptions and suggestions on the principle of keeping high ability students in class with the ordinary students and abreast of what is being taught them while enriching their study all the time. Teachers may also encourage acceleration through a course and into subsequent courses by allowing able students to proceed as fast as they can. Periodic checks of their progress to ensure mastery can be made. An example of this adaptation of classroom instruction is described by Latino (1956). Having identified students of high ability in his ninth-grade algebra class, Latino sounded them out as candidates for his accelerated program with questions and suggestions like the following (p. 181):

1 I see that you are doing well in here and that you seem to like mathematics.

2 I noticed that sometimes you understand something and have to sit there while I explain it many times to someone else who can't see it right away.

3 How would you like to work on ahead of the class? If you get through elementary algebra before the year is over, you'll be able to go into some things that you will have next year and the year after. You'll be more ready to do them by then.

For students who opted for the accelerated program, Latino devised a sequence of assignments that moved the bright students through the algebra course more rapidly than the average students. They kept a notebook for assignments, which Latino checked for progress. He supervised their study and during classroom exposition expected the bright students to pay attention but did not expect them to do the same assignments as the other students. During the period of supervised study, the bright students worked ahead on their special assignments as fast as they desired. They came to him for help when they felt they needed it. Students who had finished the regular course were tested with tests Latino constructed and with standardized tests. Students who passed moved to advanced algebra. Those who did not went back to restudy the parts of the course they had not understood. Students who moved on to advanced algebra studied conics, quadratic functions, arithmetic and geometric series, and an intuitive study of the slope of a curved line at a given point. Both theory and applications were presented.

The results of this program were encouraging. Latino found many instances of insightful problem-solving. The students accepted responsibility for their own progress and were disposed to evaluate it rather than wait for the teacher's evaluation. The bright students covered much more subject matter than the regular students. Two students were able to finish the second course in algebra during the ninth grade. Others made substantial progress into the second algebra course.

Assistant teaching

Many mathematics teachers ask able students to aid them in their teaching by working with other students who have trouble. The able students render a service in this way and also enhance their own understanding as they explain mathematics to their classmates. Anyone who has taught will testify that one comes to know a subject better, having had to teach it to someone else.

If able students become assistants to teachers, it would be well for the teachers to discuss their role with them. Their contribution will help other students understand and develop independence. If the able students only work the problems for others or tell them how to work problems, neither goal will be attained. They will have to learn to operate much as the regular classroom teacher does, diagnosing difficulties and providing remedial and corrective instruction in a manner that does not make the students they help dependent on them.

Thought questions

1   Investigate some of the references cited in this section as appropriate for supplementary text material for students of high ability and report on them to your class.

2   Examine the nature of some articles in *The Mathematics Student Journal* and *The Mathematical Log*. How appropriate are these publications for students of high potential in mathematics?

3   An issue in mathematics education is whether to keep able students abreast of the work of the other members of an ordinary class, stimulating them with enrichment material, or to allow them to proceed through a course as rapidly as they can with comprehension. What are the advantages and disadvantages of each practice? Which alternative do you favor? Why?

4   Some educators argue that using superior students to teach less able students is exploitation. Do you agree?

5   Many students of high ability enjoy projects of independent study. Suppose there are such students in each of the following courses. For each describe three possible topics or problems amenable to independent study:
    a   Seventh-grade mathematics
    b   The first course in algebra
    c   Geometry
    d   The twelfth-grade course in mathematics

The teacher of high-ability students

Not every teacher can work successfully with students of high quality, nor can every teacher work successfully with students of low ability. Special qualities are needed. The teacher should be sophisticated enough to recognize high potential even when superficial appraisal does not indicate its presence. The teacher may seek the help of other professionals on the school staff—the school psychologist, for example. The teacher should also be committed to adapting curriculum and instruction to stimulate students and make their formal education as profitable as possible.

The successful teacher of students of high ability most likely has a strong background in mathematics, commands the respect of students for his or her scholarship, and has broad appreciation for enrichment projects and topics for individual study. Moreover, such teachers follow the study of able students embarked on projects and study in advanced topics and can help them when they need help. Also he or she has to be able to assess the quality of learning. All this demands breadth and depth of knowledge and experience in mathematics.

The teacher of superior students has to be a secure person. It is possible that some students may outstrip the teacher both in intellectual ability and in their knowledge of certain topics in mathematics. The teacher has to be able to deal objectively with these students and not be threatened by their brilliance. It has been said that it is a great compliment to a teacher when students surpass him or her in attainment. It takes a secure person not only to accept this as a possibility but also to promote it.

When superior students attend classes along with students of less ability, the teacher has to be skilled in adapting instruction to all. The teacher should be aware of the various practices found effective by some teachers and be disposed to try some of these or invent others.

Like all teachers, the teacher of high-ability students also needs clarity in exposition, enthusiasm, a sense of humor, flexibility, and the ability to control a group of students. Teachers must set examples in many good traits. Psychologists tell us that identification is a powerful way of learning. A student who admires someone—another student, a teacher, or some other adult—may seek to become like that person or acquire the qualities he or she admires. If we can have teachers with whom students can identify, whether they are superior students or not, more will be learned than subject matter.

Self-test on the competencies

1 State characteristics of students who indicate high potential in mathematics.
  a Suppose you were designing a prognostic test to identify students of high potential in mathematics. What kinds of item would you put into the test?
  b Name some observable characteristics that a classroom teacher can use to identify students of high potential in mathematics.

2   Suggest possible institutional arrangements to ensure adequate education for students of high ability in mathematics.
     Describe some such institutional arrangements.

3   Offer suggestions for what a mathematics teacher of a few able students can do to adapt instruction for them.
     a   Consider the case of a teacher of five mathematics courses in each of which are able students. What can this teacher do to adapt instruction to enable these students to profit maximally from the time they spend in the course?
     b   A seventh-grade student has shown promise in mathematics and comes to you asking for a list of books in mathematics to read. Prepare such a list.
     c   A senior in one of your mathematics classes has habitually done good work in mathematics and now asks for a list of books to read. Prepare such a list.

References

Andrews, John J. "NSF Summer Mathematics Program for Gifted High-School Students." *The Mathematics Teacher*, 55 (1962), 377–379.

Bell, Clifford. "A Summer Mathematics Training Program for High-Ability Secondary-School Students." *The Mathematics Teacher*, 55 (1962), 276–278.

Brandwein, Paul F. *The Gifted Student as Future Scientist*. New York: Harcourt Brace Jovanovich, 1955.

Brown, Kenneth E., and Philip G. Johnson. *Education for the Talented in Mathematics and Science*, Bulletin No. 15. Washington, D. C.: U. S. Department of Health, Education, and Welfare, 1952.

Brush, Berneice E., and Edith Hunt. "Intermediate Algebra for High-Ability High School Students." *The Mathematics Teacher*, 54 (1961), 247–249.

Comprehensive School Mathematics Program. *Elements of Mathematics Program*. St. Ann, Mo.: CEMREL, 1971.

Elder, Florence L. "Providing for the Student with High Mathematical Potential." *The Mathematics Teacher*, 50 (1957), 502–506.

Fehr, Howard F. "General Ways to Identify Students with Scientific and Mathematical Potential." *The Mathematics Teacher*, 46 (1953), 230–234.

———. "Mathematical Education for a Scientific, Technological, and Industrial Society." *The Mathematics Teacher*, 61 (1968), 665–671.

Finkbeiner, Daniel T. "Summer Seasoning at Kenyon College." *The Mathematics Teacher*, 54 (1961), 241–245.

Gutzman, Wayne W. "A Description of a Summer Institute for Academically Talented High-School Juniors." *The Mathematics Teacher*, 55 (1962), 279–281.

Hollingworth, Leta S. *Gifted Children: Their Nature and Nurture*. New York: Macmillan, 1929.

Johnson, Donovan A. "Let's Do Something for the Gifted in Mathematics." *The Mathematics Teacher*, 46 (1953), 322–325.

Latino, Joseph J. "An Algebra Program for the Bright Ninth-Grader." *The Mathematics Teacher*, 49 (1956), 179–184.

Loyd, Daniel B. "Ultra-Curricular Stimulation for the Superior Student." *The Mathematics Teacher*, 46 (1953), 487–489.

National Council of Teachers of Mathematics. *Program Provisions for the Mathematically Gifted Student in the Secondary School*. Washington, D. C.: National Council of Teachers of Mathematics, 1957.

National Council of Teachers of Mathematics. *Enrichment Mathematics for the Grades*, Twenty-Seventh Yearbook of the National Council of Teachers of Mathematics. Washington, D. C.: National Council of Teachers of Mathematics, 1963.

————. *Enrichment Mathematics for High School*, Twenty-Eighth Yearbook of the National Council of Teachers of Mathematics. Washington, D. C.: National Council of Teachers of Mathematics, 1963.

National Society for the Study of Education. *Education for the Gifted*, Fifty-Seventh Yearbook. Chicago: University of Chicago Press, 1958. Part 2, Chs. 1, 8, 9, 10, and 12.

Nichols, Eugene D. "A Summer Mathematics Program for the Mathematically Talented." *The Mathematics Teacher*, 53 (1960), 235–240.

Remfer, Robert W. "Summer Institute for Mathematically Talented High-School Youth." *The Mathematics Teacher*, 55 (1962), 379–381.

Rising, Gerald R., and Richard A. Wiesen, eds. *Mathematics in the Secondary School Classroom: Selected Readings*. New York: T. Y. Crowell, 1972.

Rollins, Wilma E., et al. "Concepts of Mathematics—A Unique Program of High School Mathematics for the Gifted Student." *The Mathematics Teacher*, 56 (1963), 26–30.

Van der Linden, Algons J. "A Summer Mathematics Program for High-Ability Secondary-School Students." *The Mathematics Teacher*, 55 (1962), 369–376.

Wavell, Bruce B. "The Mathematics Summer School at Rollins College." *The Mathematics Teacher*, 55 (1962), 281–285.

Whitman, Nancy C. "Project D: Program for Talented Students in Mathematics in Secondary Schools in Hawaii." *The Mathematics Teacher*, 59 (1966), 564–571.

Wilansky, Albert. "A Research Program for Gifted Secondary-School Students." *The Mathematics Teacher*, 54 (1961), 250–254.

14

Planning for effective instruction

Everyone needs plans to facilitate the attainment of desired goals. Plans for a teacher involve making tentative decisions regarding expectations for a given course and deciding how these expectations can best be accomplished. Plans are formulated for particular units within a course and for individual lessons that compose a unit. Plans for specific lessons involve objectives, strategies, and homework assignments.

When plans are carefully constructed, a teacher is likely to accomplish established goals. Plans give the teacher better opportunity to help students understand the structure and utility of mathematics and see how various concepts, principles, and skills are related. Plans can help teachers become effective classroom leaders, since well-constructed plans facilitate efficient use of class time and provide the means by which teachers can present themselves as organized professionals. These are some reasons why it behooves teachers to spend time planning for instruction. Education is a purposeful activity and purposeful activities are best accomplished when they are the products of careful planning.

In this chapter we shall consider a systematic approach to planning instruction. To begin, we shall present various benefits a teacher can realize when lesson plans are carefully constructed. We shall then turn to various aspects of formulating plans. The first of these is the writing of objectives. As we discussed in Chapter 3, objectives provide direction for instruction and assist in decision-making. The second is selection of strategies to help attain objectives. The third is the use of instructional aids. Finally, we shall present various types of assignments along with suggestions for communicating them to students.

At the conclusion of this chapter, you should be able to demonstrate the following competencies:

1   Identify and discuss the advantages of careful planning for instruction

2   Construct a viable lesson plan for a specified mathematical topic and student population. This competency includes the following tasks:
   ***a*   Writing objectives for the topic**
   ***b*   Creating an appropriate teaching strategy to facilitate student attainment of the objectives**
   ***c*   Identifying and incorporating appropriate instructional aids in the teaching strategy**
   ***d*   Identifying different types of assignments**

Benefits derived from careful planning

The purpose of this section is explicitly to identify and briefly to discuss some benefits to be derived from careful planning. Some are related to planning in general; others involve the construction of objectives.

One advantage a teacher can derive from well-planned lessons is better projection as an organized and concerned leader interested in the development and progress of students. The importance of poise and confidence in a leader has been emphasized at various points in this text. There is no question that students are more likely to respect a teacher who projects a figure of stability, knowledgeability, and concern.

Students are likely to view a teacher who appears disorganized as unconcerned and view mathematics as a disorganized body of knowledge. They may not grasp the structural basis of mathematics and miss opportunities to gain understanding in the subject. Furthermore, the teacher who engages in teaching with little thought of strategy runs the risk of convincing students that learning mathematics is not important and should not be given serious consideration. If this occurs, much of the enjoyment to be realized from teaching will be missing. Watching youngsters fumble, fail, and take little or no pride in their work is not enjoyable.

The beginning teacher has many difficulties to overcome. The newness of teaching, subject matter, school, and students, all contribute to the uneasiness that every new teacher undergoes. Experience will alleviate some concern but most concerns can be dealt with only through extensive effort in planning and organizing instruction. An organized teacher with a definite teaching strategy will solve first-year teaching problems. Care in planning can help develop the teacher's mathematical competence, enhance confidence in front of students, and eventually provide the context for developing creative talent in teaching. The positive effect that an organized teacher has on students cannot be overemphasized.

Several benefits can accrue from carefully defined objectives. One is predicated on the belief that objectives assist teachers in selecting appropriate learning experiences and help them use class time efficiently. For example, a teacher about to teach a unit on linear equations in one variable might formulate the following two objectives:

1   The student should be able to solve linear equations in one variable with rational coefficients.
2   The student should be able to justify various steps in solving linear equations in one variable with rational coefficients.

The teacher who formulates these objectives is likely to clarify in his or her own mind what is to be expected of students at the conclusion of the unit. That is, a teacher would not only expect students to be skilled in solving linear equations (the first objective) but would also expect them to have some understanding of the procedures used in solving the equations (the second objective). With these objectives clearly established, the teacher can select exercises that will assist students in attaining them.

Teachers should not assume that activities concentrating on solving equations will necessarily help students become aware of the justification for the various steps they are using. In addition, the teacher can budget instructional time for various activities in accordance with the values he or she places on the stated objectives. In general, instructional time should be allocated in a way that is consistent with the values the teacher places on the various objectives.

Another advantage of objectives is their potential in communicating teacher expectations to students and parents. Gagné in *The Conditions of Learning* (1970) suggests, for example, that informing students of what is expected of them serves as direction that can facilitate student achievement. Walbesser and Eisenberg (1972) in a review of research on the relationship between objectives and academic achievement indicate that there is some support for the hypothesis that providing a learner with carefully defined objectives can have a positive effect on achievement.

Students do not, in general, profit from an activity that seems vague and whose duration appears unclear. When students are involved in loosely defined activities over which they will be tested, unnecessary tension can result. The students become less concerned about meaningful learning and increasingly concerned about outguessing the teacher with respect to upcoming tests. Unnecessary tension can be reduced by communicating to students precisely what is expected of them. Explicit statements of objectives can provide the means by which this communication can occur.

Ideally, teachers hope that students will master all the content in a given course. This goal is seldom realized, however, and teachers must judge what content to emphasize. Students realize that they cannot master all the content and they, too, must judge what to emphasize in their studies. Unlike the teacher who bases judgments on experience and a broad knowledge of mathematics, students usually cast their lot in accordance with what they perceive the teacher feels is important. Because students are generally perceptive and teachers generally construct tests that fairly well reflect what they have emphasized in the classroom, teachers' judgments and students' guesses are not totally incongruous. But the stakes are too high to leave such a mesh to chance. Hence, it makes sense to indicate to students their responsibilities in relation to the content being studied with objectives carefully constructed by the teacher through his own professional judgments based on his experience and education.

Parents sometimes desire a statement of objectives from teachers, too. Such statements generally consist of vague goals. This may suffice, since many parents do not wish to be burdened with specific accounts of a teacher's expectations. On the other hand, clearly defined objectives afford teachers an opportunity to communicate expectations to parents in a clear and precise way. For interested and concerned parents, such objectives serve as a means by which to evaluate their children's progress. Furthermore, parents sometimes inquire about tutorial assistance when a child is experiencing academic difficulty. By enumerating the objectives that the student has yet to attain, the teacher can provide direction for tutorial assistance.

Conferences between parents and teachers can sometimes become charged with emotional overtones because of the defensive behavior exhibited by either or both. Such an atmosphere can interfere with an objective analysis of a student's learning problems. Parents are likely to be receptive to a teacher's analysis of student progress when that analysis is based on stated objectives. A teacher is not likely to be viewed as vindictive when the instructional program and subsequent evaluation techniques are clearly seen to be based on objectives that are mathematically significant and appropriate. This is especially true when objectives are made available to both students and parents.

Thought questions

1 Assume that you are a teacher holding a conference with the irate parents of a student who is failing your algebra course. How could objectives help provide useful information for these parents?

2 Identify as many desirable outcomes as you can from a teacher spending a great deal of planning time.

3 Can a teacher spend too much time planning?

4 Suppose you were a substitute teacher entering a mathematics classroom for the first time. In this situation, what would be your reaction to the necessity of lesson plans?

5 What is likely to be the opinion of a principal when a mathematics teacher is ill and, in briefing the substitute, the principal can find no evidence of planning by the regular classroom teacher?

6   Every teacher has observed students whose papers are messy and disorganized and who appear to have no systematic method of solving problems. Discuss the analogy between this type of student and the teacher whose plans are disorganized or non-existent and who seems to have no systematic approach to instruction.

Writing objectives for individual lessons

One overriding objective in teaching mathematics is that students gain appreciation of the structure of mathematics, of the logical relationship between its topics and branches, and of the beauty of the logical consistencies inherent in the subject itself. These objectives cannot easily be expressed in terms of observable student behavior, yet they are central to desired outcomes of teaching mathematics. It is unlikely, of course, that students can appreciate the relationship between algebraic and geometric topics if they lack concepts or if their attainment of fundamental skills is insufficient to allow satisfactory performance of needed operations.

One basic use of specific objectives is, therefore, to ensure that students function intelligently in mathematics. This requires an adequate conceptual background, knowledge of basic generalizations, and skill in using algorithms. We shall treat this topic in some detail. We shall consider two vantage points from which a teacher can generate objectives. The formulation of objectives based on moves one uses in teaching mathematical concepts, generalizations, and skills will be discussed first, then the generation of objectives based on a taxonomy of cognitive behaviors.

Objectives based on moves

As has been discussed in other chapters, the nature of the knowledge one teaches is a determining factor in the moves used to teach it. Moves for teaching concepts, generalizations, and skills can also provide a basis for generating objectives for a given unit or lesson. Suppose, for example, a teacher decides that students should be knowledgeable about functions. What explicit objectives might be formulated? Consider the various moves for teaching this concept: defining a function, giving examples and non-examples of functions, accompanied perhaps with reasons, comparing and contrasting different kinds of functions, and indicating several procedures for determining whether a set of ordered pairs constitutes a function. From these possible moves, a teacher might construct the following objectives:

1   The student should be able to define a function.

2   The student should be able to give examples of relations that are functions and examples of relations that are not functions.

3   The student should be able to identify the differences and similarities of constant, linear, and quadratic functions.

4   Given a relation, the student should be able to determine whether it is a function.

This list does not exhaust the objectives a teacher could formulate. It serves to illustrate how a teacher can generate objectives and, hence, identify behavior students should exhibit when acquiring the concept. Having stipulated the objectives, the teacher can plan educational activities necessary to promote their acquisition.

Objectives for generalizations can similarly be constructed by considering the moves used in teaching this type of knowledge. A geometry teacher may decide that it is essential for students to have an understanding of the Pythagorean theorem. In planning moves to teach this generalization, the teacher might consider stating and interpreting the theorem by reviewing concepts such as hypotenuse or legs, by providing instances, by using an analysis move, and perhaps by having the students paraphrase the theorem. Justification could occur by examining additional instances or by presenting any one of a number of proofs. Finally, the teacher might have the students solve a variety of computational exercises or apply the theorem in proving other generalizations. These moves, then, could provide the impetus for constructing the following objectives:

5 The student should be able to state the Pythagorean theorem.

6 Given a right triangle of dimensions d, e, and f, the student should be able correctly to express the Pythagorean relationship using the given dimensions.

7 Given a problem or a generalization, the student should be able to determine whether the Pythagorean theorem can be used to solve the problem or prove the generalization.

8 Given the lengths of any two sides of a right triangle, the student should be able to find the length of the third side.

9 The student should be able to prove the Pythagorean theorem.

10 The student should be able to apply the Pythagorean theorem in proving geometric generalizations.

Each objective can be related to the moves for teaching generalizations.

To further illustrate how moves can help in the construction of objectives, consider the skill of finding inverses of nonsingular 2×2 matrices. (We shall assume in our discussion that the matrices have rational numbers as their elements.) Objectives will involve the speed and accuracy with which the inverses can be found. One way students can become skilled in finding inverses of 2×2 matrices of the form $A = \begin{bmatrix} a & b \\ c & d \end{bmatrix}$ is to use the formula

$$A^{-1} = \frac{1}{|A|} \begin{bmatrix} d & -b \\ -c & a \end{bmatrix}$$

where A^{-1} denotes the inverse of the nonsingular matrix A and $|A|$ represents the determinant of A. The objective pertaining to the desired skill might be stated as follows:

11   The student should be able to find the inverse of a given nonsingular matrix $A = \begin{bmatrix} a & b \\ c & d \end{bmatrix}$ by using the formula $A^{-1} = \dfrac{1}{|A|} \begin{bmatrix} d & -b \\ -c & a \end{bmatrix}$.

Speed and accuracy related to such an objective are, generally, implicitly defined. Teachers should exercise common sense as to the number of inverses a student can be expected to find on a given test and the accuracy needed to demonstrate the attainment of the objective.

A basic premise of Chapter 8 is that students should be provided a basis for understanding the procedures they are to practice and become skilled in. The extent to which a teacher emphasizes understanding is determined by a number of factors. Some are the teacher's judgment of the importance of the skill, the ability of the class, the teacher's understanding of the given process, and the value placed on teaching for understanding. A teacher may place a high value on understanding in general but decide the time needed to ensure that students understand a particular procedure is not justified. A teacher interested only in having students find inverses might simply instruct them to use the formula indicated in objective 11. Such an approach could enable them to find desired inverses rapidly with a minimum of errors, but it does little to promote understanding. Suppose, however, a teacher decides it is important that students understand some of the intricacies of the use and derivation of the formula for finding the inverse of a 2×2 matrix. The teacher might use various interpretation and justification moves, including review of what it means for a matrix to be nonsingular and for two matrices to be inverses and review of how to find the determinant of a 2×2 matrix. These moves can give rise to the following objectives:

12   The student should be able to find the determinant of a given 2×2 matrix.

13   The student should be able to identify 2×2 matrices whose inverses do not exist.

14   Given the nonsingular matrix $A = \begin{bmatrix} a & b \\ c & d \end{bmatrix}$, the student should be able to derive the formula

$$A^{-1} = \frac{1}{|A|} \begin{bmatrix} d & -b \\ -c & a \end{bmatrix}$$

15   The student should be able to solve equations of the form $Ax + B = C$, given the 2×2 matrices B and C and the nonsingular matrix A.

16   Given that two 2×2 matrices are inverses of each other, the student should be able to state the equations implied by the inverse relationship.

These objectives go beyond acquiring speed and accuracy in finding inverses. They focus on understanding the underlying skill.

Thought questions

1 Consider objectives 4, 6, 11, 13, and 16. What moves for teaching concepts, generalization, or skills would you plan to help students attain each objective?

2 Suppose you anticipate that students will have difficulty in attaining objective 6. What moves might help them attain it?

3 Answer question 2 for objective 15.

4 Objectives 5–10 stem from moves used in teaching the Pythagorean theorem. Create additional objectives from moves that could be used in teaching this generalization.

5 A student is repeatedly unable to determine whether a triangle is a right triangle given the lengths of its three sides. Does this mean that the student has not satisfied objective 8? Defend your answer.

6 Consider the concepts similar triangles, periodic functions, and prime numbers. Write objectives for students who might be learning each of these. Create them from the various moves that could be used to teach them.

7 Consider the following three generalizations:
  a In a proportion, the product of the means is equal to the product of the extremes.
  b The sum of the degree-measures of the interior angles of an n-sided convex polygon is $180(n - 2)$.
  c The sines of the angles of a triangle are proportional to the lengths of the opposite sides (law of sines).
  Write objectives for students who might be learning each of these generalizations. Create your objectives from the various moves a teacher could use in teaching them.

8 Suppose you wished to have students become skilled in graphing functions and in rationalizing denominators. Write objectives for the skill and the understanding underlying it for each of these tasks.

9 Select a chapter or unit from the following textbooks, identify the concepts, generalizations, and skills that comprise the subject matter of the unit you selected, and generate a set of objectives for teaching each type of knowledge:
  a Junior high school mathematics textbook
  b High school geometry textbook
  c Textbook designed for an advanced course in high school mathematics
  d Textbook designed primarily for slow learners

Objectives based on a taxonomy of cognitive behavior

When objectives are predicated on moves for teaching concepts, generalizations, or skills, they usually encompass a variety of cognitive behaviors ranging from recalling statements to applying theorems in the generation of additional knowledge. There is always the risk, however, in creating objectives, that only lower level cognitive behaviors such as recalling facts or following given algorithms will be emphasized. If this occurs, much of the significance of mathematics may be obscured. To help ensure that a wide range of useful objectives have been created, they should be reviewed or generated by considering a variety of levels of cognitive behavior. In the following discussion we shall focus on generating objectives through the use of a taxonomy of cognitive behavior.

A student who solves a quadratic equation such as

$$x^2 - x - 12 = 0$$

by factoring is employing some arithmetic facts, using the concept of factors, and applying the mathematical generalization

If the product of two factors is 0, then at least one of the factors is 0.

Applying this generalization is a more complex behavior than, for example, identifying 3 and 4 as factors of 12. In writing objectives, it is desirable to identify behavior that requires complex thought processes as well as behavior that requires only memorization or straightforward application of rules.

Each classification scheme or taxonomy of cognitive behavior involves arbitrary divisions of the thinking process. One taxonomy that has influenced many other methods of classifying cognitive behavior is described by Bloom (1956) in the classic work *Taxonomy of Educational Objectives*. Bloom describes six major categories of cognitive thought and arranges them in a hierarchy, the lowest first:

1   Knowledge: recall of specifics, universals, methods, and patterns

2   Comprehension: basic understanding of material such that it can be transformed into another mode, interpreted, summarized, or cast into simple outcomes

3   Application: using abstractions and knowledge to solve specific or straightforward problems

4   Analysis: comprehending the elements in a communication, identifying their interactions, and distinguishing its structure

5   Synthesis: producing a novel structure given its constituent parts

6   Evaluation: using internal and external evidence to make judgments according to certain criteria

Each level after the first is viewed as requiring more complex mental behavior than the preceding level. For example, according to Bloom, application represents more complex behavior than comprehension but neither of these is as complex as synthesis.

One adaptation of Bloom's taxonomy for school mathematics has been developed by the staff and consultants of the School Mathematics Study Group's National Longitudinal Study of Mathematical Abilities (NLSMA). Four levels of cognitive behavior are identified: computation, comprehension, application, and analysis. Wilson (1971, p. 660) provides the following description of the first of these levels:

The computation level represents the least complex behaviors which we expect from students as outcomes of instruction in mathematics. The computation level should be described so as to include exercises of simple recall and exercises of routine manipulation. The level represents primarily those outcomes which require of the student no decision making or complex memory.

For Wilson, this category includes the recognition or recall of specific facts and terminology and the ability to perform a given algorithm in a familiar context. Objectives are classified as computational when they require the student to reproduce or recognize material in almost the exact form presented in the instructional setting.

Wilson describes comprehension in the following way (p. 660):

Comprehension is designed to be a more complex set of behaviors than computation, although the dividing line between the categories is artificial and vague and computation-level behaviors are sometimes assumed or incorporated within comprehension-level behaviors.

Included in this category is behavior that requires knowledge of concepts, generalizations, and rules in contexts other than those limited to memorized responses. Other subcategories of comprehension include the ability to translate a verbal description to a pictorial representation, the ability to communicate mathematics, and the ability to read and interpret problems. The latter behavior does not include solving mathematical problems.

The next level of cognitive behavior identified by NLSMA is called *application*. Wilson (p. 661) states:

The application-level behaviors involve a sequence of responses from the student; this characteristic distinguishes them from computation-level or comprehension-level behaviors. On the other hand, the application-level behaviors are to be closely related to the course of study; they deal with activities that are routine in the sense that items like these application-level items (not identical to them) would have been studied. The transfer to new situations is minimal.

Application refers to solving routine exercises in which the student must select and carry out the appropriate algorithm. If the selection is not obvious and its identification requires insight, then a higher level of cognitive behavior is involved. Wilson identifies several subcategories of behavior at the application level. One is making comparisons between concepts and generalizations. Another subcategory involves gathering and analyzing information and includes separating a problem into its constituent parts, identifying relevant information for solving a problem, and recognizing analogous problems. This level of thinking also refers to recognizing patterns or relationships, providing the recognition involves patterns similar to patterns previously studied. To generate new patterns or relations involves analysis, the highest level of cognitive behavior.

Analysis refers to behavior that necessitates insight in the solution of problems, discovering and verifying new relations, and constructing and criticizing proofs. Wilson (p. 662) writes:

> This behavior level is the highest of the cognitive categories—comprising the most complex behaviors. It includes most behaviors described in the *Taxonomy* (Bloom 1956) as analysis, synthesis, or evaluation. It includes what Avital and Shettleworth (1968) have called "open search." Here we will include nonroutine problem solving, discovery experiences, and creative behavior as it relates to mathematics. It differs from application-level or comprehension-level behaviors in that it involves a degree of transfer to a context in which there has been no practice. In order to respond satisfactorily to test items at this level, there must be a greater reliance on heuristic behavior. Many of the "ultimate" objectives of mathematics instruction are at the analysis level.

Let us now apply this method of generating objectives to a unit on real roots of real numbers. The unit appears in most second-year algebra courses and generally involves such topics as using radicals to express roots of equations, defining the symbol $\sqrt[n]{b}$, including the conditions under which this symbol has meaning, approximating roots of rational numbers by graphing, stating and proving the rational root theorem, and applying this theorem to prove the irrationality or rationality of a given number.

The following two objectives could be constructed to represent a basic level of understanding for this unit:

17 The student should be able to define the nth root of b where n is an odd positive integer and b is any real number or n is an even positive integer and b is a nonnegative real number.

18 The student should be able to state the rational root theorem.

These objectives could be classified as computational on the assumption that knowledge would be presented to students and they would be expected to memorize definitions and theorems for later recall or application.

The following two objectives could also be classified as computational, providing students practiced the techniques identified in the objectives:

19 The student should be able by graphing to find to the nearest tenth a rational approximation of the square or cube root of a positive rational number.

20 The student should be able to determine the set of possible rational roots of a given polynomial equation with rational coefficients by using the rational root theorem.

The next level of cognitive behavior in the NLSMA taxonomy is comprehension. This involves the basic concepts and generalizations of a given unit of instruction. Objectives at this level specify behavior that indicates a greater depth of understanding than would be indicated by recall. Whether a given objective requires the student simply to recall information or to go beyond recall is a function of what takes place in the classroom. Objectives 21, 22, and 23 require only recall if a teacher plans on stating the information for the students and then expects them to memorize it. On the other hand, if the teacher expects to discuss the meaning of having an nth root of a number and intends to provide students with activities related to the definition, then it is more likely that the following objectives involve comprehension:

21 The student should be able to specify the conditions under which $\sqrt[n]{b^n} = b$.

22 The student should be able to state the conditions necessary for the roots of a polynomial equation to be integral.

23 The student should be able to discuss the conditions under which $\sqrt[n]{b}$ exists in the set of real numbers.

Let us turn now to the next level of cognition, application. As we stated earlier, behavior on this level requires the student to select and use operations previously acquired. Unlike computation, however, application requires the student to decide which method or technique to apply to a given situation. Computation requires only that the student follow a given algorithm. Application necessitates that the student employ a search procedure to select relevant knowledge and algorithms.

Consider, now, some objectives that could be classified as application objectives. In making such a classification, it is assumed that students are proficient in using the rational root theorem:

24 Given the expression $\sqrt[n]{\dfrac{a}{b}}$ where n, a, and b are positive integers, the student should be able to determine whether the given expression is irrational.

25 Given a polynomial equation and a root to this equation, the student should be able to show that the root is irrational or rational.

Finally, we come to the highest level of cognitive behavior, referred to as *analysis* in the NLSMA taxonomy. For an objective to be classified as analysis, a teacher must view the objective as requiring problem-solving behavior. In considering the objectives below, assume that the specific proofs indicated had not previously been seen by students. With this restriction, the following objectives might then be classified as analysis:

26 The student should be able to prove the rational root theorem.

27 The student should be able to explain why the graph of a given function in a given interval lies below or above the line $y = x$.

We have discussed two methods by which objectives can be generated for mathematical units or lessons. When generating objectives by either method, two considerations should remain foremost in the teacher's mind. The teacher must first always consider what is deemed mathematically important for a given set of students. The teacher should also consider the mathematical maturity of the students. Formulating objectives that are mathematically significant and pedagogically appropriate can help ensure that students will attain needed competence in mathematics.

Thought questions

1   Discuss why it is possible for an objective to be categorized as analysis in one instructional context and computation in another. Relate your discussion to objectives 9 and 14.

2   Which of the first sixteen objectives would you classify as
    a   computation?
    b   comprehension?
    c   application?
    d   analysis?
    State the assumptions concerning the instructional context you make in your classification.

3   Discuss an instructional context in which the construction of a proof of the irrationality of $\sqrt{3}$ would be application. Under what conditions would the construction of this proof require analysis?

4   Write three objectives at each of the different levels in the NLSMA taxonomy for geometry students studying a unit on similar triangles.

5   Answer question 4 for first-year algebra students studying a unit on systems of two-linear equations in two unknowns.

6   Select a seventh-grade mathematics textbook and with the NLSMA taxonomy generate a set of objectives for a geometry chapter.

7   Select a second-year algebra textbook and with the NLSMA taxonomy generate a set of objectives from a chapter on solving quadratic equations and inequalities.

8   Discuss the merits and shortcomings of the position of each teacher below:

    T_1 I never write down objectives. I don't want my students to memorize for my tests. I want them to think at a much higher level.

    T_2 I always duplicate copies of my objectives for students. They appreciate knowing what I expect of them.

    T_3 When I plan my lessons, I write down my objectives. But I would never let my students see my objectives! They would quit listening to what I have to say.

Planning strategies to help students attain objectives

Once objectives have been created, the teacher should devise a strategy to assist students in realizing them. In Chapters 5–8 we incorporated competencies relative to planning lessons for teaching various types of mathematical knowledge. To help you attain these competencies, each chapter contains questions to ask yourself as you construct lesson plans. In Chapters 5, 6, and 8, these questions focus on moves in teaching concepts, generalizations, and skills. In addition, we presented discussions relative to formulating viable teaching strategies in each chapter. These questions and discussions are found near the close of each chapter. In Chapter 7 we gave suggestions for deciding whether to teach a generalization by exposition or by guided discovery. Furthermore, we presented and discussed considerations for planning and conducting guided-discovery lessons. We urge you to consider these sections when constructing lesson plans.

In planning lessons it is particularly important to determine students' mastery of prerequisite knowledge. Many well-intended lessons have gone awry because students lacked the prerequisite concepts, principles, or skills. Ausubel underscores the importance of determining the prerequisite knowledge that students possess in his statement on the frontispiece of his book *Educational Psychology: A Cognitive Viewpoint* (1968):

> If I had to reduce all of educational psychology to just one principle, I would say this: The most important single factor influencing learning is what the learner already knows. Ascertain this and teach him accordingly.

A teacher should plan on ascertaining at an appropriate time what students do and do not know. Review moves, perhaps in the form of questions, can help determine what prerequisite knowledge students possess and if there is a need for remedial teaching. This aspect of planning should be given major consideration.

One key to success in any teaching strategy is student involvement. Questions usually involve students in classroom discussions, but their effective use is not always easy, especially for beginning teachers. Classroom management problems and inexperience with subject matter are concerns that render it difficult for a beginning teacher spontaneously to identify questions that stimulate class discussions and involve all students.

A beginning teacher can take steps to offset this difficulty by identifying and writing questions in a lesson plan. To refer to notes in the process of teaching is a sign not of weakness but of strength. Good thoughts conceived the night before can soon vanish in the hustle-bustle of classroom activity if they are not recorded. The beginning teacher will be not only more likely to have better lessons by jotting down appropriate questions but also more proficient in asking questions.

Here are some questions that might be appropriate for algebra students studying quadratic equations:

1 What kind of equation is $x^2 = 10$?
2 How many roots should such an equation have?
3 How can you find the roots?
4 What do we mean when we say two equations are equivalent?

5 How can you find the roots of $4 + 3x^2 = 31$?

6 Are the equations $3x^2 - 10 = 5$ and $x^2 = 5$ equivalent? Why?

7 Explain why $x^2 + 9 = 36$ and $x + 3 = 6$ are not equivalent equations.

Correct responses to these usually require various levels of thought. Most likely questions 1, 2, 3, and possibly 4 require thought in computation or comprehension. These would be appropriate to get the low achiever involved in class discussion. Questions 5 and possibly 6 call for thought at the application level. It might be difficult for some students to determine the roots of the equation given in question 5, but the teacher might ask for the first step or the plan for solving the equation. Students having difficulty would then have a chance to respond correctly and would have a vested interest in the exercise. Hence, they would be more likely to follow the steps in solving such equations. Question 7 is more difficult and could be used appropriately to challenge more able students.

Thought questions

1 Suppose you were teaching an introductory unit on percent to a junior high school class. Discuss how you would relate this topic to mathematics the students had learned previously and to mathematics they would be expected to learn.

2 Answer question 1 as if you were teaching to a tenth-grade geometry class the principle that the sum of the measures of the angles of a triangle is 180.

3 Identify the prerequisite knowledge beginning algebra students would need to attain the following objective: The student should be able to factor trinomial expressions over the rational numbers.

4 Identify the prerequisite knowledge an advanced senior class would need to attain this objective: The student should be able to determine whether a given infinite geometric series converges.

5 There are several algorithms with which to divide fractions, but let us assume that you are expecting students to convert the division problem to a multiplication problem by inverting the divisor and then proceeding as in the multiplication of fractions. What knowledge is required for students to learn how to divide fractions in this way?

6 If students are to construct a tangent from a point to a circle, what knowledge is prerequisite? If students are expected to understand the significance of the steps in this construction what additional knowledge is prerequisite?

7 Consider objective 14 on page 392. Write down several questions of varying difficulty that you might ask students who were trying to attain this objective.

8 Answer question 7 for objective 19.

9 Answer question 7 for objective 23.

Selecting instructional aids

Student interest can be captured and learning facilitated when instructional aids are used in conjunction with a teacher's presentations. These include the chalkboard and multicolored chalk, films, filmstrips, overhead and opaque projectors, television, audio- and video-recorders, geoboards, multibase blocks, models, and special displays such as charts, maps, and overlays for an overhead projector. Periodicals such as *The Mathematics Teacher*, *The Arithmetic Teacher*, and *School Science and Mathematics* frequently contain articles on the use of commercial and homemade teaching aids. Commercial aids are advertised in these journals too. Many audio-visual aids can be constructed from inexpensive items and a little ingenuity.

Aids must be used judiciously if they are to have sustaining impact on students. In trying to decide whether to use an aid the teacher should consider two basic questions. Does it appear likely that it will help students attain the desired objectives? Does its use represent an improvement over what the teacher might ordinarily do without the aid? Sometimes films and other aids can better demonstrate a point than can a teacher at a chalkboard. Three-dimensional displays and the intersection of sets are examples. Some other topics, particularly algorithms, can usually be demonstrated better by the teacher, who can give advice as questions arise. Some visual aids present material in essentially the same way that textbooks do and such aids may not make the best use of class time.

The teacher who decides to incorporate aids into a lesson should adhere to several guidelines. First, all aids to be used should be carefully reviewed before they are implemented. Advertised promises and descriptions of films and filmstrips are often misleading and cannot always be relied on. Aids that have been reviewed and considered appropriate should be made ready for use when the class arrives. Projectors should be ready to run; geoboards should be ready to distribute. Any room rearranging should be done and additional equipment (screens, pencils, graph paper) should be secured. A disorganized teacher scurrying around frantically trying to get equipment ready for use while the students are present can lead to confusion and mismanagement.

The teacher is also wise to indicate to the class the purpose of using the aid. The class should be alerted to the special points of interest in a film. This is another reason why films and filmstrips should be carefully previewed before use. If the aids are materials for students to use, they should be explicitly informed as to purposes and methods. Such instruction will facilitate the learning experience and also better enable the teacher to be a forceful and confident classroom leader.

To further maximize the benefit derived from using an aid, a teacher should identify questions and important points that it will exhibit. These should be incorporated into the lesson plan. If a film or filmstrip is used, the teacher should plan questions for students to consider before the showing and questions for a follow-up activity as well.

Finally, the teacher should evaluate aids after they have been used. Audiovisual aids may hold great promise and yet even with careful planning the lesson may not be enhanced. One cannot always determine in advance how students will react. Should a lesson go well and an aid be viewed as

Figure 14.1

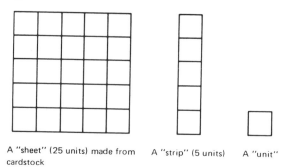

A "sheet" (25 units) made from   A "strip" (5 units)   A "unit"
cardstock

Figure 14.2

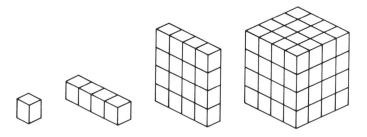

Aids such as these can be made from sugar cubes
to illustrate various numeration systems.
What numeration system is illustrated above?

Figure 14.3

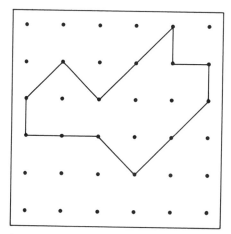

Can you determine the area of the region enclosed
by the polygon?

helpful, then the teacher may wish to note its success and use it again when teaching a similar lesson.

Thought questions

1   Indicate how you might use the overhead projector as an aid in a lesson on the graphing of linear and quadratic inequalities.

2   Construct a series of exercises that would emphasize the basic concepts of place value and position in a numeration system using materials such as those exhibited in Figures 14.1 and 14.2.

3   The geoboard (see Figure 14.3) can be used to illustrate basic concepts and generalizations concerning area, perimeter, and slopes of line segments. Determine the area and perimeter of the polygon in Figure 14.3. Describe how the geoboard could be used with junior high school students to develop concepts and generalizations concerning area of other geometric shapes (triangles and trapezoids). Describe how the geoboard could be used to teach concepts and generalizations concerning the slope of line segments to ninth-grade algebra students.

4   Identify in a high school geometry textbook two theorems whose proofs would be enhanced by the use of multicolored chalk and discuss your projected use of the chalk.

5   Recall from your own student experiences situations in which the teacher used instructional aids. Were they used effectively? Discuss.

Planning assignments

After objectives have been established and a teaching strategy has been determined, the teacher should carefully consider the assignment to be given students. It may consist of exercises or problems to be done in or outside class. Decisions about the length and nature of assignments should be made while planning a lesson and not during the stress of classroom teaching. Assignments that are unclear, confusing, or unrealistic will only inhibit learning and alienate students and cause them to dislike the subject, the teacher, and perhaps both.

A primary and obvious purpose of assignments is to provide activities in mathematics. Problems and exercises provide a context for applying generalizations and for practicing algorithms basic to development of mathematical skills. Students learn mathematics by being actively involved in doing it. When application and practice are absent, students are likely not to attain the desired levels of competence.

Teachers can use assignments as barometers of student achievement. That students are not completing assignments or are not doing them correctly may signify that they are too long or the directions are confusing. Teachers can use assignments or, more precisely, students' work in doing assignments, as a diagnostic tool. The identification of types of student errors can provide the teacher with valuable information for future lessons, reteaching, and constructing follow-up activities.

Types of assignment

One way to construct assignments is differentiation, described in Chapter 12 in the context of helping slow learners in heterogeneous classes. A differentiated assignment entails one basic assignment for all students, other, more challenging problems for able students, and exercises for the students who need review and additional practice.

Laing and Peterson (1973) discuss four kinds of assignments. The first involves work on a given topic only when that topic is being taught. When the teacher begins teaching a different topic, then the assignment focuses on the new material and does not involve explicit review of the first topic presented. The second entails not only assigning problems and exercises on the topic being discussed but also reviewing material previously covered and, in addition, exploratory exercises or reading material based on forthcoming lessons. A third type of assignment involves review material as well as exercises related to the immediate topic but no exploratory work. The manuals of several high school mathematics textbooks suggest this kind of assignment.

The fourth kind of assignment involves exercises or problems that relate directly to the topic being discussed and exploratory work or reading on topics that are yet to come. This kind of an assignment does not explicitly provide for review of previously learned mathematics.

Informing students of assignments

It is imperative that work be assigned when the teacher has the full attention of students. Assignments given while students are "packing up" and leaving or while they are busy attending to other matters will only serve to promote confusion and misunderstanding. When students perceive confusion, they have a ready-made alibi, not totally unjustified, for not doing their work.

The students must also be clear about procedure. Work that entails unfamiliar algorithms or applications of principles that are not yet understood will only contribute to student discontent or to copying and will undermine the teacher's intent. Ideally, homework assignments should be given in class while students still have time to start work under the supervision of the teacher.

The teacher should try to provide motivation for assignments. Extrinsic rewards such as special recognition or privileges might be helpful for younger or less mature students. Extrinsic rewards can also consist of grades, either for their own sake or as a means of avoiding confrontations with parents or school personnel. It is hoped that students will develop intrinsic motivation to do their work. However, most students are initially orientated toward immediate goals and need some form of teacher encouragement. One technique of motivating students when problems or exercises are assigned is to provide them with some of the answers so that they can determine when they have completed an exercise or problem correctly and subsequently gain confidence that they have also worked other exercises or problems correctly.

As a check that an assignment is explicit and clear, the teacher might reflect on the following questions:

Have I told the students what is to be done?
Have I provided them with a reason for doing the assignment?
Have I told them how the assignment is to be done?
Have I told them when the assignment is due?

If the answers are affirmitive, then the assignment has probably been communicated clearly.

Thought questions

1 Select some secondary school mathematics textbook and within the text identify some topic. Write four assignments that seem reasonable for a given population of students using the textbook such that each assignment exemplifies the four types of assignments identified by Laing and Peterson.

2 Consider the following three exercises:
   a 5 is what percent of 20?
   b 25 percent of 30 is what?
   c 35 percent of what number is 10?
   If you were teaching students to solve such exercises would it be advantageous to make assignments of all three types of exercise or would it be better to give assignments dealing with only one type at a time? Justify your position.

3 Discuss the advantages and disadvantages of giving long-range assignments—for example, assignments for an entire chapter when beginning work in it.

4 Discuss the relative advantages and disadvantages of giving assignments at the beginning of the class period rather than near its end.

5 What factors in a student's home environment can affect his or her performance in doing assignments? Can you conceive of conditions in which you would not require a particular student or groups of students to do homework? Discuss.

6 What is likely to happen to the efforts students make outside class on assignments when the teacher does not in some way check their work?

7 Some teachers collect and grade assignments. Others check them randomly and give short quizzes based on the assignment. What are the merits and drawbacks of each of these procedures?

8 In what context would you make adjustments in assignments that had already been announced? Why is it sometimes bad policy to add problems or exercises to an assignment that has already been given?

Writing lesson plans

Thus far, we have identified various steps one can take to facilitate a systematic approach to instruction. Planning consists of recording objectives, developing teaching strategies to reach them, including the use of aids, and designing assignments. The method by which a teacher records this information is a matter of personal taste. The lesson plan for beginning algebra students given in Figure 14.4 is only an illustration of one way in which such plans can be constructed.

In general, written plans should contain the information that will highlight key points of given lessons. The beginning teacher may feel initially more comfortable with detailed plans. The one illustrated in Figure 14.4 may then be desirable. Caution must be exercised, however, so that the written plan does not become so extensive that teaching becomes stilted and confined only to the interactions specified in writing. It must be realized that the purpose of a plan is to enable teachers to facilitate learning and not simply rigidly to follow preestablished directives.

Sometimes it is helpful to specify the approximate time to be spent on various aspects of a lesson. This has the advantage, especially for the inexperienced teacher, of promoting efficient use of class time. The specification of time for given activities can serve as a guideline and keep the teacher from rambling, but the danger inherent in allocating time is that the teacher may feel confined. It would be unfortunate for a teacher to abort an interesting discussion because of preestablished time constraint.

Figure 14.4

A sample lesson plan

Objectives:
    a. The student should be able to state what proportion is and give examples of proportions.
    b. The student should be able to identify the means and the extremes in a given proportion.
    c. The student should be able to state, apply and prove the generalization :
       In a proportion, the product of the means is equal to the product of the extremes.

Strategy:
    1. Present the students with the following question, "I have here two boxes of the same brand of detergent. One box contains 38 oz. and sells for 90¢. If a 12-oz. box is to represent the same value, what should it sell for?"
    2. Discuss this problem and the use of proportions to solve other such problems.
    3. State the objectives above for the students.
    4. Give a definition of proportion and give or elicit from students examples and non-examples of proportions.
    5. Write the generalization on the chalkboard.
    6. Give instances and identify the means and the extremes of the proportions given.
    7. Have the students use the generalization to solve equations such as

$$\frac{5}{8} = \frac{x}{24} \quad \text{and} \quad \frac{5}{12} = \frac{x}{16}$$

    8. Prove the generalization. Have students supply the reasons for the steps that are given.
    9. Have them work on this problem. Given only string, a globe, and the fact that the earth is approximately 25,000 miles in circumference at the equator tell how you could find the distance from Chicago to London.

Assignment: Review exercises on ratios, p. 176, nos. 5, 8, 10, 15.
                Do exercises on proportions, p. 180, nos. 1, 2, 4, 5, 10, 12.

Thought questions

1 Questions 1–7 refer to the lesson plan in Figure 14.4. Estimate the time you would spend on the various aspects of the lesson identified in the plan. Assume the lesson is intended for average eighth-grade students. Do you think allocating time is a good idea in planning?

2 On the basis of what was planned, what moves are likely to be used?

3 How do you think the objectives for the lesson were generated—that is, by what method discussed in this chapter?

4 Identify several key questions that you think a teacher using this lesson would ask students.

5 Which of the types of assignments appears to be indicated in the plan?

6 Identify an alternative teaching strategy that might be used in attaining the stated objectives.

7 When you construct your own lesson plans, would you prefer more or less detail than that given in Figure 14.4? Why?

8 Create a lesson plan that you might use for some topic for high school geometry students.

9 Create a lesson plan that you might use for some topic for second-year algebra.

Self-test on the competencies

1 Identify and discuss the advantages of carefully planning for instruction.
   a Create a dialogue between two mathematics teachers debating the advantages of creating and using objectives. Each teacher should state and defend a position and attempt to counter the points made by his or her colleague.
   b How might a teacher use previously written lesson plans when discussing with a parent the learning difficulties that beset a student?

2 Construct a viable lesson plan for a specified mathematical topic and student population. This competency includes the following tasks: (a) writing objectives for the topic; (b) creating an appropriate teaching strategy to facilitate student attainment of the objectives; (c) identifying and incorporating approximate instructional aids into the teaching strategy; (d) identifying different types of assignments.
   a Select a topic from a school mathematics textbook. Construct objectives and create a strategy that would help students attain them. Write three different types of assignment you might give students studying the topic.
   b Design aids you might use to teach the following topics:
      (1) Squaring a binomial
      (2) Intersection and union of sets
      (3) Euler's formula
      (4) Pythagorean theorem
   c Select some mathematics topics you might teach to beginning algebra students. Create a lesson plan in as much detail as necessary.

References

Ashlock, Robert B. *Error Patterns in Computation: A Semiprogrammed Approach.* Columbus, Ohio: Merrill, 1972.

Ausubel, David P. *Educational Psychology: A Cognitive View.* New York: Holt, Rinehart and Winston, 1968.

Beger, Emil J., ed. *Instructional Aids in Mathematics*, Thirty-Fourth Yearbook of the National Council of Teachers of Mathematics. Washington, D. C.: The Council, 1973.

Bloom, Benjamin S., ed. *Taxonomy of Educational Objectives: Cognitive Domain.* New York: David McKay, 1956.

Dolciani, Mary P., et al. *Modern Algebra Structure and Method, Book I*, Modern School Mathematics Series, Teacher's Edition. Boston: Houghton Mifflin, 1965.

Fitzgerald, William M., and Irvin E. Vance. "Other Media and Systems." *The Teaching of Secondary School Mathematics*, Thirty-Third Yearbook of the National Council of Teachers of Mathematics. Washington, D. C.: The Council, 1972.

Gagné, Robert M. *The Conditions of Learning.* New York: Holt, Rinehart and Winston, 1970.

Higgins, Jon L. "Sugar Cube Mathematics." *The Arithmetic Teacher*, 16 (1969), 427–431.

Hines, Vynce A. "Homework and Achievement in Plane Geometry." *The Mathematics Teacher*, 50 (1957), 24–29.

Johnson, Donvan A., and Gerald R. Rising. *Guidelines for Teaching Mathematics.* Belmont, Calif.: Wadsworth, 1972. Ch. 24 and App. A, C, and D.

Laing, Robert A., and John C. Peterson. "Assignments: Yesterday-Today, and Tomorrow-Today." *The Mathematics Teacher*, 66 (1973), 508–518.

Popham, W. James, and Eva L. Baker, *Systematic Instruction.* Englewood Cliffs, N. J.: Prentice-Hall, 1970.

Small, Dwain, Boyd Holton, and Edward J. Davis. "A Study of Two Methods of Checking Homework in a High School Geometry Class." *The Mathematics Teacher*, 60 (1967), 149–152.

Vargas, Julie S. *Writing Worthwhile Behavioral Objectives.* New York: Harper & Row, 1972.

Walbessor, Henry H., and Heather L. Carter. "Behavioral Objectives." *The Slow Learner in Mathematics*, Thirty-Fifth Yearbook of the National Council of Teachers of Mathematics. Washington, D. C.: The Council, 1972. Pp. 52–103.

———, and Theodore A. Eisenberg. *A Review of Research on Behavioral Objectives and Learning Hierarchies.* Columbus Ohio: ERIC Information Analysis Center for Science, Mathematics, and Environmental Education, 1972.

Wilson, James W. "Evaluation of Learning in Secondary School Mathematics." *Handbook on Formative and Summative Evaluation of Student Learning,* Benjamin S. Bloom, ed. New York: McGraw-Hill, 1971. Pp. 643–696.

Selected vendors of educational films

Bailey Films, Inc., 6509 Delonpre Ave., Los Angeles, Calif.　90028
Davidson Films, 1757 Union St., San Francisco, Calif.　94123

Walt Disney Productions, Educational Film Division, 350 S. Buena Vista Ave., Burbank, Calif.　91503

International Film Bureau, 332 S. Michigan Ave., Chicago, Ill.　60604

Knowledge Builders, 31 Union Square West, New York, N. Y.　10003

Modern Learning Aids, 16 Spear St., San Francisco, Calif.　94105

Moody Institute of Science, Educational Films Division, 1200 E. Washington Blvd., Whittier, Calif.　90606

National Council of Teachers of Mathematics, 1906 Association Drive, Reston, Va.　22091

Science Research Association, 259 E. Erie St., Chicago, Ill.　60611

Selected suppliers of instructional aids
(Catalogues available from vendor)

Creative Publications, P. O. Box 10328, Palo Alto, Calif.　94303

Midwest Publications Company, Inc., P. O. Box 129, Troy, Mich.　48084

Sigma Scientific, Inc., P. O. Box 1302, Gainesville, Fl.　32601

The Math Shop, 5 Bridge St., Watertown. Mass.　02172

15

Evaluating student and teacher performance

Teachers and administrators are frequently called on to evaluate the performance of students. With the thrust toward accountability in teaching, the performance of teachers, too, is evaluated. Hence it is appropriate to give some consideration to the means by which students and teachers can be evaluated. In this chapter we shall deal first with evaluating student performance and then with teachers.

In the first section we shall present cognitive and affective considerations for assessing student performance. For many teachers, consideration of how well students do on tests is the major item in assessing performance. We shall discuss this at some length. We shall first consider the construction of tests to measure attainment of objectives and then their administration and grading. This will lead us into such issues as partial credit, curving grades, and cheating. Following this we shall consider completion of assignments, class participation, work in addition to regular assignments, and the teacher's perception of what is best for particular students.

In the second section, we shall consider four factors in evaluating teacher performance, including student achievement, student attitudes, judgments of the appropriateness of teaching strategies, and the efficiency with which administrative matters are conducted. In this section we shall also discuss the issue of accountability in education.

At the conclusion of this chapter, you should be able to demonstrate the following competencies:

1 Write test items at various cognitive levels that reflect stated objectives

2 Discuss the advantages and disadvantages of curving grades and giving partial credit

3 State reasons for and concerns associated with considering student assignments, class participation, attitude and effort, extra credit, and individual needs in evaluating progress

4 Discuss how student performance on tests, attitudes and conduct, teaching methods, and administrative matters can be used to evaluate a teacher's performance

5 Identify merits and concerns associated with accountability in education

Evaluating student performance

In most educational settings teachers are called on to evaluate the performance of their students. Assigning grades, writing letters of recommendation to prospective employers and educational institutions, and recommending students for special programs and courses are some of the ways teachers are asked to express their opinions of students. Realizing that the consequences of their evaluations can influence the lives of students, many teachers choose to consider a number of factors in their judgments. We begin with the construction and use of tests.

Test construction

In the preceding chapter we were concerned with objectives for planning activities, carefully formulated objectives to provide guidelines for selecting learning experiences and planning for units of instruction and individual lessons. Objectives can make teachers explicitly aware of the content they deem most important.

When objectives provide the basis for examinations, there is less chance that students will miscalculate what mathematics they should emphasize and review. When they realize that test questions are manifestations of previously stated objectives, they tend to be less anxious and antagonistic to testing situations in particular and the teacher in general. When students perceive that tests are constructed in the eleventh hour and are products of a teacher's whims, their strategy for studying is likely to become predicated on guessing what content will be emphasized. Furthermore, tests constructed in such a manner encourage students to rationalize the futility of studying and preparing for tests.

Poorly designed tests can result in unsatisfactory student performance. This is upsetting to teachers because students have seemingly learned so little. Similarly, students become discouraged or angry when tests are, in their view, unfair. The teacher may then reteach or retest the unit or continue with new material with no clear evidence that students have mastered prerequisite knowledge. It does not take long for such situations to engender an atmosphere of tension and hostility between teacher and students.

Eventually, students resort to cheating to counter what may be in their eyes a vindictive teacher bent on testing what they do not know. Of course, not all teaching and testing situations dissolve into chaos. However, the testing situations that are most profitable for teachers and students are generally products of teachers carefully identifying the mathematics for which students should be responsible.

It is generally easier to write test items when objectives have already been constructed. In some cases, test items are in a sense restatements of objectives. For example, the objectives:

> The student should be able to prove DeMoivre's theorem.

> The student should be able to state the conditions under which a transformation represents a congruence.

> Given a unit of length, the student should be able to construct a line segment of length $\sqrt{3}$.

could give rise to the following test items:

> Prove De Moivre's theorem.

> State the conditions under which a given transformation describes a congruence.

> Using $1''$ to represent a unit of length, construct a line segment of length $\sqrt{3}$.

It is also possible for test items to be based on an objective but not be simply a restatement of that objective. Suppose students in an algebra class have been exposed to the traditional method of proving that $\sqrt{2}$ is irrational. A teacher might have formulated the objective: The student should be able to prove that the $\sqrt{2}$ is irrational. Besides the obvious test item, others can be developed:

> Explain why the square root of an even perfect square must be even.

> If one tried to prove that $\sqrt{4}$ is irrational and tried to use an indirect proof similar to the one used in class, where would the attempted proof fail?

For students who are well versed and fully understand how to prove $\sqrt{2}$ irrational by using the traditional method, the questions above should require only minimal transfer. For students not fully acquainted with the proof, these items could represent a rather formidable challenge.

To further illustrate writing test items from objectives, consider the following objective, which might be given to junior high school students:

> The student should be able to find the surface area of a sphere, given its diameter or radius.

The following test items could be based on this objective:

Find the surface area of a sphere if its diameter is 7 inches.

If the diameter of a sphere is doubled, what is the corresponding effect on the surface area?

If a gallon of paint can cover 400 square feet of surface area, how many gallons would be needed to paint a hemispherical tank of radius 100 feet?

The first item would be straightforward in view of the stated objective; the last two items require an extension of ability to compute the surface area of a sphere. Depending on the instructional context, these items might be classified at the comprehension and application levels, respectively, whereas the first question would most likely be classified as computational in view of the stated objective.

A teacher must be careful that test items that are not restatements of an objective do in fact measure attainment of the objective. Assume that a teacher has stated:

The student should be able to apply the Pythagorean theorem.

Which of the following test items measure this objective?

Given that $\triangle ABC$ has a right angle and the length of the shortest and longest sides are 10 inches and 26 inches respectively, find the length of the third side.

Which of the following lengths determine sides of right triangles? (1) 15, 20, 25; (2) 8, 12, 15; (3) 16, 30, 34

Prove the Pythagorean theorem.

Find the length of the longest stick that can be placed in a box of dimensions 6 inches by 4 inches by 3 inches.

The first question reflects the intent of the given objective. The second item requires students to employ the converse of the Pythagorean theorem and, hence, is not a measure of the given objective. While the third question may be fair in light of the instruction students may have received, it does not reflect the objective. Proving the Pythagorean theorem does not indicate a student's ability to apply this theorem in various contexts. The last test item is based on the objective. It represents an extension of the objective in that to solve the problem the Pythagorean theorem must be applied twice. As a test item it measures ability to attain the desired objective.

Suppose now we are about to teach a unit on the geometry of the *xy*-plane appropriate for a geometry or algebra class. Involved in this unit are concepts such as distance, slope, parallel and perpendicular lines, points and their coordinates, equations and graph of lines, intercepts and collinearity of points. Basic definitions and generalizations would include the definition of slope, the distance formula, and the relation between the slopes of parallel and perpendicular lines. Skills could involve the graphing of points and lines, determination of the slope of a given line, writing equations given appropriate information, and determining whether points are collinear.

The following objectives might be formulated. In communicating these objectives to students, it should be emphasized that the objectives pertain to the geometry of the xy-plane:

The student should be able to:

1   Graph points given the coordinates and give the coordinates of a designated point

2   Define *slope* and determine the slope of a line passing through two given points

3   Determine the slope of a line given its equation by transforming the given equation to the form $y = mx + b$

4   Develop the distance formula

5   Apply the distance formula

6   Determine the x- and y-intercepts of a line given the equation describing the line

7   State and apply the relation between slopes of parallel lines and slopes of perpendicular lines

8   Determine an equation of a line given two points through which the line passes

9   Determine an equation of a line given the slope of the line and a point through which the line passes

10   Determine whether three points are collinear

11   Find the distance between a point and a line

12   Find the midpoint of a line segment given the coordinates of its endpoints

From these objectives, the following representative test items could be constructed:

1   Graph the following points $(4,-5)$, $(-2,0)$, $(5,-4)$, $(-3,-6)$, and $(-2,+6)$.

2   Write an expression for the slope of a line passing through the two points (a,b) and (c,d) where a, b, c, and d are real numbers.

3   What is the slope of a line that is perpendicular to a line having a slope of 4?

4   Two lines are parallel (or coincident) if their slopes are _____.

5   Find the slope of the line defined by the equation $2x + 3y = -10$.

6   Write an expression that gives the distance between the points (p,q) and (r,s).

7   Determine the nature of the triangle whose vertices are $(-2,-2)$, $(4,4)$, and $(3,-1)$.

8 Write an equation of any line parallel to the line determined by the equation $5x + 2y = 8$.

9 Consider the lines determined by the equations $4x - 6y = 6$ and $2x + 8y = 3$. Are these lines parallel, perpendicular, or oblique?

10 Determine an equation of a line that contains the points $(4, -2)$ and $(-3, 10)$.

11 Determine an equation of a line passing through the point $(10, -4)$ and parallel to the line defined by the equation $x + \frac{1}{2}y = 10$.

12 Find the distance between the points $(5, -2)$ and $(-4, -6)$.

13 Determine whether the points $(4, -3)$, $(7, 0)$, and $(10, 3)$ are collinear.

14 Determine a point that is collinear with $(-2, 10)$ and $(8, 4)$.

15 Find an equation of a line that is the perpendicular bisector of the line segment joining the two points $(4, 8)$ and $(-2, 6)$.

16 Find the shortest distance between the point $(-2, 3)$ and the line whose equation is $x + 3y = 6$.

17 Find an equation of a line whose x-intercept is -4 and whose y-intercept is $+6$.

18 Classify the quadrilateral whose vertices are the points $(1, 1)$, $(3, -3)$, $(-1, -5)$, and $(-3, -1)$. Justify your classification.

19 Suppose we had a coordinate system in 3-space consisting of an x-, y-, and z-axis. The ordered triple $(3, -1, 4)$ identifies a point 3 units on the x-axis, -1 units on the y-axis, and 4 units on the z-axis. Find the distance between two points whose coordinates are $(-2, 5, 1)$ and $(4, -2, 6)$.

In constructing such a test, the teacher should make sure that the test items reflect given objectives. Some will involve more than one objective, particularly more difficult items. After constructing such a test many teachers will make value judgments concerning the points assigned to each test item in measuring student's performance on this test. Assigning points will result in an ordinal scale. After a measurement or score is assigned to each test, teachers will then make another value judgment and assign a letter grade.

Let us now analyze this test by matching each test item with the objective that it is intended to measure and by determining the level of thought required by each item. It is easy to identify the objectives measured by some of the test items. For example, questions 1–6, 10, 12, and 13 are directly related to objectives 1, 2, 7, 7, 3, 5, 8, 5, and 10, respectively. Each test item is basically an immediate implication of its related objective. Other test items measure only a single objective but in a more complicated context than does the previous set of questions. Question 7, for example, is primarily a reflection of objective 5. At first glance, it appears that question 17 measures objective 6 but this is not the case. Objective 6 requires the student to find the intercepts given the equation, whereas question 17 asks the student to find the equation of a line given its intercepts. Is, then, this test item unfair? The answer depends on whether the item can be based on any other objective.

Test items 11, 14, 15, 16, and 18 are based on more than one objective. Which objectives are involved is to some extent a function of what procedures are employed to answer each question. Question 18, for example, can be answered by using the concept of slope (objectives 2 and 7) or the concept of distance (objective 5). Some students might use both approaches—that is, determine whether the opposite sides are parallel by using slope and then apply the distance formula to determine the lengths of the diagonals. Each approach is based on the student's ability to graph points (objective 1) for otherwise the student would have difficulty in determining which lines are sides of the quadrilateral and which are diagonals. Test item 19 is related to objectives 4 and 5. This item is difficult because it requires behavior that reflects an extension of these objectives. By constructing a tally sheet, a teacher can determine the number of times each objective is being tested or whether some objectives are not being tested at all. On the basis of the results of such a tally, the teacher may wish to revise the test by changing, adding, or deleting some items.

Another factor to be considered in constructing a test is the cognitive level of behavior required in responding to the test questions. If a test consistently requires responses at the application and analysis levels of thought, then a teacher ought not to be surprised when students miss a large number of items. On the other hand, a test on which most students score greater than 90 percent may not represent outstanding success if the vast majority of the test items reflect only a low level of cognitive behavior.

Of course, a test can be difficult even though it is composed of items that largely require low-level cognitive behavior. Although it is true that analysis items tend, on the whole, to be more difficult than computation items, they are not necessarily so. For example, asking students to compute the volume of a sphere whose radius is 12.619 is not conceptually difficult if students are versed in using the formula $V = \frac{4}{3}\pi r^3$. Were such an item given to junior high school students, it is likely that many would miss it. The item requires low-level cognitive behavior but is nevertheless difficult because of the extensiveness of the computation. Thus, the difficulty of each item should also be considered in constructing tests.

It is important, then, for a teacher to consider the cognitive levels of behavior required of students and the difficulty of each test item. If a test is weighted with questions of a particular type, the results may be skewed and not provide information necessary to evaluate achievement accurately and fairly. Fortunately, most teachers use good judgment and common sense to construct fair tests. However, if test items are constructed from the perspective of established objectives and require a variety of levels of cognitive behavior and difficulty, the test is likely to represent a fair and comprehensive measure of student achievement.

To classify test items by levels of cognitive behavior, one must be aware of instruction before the test. To enable us to classify the test items above, let us assume that the instruction has been aimed primarily at the stated objectives and has not been explicitly concerned with tasks that involve a combination of objectives or extensive application of the objectives. With this assumption in mind, we shall classify the various test items with the NLSMA taxonomy. Undoubtedly some items are ambiguous with respect to their classification; different judges would make different classifications. The importance of the overall task is not how an individual question is classified but whether the test generally calls for the levels of cognitive behavior deemed important and appropriate.

Questions 1, 4, and 12 are computation items. They require either recall of knowledge or use of a practiced algorithm in a familiar context:

1   Graph the following points $(4,-5)$, $(-2,0)$, $(5,-4)$, $(-3,-6)$, and $(-2,+6)$.

4   Two lines are parallel (or coincident) if their slopes are _____.

12   Find the distance between the points $(5,-2)$ and $(-4,-6)$.

Are there any other items that might be classified as computation? Comprehension items would include items 2 and 6:

2   Write an expression for the slope of a line passing through the two points (a,b) and (c,d) where a, b, c, and d are real numbers.

6   Write an expression that gives the distance between the points (p,q) and (r,s).

These items require an understanding of basic concepts and generalizations. If a student has these understandings, then the questions are relatively easy to answer. Sometimes it is difficult to distinguish between computation and comprehension items. An item may be simply recall for one student and yet require some degree of insight for another. Are there any other items that might be clasified as comprehension items?

Items 11, 15, 16, and 18 would most likely be classified as application items:

11   Determine an equation of a line passing through the point $(10,-4)$ and parallel to the line defined by the equation $x + \frac{1}{2}y = 10$.

15   Find an equation of a line that is the perpendicular bisector of the line segment joining the two points $(4,8)$ and $(-2,6)$.

16   Find the shortest distance between the point $(-2,3)$ and the line whose equation is $x + 3y = 6$.

18   Classify the quadrilateral whose vertices are the points $(1,1)$, $(3,-3)$, $(-1,-5)$, and $(-3,-1)$. Justify your classification.

Each of these questions requires students to use an algorithm that they have practiced. Unlike computation items, however, these questions require students to decide which algorithms to employ and in what way they are to be used. When students are confronted with such decisions, something higher than a computation level of thought is required of them. The difficulty in distinguishing between computation and application rests with the determination of the extent to which the test question immediately triggers a procedure known to the student. If the question is housed in a context that is basically a restatement of the objective, then the item is probably a computation item. However, if the question is presented in a context that requires an extension of what is stated in a given objective, then it is an application item. In view of this distinction how should items 5, 8, 10, and 17 be classified?

5   Find the slope of the line defined by the equation $2x + 3y = -10$.

8   Write an equation of any line parallel to the line determined by the equation $5x + 2y = 8$.

10   Determine an equation of a line that contains the points $(4,-2)$ and $(-3,10)$.

17   Find an equation of a line whose x-intercept is -4 and whose y intercept is $+6$.

Analysis items are usually difficult to write since they require the use of knowledge in a way that has not been previously presented to students. Test question 19 is the only item that fits this description:

19   Suppose we had a coordinate system in 3-space consisting of an x-, y-, and z-axis. The ordered triple $(3,-1,4)$ identifies a point 3 units on the x-axis, -1 units on the y-axis, and 4 units on the z-axis. Find the distance between two points whose coordinates are $(-2,5,1)$ and $(4,-2,6)$.

Once test items have been classified according to some taxonomy of cognitive behavior and the difficulty of each item has been assessed, a decision can be made relative to the appropriateness of a given test in assessing student achievement. From such analysis, the teacher can predict the expected distribution of test scores. If it appears that the distribution is skewed because of the preponderance of easy or difficult items or that, in the teacher's judgment, the test has overemphasized a particular level of cognitive thought, then appropriate revisions can be made. The importance of analyzing a test before its administration cannot be overemphasized.

Thought questions

1   If you did not know a teacher's objectives or if they had never been explicitly formulated, how could an analysis of the teacher's test reveal her objectives—that is, what the teacher values in teaching mathematics?

2   Conjecture why students would make the following comments: "I don't study for his tests. It's no use," and "Sure, I cheated. After all, he's out to get us."

3   What kinds of test question can give students the impression that a test was constructed at the last minute or from the teacher's impulses?

4 Suppose the only proof of the irrationality of $\sqrt{2}$ presented to students has been based on the rational root theorem. Would the test items given early in this section concerning the square root of an even perfect square and the failure of the proof of the irrationality of $\sqrt{4}$ be measures of an objective calling for students to be able to prove $\sqrt{2}$ is irrational? Justify your answer.

5 Consider the following objective for junior high school students.

   The student should be able to find the least common multiple of a given set of whole numbers.

   Which of the following test items measure attainment of this objective?
   a   Find the least common multiple of 4, 7, and 8.
   b   Find the largest integer that divides 10, 15, and 20.
   c   If each element of a set of whole numbers is doubled, is their least common multiple also doubled?
   d   When is the least common multiple of a set of whole numbers one of the elements of this set?

6 It was pointed out earlier that question 17 was not based on objective 6. On which objective is this item based?

7 Construct a tally sheet that gives the matchings between test items 1–19 and objectives 1–12. Include on the tally sheet a classification of each item according to the NLSMA taxonomy of cognitive behavior. How can such a tally sheet be used to suggest modifications on a test?

8 Select a set of objectives that you have previously constructed or create a new set of objectives for some unit at a designated grade level. Write test items based on these objectives. Classify each test item by the NLSMA taxonomy. From this analysis, do you believe the test is fair? Justify your position.

9 State and defend your position on the use of test questions that require analysis.

10 Why is it desirable to analyze a test before its administration?

11 Some educators argue that it is improper to add the measures of various levels of cognitive behavior and assign one number to a student's performance on a given test. They maintain that it is appropriate to consider a student's computation, comprehension, application, and analysis scores separately rather than additively. React to this contention. What are its merits and drawbacks?

Thus far in this section of the chapter we have discussed the creation of a fair test—one that reflects objectives determined by the teacher. After a test is constructed, the teacher is usually responsible for administering it and making value judgments in determining students' grades. Teachers must come to grips with several issues in evaluating tests. These include partial credit, curving grades, and cheating.

Test evaluation

We shall consider some of the problems associated with grading tests and alternative procedures for handling concomitant problems. Consider first the question of partial credit.

The following two statements exemplify two somewhat extreme positions:

T₁   I never give partial credit. To me, an answer is either right or wrong, and I grade accordingly. In life, it doesn't do any good to be half right.

T₂   I believe in giving partial credit. The process of getting an answer is always more important than the actual answer itself. A student should get credit for what he knows.

Each position has its relative advantages and disadvantages. What strategy are students likely to use when taking a test for T_1? Are they likely to attempt to answer a question if they believe they cannot give a completely correct response? Since T_1 does not give partial credit, he or she will have fewer decisions to make and, hence, will finish grading test papers in shorter time. This is appealing, but it may tempt teachers to check only answers. What dangers are inherent in grading papers in this way? Which position provides more encouragement for students to check their own work?

If a teacher gives partial credit, then several decisions and value judgments must be made. For example, each of the following attempts to solve the equation

$$2(x - 10) - (12x - 4) = 20$$

contains an error. Identify each error. In one method, the error occurs in the beginning of the attempted solution. In another, the error occurs late in the student's work, and in the remaining procedure the error occurs at some point near the middle. How should the teacher evaluate and assign

a. $2(x-10)-(12x-4)=20$
$2x-20-12x+4=20$
$-10x-16=26$
$-10x=26+16$
$-10x=\overset{16}{42}$
$\boxed{x=-4.20}$

b. $2(x-10)-(12x-4)=20$
$2x-10-12x-4=20$
$-10x-14=20$
$-10x=34$
$x=\dfrac{34}{-10}$
$\boxed{x=-3\tfrac{2}{5}}$

c. $2(x-10)-(12x-4)=20$
$2x-20-12x+4=20$
$-10x-16=20$
$-10x=20+16=36$
$-10x=36$
$x=\dfrac{-36}{10}$
$x=-3+\dfrac{3}{5}=-2\tfrac{2}{5}$
$\boxed{x=-2\tfrac{2}{5}}$

credit to each of these efforts? Should the procedure with the error near the end of the attempted solution be assigned more points than the procedure with the error at the beginning?

Another concern in giving partial credit involves the reason for students' miscues. In example a, the student was apparently the victim of his or her own careless handwriting. However, in examples b and c it is not clear whether the students were careless in using the distributive property or whether they lacked understanding. When students are not available for questioning, it is difficult for the teacher to ascertain the source of an error. One indication that an error occurs because of a misunderstanding rather than from carelessness is the frequency of the same type of mistake. A careless error is not likely to be repeated consistently, whereas an error based on misunderstanding is likely to appear more than once. Thus, the problem of facing a teacher giving partial credit is twofold. First, how can one ascertain what is the source of the error? Second, if such determination can be made, how should each type of error be valued in grading the exercise?

The problem of assigning partial credit becomes even more severe in grading proofs. Consider the following attempted proofs of a problem a teacher might present to students. The reader is expected to supply the justification for each individual step and find the errors. Both attempted proofs are based on the diagram in Figure 15.1. Each attempted proof involves errors with respect to the construction of $\overleftrightarrow{c}$. In example d the construction is not possible except for special cases. The information derived from the assumed angle bisection, however, is not an integral part of the deductive argument. In view of this, how should the proposed proof be evaluated? In example e the construction of $\overleftrightarrow{c}$ is also in error because of the number of conditions placed on the constructed line. If $\overleftrightarrow{c}$ is constructed parallel to $\overrightarrow{a}$, then it remains to be shown that $\overleftrightarrow{c}$ is parallel to $\overrightarrow{b}$. How should this error be evaluated? On a ten-point scale, how many points should be assigned to each attempted proof? Such situations help exemplify some of the difficulties associated with giving partial credit.

One way for a teacher to decide whether to give partial credit is to examine its probable consequences. A teacher who does not give partial credit may encourage students to work carefully and check their work when answers have been obtained. The same teacher runs the risk of encouraging students to focus all their attention on obtaining a correct result and discouraging students from attempting any work they feel they cannot complete. The teacher who gives partial credit is better able to encourage students to attempt problems that at first glance appear to be beyond their grasp. Students are more likely to feel they have been treated fairly when they have received credit for work that has been done correctly. It is generally devastating for students to receive no credit when they made only a minor arithmetic error in attempting to solve a complex exercise. On the other hand, a teacher who gives partial credit may be encouraging students to be

Figure 15.1

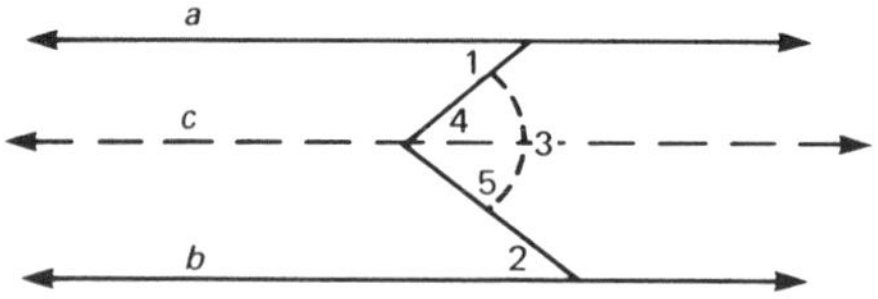

d. Given: $a \parallel b$

Prove: $m\angle 1 + m\angle 2 = m3$

Proof: $\overleftrightarrow{a} \parallel \overleftrightarrow{b}$

Construct $\overleftrightarrow{c}$ parallel to $\overleftrightarrow{a}$
and bisecting $\angle 3$.

$m\angle 4 = m\angle 5$
and $m\angle 1 = m\angle 4$.

Also $c \parallel b$

$m\angle 2 = m\angle 5$
$m\angle 1 + m\angle 2 = m\angle 4 + m\angle 5$
$m\angle 3 = m\angle 4 + m\angle 5$
$\therefore m\angle 1 + m\angle 2 = m\angle 3$

e. Given: $\overleftrightarrow{a} \parallel \overleftrightarrow{b}$

Prove: $m\angle 1 + m\angle 2 = m\angle 3$

Proof: $\overleftrightarrow{a} \parallel \overleftrightarrow{b}$

Construct $\overleftrightarrow{c}$ parallel to $\overleftrightarrow{a}$
and to $\overleftrightarrow{b}$.

It follows that:
$m\angle 1 = m\angle 4$ and
$m\angle 2 = m\angle 5$
$\therefore m\angle 1 + m\angle 2 = m\angle 4 + m\angle 5$

Since $m\angle 3 = m\angle 4 + m\angle 5$
it follows that:
$m\angle 1 + m\angle 2 = m\angle 3$.

unconcerned about making careless errors. Furthermore, students may continue to commit the same type of error if they realize that partial credit will always be given. Another disadvantage of giving partial credit is the difficulty of assigning credit that, in the eyes of the students, is fair and impartial.

Another issue related to grading tests is the concern of whether to base grades on a pre-established standard of achievement or to curve them. These two positions are exemplified by Teacher$_3$ and Teacher$_4$, respectively, in the utterances below:

T_3 I base my test grades on a strict percentage, 90 percent or better is an A, 80–89 percent is a B, and so on. This keeps my standards high and consistent from test to test.

T_4 In grading tests, I always give so many A's, so many B's, and so on, regardless of the test scores. I don't think it's always possible or desirable to construct tests in which students will obtain scores in the 90's, 80's, and so on.

One way to reach a decision on this issue is to identify the assumptions underlying each teacher's position and the probable consequences of each position. T_3 is assuming that he or she has constructed tests in such a way that results will range over a predetermined scale. The consequences of the decision of T_3 dictate that if most students obtain a score of 90 percent or better, then they should all be rewarded with a grade of A. Similarly, if most students do poorly on a test, only a few scoring 80 percent or better, then the majority of the students would receive a grade of C or lower. On some occasions T_3 may be displeased with these consequences. Whenever the scores on a given test are skewed in one direction or another, the assumptions accepted by a teacher like T_3 must be carefully examined. If test scores are unusually low, it may be because there are too many difficult test items. Should test scores run unusually high then a teacher may be rewarding students for only low-level cognitive behavior. A teacher whose test grades are consistently high or low may encounter criticism from students, parents, and school officials.

These are some of the concerns relative to grading by fixed percentage. What are the concerns of "curving grades"? First is the assumption that achievement within a class is distributed according to some preconceived notion. For example, a teacher might assume student achievement is normally distributed. A second assumption is that a given range of achievement scores represents a quality of comprehension ranging from superior to unsatisfactory.

In advanced courses and in honors classes as well as in remedial sections, the consequences of accepting the second assumption may be disturbing to T_4. The acceptance of the second assumption implies that the lowest test score in an honors class reflects unsatisfactory comprehension. It also implies that a top score of 40 percent in any class represents achievement commensurate with a grade of A. Thus, both methods of grading involve certain assumptions and consequences. A teacher must weigh the relative merits of each position before deciding which method, if either, can best provide assessment of student progress.

Another concern in evaluating student performance on tests centers on cheating. When cheating occurs, the problem of evaluation is greatly confounded, sometimes to the extent that it is not possible to assess students' work accurately. When evidence of cheating is unmistakable, the students involved can be warned, reprimanded, or perhaps retested. Evidence of cheating is usually equivocal, however, and the task of deciding what a student accomplishes represents a formidable and perhaps impossible task. It is therefore desirable that preventive techniques to thwart cheating be used in order to obtain measures reflecting each particular student's achievement.

First, and perhaps foremost, students must recognize that tests are fair and reflect classroom instruction. By demonstrating to students that test items reflect established objectives, the groundwork for inhibiting cheating has been laid. Students are most likely to cheat when they are under pressure. If, in addition, they perceive that a teacher's tests are unfair, then they will quickly rationalize as acceptable the dishonest behavior of cheating.

Teachers can inhibit dishonest behavior by making the directions to tests clear and concise so that confusion does not occur after students have begun work. Teachers should also insist that students show all their work in obtaining answers. This directive can be further emphasized when the teacher has convinced students that the entire response has been evaluated rather than just the final results. Students are quick to perceive when a teacher simply grades answers. Cheating is fostered when credit is given for answers that do not logically follow from the methods used.

Teachers can also thwart cheating by moving around the classroom, observing students and being alert for signs of dishonest practice such as note-passing and glancing at crib notes. A teacher who allows individual students to monopolize his time during a test or who uses the examination period as an opportunity to grade papers or prepare for another class invites students to become engaged in fraudulent behavior. Moving through the room during examinations has another advantage: it can help the teacher gain insights into the ways students solve problems and the kinds of errors they make. This information can help the teacher provide additional instruction for the knowledge in question. Sometimes this information is lost when students erase or scratch out their abortive efforts at solutions. Teachers can use this information to help convince students that they are sincerely interested in their progress.

A more drastic technique a teacher can use to inhibit cheating is to give students alternate forms of the same test. Distributing these forms so that students in adjacent seats have different tests makes it difficult for students to copy. Placing each student's name on tests before distribution ensures that test papers cannot be exchanged to negate the distribution of alternate forms of an examination. If alternate forms of a test are constructed, care must be taken to ensure that the tests are of equal difficulty and that they measure the same objectives.

Sometimes teachers suspect cheating but are unable to identify the culprit. What action should be taken? A brief comment such as "O.K., John, now let's keep our eyes on our own paper now" may keep a student from cheating. Sometimes the essence of this message can be transmitted by nonverbal means—a stare or a frown or even the physical presence of the teacher standing next to the student. If a teacher encounters two test papers (or two homework papers) that are remarkably alike the teacher might write on one paper, "Your solution is a lot like John's" and on the other write, "Your solution is a lot like Jane's." Of course, a teacher must use such techniques with discretion, because they imply that cheating does in fact exist. The advantage of such techniques is that teachers serve notice to the students of suspicion of cheating but do not place themselves in a position of making unprovable accusations.

Such corrective measures are often effective because students usually wish to avoid a direct confrontation with teachers, parents, and school personnel. The teacher who decides to take punitive action against a student suspected of cheating should first have explicit and unequivocal evidence before confronting student, parents, or school administration. To do less only invites the wrath of parents and school officials and serves to undermine the teacher's authority in the eyes of other students.

Despite extensive preventive and corrective measures, every class is destined to have some cheating. As long as grades are important to students or their parents, and as long as society and schools place a premium on grades, there will undoubtedly be students who will attempt to improve their positions dishonestly. Therefore, teachers should not be surprised or take it as a personal affront when they perceive that dishonest behavior has occurred. It does not follow that every instance of cheating is caused by a teacher failing to meet responsibilities.

Thought questions

1 React to the positions exemplified by the dialogue given below. Consider the probable consequences of each teacher's policy.

T_1 In my class a kid needs 90 percent or better to get an A. You gotta draw the line someplace.

T_2 In my class I assign grades on the basis of where there is a natural gap in the test scores.

T_1 You mean if the scores were 99, 98, 97, 91, 90, and so on, the 97 gets an A and the 91 gets a B?

T_2 Right. That's a lot better than trying to haggle over whether 89.9 or 90.1 is an A or a B. After all, test scores just aren't reliable enough to differentiate between scores of 89 and 90.

T_1 O.K. But sometimes you will give kids an A for a score of 97 and another time give an A for an 85. That seems pretty inconsistent to me.

2   React to the contention that a teacher should not give partial credit if a student could check his or her answer in some way other than by reworking the problem in the same way it was worked initially.

3   Should a geometry teacher penalize students for having irrelevant but correct steps in their proofs? Defend your answer in terms of probable consequences.

4   Suppose the work shown below appeared on the papers of three algebra students, each trying to solve the following problem. Suppose further that you are expecting an algebraic solution in light of what has transpired in class. However, students were not given instructions to submit only algebraic solutions. On the basis of 10 points evaluate each student's work. Then evaluate it on the basis of 3 points. The problem is: The sum of three consecutive odd integers is 81. Find the three integers.

a. Let x = 1st odd integer
. $x + 1$ = 2nd odd integer
    $x + 2$ = 3rd odd integer
    $x + x + 1 + x + 2 = 81$
    $3x + 3 = 81$
    $3x = 78$
    $x = 26$
∴ The integers are
26, 27, 28.

b. Let x = 1st odd integer
    $x + 2$ = 2nd odd integer
    $x + 4$ = 3rd odd integer
    $x + x + 2 + x + 4 = 81$
    $9x = 81$
    $x = 9$
∴ The integers are
9, 11, and 13.

c.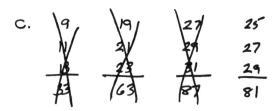

The integers are 25, 27, 29.

5   Is a teacher who penalizes students for using trial and error for successive approximations rather than algebraic methods (refer to solution c in question 4) discouraging problem-solving behavior that would be applauded in other contexts? Explain your position.

6   Evaluate the following work of junior high school students first on a 10-point scale and then on a 3-point scale.

(a) $\frac{5}{12} = \frac{5}{12}(3) = \frac{15}{36}$

$\frac{7}{8} = \frac{7}{18}(2) = \frac{14}{36}$

$\boxed{\frac{29}{36}}$

(b) $\frac{5}{12} + \frac{7}{18} = \frac{90 + 84}{12 \times 18} = \boxed{\frac{174}{216}}$

(c) $\frac{5}{12} + \frac{7}{18} = \frac{15}{36} + \frac{14}{36} = \frac{28}{36} = \frac{14}{18} = \boxed{\frac{7}{9}}$

(d) $\frac{5}{12} + \frac{7}{18} = \frac{12}{30} = \boxed{\frac{2}{5}}$

7   Evaluate the following work of the students in an advanced mathematics course who are trying to solve the following exercise. Base your evaluation on a 10-point scale and then on a 3-point scale. The problem is : Find an equation of the line through the intersection of the lines $3x - y - 2 = 0$ and $x - 2y + 6 = 0$ and with a slope of $\frac{2}{3}$.

(a) $3x - 2y - 2 = 0$
$\underline{\quad x - 2y + 6 = 0}$
$\quad 2x \quad -8 = 0$
$\therefore x = 4$
$\therefore y = -5$

$\therefore$ Lines intersect at $(4,5)$. Hence desired equation is
$$\frac{2}{3} = \frac{y - 5}{x - 4}$$

(b) $3x - 2y - 2 = 0$
$\underline{\quad x - 2y + 6 = 0}$
$\quad 2x - 8 = 0$
$\therefore x - 4 = 0 \text{ or } x = 4$
and $y = -5$
Lines intersect at $(4,5)$
$\therefore \frac{2}{3} = \frac{y - 5}{x - 4}$
or $2x - 8 = 3y - 15$
or $2x + 3y = -7$

8   Conjecture situations in which students are likely to feel compelled to cheat. How might a teacher avoid placing students in such contexts ?

Assignments

A factor that many mathematics teachers consider in evaluating student progress is work on assignments outside class. It is generally agreed that mathematics is not a spectator sport and that students need practice solving problems and completing exercises related to the subject matter. Many teachers assign more problems and exercises than students can do in class and expect them to complete this work before the next class meeting. Since subsequent class meetings often involve work that has been assigned, teachers become aware of students who have spent effort on assignments. Some teachers obtain this information by collecting and, in some cases, grading the students' papers. Others rely on quizzes or questions and answers from the students during class discussion. In any event, the amount of effort and the quality of individual work makes an impression on the teacher, and this influences the value judgments about progress. Some teachers consider grades on assignments along with test scores in making final grades. Others use their evaluation of students' efforts on assignments to help make judgments when they have some question as to which of two grades to assign. Still others claim they ignore this factor and consider only test scores, the purpose of assignments being to help students obtain satisfactory test grades.

It may be enlightening for a teacher to consider decisions relative to the use of assignments in evaluations in light of its probable consequences. Some students will do well on assignments; their work will be relatively complete and on time. Yet some of these students may do poorly on tests. Is it the case that they freeze on tests or is it that they cannot function adequately in mathematics without recourse to textbook, answers, or advice and assistance from others? A teacher who does not consider efforts on assignments may make the first type of student even more anxious on tests and encourage dishonest behavior. On the other hand, some students may become dependent on having answers or assistance at their disposal. The teacher who weights assignments too heavily runs the risk of encouraging such dependence. The problem is compounded by the fact that these two situations are not mutually exclusive. A teacher's judgment must prevail as to the extent assignments should be considered.

A teacher is also likely to have a few students who apparently put forth minimal effort on assignments outside class and yet obtain adequate, perhaps even outstanding, test scores. Consider for a moment the case a student (and perhaps his or her parents) will make if a grade of C or B is assigned when the student's test scores are among the highest in the class. The teacher who cannot rightfully claim that this student's test scores were obtained by improper behavior will have to contend that evaluation of the student's performance reflects more than academic achievement. While such a contention often meets with approval in situations where a teacher has used other factors to raise a student's grade, this contention is likely to meet with resistance when it is used to justify a grade that is lower than supposedly objective measures indicate.

Class participation

Another factor that teachers may take into account in evaluating student performance is the contributions students make to the academic activities in the classroom. Assessment of the quality of a student's contribution in this area is highly subjective and, therefore, should be viewed judiciously in evaluation deliberations.

The degree to which class participation should be considered in evaluation faces every teacher. One approach to dealing with this issue is to view it from the perspective of plausible consequences. Suppose a teacher rewards with grades students who continually make verbal contributions to class discussions. This practice encourages students to participate actively in classroom discussions. Such interactions provide the teacher with evidence for diagnosis and response to student's needs.

The teacher who overemphasizes classroom interaction, however, runs the risk of encouraging superfluous responses and questions. That is, students will be eager to participate solely for the purpose of demonstrating to the teacher that they are paying attention. On the other hand, the teacher who does not consider class participation may engender a passive attitude in students. They may become discouraged if they conscientiously participate and yet their evaluations are no higher than students who respond only minimally in class.

The teacher should exercise good judgment in rewarding class participation. Teachers should neither ignore students' contributions nor should they tally points for every question, answer, or comment students make. Teachers can reinforce student engagement in discussions by nonverbal gestures such as a smile or a nod, by compliments during or after class as well as by taking students' participation into account in formal assessments.

Attitude and effort

Sometimes a teacher, especially of slow learners, may wish to consider the attitude and effort of students in evaluating performance. Student attitude is often inferred from attendance, punctuality, willingness to work on assignments, and care of materials and conduct. There are at least two reasons why a teacher considers such things as attendance and conduct in determining grades and making other evaluations.

First, the subject matter may be difficult for some students and a teacher may consider such behavior as punctuality and care of materials to be something they can and, perhaps, need to learn to do. The teacher then feels justified in rewarding this behavior. A second reason, related to the first, is that in some classes the teacher may have difficulty getting students to come to class, work on assignments, and exhibit socially acceptable conduct in the classroom. Making students aware that their attitude and efforts contribute toward their grades may induce them to exhibit desirable classroom behavior.

What are the consequences of using student attitudes and efforts in evaluating their progress? A positive result may be an improvement in attendance and effort in doing class work. The extent to which this occurs depends on the value that the students place on grades. Once patterns of punctuality and conscientious efforts are established, however, they may become habitual.

One concern in basing grades, even partly, on attitude and effort is that grades are less reflective of academic accomplishment. In some instances this may be of little import, but if it must be determined whether a particular student should continue in mathematics, then grades based partly on attitude may not accurately indicate mastery of necessary prerequisite knowledge.

Extra credit work

At various times throughout a school year students are interested in doing extra credit work, some because of the challenge, others because it provides them a means by which positively to influence the teacher's assessment of their performances. Some teachers regularly announce problems that can be worked for extra credit; some may come from the textbook, others may arise in classroom discussions.

Not all extra credit work has to be in the form of problems. In some cases students who lack problem-solving skills can do extra credit work by constructing models and other visual aids. In other instances, teachers who believe that a student could profit from extra practice may decide to give students extra credit for working additional sets of exercises. Researching some event of significance in the history of mathematics, reporting on the life of a mathematician, and illustrating an application of mathematics are other activities distinct from problem-solving that can be undertaken for extra credit.

While extra credit work can provide valuable experiences for students, a problem arises when a teacher must determine to what extent such work should contribute to a student's grade. Some teachers do not consciously consider extra credit work in determining grades. Others use it to enable borderline students to receive a higher mark. Still others allow students to use extra credit work to compensate for deficiencies in test performances and homework assignments.

In the latter case, the teacher may be encouraging students to work on extra credit problems or projects to the exclusion of regular classroom work. For some students, this practice may be deterimental to acquistion of mathematical concepts, principles, and skills. On the other hand, if extra credit work is not rewarded in some way, students may be reluctant to pursue such assignments. The teacher must realize that the amount of time and effort students will expend on extra credit projects will be influenced by the way they are rewarded for it.

Needs of students

We will consider one additional factor that teachers sometimes take into consideration when evaluating student work—particularly when assigning grades on official school reports. On some occasions when a student's work places him or her on the borderline between two possible grades, a teacher may assign the higher grade, believing that encouragment or a vote of confidence will promote additional effort. On the other hand, the lower of two possible grades may be assigned to emphasize to the student and perhaps to parents that he or she is working considerably below ability.

These practices should be employed discretely and with the realization that in either case the results may differ from what the teacher intended. Students can perceive a vote of confidence as an indication that they have little to be concerned about or that the mathematics course in question is going to be easier than expected. Students can also perceive what the teacher intends to be a warning as an indication that the teacher is unfair or determined to harass them. The teacher can help avert such undesirable situations by conferring with a colleague, the principal, the student, and in some cases parents before actually taking action. Conferences themselves can lead to a change in student behavior.

Thought questions

1   Is it ethical for a teacher to grade students in the same class according to different criteria—for example, to consider only the test scores of some students and to consider test scores along with homework, class participation, and attitude and effort for other students? Defend your answer.

2   What are the advantages and disadvantages of collecting and correcting homework? By what alternative procedures can a teacher ascertain the quality of homework assignments?

3   What can be done to help students who freeze on tests?

4   Conjecture why some students are indifferent toward grades. How can this pose problems for the teacher? How can such students be encouraged to learn mathematics?

5   Suppose you were teaching a seventh-grade mathematics class and had a few students that were on a third- or fourth-grade level in arithmetic achievement. How would you evaluate the progress of these students if you gave them work on their level?

6   Are extra credit assignments appropriate for all students? Would you permit a student who is failing to use extra credit work to compensate for regular assignments?

7   Under what conditions would you give a student the higher of two grades? Under what conditions would you give the lower of two grades? What assumptions would your decision be predicated on?

Evaluating a teacher's performance

A teacher's performance is evaluated informally by students, parents, school officials, colleagues, and the teacher. In many schools, teachers are also formally evaluated by the principal, a supervisor, and evaluators from outside the school. In some settings teachers actively participate in constructing formal evaluation procedures and in rating their own performances with respect to previously established standards or criteria. Methods of evaluation include introspection, questionnaires for students, examinations of video and audio recordings, and ratings by peers or supervisors. Teachers have the responsibility of examining their performance and striving to improve effectiveness. In this section we shall consider four factors that can be used in formal or informal evaluations: student achievement, student attitudes, judgments relative to the appropriateness of teaching strategies, and the efficiency with which administrative matters are conducted.

Student performance on tests

While test scores provide a means of determining student progress, they can also be used as one means of evaluating a teacher's performance. Most teachers are well aware of how their students perform on chapter and unit tests. In addition, class averages and scores from departmental, systemwide, or standardized tests administered at the beginning and end of the school term can be ascertained. Such information is relatively easy to obtain and is often considered to be an objective measure of a teacher's effectiveness. In situations in which a teacher is accountable for producing measurable academic growth, test scores can become a critical factor in teacher evaluation.

If test scores indicate students are making satisfactory academic progress, it can generally be inferred that the teacher's performance is also satisfactory and responsive to students' academic needs. Students, parents, and administrators who are basically pleased with students' marks on tests are likely to view the teacher as effective. On the other hand, if student performances on tests tend to be unsatisfactory and if as a result students, parents, and administrators are displeased, then the teacher would be wise to reflect on his or her teaching methods and expectations. Clearly, if students are not making satisfactory academic progress something is amiss. The question then becomes to what extent the factors contributing to this situation are under the control of the teacher.

Some of these are the validity of the tests, the selection of subject matter, and the determination of teaching strategies. If students seem not to be responding to a teacher's efforts, as evidenced by their test results, then the teacher might review these three factors. Perhaps the tests do not measure what they are intended to measure, do not adequately reflect established objectives. The situation may be resolved by more careful analysis in constructing tests. Perhaps the teacher's initial judgments were in error and the material is too difficult for the students. If the teacher or a consensus of colleagues determine that this is the case, then appropriate adjustments can be made. Finally, the teacher might reflect on the strategies used to teach the content.

Other factors partially beyond the control of a teacher can influence students' test scores. An individual teacher has only partial control over attitudes, attendance, willingness to participate in instructional activities, and, in general, the conditions under which teaching is to take place. An individual teacher has virtually no control over a student's home environment, physical and mental health, basic intelligence, and previous mathematics achievement. Begle (1973) in summarizing a five-year study of mathematics learning cites previous mathematics achievement as the single best predictor of how students will perform on mathematics achievement tests. Thus, inferences concerning a teacher's effectiveness predicated on test results, whether good or bad, should be viewed in light of the conditions under which students come to the teacher.

In professions other than teaching, it is considered absurd to hold the practitioner responsible for the final state of a client without considering the conditions under which the client comes to be helped, the resources available to the professional, the client's willingness to follow advice, and the things that happen to the client while not under the direct supervision of the professional. Who would hold a physician accountable for the final state of a patient's health if the patient did not participate in scheduled therapy, take prescribed medication, or change behavior in ways specified by the professional? This should not be interpreted to mean that measuring students' academic progress in terms of test results is inappropriate in evaluating a teacher. When tests reflect what the teacher has taught and test scores are considered in light of the conditions under which teaching has occurred, student achievement is one indicator of a teacher's effectiveness. A teacher might also ask questions such as the following in reference to student performances on tests:

What percentage of my students are doing unsatisfactory work? Outstanding work?

Are my students achieving at a level that is commensurate with their ability as evidenced by previous grades and aptitude measures?

Are my students generally pleased with their progress?

Can they explain and apply the mathematics I have taught?

How are these students doing in this class in comparison to their other classes?

Student attitudes and conduct

Another indicator of teacher performance lies in the social aspects of the classroom environment. A teacher can partly ascertain the classroom atmosphere by determining whether students are punctual, prepared for class, and willing to work or whether they frequently cut class, are tardy, unprepared, obstreperous, and indifferent. Other evidence can be obtained more subjectively. The amount of praise, encouragement, acceptance, defensive behavior, hostility, and sarcasm in a classroom indicates the climate that characterizes the social interactions. It is difficult for a teacher to make such determinations alone, however. Hence, it may be helpful to obtain an observer's opinion with regard to these considerations. Teachers who have confidence in their own ability to be perceptive can record class discussions and analyze them at a later time.

To assist in evaluating teaching in reference to the social climate, a teacher could pose questions similar to the following:

Are students prompt in coming to class and in getting settled to work?

Do they have the necessary materials?

What percentage of the students have their assignments completed?

Do students employ excessive defensive behavior when I call on them?

Are they hostile when they or I make a mistake?

Are they willing to venture conjectures, try to answer challenging questions, or attempt extra credit problems?

Do their questions and tone of voice convey respect for themselves, fellow students, and the teacher?

When they get stuck on an assignment, do they try or just give up?

Do students frequently ask, "Why are we studying this?"

Do students initiate discussions concerning mathematics?

Are students constantly misbehaving?

What happens if I step out of the room for a minute?

How do they conduct themselves in their other classes?

Do I anticipate and thwart potential problems with nonverbal techniques?

Do I keep disturbances in perspective and where possible avoid confrontation concerning behavior?

Are my punitive measures appropriate for each particular disturbance?

Am I consistent in dealing with behavior problems?

Do I administer group punishment when it is uncalled for?

Answers to questions similar to these can be formed on the basis of observable behavior and value judgments. Answers are also influenced by the nature of the student population in each classroom. In situations in which someone other than the classroom teacher is involved in the evaluation, judgments should be based on a series of observations. Frank and open discussions of the answers to such questions and constructive criticism of the teacher's actions by both the teacher and the observer can provide invaluable means for professional improvement.

Methods of teaching

In addition to examining student academic and social behavior in judging teacher effectiveness, it is appropriate for the teacher to analyze the teaching strategies employed. Since a significant portion of a teacher's planning efforts and behavior in the classroom is consciously directed toward the teaching of concepts, generalizations, and skills, it is appropriate to judge the effectiveness of the way in which this content is handled. In teaching a generalization by exposition questions similar to the following can provide a structure for evaluation:

Do I clearly assert the generalization?

Do I provide motivation?

Is the generalization interpreted so that the students appear to understand the hypothesis and the conclusion?

In particular, are sufficient instances presented and discussed?

Does the justification seem to be appropriate and effective?

Do I ask my students to apply the generalization?

If the generalization is taught by guided discovery, value judgments about the appropriateness of the instances presented for the students to form abstractions and generalizations would be of concern. Also of concern would be the quality of the questions posed to foster generalizations or deductions. A value judgment concerning the placement of the assertion move in relation to the frustration level exhibited by the students could also be formed.

If the development of a mathematical skill is the object of instruction, evaluation of the teacher's behavior could include questions similar to the following:

Are the students given sufficient opportunity to practice?

Does the practice incorporate feedback?

Do I provide motivation for skill acquisition?

If understanding the procedures involved in performing a skill is the object of instruction, then value judgments concerning the appropriateness and effectiveness of the teacher's efforts to interpret and justify this knowledge would be relevant to the evaluation.

Judgments relative to the effectiveness of teaching strategies are necessarily highly subjective. Student performance on tests should not be the sole source of relevant data. Because of the difficulty of analyzing one's own teaching behavior, it may be desirable for a teacher to secure judgments formulated by a knowledgeable observer, perhaps one's colleague. Sometimes it is difficult to obtain the services of an observer. An alternative approach is to videotape or audiotape a lesson and analyze the teacher's behavior with questions similar to those above. It is possible and relevant to structure part of the evaluation of a teacher's performance around the seeming appropriateness of the deliberate actions relative to the knowledge being taught and the method of instruction being used.

Administrative matters

In evaluating their own performance, teachers can consider management of routine matters and instructional activities. Grading and returning papers, taking attendance, and having materials ready for use can often set the tone for the classroom atmosphere. The teacher who continually fails to start class on time, fails to reach closure, or neglects tasks such as taking attendance is likely to be viewed by students and administrators alike as inefficient, unreliable, and lacking in leadership qualities. Thus, although administrative concerns are not of paramount importance in view of the total instructional program, the ability to perform them effectively provides a context enhancing other, more central instructional activities.

The questions below can provide a basis from which to ascertain whether or not a teacher is effective administratively. Some questions can be reliably answered by the teacher. For others the teacher may wish to obtain judgments from colleagues or supervisors:

Are matters relating to attendance, reading announcements, and other routine tasks dispensed with quickly and before instructional activities begin?

Are students quick to settle down once routine matters are finished?

Are assignments clearly communicated both orally and by written word?

Do students begin to work on their assignments quickly and with a minimum of delay?

Do students seem to understand what is expected of them in class, what they are to do, and where they are to obtain needed materials?

Is closure obtained for most lessons—that is, are explanations and assignments given without getting caught by the bell?

Are students aware of grading procedures?

Are homework papers and test papers returned promptly?

Does the teacher have all necessary instructional aids at hand and are they in good working order?

The collective responses to these questions can provide some information as to how effectively the teacher is using class time.

The four factors presented here are means by which teachers can evaluate their own teaching through value judgments, formed by either themselves or other observers, by considering what the sum total of the responses seems to suggest. Perhaps the most difficult task for all human beings is subjection to self-criticism or criticism by another person. It is all too easy to rationalize and explain away others' criticism of one's own teaching. It is even easier to fool oneself into believing that one's classroom conduct is consistent with stated objectives and meets the needs of individual students when in fact they do not. A truly professional teacher can objectively discuss weaknesses of his own instructional efforts. Often a teacher's only real source of evaluation is through introspection. The perceptive teacher adjusts, matures, and develops into a professional teacher respected by students, parents, and administrators alike.

Thought questions

1   Should a teacher take steps to evaluate his or her own performance apart from or beyond formal evaluation procedures? Why?

2   Suppose you were constructing a questionnaire for your students to evaluate your teaching. Create four questions that you would ask. Would you ask different questions of different level classes? If so, give an illustration. At what time or times during the year would you consider using such a questionnaire?

3   To what extent should a teacher feel responsible for changing his or her behavior in response to the results of a questionnaire? Would you do so if many students comment that your expectations are too high?

4   How do you react to the idea of a secondary school student council evaluating teachers and courses and publishing this information in a student handbook, as is done at some universities? How would most secondary school teachers react to this idea?

5   Suppose $Teacher_1$'s classes consistently outperformed $Teacher_2$'s classes on achievement tests. Does this indicate that $Teacher_1$ is a better teacher than $Teacher_2$? Justify your answer.

6   Assume that you are teaching first-year algebra and have been informed that your students will be given a standardized test at the end of the term and that, largely on the basis of their performance, decisions will be made concerning your subsequent employment and salary. What further information would you seek concerning this matter? Would your teaching be affected by this procedure? In what way?

7   Under what conditions would small gains in student achievement indicate that a teacher is ineffective? Under what conditions would small gains indicate a teacher is effective?

8   In addition to visiting classes, an outside observer can interview individual students or small groups of students concerning their perceptions of the quality of their interactions with a particular teacher. Do you think that such practice should be a part of the procedures used to evaluate teachers? Justify your response.

9   What qualifications would you expect of a person who is responsible for observing and evaluating your teaching?

10 In this chapter we presented a number of questions designed to provide a structure for evaluating the teaching of generalizations and skills. What additional questions could be included in these lists?

11 Create a set of questions that could be used to structure an evaluation of a teacher's behavior when this teacher is engaged in teaching a concept.

12 If you were charged with the responsibility of evaluating a teacher's classroom performance, would you wish to consider factors distinct from student achievement, student attitude and conduct, teaching methods, and administrative matters? Discuss your answer.

Accountability

Today perhaps more than ever before there is a trend to hold corporations, politicians, and social agencies accountable for their actions. The term *accountability* has become commonplace in our language. Generally, it refers to the condition of being accountable, liable, or responsible for actions taken.

When applied to education, accountability means that the administrators of instructional programs are to be held responsible for their educational products, usually determined by student achievement. Those who advocate holding educational institutions and educators accountable for the progress of their students maintain that it is the right of the people who finance public education to judge the quality of their investment. Proponents of accountability also claim that such measures lead to improvement in efficiency and the products of schools. This conclusion is based on the assumption that the removal or replacement of incompetent or inefficient teachers, administrators, and programs will be followed by the appointment or implementation of better personnel and courses of study. Those who oppose accountability measures tend either to oppose the notion of primarily judging educational endeavors in terms of output or are concerned that accountability practices will be focused on only one element in the educational process (the classroom teacher) or are suspicious of the measures to be used to judge the merits of educators.

In any event, educational accountability entails evaluation of teachers' performances and students' performances. Consider some of the contentions of advocates and opponents of educational accountability.

Projected benefits of educational accountability

Proponents of accountability feel that it is beneficial to hold educators directly responsible for products the educational system delivers. It is believed that this will ensure that students will remain the most important element in the system. It is held that by forcing educators to specify outcomes, students are more likely to be assured they will be competent in fundamental skills. In addition, when teachers and administrators are answerable for student progress, they will be forced to give high priority to instructional concerns, stay abreast of the development of new programs and materials, and in general be more efficient.

Some argue that teachers judged most efficient by whatever accountability measures are adopted should be rewarded economically. Although merit pay increases have sometimes been viewed with suspicion and concern, proponents of accountability maintain that merit pay is an integral factor in upgrading educational institutions. The position is that salary increases should be tied to demonstrable student progress rather than years in service or academic training.

Advocates of accountability maintain that the financial support for any aspect of education is more easily obtained when educators can demonstrate the effectiveness of their programs. Hence, they argue that accountability can provide the means of generating and maintaining adequate monetary resources needed to educate the population.

Concerns associated with educational accountability

Parties opposing the accountability movement in education maintain that the attainment of some significant and desirable educational outcomes cannot be ascertained by objective measures of student academic performances. Such affective considerations as developing a healthy self-concept and being able to relate positively to others in society are viewed as worthy educational goals. But these goals are somewhat vague. Furthermore, how does one ascertain, for example, whether a mathematics student has developed an appreciation of the power and usefulness of deductive reasoning? Which teachers or courses of study are responsible for changes in a student's self-concept or ability to solve problems? Adversaries of accountability are quick to point out that these are examples of important questions that are highly resistant to resolution by standard measurement techniques.

Since the attainment of skills and factual content is readily measurable by standardized tests, it is conceivable that those charged with evaluating the effectiveness of schools will be disposed to place an inordinate amount of weight on fact and skill learning. Opponents of accountability measures predict that this will be the case and fear that the use of standardized tests will dictate that teachers teach for the tests to the exclusion of other important educational outcomes. In conjunction with this concern is the cry over dehumanizing education. There is a belief by some that the net effect of holding teachers accountable for student academic performances will result in neglect of individual student needs.

Another issue raised by opponents of accountability concerns the scope of the responsibility for student performance. It is apparent that teachers have responsibility for designing and conducting learning experiences, diagnosing students' learning difficulties, and providing remediation. It is also clear that teachers can be held accountable for student learning and rewarded or penalized with salary, recognition, or dismissal. However, the responsibility of other parties in the performance of students and measures to be taken to reward or penalize these parties is not clear. Other parties directly involved in the educational process include the individual student, the student's family, school and district administrators, as well as those providing the financial support for education. To what extent are students or parents responsible for student participation in lessons? What responsibility do administrators, schoolboard members, and the financers have with respect to student achievement? Should teachers be held accountable for student progress if the community at large does not provide the means by which they can teach effectively? Such unanswered questions form a basis of concern for some educators grappling with the issue of educational accountability.

Thought questions

1   Should schools be fully funded and then be evaluated on the basis of their educational products or should schools be required to demonstrate their effectiveness and then be funded accordingly?

2   React to the following teacher's statement : It is a mistake for us to consider ourselves professionals. Professionals set their own fees, working conditions, and professional standards. We would be better off to consider ourselves as hired hands, just as if we were paid to produce a product.

3   State and defend your position on the following claim : The accountability movement holds great promise for moving education away from its mediocre course. When education can be businesslike, students, teachers, administrators, and taxpayers will benefit.

4   Suppose you were on a committee charged with designing a plan for teacher accountability. Discuss your recommendations for the committee's consideration. Identify actions for which teachers should be held accountable and how evaluation could be conducted.

5   Identify factors outside of the control of a teacher that can influence student academic performances. What relevance do you think these factors have concerning the accountability issue?

Self-test on the competencies

1   Write test items at various cognitive levels that reflect stated objectives.
    Write a computation and an application test item for the following objectives :

    The student should be able to find the volume of a right circular cone given its radius and height.

    The student should be able to utilize Cramer's rule to solve systems of linearly independent equations.

2   Discuss the advantages and disadvantages of curving grades and giving partial credit.
    a   Describe a set of circumstances that would seem to indicate that curving grades would be preferable to grading on a fixed percentage basis.
    b   What value judgments are implicit when a teacher decides to give partial credit?

3 State reasons for and concerns associated with considering student assignments, class participation, attitude and effort, extra credit, and individual needs in evaluating student progress.

What are the advantages and disadvantages of using homework, class participation, attitude and effort, and extra credit work in evaluating student performance?

4 Discuss how student performance on tests, attitudes and conduct, teaching methods, and administrative matters can be used to evaluate a teacher's performance.

   a Suppose you wish to evaluate your own teaching. What relative importance would you give to each of the four factors identified in this chapter? Defend your answer.

   b Design instruments that could be used to gather information on each of the four factors.

5 Identify merits and concerns associated with accountability in education.

   a Construct a brief argument supporting accountability in education.

   b Construct a brief argument opposing accountability in education.

References

Begle, E. G. "Some Lessons Learned by SMSG." *The Mathematics Teacher*, 66 (1973), 207–214.

Bloom, Benjamin S., J. Thomas Hastings, and George F. Madaus. eds. *Handbook on Formative and Summative Evaluation of Student Learning*. New York: McGraw-Hill, 1971.

Carroll, J. A. "A Model of School Learning." *Teachers College Record*, 64 (1963), 723–733.

Epstein, Marion G. "Testing in Mathematics: Why? What? How?" *The Arithmetic Teacher*, 15 (1968), 311–319.

Evaluation in Mathematics. Twenty-Sixth Yearbook of the National Council of Teachers of Mathematics. Washington D. C.: The Council, 1961.

Hamachek, Don E. "What Makes a Good Teacher?" *Phi Delta Kappan*, 50 (1969), 341–345.

Hatfield, Larry. "Patterns for Professional Progress: Report of The Minnesota Council of Teachers of Mathematics." *The Mathematics Teacher*, 62 (1969), 497–503.

Johnson, Donovan A., and Gerald R. Rising. *Guidelines for Teaching Mathematics*. Belmont, Calif.: Wadsworth, 1972. Chs. 8 and 9.

Myers, Sheldon S. *Mathematics Tests Available in the United States*. Washington, D. C.: National Council of Teachers of Mathematics, 1970.

Romberg, Thomas A., and James W. Wilson. "The Development of Mathematics Achievement Tests for the National Longitudinal Study of Mathematical Abilities." *The Mathematics Teacher*, 61 (1968), 489–495.

Weaver, J. F. "Evaluation and the Classroom Teacher." *Mathematics Education*, Sixty-Ninth Yearbook of the National Society for the Study of Education. Chicago: University of Chicago Press, 1970. Ch. 9.

Wilson, James W. "Evaluation of Learning in Secondary School Mathematics." *Handbook on Formative and Summative Evaluation of Student Learning*, ed. by Benjamin S. Bloom et al. New York: McGraw-Hill, 1971. Ch. 19.

Index